8 MINUTOS DIARIOS
PARA ADELGAZAR
EN LA MITAD INFERIOR DEL CUERPO

Dr. Philippe Blanchemaison

8 MINUTOS DIARIOS

PARA ADELGAZAR
EN LA MITAD INFERIOR DEL CUERPO

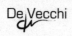

De Vecchi

Obra publicada bajo la dirección de Laure Paoli.

Traducción de Sonia Saura Martínez.

Diseño gráfico de Marie-Christine Pinaux.

Ilustraciones de Christiane Schaeffer Cinqualbre.

Título original: 8 minutes par jour pour maigrir du bas.

© Éditions Albin Michel, S. A. - París 2004
© Editorial De Vecchi, S. A. U. 2006
Balmes, 114. 08008 BARCELONA
Depósito Legal: B. 19.609-2006
ISBN: 84-315-3440-0

Índice

Introducción

D os de cada tres mujeres padecen celulitis, creen que tienen problemas de retención de líquidos y les atemoriza mostrar una silueta deformada en la mitad inferior de su cuerpo, esto es, en la zona de las caderas, los glúteos, los muslos, las pantorrillas y los tobillos. Este problema afecta incluso a las mujeres de constitución delgada, que, a pesar de tener una cara, unos hombros y un busto estilizados, acumulan líquidos y grasas de cintura para abajo.

Ahora bien, adelgazar de cintura para abajo es una tarea difícil: las dietas clásicas inciden muy poco en la retención de líquidos y, por otra parte, la grasa celulítica es muy resistente a la gimnasia clásica.

A pesar de todo, desde hace algunos años, la investigación ha dado grandes pasos en la percepción de estos dos fenómenos y, gracias a los nuevos descubrimientos, se ha podido tener acceso a métodos eficaces para mejorar la situación.

El objetivo de esta obra consiste en ofrecerle una explicación clara y detallada de los complejos mecanismos que dan lugar al fenómeno de la retención de líquidos, el único responsable de que en la mitad inferior del cuerpo se registre un aumento medio de peso de entre 4 y 7 kg. La retención se asocia a trastornos de retorno venoso o linfático, o a un desequilibrio hormonal, y, además, es la única culpable de que las piernas presenten ese aspecto hinchado, tumefacto y acolchado, así como de que la silueta parezca deformada.

Asimismo, se sabe que los músculos desempeñan un papel importante en este fenómeno y, de hecho, estudios recientes han demostrado que algunos, los músculos posturales, tienen una función más importante que otros en lo que a la mejora de la circulación sanguínea y la celulitis se refiere. Evidentemente, la práctica semanal de 2 o 3 horas de gimnasia realizada de forma correcta les garantiza una cierta tonicidad, aunque muchas mujeres no tienen la posibilidad, ni las ganas, de practicar deporte. Por esta razón, le proponemos que, mediante una gimnasia rápida y periódica de 8 minutos al día, entrene estos músculos posturales profundos (muy próximos a los huesos, al contrario que los músculos cercanos a la piel, que son los «responsables» del contorno curvado). Como es lógico, estos movimientos no la convertirán en una atleta de alta competición, aunque este entrenamiento, al que hemos denominado Fast Gym (gimnasia rápida), será suficiente para garantizar el apoyo de las venas profundas, según los mecanismos que especificaremos en las siguientes páginas.

Por otra parte, el reciente descubrimiento de la misión de algunas proteínas mal digeridas que producen un efecto «esponja» en los tejidos y retienen líquido en la misma medida que la sal o el azúcar industrial nos ha animado a proponerle una nueva disciplina alimentaria que consiste, básicamente, en reconocer y evitar estos alimentos «esponja» en la dieta de hoy en día, y en favorecer los alimentos drenantes.

En definitiva, lo que le proponemos es una auténtica dieta para contrarrestar la retención de líquidos y depósitos adiposos. De forma complementaria, realizaremos un rápido repaso de los métodos de fisioterapia moderna que utilizan los médicos y fisioterapeutas, y de las novedades como, por ejemplo, el drenaje acuático linfático asociado a los casos graves de administración de medicamentos, que han permitido definir un verdadero programa para contrarrestar la retención de líquidos (PCRL).

El método que le presentamos en este libro permite, gracias a un tratamiento de choque de 15 días, actuar sobre los parámetros que se han identificado como los culpables del «aumento de peso de cintura para abajo». En definitiva, permite:

— fortalecer las paredes venosas,
— fortalecer los músculos posturales (con el programa de Fast Gym de 8 minutos diarios),
— reequilibrar el sistema hormonal y linfático, y
— eliminar los alimentos «esponja».

En 15 días puede estimularse una pérdida de entre 1 y 3 kg, que irá acompañada de un programa de mantenimiento basado especialmente en eliminar la acumulación de agua y grasa celulítica.

Capítulo 1

Protagonista:
el agua

El fenómeno del aumento de peso es complejo, ya que existen numerosos parámetros implicados (genéticos, de conducta, fisiológicos o psicológicos). No obstante, intentaremos ofrecerle una explicación partiendo del principio de que reconocer los mecanismos del aumento de peso es sinónimo de armarse para luchar con éxito contra los mismos.

Para empezar, hablaremos del agua, que constituye entre el 50 y el 60 % del peso total del cuerpo humano; dicho de otro modo, una mujer de 40 años y 55 kg de peso alberga alrededor de 30 litros (es decir, 30 kg) de agua. De estos 30 litros de agua, las 3/5 partes participan en la composición de los músculos, los huesos, la piel, etc. Esta agua recibe el nombre de «líquido intracelular» y es indispensable para el buen funcionamiento del organismo, por lo que no podemos ni debemos eliminarla.

En consecuencia, quedan 12 litros de «agua extracelular» circulando por todo el cuerpo, de los cuales 4 litros se encuentran en la sangre, los fluidos digestivos, la saliva, la médula espinal, etc.

Los 8 litros de agua (de media) restantes constituyen lo que conocemos por el nombre de «líquido intersticial», que es el líquido en el que flotan nuestras células y que se encuentra, en principio, en constante movimiento, aunque comprobaremos que no siempre es así y que esto puede ser la causa de las molestias que muchos de nosotros experimentamos.

Todos los días esos 8 litros de agua salen de nuestras arterias, lavan nuestras células y, seguidamente, son reabsorbidos a través de las venas y los vasos linfáticos. Esta extraordinaria actividad de lavado diario se produce a través de un equilibrio perfecto: la misma cantidad de agua debe salir de las arterias y ser reabsorbida por las venas y los vasos linfáticos. Por tanto, se procurará que nunca haya más de 8 litros de agua entre las células en los espacios intersticiales. Al mínimo desequilibrio, es decir, cuando sale demasiada cantidad de agua o se reabsorbe una cantidad insuficiente de la misma —debido a un mal retorno venoso, por ejemplo, a una mala circulación linfática o también porque nuestros vasos son demasiado permeables (estado producido por un desequilibrio hormonal, al que ya nos referiremos más adelante)—, el exceso de agua se acumula y estanca entre las células, y se produce el fenómeno que conocemos con el nombre de retención de líquidos. En el peor de los casos, la cantidad de líquido intersticial puede incluso duplicarse, y este exceso de agua es el causante de la deformación de la silueta y de que, de cintura para abajo, el cuerpo se hinche como si de cúmulos de grasa se tratase. Por tanto, dicho exceso será el que podremos y deberemos combatir.

Este ciclo de agua que tiene lugar en nuestros cuerpos es uno de los mecanismos del metabolismo más minuciosamente regulados, por lo que ahondar en su conocimiento es indispensable para actuar desde el principio, desde que se produce un desajuste.

Una cuestión
de circulación

La extraordinaria actividad de lavado de los tejidos está condicionada por la calidad de nuestra circulación sanguínea. Veremos cómo una mala circulación sanguínea puede ser la causante de un desequilibrio en el ciclo del agua y, en definitiva, de la retención de líquidos.

Pero, en primer lugar, ¿qué entendemos por mala circulación?

Sin duda, esta expresión es demasiado genérica. Hay cuatro tipos de vasos: las arterias, las venas, los capilares y los linfáticos. Por tanto, al hablar de mala circulación, hay que precisar si se está hablando de circulación arterial, venosa, capilar o linfática, ya que cada una de estas disfunciones se manifiesta con efectos diferentes.

La mala circulación arterial

Se manifiesta en las piernas en forma de dolor en las pantorrillas al caminar. Este dolor puede ser lo bastante intenso como para obligar a la persona que lo sufre a detenerse de forma reiterada, y está asociado a lo que se denomina «arteritis», dolencia que no influye de ningún modo en el fenómeno de retención de líquidos.

La mala circulación capilar

En este caso, se manifiesta en las piernas en forma de sensación de frío en los pies o de un aspecto hinchado de la piel. Este problema tampoco provoca retención de líquidos.

La mala circulación venosa

Se relaciona con la sensación de piernas cansadas, la aparición de varices o varicosidades en las mismas, o de moratones espontáneos, y es la responsable del problema que nos ocupa.

La mala circulación linfática

Se manifiesta en pies y tobillos hinchados, fenómeno que puede llegar a ser muy importante y extenderse hasta los dedos de los pies, lo que es sinónimo de una afección linfática. También puede provocar retención de líquidos, aunque es mucho menos frecuente que en el caso de la mala circulación venosa.

Test 1

¿Tiene problemas
de circulación venosa?

El siguiente test le permitirá determinar si usted padece o no problemas de retorno venoso. Para ello, debe responder a las preguntas y sumar el total de los puntos que figuran a la derecha de las cuestiones. Remítase a continuación a los comentarios.

1 ¿Es usted...?

Hombre	0
Mujer	1

2 ¿Qué edad tiene?

Menos de 14 años	0
Entre 14 y 29 años	1
Entre 30 y 45 años	2
Más de 45 años	3

3 ¿Cuánto tiempo hace que lleva una vida sedentaria (no practica deporte, utiliza de forma sistemática el coche, los ascensores, etc.)?

No llevo una vida sedentaria	0
Entre 1 y 3 años	1
Entre 4 y 10 años	2
Más de 10 años	3

4 **¿Presenta usted un exceso de peso en relación con el que le correspondería para estar en forma?**

No	0
Sí, entre 1 y 5 kg	1
Sí, entre 6 y 10 kg	2
Sí, más de 10 kg	3

5 **¿Cuántos embarazos ha tenido?**

No he tenido embarazos	0
1 embarazo	1
2 embarazos	2
Más de 2 embarazos	3

6 **En caso de trabajar, ¿en qué posición suele hacerlo?**

En posición sentada, de pie o sin moverse menos de 4 horas al día	0
En posición sentada, de pie o sin moverse entre 4 y 8 horas al día	1
En posición sentada, de pie o sin moverse más de 8 horas al día	2
En posición sentada, de pie o sin moverse más de 8 horas al día, con trayectos largos frecuentes en coche, tren o avión	3

7 **¿Tiene antecedentes familiares (padre o madre) con varices?**

No, ninguno	0
1 familiar con varices	1
2 familiares con varices	2
2 familiares con varices y uno de ellos con complicaciones	3

8 ¿Sale a caminar o practica natación, bicicleta, *footing* o gimnasia?

Sí, al menos 3 horas por semana	0
Menos de 3 horas por semana	1
De forma irregular (en vacaciones)	2
Nunca	3

9 ¿Tiene la sensación de tener las piernas cansadas?

No, nunca	0
Sí, ocasionalmente	1
Sí, a menudo	2
Padezco dolores fuertes de forma casi permanente	3

10 Si padece sensación de piernas cansadas, esta aumenta con:

El calor	1
La píldora y los tratamientos hormonales	2
De forma sistemática durante la regla	1

11 ¿Se le hinchan los tobillos?

No, nunca	0
Solo en épocas de mucho calor o en largos trayectos en avión, tren o coche	1
Sí, casi todos los días, pero sólo por la noche	2
Sí, todos los días desde por la mañana	3

Resultados

Si su resultado total es:

Inferior o igual a 11

Se arriesga levemente a padecer una insuficiencia venosa. Siga los consejos de estilo de vida que le presentamos a continuación para conservar el buen estado de salud de las venas.

Entre 12 y 22

Se arriesga a padecer una insuficiencia venosa o esta dolencia ya se ha manifestado en usted mediante algunos síntomas que ponen de relieve la delicadeza de sus venas.

Es hora de actuar de forma activa y personal (deporte y normas de disciplina venosa), así como médica (venotónicos, contención, drenaje linfático, etc.).

Igual o superior a 23

Padece una insuficiencia venosa grave o un riesgo elevado de sufrirla algún día. Debe detener la evolución de la enfermedad mediante un tratamiento médico (esclerosis, cirugía, láser) y consolidar los resultados obtenidos respetando las normas de estilo de vida que le indicaremos más adelante.

¿Cómo se produce la retención de líquidos?

Ahora le invito a realizar un viaje por el interior de las piernas, en lo más profundo de los vasos.

He intentado que esta demostración sea lo menos complicada posible. No obstante, si no desea conocer todos y cada uno de los detalles, puede pasar a la lectura del capítulo siguiente.

Un circuito muy preciso

La función de las arterias consiste en transportar una cantidad de sangre roja activa repleta de nutrientes y de oxígeno a las células que van a alimentar. Posteriormente, dichas células, tras haber utilizado el oxígeno y los nutrientes para funcionar, expulsan residuos y dióxido de carbono.

A continuación, las venas profundas toman el relevo y recogen, desde los pies hasta el corazón, la sangre inservible, que presenta un color rojo oscuro debido a que está cargada de toxinas. Si todo este proceso se sucede correctamente, el mecanismo funciona como un reloj, aunque puede ocurrir que dicho mecanismo se «paralice», en particular cuando el individuo sufre molestias circulatorias.

Problemas circulatorios

Los problemas circulatorios de las arterias y de las venas profundas son muy diferentes. Cuando una arteria se estropea, se encoge y se endurece, y hablamos entonces de arterosclerosis. En cambio, cuando una vena se deteriora, al contrario que ocurre con las arterias, se ablanda, se ensancha, se dilata, ya que su misión es totalmente distinta: se encarga de drenar las toxinas y el agua de lavado de las células. Ahora bien, recoger la sangre desde los pies hasta el corazón todos los días, luchando contra el fenómeno de la gravedad, es una tarea problemática.

Nuestra vida se desarrolla de pie o sentados de forma prolongada y nuestra sangre presenta un determinado peso, por lo que tiende a volver a bajar hacia los pies y, en consecuencia, a dilatar las venas. Para que lo entienda, imagínese un globo de goma con forma de salchicha lleno de agua. Si lo mantiene de forma vertical, las paredes del mismo no mantendrán una forma paralela, sino que adquirirán más bien la forma de una pera o una gota de agua; lo mismo ocurre con las venas: si las paredes no son lo suficientemente sólidas (la causa puede ser hereditaria), aquellas irán dilatándose progresivamente. Se trata del principio de un círculo vicioso, ya que, cuanto más se dilaten, más cantidad (y por tanto, más peso) de sangre podrán albergar. En consecuencia, cada vez será más complicado volver a hacer subir la sangre hacia el corazón, por lo que la sangre venosa se estancará en las piernas. Como veremos más adelante, dicha sangre será la causante de la retención de líquidos.

Músculos, venas superficiales y venas perforantes

Prosigamos con nuestro viaje. Ahora, las arterias y las venas profundas irán acompañadas de otros dos agentes esenciales en la circulación venosa: los músculos y las venas superficiales.

Las venas profundas están rodeadas de músculos, de los cuales los más importantes son los músculos profundos, también denominados músculos posturales. Estos músculos rodean y sostienen a las venas. En caso de que estas últimas sean demasiado frágiles y se dilaten con demasiada facilidad por el peso de la sangre, los músculos actuarán como una auténtica contención natural.

Debido a esto, se comprende en seguida lo importante que es tener un buen tono y una buena actividad muscular. Ahora bien, las venas profundas, que están en nuestros músculos y no son visibles, representan el 80 % de la totalidad de las venas de nuestras piernas. El 20 % restante se encuentra en o bajo la piel, en el tejido adiposo. Cuando las venas superficiales enferman, se dilatan y pueden formar varicosidades (pequeños capilares violáceos visibles en las piernas) o varices (grandes venas moradas y arqueadas, visibles a través de la piel).

No olvidemos, además, que pasamos la mayor parte del tiempo en posición vertical, de pie o sentados, y que la presión en las venas, es decir, el peso de la sangre, puede aumentar significativamente si estas se dilatan. Ahora bien, las venas profundas y las superficiales se comunican a lo largo de la pierna a través de un tercer tipo de venas, las llamadas venas perforantes. Según el célebre principio de los vasos comunicantes, cualquier distensión de las venas profundas en los músculos repercutirá en las venas superficiales, lo que favorecerá la retención de líquidos en la piel y la celulitis.

La primera conclusión tras esta primera etapa transcurrida en lo más profundo de nuestras células es que no cabe esperar un resultado duradero en un tratamiento de retención de líquidos con una paciente que presente una dilatación considerable de las venas profundas, sino que hay que fortalecer el soporte muscular de estas venas, es decir, hay que reforzar los músculos profundos posturales. Los 8 minutos diarios de Fast Gym que se describen en el capítulo 4 podrán contribuir en el logro de dicho resultado.

Por último, hablaremos de otro agente de la circulación sanguínea en las piernas: los vasos linfáticos. La mayoría de ellos se extiende por las venas superficiales de las extremidades inferiores, y tienen como función recoger el exceso de agua de las piernas y llevarlo hasta el corazón. En cierto modo, actúan como una válvula de seguridad que, cuando funciona perfectamente, evita la retención de líquidos.

Resumen

Las condiciones de una buena circulación

• La sangre fresca, cargada con nutrientes y oxígeno, desciende por las arterias desde el corazón hacia las piernas para alimentar a los tejidos.

• Las células expulsan residuos, toxinas y dióxido de carbono, sustancias que las venas profundas y las superficiales trasladarán desde los pies hasta el corazón. Este retorno venoso se efectúa en contra de la presión de la gravedad, por lo que hay que luchar contra el peso de la sangre que tiende a dilatar las venas.

• De forma paralela a esta función de la circulación, que consiste en transportar los nutrientes para alimentar a las células y llevar los residuos al corazón, la segunda función que le corresponde es la
de trasladar el agua necesaria a los tejidos a fin de
que se produzca el lavado diario de todas las células. Cada día, 8 litros de agua salen de nuestras arterias para lavar las células. El 90 % de esta agua es
reabsorbida por las venas, y el 10 % restante, por
los vasos linfáticos.

Imagínese ahora que el agua que sale de las arterias no
sea reabsorbida totalmente por las venas ni por los vasos
linfáticos, sino que toda esta agua se queda en los tejidos
intersticiales, entre las células, concretamente en los pies
y los tobillos.

Si esta retención de líquidos es importante, se hará visible y será la causante de la hinchazón de los tobillos, dolencia conocida con el nombre de edema.

En la mayoría de los casos, la retención afectará a toda
la pierna y se instalará principalmente en las caderas, las
caras externas de los muslos y las internas de las rodillas,
así como en los tobillos.

Esta retención se asociará a la acumulación grasosa y
ofrecerá el aspecto hinchado de piel de naranja; asimismo, podrá infiltrarse en los tejidos sin causar un verdadero edema e instalarse en los dedos, las manos, los párpados, etc.

Mecanismos que impiden
la reabsorción del agua

Intentemos ahora comprender por qué en algunos casos la totalidad del agua que sale de las arterias no puede ser reabsorbida ni por las venas ni por los vasos linfáticos; dicho de otra manera: ¿cuáles son los mecanismos que pueden provocar retención de líquidos?

Una circulación venosa defectuosa

Tal y como hemos visto antes, si las venas están demasiado dilatadas, aumentará el peso de la sangre en las mismas. Se trata de una ley puramente física: una excesiva presión en las venas impide la reabsorción de la totalidad del agua que sale de las arterias.

Un fallo de la circulación linfática

Normalmente, si las venas no funcionan bien, la naturaleza nos ha proporcionado un sistema de seguridad: los vasos linfáticos. La misión de estos consiste en aumentar la proporción de líquidos que van a transportar hacia el corazón a fin de evitar que se acumule un exceso de agua en los tejidos. Si los vasos linfáticos no funcionan convenientemente, se pone en marcha un segundo mecanismo: la retención de líquidos. Hablamos de linfedema cuando se produce una disfunción importante.

Presencia de moléculas en el tejido intersticial

Se trata de grandes moléculas que pueden ser proteínas mal digeridas, azúcar o sal. Estas moléculas producen un efecto «esponja», ya que retienen los líquidos.

Para comprenderlo mejor, volvamos al ejemplo del globo con agua y sumerjámoslo en un recipiente lleno con la misma agua. El globo, mantenido por la presión del agua exterior, la del recipiente, ya no se dilatará en forma de gota, sino que mantendrá su forma de salchicha con extremos paralelos.

Imaginemos ahora que en el agua del recipiente vertemos proteínas de gran tamaño, azúcar o sal. En tal caso, se producirá un fenómeno conocido con el nombre de «presión osmótica».

Se trata de una ley física según la cual el agua se dirige siempre del medio menos concentrado al más concentrado. De este modo, las proteínas, la sal o el azúcar que se encuentran en el agua del recipiente producirán un efecto «esponja» y atraerán el agua del globo hacia el recipiente.

Ocurre lo mismo en nuestro sistema venoso: si existen proteínas, azúcar o sal en los espacios intersticiales, el agua saldrá de las venas para dirigirse al medio más concentrado. Este efecto «esponja» es el causante de la retención de líquidos que se manifiesta en las personas que presentan una intolerancia a determinados alimentos, los cuales se mantendrán en los tejidos en forma de grandes proteínas al no ser completamente digeridos por el tubo digestivo.

La lucha contra la relajación
de la pared venosa

Volviendo al ejemplo del globo de hace un momento, el que se dilata en forma de gota de agua, una de las soluciones para impedir que este fenómeno ocurra consiste en fortalecer las paredes.

Por tanto, sustituyamos el globo de goma flexible por un globo de material mucho más grueso y resistente, es decir, poco deformable.

Si se coloca el globo en posición vertical, este mantendrá una forma regular a pesar de que se produzca el aumento de la presión.

Lo mismo sucede en las piernas de cualquier persona cuando las venas, al igual que el globo, presentan unas paredes suficientemente sólidas.

Imaginemos ahora que este globo que representa nuestras venas está envuelto en un refuerzo lo suficientemente resistente como para evitar las deformaciones en las piernas.

La naturaleza ya nos ha provisto de este mecanismo al colocar el 80 % de las venas de nuestras piernas en el interior de los músculos.

Estos últimos actúan como un refuerzo en caso de que las paredes venosas sean excesivamente débiles.

Finalmente, en caso de que, como consecuencia de una vida demasiado sedentaria, los músculos tampoco muestren una tonicidad suficiente debida, por ejemplo, a su poca actividad, las venas perderán este otro sistema de seguridad.

Venas permeables:
un caso especial

Vamos a ilustrar otro mecanismo responsable de la retención de líquidos. Volvamos a utilizar el ejemplo del globo e imaginemos esta vez que las paredes del mismo son porosas y el agua pasa a través de las mismas. En nuestro cuerpo, el aumento de permeabilidad de las venas está especialmente condicionado por el equilibrio hormonal entre los estrógenos y la progesterona. Tanto el exceso de estrógenos como la carencia de progesterona pueden desembocar en una permeabilidad excesiva de las venas, lo que ocurre principalmente durante el síndrome premenstrual: hinchazón que algunas mujeres experimentan antes de la regla, tensión en los senos, hinchazón de pies y tobillos, y sensación de congestión en piernas y pelvis.

Test 2

¿Padece retención de líquidos?

Responda a las 5 preguntas siguientes:

I. ¿Su peso puede variar entre I y 3 kg en menos de una semana?

SÍ   NO

2. Si realiza una dieta severa, ¿suele perder más peso de cintura para arriba que de cintura para abajo?

SÍ   NO

3. ¿Se le hinchan los pies o los tobillos en época de calor?

SÍ   NO

4. ¿Se le hinchan los pies o los tobillos cuando realiza largos trayectos en avión?

SÍ   NO

5. Si apoya el pulgar sobre la piel de los tobillos, ¿la huella del pulgar permanece visible durante más de 2 segundos?

SÍ   NO

COMENTARIO

Si ha respondido afirmativamente a más de 2 preguntas, puede que padezca molestias relacionadas con la retención de líquidos, es decir, cuando las células de su cuerpo se someten al lavado del líquido que sale de las arterias, ni las venas ni los vasos linfáticos pueden absorber la totalidad del mismo.

Capítulo 2

Causas de la hinchazón de las piernas

A cabamos de ver cómo la presencia de un exceso de líquidos en los tejidos intersticiales puede asociarse a tres causas:

Una mala circulación venosa o linfática

Las venas se encuentran demasiado dilatadas debido a que su pared es frágil, bien por razones hereditarias, bien por razones ligadas a una sensibilidad a los factores del estilo de vida actual como la alimentación moderna, el sedentarismo, el estrés, etc.

Un exceso de permeabilidad de los vasos

Una cantidad excesiva de agua, superior a los 8 litros previstos inicialmente por la naturaleza, se filtra a través de las venas hacia los tejidos intersticiales. Hay varios factores que pueden hacer que nuestros vasos se vuelvan demasiado permeables, y uno de ellos es la inflamación. Cuando sufrimos un traumatismo como, por ejemplo, un esguince de tobillo, este último se hincha. Se trata de un mecanismo de defensa del organismo: para acelerar la cura de los ligamentos que se han estirado durante el esguince, la sangre hace llegar a la zona unas sustancias denominadas «mediadores de la inflamación». Estas sustancias se encargan de hacer que el vaso sea más permeable para facilitar el paso de los glóbulos blancos desde los vasos hacia los tejidos y, de este modo, reparar las células o atacar los posibles gérmenes que puedan haberse introducido si se ha producido una herida.

Esta introducción de glóbulos blancos va acompañada obligatoriamente de agua debido al aumento de la permeabilidad del vaso, y este es el motivo de que se produzcan las hinchazones que pueden observarse en cualquier reacción inflamatoria. Por otra parte, el enrojecimiento que se observa se debe a la dilatación de los vasos, que se produce para aportar una mayor cantidad de sangre (y por tanto de glóbulos blancos) a la zona.

Un desequilibrio hormonal

La causa más frecuente del aumento de permeabilidad de los vasos va asociada a un desequilibrio hormonal que se produce entre los estrógenos y la progesterona, tal y como hemos indicado anteriormente. Cuando hay una excesiva cantidad de estrógenos en la sangre en comparación con la de progesterona, los vasos se hacen más permeables y se experimenta por tanto una sensación de hinchazón, obstrucción y retención de líquidos. Las mujeres que lo padecen sufrirán, antes de la regla, hinchazón en cara, dedos y piernas, y también sentirán dolor en los senos.

Test 3

¿Padece un desequilibrio hormonal?

Responda a las 5 preguntas siguientes:

1. ¿Presenta quistes en los senos?
>   SÍ   NO

2. ¿Sus reglas son irregulares?
>   SÍ   NO

3. ¿Sus reglas son demasiado abundantes?
>   SÍ   NO

4. ¿Siente dolor en la pelvis durante la regla?
>   SÍ   NO

5. ¿Siente dolor en los senos durante la regla?
>   SÍ   NO

COMENTARIO

Si ha respondido afirmativamente a más de 2 preguntas, puede que padezca un desequilibrio hormonal. Su ginecólogo podrá confirmarle el diagnóstico, averiguar la causa y encargarse de equilibrar sus hormonas mediante un tratamiento adecuado.

Presencia de moléculas «esponja»

Como hemos visto con el ejemplo del globo, la sal y el azúcar pueden «aspirar» y retener líquidos. Por ello, hay que evitar una alimentación con demasiada sal y también el exceso de azúcar industrial de los pasteles, dulces, refrescos y productos lácteos edulcorados.

No obstante, se ha confirmado que algunas proteínas también tienen parte de culpa, a pesar de la buena reputación de la que suelen gozar por encargarse de la formación de tejidos, huesos, músculos y piel. Entonces, ¿por qué en ocasiones pueden resultar perjudiciales?

Importancia de la digestión de las proteínas

Una proteína es una gran molécula que, en realidad, es un entramado de aminoácidos. En este caso, la comparación puede realizarse con una casa de ladrillos, donde cada ladrillo es un aminoácido.

Normalmente, durante la digestión, las enzimas digestivas que se encuentran en el tubo digestivo se encargan de separar cada uno de los ladrillos, que a continuación serán asimilados para la elaboración del cabello, las uñas, la piel y los huesos. Si una proteína no se ha digerido completamente, bien porque su forma química es demasiado compleja, bien porque no disponemos de suficiente capital enzimático digestivo, quedan algunos entramados de aminoácidos que reciben el nombre de **péptidos**.

Por tanto, un péptido es un entramado de aminoácidos que puede proceder de una proteína que no se ha digerido completamente.

Proteínas cada vez más químicas

Los productos procesados de la alimentación moderna han experimentado extraordinarios avances en materia de conservación, de eliminación de bacterias y también de sabor. Cuanto más se transforma, refina y conserva un producto, más se altera su sabor. No obstante, el sabor de un alimento que ha quedado demasiado insípido o demasiado seco puede mejorar añadiendo productos químicos que retienen el agua o la grasa como, por ejemplo, los productos emolientes, que pueden ablandar o suavizar un producto seco o demasiado duro. Asimismo, este tipo de productos puede actuar sobre uno de los parámetros que configuran el sabor: la untuosidad.

A las nociones básicas que aprendemos en secundaria sobre el sabor —dulce, salado, ácido, etc.— se añaden otras nociones que el sector agroalimentario examina y controla perfectamente en la actualidad. La untuosidad forma parte de dichas nociones: se obtiene a partir de un alimento mediante la adición de un elemento graso o de agua, con lo que se mejora la sensación de «suavidad». Tomemos el jamón como ejemplo: si está demasiado seco, no está bueno. Su sabor puede mejorarse con elementos grasos o asociándolo a productos emolientes y humectantes que aumentarán la cantidad de agua. Este proceso permitirá, por una parte, mejorar la untuosidad y, por otra, incrementar el peso del producto (para que esté a gusto de todos). Hoy en día, podemos encontrar productos emolientes en cualquier alimento, hasta en las galletas secas, para que no estén tan... secas.

Una diferencia incuestionable

La mayoría de las personas metaboliza muy bien los productos químicos que proceden del sector agroalimentario y que se encuentran en la mayor parte de los productos procesados y conservados, concretamente en los productos complejos como los platos precocinados, las sopas, etc.

No obstante, algunas personas no pueden asimilar completamente estas proteínas químicas en el tubo digestivo, con lo que, en lugar de transformarse en ladrillos de aminoácidos, permanecerán agrupadas en pequeños bloques de ladrillos como si, retomando el ejemplo anterior de la casa, esta se hubiese derruido parcialmente, diseminada en pequeños grupos de ladrillos, con algunos de ellos todavía unidos.

El equivalente en nuestro organismo de estos pequeños grupos de ladrillos unidos son los famosos péptidos, que podemos encontrar en la sangre y, posteriormente, en los tejidos intersticiales, y que en presencia de líquido se comportan como auténticas esponjas y los retienen en los tejidos.

Podría tratarse de aditivos alimentarios emolientes, humectantes, aunque también de agentes de carga, productos secuestrantes, endurecedores, estabilizantes, potenciadores del sabor, emulgentes o edulcorantes. En numerosos productos que las mujeres modernas apre-

Ejemplo

de chica joven
de 18 años...

... que padece una retención de líquidos dispersa por el cuerpo, lo que le provoca una sensación de obstrucción generalizada. Por las mañanas, al despertarse, se levanta con los párpados y los dedos un poco hinchados, y ya presenta una celulitis congestiva con retención de líquidos en los muslos y en la cara interna de las rodillas.

Como muchas jóvenes de su edad, sigue una dieta moderna y, a pesar de que procura consumir una buena cantidad de frutas y verduras, en su alimentación podemos encontrar algunos de los productos del sector agroalimentario que sus amigas soportan muy bien, pero que ella no digiere completamente, sino que, en su caso, estos alimentos se convierten en **«esponjas»**.

cian de forma especial (sopas preparadas o platos precocinados) hay elementos espesantes y almidones modificados, así como pectinas utilizadas por sus propiedades gelificantes. Al igual que el resto de los polisacáridos, mejoran considerablemente la sensación de untuosidad en la boca e incluso consiguen dar una consistencia similar a la de los productos ricos en materias grasas, con la diferencia de que no las tienen.

Por otra parte, para estabilizar las proteínas se utilizan numerosas sustancias químicas que parecen inofensivas como la sacarosa, el glicerol, el sorbitol, el manitol y sales como el sulfato de amonio. Puede que, sin darse cuenta, las personas que consumen estas sustancias no las toleren ni las digieran.

Numerosos productos de nuestro entorno alimentario, ya sea por un mecanismo de intolerancia alimentaria, de alergia o de digestibilidad incompleta de molécula química, pueden dar lugar a una reacción de retención de líquidos que, combinada con la grasa, provocará un aumento de peso.

Este volumen de líquido representará una masa importante de entre 4 y 7 kg (e incluso de hasta 15 kg en algunos casos extremos) que no podrán eliminarse con una dieta hipocalórica clásica, puesto que con este tipo de dietas tan solo llega a eliminarse la grasa de la parte superior del cuerpo.

Incluso algunos aditivos alimentarios como los sulfitos, que se encuentran en los frutos secos, los copos de puré, la mostaza, los zumos de limón preparados o las olivas en lata, es decir, en alimentos que gozan de buena reputación por lo beneficiosos que resultan para la salud, pueden dar lugar, en algunas personas, a una retención de líquidos a través de un proceso alérgico.

Ocurre algo similar con los benzoatos, sustancias presentes en la mayoría de las bebidas refrescantes, incluyendo las *light*.

Causas de enfermedades más graves

Hemos visto cómo algunas proteínas mal digeridas podían formar péptidos que se instalaban en los tejidos intersticiales y retenían líquidos. En el proceso inverso, la falta considerable de proteínas en la dieta también puede desembocar en una situación de retención de líquidos, ya que el fenómeno, en lo más profundo de su mecanismo, es aun más delicado y complejo. De hecho, la diferencia de concentración de proteínas entre la sangre y el tejido intersticial es la causante de la retención de líquidos en los tejidos. Un exceso de proteínas en el tejido intersticial (alimentos «esponja») puede llegar a desembocar en una situación de retención de líquidos; sin embargo, ocurrirá lo mismo en caso de no existir una cantidad suficiente de proteínas en la sangre. Una persona que prácticamente no las come o que lo hace en muy poca cantidad puede llegar a padecer edemas. Este es el caso de los niños africanos que están totalmente desnutridos y, sin embargo, presentan una barriga hinchada. La barriga está llena de agua debido a la ausencia total de proteínas en su alimentación y, por tanto, en la sangre.

Asimismo, pueden padecerse hinchazones cuando los riñones o el hígado no funcionan correctamente. Una enfermedad renal denominada síndrome nefrótico conlleva una pérdida de proteínas por medio de la orina que provoca hinchazón y retención de agua debido a la escasez de proteínas en la sangre. Además, las personas que tienen problemas con el alcohol o que padecen cirrosis de hígado pueden sufrir problemas de retención de líquidos y edemas debido a una insuficiente síntesis hepática de las proteínas.

Por último, determinados medicamentos como los inhibidores cálcicos que se prescriben para la hipertensión arterial también pueden generar situaciones de retención de líquidos.

Como hemos visto, incluso en enfermedades graves, la alimentación o un problema de metabolismo de las proteínas suele estar implicado como el origen de estos desajustes de retención de líquidos.

Celulitis, una antigua
reserva sin sentido

La tercera causa está asociada a la retención de la grasa, que puede situarse justo encima de la piel y que se denomina celulitis, o que también puede instalarse en una zona un poco más profunda encima de los músculos y que denominamos en tal caso esteatomeria. Estos depósitos adiposos se localizan en las caderas, la cara interna de los muslos, la cara interna de las rodillas y, a menudo, a lo largo de las piernas y de la barriga de forma dispersa. Las retenciones de agua y de grasa suelen manifestarse de forma conjunta en determinadas formas de celulitis.

La predisposición genética está ligada a la actividad de una enzima que se encuentra en nuestras células adiposas y que se denomina lipoproteína lipasa, encargada de regular la cantidad de grasa que, día a día, se irá almacenando o que, por el contrario, se utilizará para producir energía.

Este mecanismo se ha ido programando a lo largo de nuestra evolución a fin de que nos afecten menos los periodos de hambruna que conocieron nuestros ancestros en la época de las cavernas entre dos periodos de caza o en condiciones de variaciones climáticas. Las mujeres en particular han desarrollado este mecanismo de almacenamiento de energía para poder enfrentarse a las necesidades energéticas de un posible embarazo. La actividad de esta enzima puede programarse de forma genética. En algunas mujeres, esta enzima funciona principalmente para almacenar grasa y, en otras, para utilizar la grasa en caso de que el cuerpo necesite energía.

En la actualidad, esta grasa de reserva carece de sentido, puesto que ya no padecemos periodos de hambruna, al menos en los países industrializados. No obstante, en caso de existir un excedente alimenticio que supere nuestras necesidades, este mecanismo sigue funcionando y, aunque la grasa depositada en los muslos deforma la silueta y produce un perjuicio estético, sigue siendo menos nociva que si se depositara en las arterias hasta obstruirlas.

La aparición de la celulitis no se debe a la cantidad de alimentos ingeridos, sino a la calidad de los mismos, en particular:

Mala calidad de las grasas

Las peores son las grasas cocidas y los ácidos grasos saturados, ya que presentan un proceso de metabolismo más complicado y se almacenan directamente en la celulitis. Antiguamente, en las facultades de medicina se enseñaba que el peor enemigo, en lo que a la grasa se refería, era el colesterol. Actualmente, existen cuatro condiciones que propician los riesgos:

— La presencia de colesterol que, en exceso, favorece la arteriosclerosis y obstruye las arterias.
— La presencia de grasas cocidas, que deberían evitarse en la medida de lo posible.
— La utilización de ácidos grasos saturados como la mantequilla, el aceite de cacahuete, las grasas animales de los productos de charcutería y las carnes grasas.
— La ausencia de omega 3, los famosos ácidos grasos protectores que se encuentran en el pescado de agua fría (caballas, arenques y salmones salvajes) y en algunos aceites vegetales como el de colza.

Por tanto, las grasas beneficiosas cumplen cuatro requisitos: son grasas crudas, ricas en omega 3, pobres en colesterol y ricas en ácidos grasos poliinsaturados. Se metabolizan mejor, refuerzan las membranas de las células y hacen que la sangre fluya con mayor facilidad. Las grasas perjudiciales, en particular las grasas cocidas, pueden almacenarse directamente en las zonas celulíticas.

Exceso de azúcares industriales

Las grasas no son las únicas culpables de la aparición de la celulitis. Actualmente, los azúcares industriales también están implicados de forma directa. Efectivamente, se han descubierto receptores de insulina, la hormona que regula la cantidad de azúcar en la sangre, en las membranas de las células adiposas: los adipocitos, presentes en la celulitis. Los azúcares industriales, en particular la sacarosa, pueden agravar la celulitis. Son preferibles los azúcares naturales como los de las frutas, las verduras y los cereales, que, en forma integral y no procesada, pueden metabolizarse correctamente gracias a la rica cantidad de vitaminas y minerales que presentan.

Ausencia de vitaminas

La ingestión diaria de una cantidad suficiente de vitaminas y minerales es necesaria, y su falta es perjudicial. Efectivamente, los grandes nutrientes como las proteínas, los azúcares (glúcidos) y las grasas (lípidos) necesitan vitaminas y minerales para su correcta digestión.

Cada uno de estos grupos de alimentos está constituido por pequeños ladrillos. Por ejemplo, los ladrillos de las proteínas son aminoácidos. Una proteína es un conjunto de aminoácidos unidos los unos a los otros como los ladrillos de una casa, tal y como hemos visto antes.

Los ladrillos de los azúcares son las moléculas de glucosa o de fructosa que, agrupadas entre ellas, forman los glúcidos, los polisacáridos o los almidones. Para digerir correctamente los glúcidos, sobre todo los de origen industrial, debemos utilizar una gran cantidad de vitaminas y minerales, a fin de poder separarlos en pequeños ladrillos que seguidamente utilizarán nuestras células.

Los ladrillos de grasa se denominan ácidos grasos. Las grasas, o lípidos, son un conjunto de ácidos grasos unidos y, en función de la forma de dicha unión, hablaremos de grasas saturadas o poliinsaturadas. Los ácidos grasos saturados presentan un proceso de metabolismo más complicado, ya que se depositan en el tejido celulítico. Por el contrario, su naturaleza rígida los hace resistentes al calor y a la cocción, lo que explica que estén tan presentes en los aceites de cocina. En cambio, las grasas poliinsaturadas, entre las que se incluyen las omega 3, son flexibles, suaves, frágiles y sensibles a la cocción. Diluyen las membranas de las células y se metabolizan muy fácilmente, por lo que no se acumulan en la grasa celulítica.

Por todo ello, ya puede imaginarse qué dieta influirá de forma determinante en la acumulación de grasa en la parte inferior del cuerpo: deberá huir de los productos químicos que el sistema digestivo digiere de forma incompleta, y de las grasas cocidas y los ácidos grasos saturados, así como evitar o reducir en la medida de lo posible los azúcares industriales y, finalmente, aumentar el consumo diario de vitaminas y minerales.

Por tanto, puesto que lo que beneficia a una mujer puede perjudicar a otra debido a las capacidades digestivas, a los gustos y a la predisposición genética de cada una, deberá determinarse la alimentación más afín a la necesidades psicológicas naturales de cada una, la menos procesada, intentando sacar partido de los avances incontestables del sector alimentario y, sobre todo, incrementando el aporte de vitaminas y minerales que requiera cada persona.

La alimentación moderna ideal todavía está por descubrir. En la actualidad, el sector agroalimentario nos ha aportado avances innegables al ofrecernos alimentos exentos de bacterias, de una amplia variedad, en cualquier estación del año, y envasados de forma que no perdamos nada de tiempo.

Todo ello nos permite adaptarnos a la vida moderna, en la que el tiempo que antes pasábamos en ir al mercado y pelar las verduras ha sido sustituido por el tiempo que dedicamos a trasladarnos, trabajar y organizarnos.

Estos avances nos proporcionan unas amplias posibilidades de elección, aunque, como ocurre con todo, también tienen sus inconvenientes, ya que si consumimos demasiados alimentos procesados podemos caer en una alimentación demasiado rica, demasiado grasa o demasiado química.

Todo ello se traduce de forma muy clara en la aparición de auténticas alergias, debido a la degradación incompleta de las moléculas que se más tarde transformarán en elementos «esponja» y darán lugar al fenómeno de retención de líquidos.

Ahora que somos completamente conscientes de que podemos engordar de cintura para abajo por motivos asociados no sólo a la genética, sino también a la retención de líquidos o a la de grasas, deberá conocer cómo pueden combinarse dichos elementos y dar lugar a diferentes tipos de celulitis.

No hay un solo tipo de celulitis,
sino varios

La celulitis es una grasa «concentrada» que se instala justo debajo de la piel y que suele ir acompañada de problemas de retención de líquidos y fibrosis. Existen tres tipos de celulitis: la adiposa, la infiltrada y la fibrosa.

Tres tipos de celulitis

En función de cuál sea el componente mayoritario, hablaremos de uno u otro tipo de celulitis: cuando es el componente adiposo, tenemos una celulitis **adiposa** o de lipodistrofia; cuando es el componente que retiene el agua, se trata de celulitis **infiltrada** o de hidrolipodistrofia, y cuando es el componente fibroso el mayoritario, lo que se presenta es una celulitis **fibrosa** o fibrolipodistrofia.

Tanto si padece usted una celulitis adiposa o infiltrada con retención de líquidos, ambas se mostrarán suaves al tacto. En cambio, si al tocarse nota que la consistencia de la celulitis es dura (es decir, que se endurece al pasar la mano), entonces será fibrosa. Asimismo, pueden manifestarse celulitis mixtas, es decir, adiposas e infiltradas a la vez.

Los tratamientos propuestos también difieren en función del tipo de celulitis. Las celulitis adiposas se sensibilizarán con la aplicación de cremas que contengan cafeína, una sustancia conocida por su capacidad para acelerar la eliminación de grasas, con la inyección de medicamentos lipolíticos, que también permiten reducir las grasas, o con la liposucción, que, para este caso en concreto, es la técnica más eficaz.

En el caso de la celulitis infiltrada acompañada de retención de agua, los métodos de drenaje como el drenaje linfático, el drenaje linfático en piscina, la presoterapia o el aparato Cellu M6 han conseguido hacerse un hueco.

Sin embargo, en el caso de la celulitis fibrosa, endurecida, tan sólo el aparato Cellu M6 ha dado buenos resultados.

Un caso particular: la celulitis hereditaria

Determinados tipos de celulitis consiguen sortear cualquier técnica correctora y, en consecuencia, sólo pueden controlarse mediante esfuerzos constantes: las mujeres cuyas madres o abuelas presentaban las piernas «deformadas» debido a la celulitis deberán realizar más ejercicio físico o evitar cualquier desliz en la dieta que otras personas. Se trata de la injusticia de las variaciones interindividuales que se manifiestan en todos los sistemas biológicos.

En lo que a problemas circulatorios y desequilibrios hormonales se refiere, también existen varias posibilidades, que harán que algunas mujeres sean sensibles a un reequilibrio y otras ofrezcan más resistencia.

Un equilibrio personalizado

Finalmente, aunque las medidas relativas a la alimentación pueden parecer simples, estas se enfrentan a la cultura, la educación en cuanto al sabor, las costumbres y el estrés diario; en definitiva, unas condiciones que conducen, en caso de bajar la guardia, a volver a caer en los mismos errores. Lo ideal sería poder disfrutar con una alimentación sana y equilibrada. No obstante, a pesar de que uno puede volverse loco de placer comiéndose el gajo de una naranja, esto también puede ocurrir con un trozo de chocolate, que, aunque es cierto que contiene una pequeña cantidad de magnesio, desafortunadamente también incluye una gran cantidad de grasas y azúcares perjudiciales.

Nuevamente, la cuestión vuelve a girar en torno al equilibrio y a la tolerancia de cada uno. Así, algunas personas podrán tomar varios trozos de chocolate todos los días y compensarlo por otra parte con una alimentación equilibrada. Sin embargo, a otras personas les afectaría el primer trozo, ya que las grasas saturadas y los azúcares industriales de este irían a acumularse directamente en zonas no deseadas.

Definir un programa de adelgazamiento que actúe sobre la mitad inferior del cuerpo significa poner en marcha una balanza que intentará equilibrarse de forma personalizada.

Test 4

¿Qué tipo de celulitis padece?

Responda SÍ o NO a las 5 preguntas siguientes:

1. Su celulitis no se localiza únicamente en la parte superior de las piernas (caderas y cartucheras), sino que también aparece en la cara interna de las rodillas y de los tobillos:

SÍ   NO

2. ¿Le suelen doler las piernas?

SÍ   NO

3. ¿Se le suelen hinchar las piernas durante la regla?

SÍ   NO

4. ¿Suelen aparecerle cardenales en las piernas al más mínimo golpe?

SÍ   NO

5. ¿Presenta pequeñas varicosidades de color rojo o violáceo que sean visibles en las piernas?

SÍ   NO

COMENTARIO

Si ha respondido afirmativamente a 2 o más preguntas, puede que padezca una celulitis infiltrada, es decir, acompañada por una retención de líquidos asociada a uno de los mecanismos que hemos visto antes: una circulación venosa o linfática defectuosa, un desequilibrio hormonal o una intolerancia a los alimentos «esponja».

Capítulo 3

Fortalecimiento de los músculos posturales

L a acumulación de peso en la mitad inferior del cuerpo constituye una forma de desequilibrio visible. En la balanza, deberá encontrarse un equilibrio entre, por un lado, los elementos que tienden a hacer engordar de cintura para abajo (la genética, la retención, los desajustes hormonales, etc.) y, por otro, los elementos de compensación (Fast Gym para entrenar los músculos posturales profundos, las plantas drenantes, etc.). En última instancia, podrá recurrirse a los medicamentos que hacen posible la pérdida de líquidos o de grasas.

La balanza puede presentarse de esta forma:

Elementos negativos	Elementos positivos
• Genética	• Fast Gym
• Estilo de vida sedentario	• Plantas drenantes
• Grasas cocidas	• Drenaje en agua
• Azúcares industriales	• Drenaje linfático
• Alimentos «esponja»	• Cellu M6
• Estrés	• Contención
• Falta de tiempo	• Medicamentos

8 minutos
al día

Este es el tiempo necesario para efectuar los ejercicios de gimnasia postural denominada Fast Gym.

Tampoco necesitará mucho más tiempo para eliminar de su dieta las grasas cocidas o los azúcares industriales, establecer una agenda alimentaria de todo lo que come al día (durante 6 semanas) para poder identificar los alimentos «esponja», es decir, los que no le convienen y que pueden variar totalmente de una persona a otra.

Necesitará unos cuantos segundos más para tomarse 2 o 3 cápsulas de plantas con propiedades drenantes y vitaminas que favorezcan las reacciones metabólicas como la vitamina E, la vitamina C, el selenio y el cinc.

No obstante, puede que deba modificar el uso que hace de sus horas para aumentar el tiempo diario que pasa caminando, renunciar a los ascensores, practicar 1 o 2 horas de gimnasia, comprar dos veces por semana productos frescos y dedicar un poco de tiempo a preparar sopas, pelar zanahorias y exprimir algún que otro zumo de naranja, pomelo o limón.

Hemos comprobado que el 80 % de las venas de las piernas se encuentran en el interior de masas musculares. Diferentes estudios han demostrado el estrecho vínculo que existe entre los músculos y la circulación venosa de las extremidades inferiores.

En la actualidad, se sabe que existe un estrecho vínculo entre el tono muscular de las pantorrillas y el diámetro de las venas situadas en el interior de estos músculos. Sin embargo, hasta hace poco se desconocía que no todos los músculos tenían la misma predisposición frente al retorno venoso. Los grupos musculares más eficaces a la hora de garantizar una buena circulación venosa son los músculos posturales, esto es, los músculos profundos de las piernas, los muslos y la pelvis.

Músculos posturales

Una de las características del cuerpo humano es la de poder mantenerse de pie. Coja el palo de una escoba e intente mantenerlo en posición vertical apoyado en el suelo: el palo no se mantendrá en pie por sí solo, sino que hay que sujetarlo; asimismo, se habrá dado cuenta de que es mucho más fácil mantenerlo de pie por la parte superior que por la inferior. Pues bien, el cuerpo humano sí se mantiene en pie, aunque se sostiene por la parte inferior. Por muy pequeña que sea la superficie de contacto con el suelo que el pie representa, esta es suficiente para proporcionar una estabilidad.

Esta extraordinaria capacidad es posible gracias a los músculos posturales, los cuales, al estar cerca de los huesos, mantienen el esqueleto en la posición mencionada, al igual que hacen los obenques, esto es, los cables metálicos que sujetan el mástil de una embarcación.

Si realizamos un recorrido de arriba abajo, los músculos posturales son: los **sóleos**, que se encuentran en las pantorrillas; los músculos **pectíneos** y los **aductores**, que están en los muslos, y los **psoas** y los **piramidales**, situados a la altura de la pelvis. Asimismo, existen otros músculos posturales muy importantes que se extienden a lo largo de la columna vertebral hasta llegar al cráneo.

Todos estos músculos posturales son los responsables de nuestra actitud, nuestra apariencia, nuestra pose en general. Se trata de músculos muy superficiales que, en consecuencia, conocemos mucho más, ya que se encuentran directamente bajo la piel, y que confieren a las pantorrillas, los muslos y las nalgas su contorno curvado.

Por tanto, los músculos posturales tienen una función similar a la de los obenques: mantienen la estructura vertical de forma sólida y son cuatro veces más eficaces en su acción sobre el retorno venoso que los músculos superficiales.

Los deportistas

• Un ejercicio muscular intenso implica un aumento de la irrigación sanguínea arterial, necesaria para nutrir el músculo cuyo metabolismo se está aumentando. De forma paralela, el diámetro de los troncos venosos colectores se incrementa a fin de garantizar el drenaje de este aflujo sanguíneo. Aumentará en particular el diámetro de las venas de los gemelos, entre un 25 y un 40 %, mientras que el de las venas de los músculos posturales crecerá poco.

• Por el contrario, si un individuo que participa en competiciones con 20 años deja de practicar deporte en la cuarentena, se observará una disminución del tono muscular. La dilatación de las venas que se adquiere durante la juventud puede, posteriormente, convertirse en patológica y favorecer el desarrollo de una enfermedad venosa.

• Recientemente estos datos se vieron confirmados por los estudios llevados a cabo por el CNES francés (Centro Nacional de Estudios Espaciales) en astronautas, basados en pasar largos periodos de varios meses en estaciones espaciales, y por los estudios *bed-rest* en individuos con un buen estado de salud que se presentaron como voluntarios para participar, fundados en permanecer postrados en cama durante 3 meses.

• En efecto, la ingravidez (o microgravedad) es la responsable de la pérdida muscular de los músculos posturales y de la dilatación de las venas intramusculares, acompañada de un aumento de su distensión.

• Estas experiencias han puesto de relieve, en relación con las venas, la función fundamental de la gravedad sobre la tonicidad de la pared venosa por medio del tono muscular. Si la gravedad desaparece, la pared venosa pierde su tono en varias semanas y se dilata cada vez más a medida que la atrofia muscular aumenta.

• El espacio y los estudios *bed-rest* se presentan como un extraordinario observatorio que permite crear en varias semanas unas condiciones similares a las observadas en los pacientes que padecen enfermedades venosas, a pesar de que, en estos pacientes, dichas condiciones se desarrollan a lo largo de varias decenas de años.

Utilidad de la Fast Gym

Una mujer deportista que practica entre 2 y 3 horas de gimnasia por semana entrena los dos grupos musculares mencionados: los superficiales y los profundos. La gimnasia Fast Gym, que tan sólo ejercita los tres principales grupos de músculos posturales de las piernas, se realiza en 8 minutos al día, de ahí su nombre, y va dirigida a las personas que no tienen tiempo o no tienen la afición de practicar una actividad deportiva.

Origen de la Fast Gym

Esta práctica deportiva surgió como resultado de unos trabajos realizados en entornos hospitalarios durante los mencionados estudios *bed-rest*, según los cuales, en el transcurso de más de 3 meses, grupos de pacientes permanecieron en observación guardando cama, lo que significó para estos una pérdida de más del 20 % de la masa muscular en piernas y pelvis.

Asimismo, gracias a mediciones del diámetro de las venas, se detectó que, de forma paralela a la pérdida muscular, las venas profundas tendían a dilatarse más, al no contar con el apoyo que le ofrecían los músculos que las rodeaban.

Por tanto, se llegó a la conclusión evidente de que, a fin de reestablecer la situación, era necesario someterse a un entrenamiento, que incidiera especialmente sobre los músculos profundos posturales, aunque este no debía ser un entrenamiento cualquiera.

Principios de la Fast Gym

En materia de circulación venosa, algunos movimientos son más eficaces que otros. Se trata de los ejercicios musculares efectuados contra una resistencia, en los que participan músculos posturales agonistas y antagonistas de forma amplia y rítmica.

A fin de garantizar un buen retorno venoso, las venas tan sólo deben entrenarse un mínimo de 8 minutos diarios con la práctica de una gimnasia de resistencia en la que se ejerciten los músculos posturales.

Por otra parte, son preferibles los movimientos en los que, en un mismo ejercicio, participen los músculos **agonistas** y **antagonistas**. La bicicleta, por ejemplo, conocida por sus excelentes efectos sobre la circulación venosa, tan sólo ejercita los músculos agonistas, ya que el pie, al empujar uno de los pedales, hace que no haya una resistencia del pedal que sube. A fin de optimizar este ejercicio, se ha creado la bicicleta acuática que, gracias a la resistencia del agua, permite actuar simultáneamente sobre los dos grupos musculares de las piernas, los agonistas y los antagonistas.

Finalmente, los movimientos amplios y completos son preferibles a los rápidos y de amplitud parcial como los que se realizan a veces con música en una sala de gimnasia. Efectivamente, los músculos se encuentran envueltos por una capa que se denomina **fascia** o **aponeurosis**, que pierde su flexibilidad con el paso de los años. A través de este envoltorio pasan numerosas venas que drenan el tejido adiposo superficial y la piel. Si estas famosas fascias se retraen o llegan a padecer fibrosis, el drenaje de la sangre venosa desde la celulitis hacia las venas profundas se llevará a cabo de forma más defectuosa. Por ello es importante que conserven su gran flexibilidad mediante movimientos de estiramiento y de relajación, en particular de toda la cadena muscular posterior de la pierna y el muslo. Estos movimientos son los que se proponen en las sesiones de estiramiento o de yoga, dos prácticas excelentes para mantener un buen retorno venoso.

Y además...

El programa propuesto por la Fast Gym permite, en tan sólo 8 minutos al día, mantener el tono muscular de los músculos profundos posturales y la flexibilidad de las fascias que los recubren.

Evidentemente, en materia de actividad física, si se desea mejorar el funcionamiento del corazón y, de forma especial, de la pareja formada por este y los pulmones, así como la resistencia física, se hace necesaria la práctica de ejercicios de fondo de resistencia de una duración mínima de 40 minutos. Asimismo, si se desea desarrollar el volumen muscular y mejorar el contorno curvado de las piernas, también deberán practicarse ejercicios repetitivos de resistencia en serie, de una duración global de 40 minutos.

No obstante, si tan sólo se trata de contribuir a mejorar la circulación venosa al tiempo que se conserva el tono de las piernas, y cuando no se tiene ni tiempo ni ganas de efectuar 2 o 3 sesiones semanales de gimnasia, la Fast Gym constituye una respuesta. Aunque no convertirá a ninguna mujer en atleta de alta competición, permitirá conservar el nivel mínimo exigido de buen equilibrio.

Capítulo 4

Movimientos de la Fast Gym

L a aplicación de todos los principios desarrollados en esta obra nos ha llevado a la definición de una gimnasia vascular activa (GVA) que permite obtener en poco tiempo un efecto máximo sobre la circulación venosa, es decir, en las piernas cansadas, en los fenómenos de retención de líquidos, en las varicosidades y en la celulitis, dolencias asociadas a un retorno venoso defectuoso.

• **La estimulación de la pareja muscular formada por los psoas y los músculos piramidales** (véanse las págs. 68-69) se consigue con un ejercicio que se realiza de pie y que consiste en levantar lo más alto posible la rodilla contra resistencia, utilizando una goma elástica o fijándose un peso al tobillo.

• **A la altura del muslo, puede estimularse la pareja formada por el pectíneo y los aductores** (véanse las págs. 70-71), en posición sentada o estirada, con movimientos de acercamiento contra resistencia de ambas rodillas.

• **La estimulación del músculo sóleo de la pantorrilla** (véanse las págs. 72-73) se obtiene con movimientos de flexión y extensión, apoyándose sobre la punta de los pies encima de algo que permita un levantamiento del antepié con respecto al talón.

• Seguidamente se realizan los **estiramientos** (véanse las págs. 74-75) de estos tres grupos musculares.

Esta serie de cuatro ejercicios debe realizarse a un ritmo relativamente constante (unos 1,5 segundos por movimiento). Puede, no obstante, que al principio deba realizarse un calentamiento con una veintena de flexiones-extensiones cambiando de una posición de cuclillas a una posición de pie.

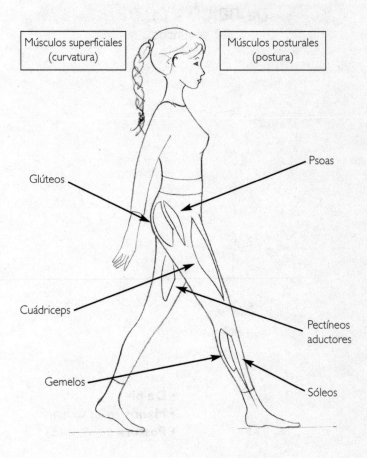

Músculos superficiales
(curvatura)

Músculos posturales
(postura)

Psoas

Glúteos

Cuádriceps

Pectíneos
aductores

Gemelos

Sóleos

Desarrollo
de los músculos psoas

De 00.00 a 00.02

120 segundos

- **De pie**
- **Manos** en las caderas
- **Postura** bien erguida

- **Levante la rodilla** lo más alto posible hacia el tórax flexionando el muslo

- 20 series con la pierna derecha
- 20 series con la pierna izquierda
  Repita una sola vez

- **Ritmo:** 80 movimientos rápidos (1,5 segundos por movimiento)

Para que dichos movimientos se realicen «en resistencia», colóquese unas pulseras con peso en los tobillos (a la venta en tiendas de deporte).

Desarrollo
de los músculos
pectíneos y aductores

De 00.02 a 00.04
120 segundos

- **Posición estirada** en el suelo
- Colóquese una **pelota** grande **entre las rodillas**

- **Junte las rodillas apretando**
  la pelota, que ofrece resistencia,
  manteniendo la pelvis en el suelo

- 3 series de 20 movimientos

- **Ritmo:** 2 segundos por movimiento

Si no dispone de una pelota, siéntese, coloque las manos en la cara interna de las rodillas e intente empujarlas hacia fuera. Las personas que estén mejor equipadas podrán sustituir la pelota por una prensa (a la venta en tiendas de deporte).

Desarrollo
de los músculos sóleos

De 00.04 a 00.06
120 segundos

- **De pie, apoyada sobre una pierna,** con la punta del pie colocada en el borde de un escalón.

  - El otro pie puede colocarse **detrás del tobillo** de la pierna que se está ejercitando.

- Realice **flexiones y extensiones** sobre la punta del pie descendiendo **el talón a un nivel inferior** que el antepié

  - 20 series sobre la pantorrilla derecha
  - 20 series sobre la pantorrilla izquierda
  Repita una vez

Debe realizar 80 movimientos de 1,5 segundos cada uno.

Estiramientos

De 00.06 a 00.08
120 segundos

Estiramiento 1: los psoas
• Al comenzar, **posición de pie**

• **Estire la pierna hacia atrás,** con las manos sujetando el tobillo

---

Debe practicar cada uno de estos movimientos durante 40 segundos. Estos movimientos son muy importantes para la flexibilidad de los recubrimientos de las fascias, ya que de ellos depende el buen funcionamiento de las venas que drenan la celulitis.

El último es particularmente importante: consiste en levantar la punta del pie hacia uno mismo, lo que se conoce como flexión

Estiramiento 2:
los aductores

- **De pie,** con la pierna levantada de forma lateral y colocada sobre una mesa (o una barra fija)

- **Flexione la pierna** sobre la que reposa el peso del cuerpo a fin de estirar los músculos del interior del muslo

Estiramiento 3: los sóleos

- **Sentada** en el suelo, en posición recta

- **Desplace la punta de los pies** mediante una flexión dorsal lo más cerca de usted que pueda

---

dorsal del pie. La amplitud de la flexión dorsal disminuye con el paso de los años en las personas con un estilo de vida moderno. En las personas jóvenes es de 40°; sin embargo, a partir de la cuarentena, va disminuyendo paulatinamente a 30°, 20°, 10°... hasta alcanzar prácticamente un bloqueo de tobillo en las personas ancianas.

Capítulo 5

Alimentación para contrarrestar la retención de líquidos

En nuestra alimentación entran en juego numerosos parámetros que varían en función del individuo. Hace cuarenta años consiguió demostrarse que el colesterol era «el» mayor enemigo, por lo que se le dio caza, aunque después se llegó a la conclusión de que no era el único adversario.

Los médicos han dado cuenta de la aparición de numerosos casos de infarto en individuos con un índice de colesterol normal y, por otra parte, todos los días ven cómo otros pacientes alcanzan una edad avanzada con un índice de colesterol muy elevado durante años. A pesar de todo esto, siempre se registrarán más casos de infarto en un grupo de personas que presente colesterol.

Protesta contra los glúcidos

Posteriormente se descubrió que los glúcidos no eran aconsejables en caso de padecer diabetes, por lo que se prohibieron en todas sus formas, incluyendo los azúcares lentos, los cereales, el arroz, el pan, etc. Más tarde, nos dimos cuenta de que, sin estos alimentos, nuestra alimentación estaba descompensada y arrastraba un exceso de grasa o de proteínas, por lo que dimos marcha atrás y, en la actualidad ocurre todo lo contrario, se aconseja comer arroz, pan y frutas hasta a las personas diabéticas.

Regreso
del sentido común

Pasemos revista rápidamente a los riesgos modernos asociados a determinadas contaminaciones alimenticias. En la actualidad, nos aconsejan comer de todo un poco y se considera dieta equilibrada aquella que contiene una mayoría de glúcidos, una pequeña cantidad de grasas beneficiosas y proteínas, cuya cantidad necesaria se estima que oscila entre 0,7 y 1 g por kilo de peso al día. Basándonos en estas normas, una mujer de 50 kg de peso debe comer entre 40 y 50 g de proteínas al día y no más, ya que las proteínas, tras su digestión, pueden generar productos nitrogenados perjudiciales para la salud como el ácido úrico.

Líneas
generales...

En términos de alimentación, las líneas generales que deben seguirse son una combinación de sentido común y de adaptación a las propias necesidades, teniendo en cuenta los gustos y el tiempo disponible de cada uno, así como ser conscientes de que la conducta alimentaria es frágil y depende en gran medida del bienestar y la relajación psicológica de cada uno.

Alimentos crudos, prioritarios

En primer lugar, deben comerse alimentos crudos no procesados. Pueden consumirse en gran cantidad las frutas, las hortalizas y las verduras crudas. Asimismo, para los más fanáticos, los cereales germinados como el trigo germinado, la soja germinada o el sésamo son verdaderos regalos de la naturaleza, con muchas vitaminas y selenio, cinc, magnesio, cromo, etc., en cantidades ideales para satisfacer nuestras necesidades; no en vano nuestra evolución se basa en este tipo de alimentación.

Sin embargo, hay que tener en cuenta la flora digestiva de cada uno, ya que si alguien no está acostumbrado a comer este tipo de alimentos, ni siquiera frutas, puede tener dificultades para digerirlos. Las personas que no sean frugívoras por naturaleza, deberán introducir las frutas en pequeñas cantidades, preferentemente al margen de las comidas principales, y, sobre todo, no obstinarse, ya que existen otras soluciones, y forzarse no sirve de nada.

Las frutas pueden comerse cocidas, en compota; los cereales germinados pueden incorporarse en pequeñas cantidades en las ensaladas o en otro tipo de platos. No obstante, las compotas deben ser caseras como las sopas o las ensaladas, y deben reservarse los platos precocinados para casos de emergencia y situaciones excepcionales, es decir, para salir del atolladero, una actitud difícil de adoptar.

Una alimentación programada

Otro elemento de sentido común es tomar un buen desayuno por la mañana, un buen almuerzo a media mañana y cenar de forma más ligera por la noche, procurando, sobre todo, no hacerlo demasiado tarde. Cenar demasiado tarde y, además, hacerlo combinando grasas, proteínas y azúcares es garantía de una acumulación máxima en zonas no deseadas.

Se trata de otra de las dificultades de la vida moderna: durante nuestra jornada, las situaciones de estrés a las que estamos sometidos nos permiten aguantar mucho tiempo sin pensar ni un minuto en la comida. No obstante, cuando llega la noche, nos invade una sensación de relajación y, por otra parte, comer en familia o con amigos favorece el hecho de que comamos de forma más completa, aunque en un mal momento, el que precede al sueño.

Trampas que deben evitarse

El último de los elementos para seguir una conducta de sentido común consiste en resistir a las tentaciones que ofrece el sector agroalimentario moderno y evitar los comportamientos a los que estas inducen.

Un ejemplo de estas tentaciones son los productos de aperitivo, es decir, los pequeños tentempiés de productos precocinados o listos para comer, que permiten aplacar el hambre rápidamente. Otro ejemplo es el *craving*, es decir, el deseo intenso de comer, una pulsión alimentaria derivada de una situación difícil o estresante que se concibe como un premio de compensación tras haber experimentado una situación complicada o angustiosa.

Es una ardua tarea la de buscar en uno mismo y encontrar un medio distinto al de la comida que nos permita enfrentarnos a dichas situaciones.

En este caso, el problema es que todos somos influenciables, aunque diferentes: la mayoría de nosotros aguantamos bastante bien la alimentación moderna e, inconscientemente, influimos en aquellos que no la toleran. Así, si un día decidimos suprimir totalmente los alimentos industriales, en un momento dado nos encontraremos rodeados de personas que parecen consumirlos sin moderación y sin problemas, lo que nos hará bajar la guardia.

… pero no normas universales

En materia de dieta ideal, no existen unos grandes principios universales, ya que, mientras que tomarse una sopa por la noche puede ser una verdadera delicia para determinadas personas, para otras puede suponer una fuente de gases, a menudo no por intolerancia a las verduras de la sopa, sino a los espesantes, estabilizadores, emulgentes y conservadores que la acompañan. Asimismo, para otras personas un vaso de leche representará un alimento realmente relajante, pero para otras implicará una intolerancia alimentaria debido a la reducida actividad de sus lactasas, las enzimas digestivas que digieren la leche.

Estas intolerancias pueden manifestarse de diferentes formas: para algunos, se presentará en forma de aumento de peso o de modificación de la silueta con retención de líquidos en la mitad inferior del cuerpo, aunque para otros el fenómeno de la retención de líquidos aparecerá de otra forma. Así, determinadas personas necesitan aspirar o sonarse las mucosidades tras haber comido determinados alimentos. Este taponamiento de los senos nasales puede asociarse a la intolerancia de un determinado tipo de proteínas, del trigo o de la leche, o a un producto industrial; aunque quizás esta persona no vea el taponamiento nasal como un inconveniente porque, acostumbrada a estos efectos que la acompañan durante las comidas, los ignorará totalmente.

Mejor nueces
que queso

Un ejemplo bastante significativo de esta variabilidad de expresión de las intolerancias alimentarias es la aparición de aftas al consumir nueces o almendras. El afta es, propiamente dicho, una forma muy localizada de retención de líquidos, ya que se trata de una pequeña vesícula que se forma debajo de la mucosa de la lengua o de la encía.

Este fenómeno se asocia a una intolerancia a los productos utilizados para la conservación de las nueces: la inmersión de las mismas en soluciones ácidas para blanquearlas o en soluciones químicas para conservarlas. Si se tiene la ocasión de comer nueces recogidas directamente de un árbol, puede observarse que estas no generan aftas. Sin embargo, algunos individuos no toleran los componentes internos de las nueces, por lo que estarán inclinados a padecer aftas, con independencia del tipo de nueces.

Una falsa idea muy extendida

El ejemplo de las nueces es recurrente en una cierta cantidad de alimentos de consumo habitual. No obstante, la nuez fresca es una de las mejores fuentes de proteínas, ácidos grasos poliinsaturados, vitaminas y minerales. Se trata de un tipo de grasa excelente, superior a la que encontramos en un trozo de queso gruyer o en cualquier otro tipo de queso de pasta cocida y, a pesar de todo, suele decirse que la nuez engorda, mientras que el queso se beneficia de una buena fama por el aporte de calcio y de proteínas.

He aquí un ejemplo en el que el sentido común se ha ido corrompiendo progresivamente: un trozo de queso contiene grasas perjudiciales, saturadas, cocidas, con mucha sal. Se trata de un producto que probablemente, hace unos siglos, tuvo su sentido, ya que permitía disponer de un producto lácteo en invierno. Sin embargo, en la actualidad disponemos de productos frescos durante todo el año y los quesos no son nada interesantes desde el punto de vista dietético. Por tanto, deberían consumirse simplemente por placer, tan sólo por su interés gustativo, al igual que nos comemos una onza de chocolate. Desafortunadamente, con el paso de las generaciones, hemos desarrollado una gran apetencia por los alimentos grasos, dulces o salados, entre los que se incluye el queso, que nos parece muy sabroso.

Un error de cálculo recurrente

Algunas personas que, aunque con sobrepeso, están convencidas de comer de forma muy sana suelen cometer un error con demasiada frecuencia: tomar para cenar un poco de queso fresco con un 0 % de materia grasa y una ensalada con un trozo de gruyer.

No llegamos a comprender esta idea: ¿por qué tomar queso fresco con un 0 % de materia grasa? Mejor comerlo con un 40 % de materia grasa, lo más graso posible, ya que no hay que olvidar que dicho 40 % es la masa grasa a partir del extracto seco. Ahora bien, el queso fresco contiene más del 80 % de agua y, además, su grasa es mejor que la del queso de pasta cocida; simplemente presenta el inconveniente, al igual que este último, de ser una grasa saturada, aunque no está cocida, sino que todavía contiene todas las vitaminas liposolubles como la vitamina E, la K y la D. Además, en el queso fresco aún queda lactosuero, cuyas proteínas ofrecen el mejor valor biológico, muy superior al de la caseína (que se encuentra en la parte cuajada).

Realicemos el cálculo: un trozo de queso fresco de 500 g contiene un 80 % de agua, por lo que tan sólo hay 100 g de extracto seco con un 40 % de materia grasa, es decir, 40 g. Entonces, si comemos algo menos de la mitad del envase de 500 g, por ejemplo una porción de 200 g, habremos comido en total 16 g de grasa cruda rica en vitaminas.

En el caso del queso gruyer o del queso Comté, estos 16 g de grasa corresponden a un trocito de queso que, sin llegar a satisfacernos, nos habrá aportado 16 g de grasa cocida perjudicial, sin ningún tipo de vitaminas, aunque, efectivamente, muy rico en calcio. No obstante, es preferible obtener nuestra ración de calcio de las legumbres o del agua mineral. Para que se haga una idea, sepa que, si un yogur contiene 160 mg de calcio, en una ración de lentejas hay 200 mg. Asimismo, un vaso de agua mineral puede contener 6 veces más calcio que otra de débil mineralización, es decir, con un menor aporte de calcio. Por tanto, comer queso gruyer o cualquier otro tipo de queso de pasta cocida únicamente para aumentar el aporte en calcio no tiene sentido. La razón principal por la que se come este tipo de quesos es por el sabor, cosa que puede hacerse, aunque intentando evitar los excesos.

Sin embargo, como siempre, en este aspecto también surgen variaciones individuales. Habrá muchas personas que coman queso en cantidades considerables sin ningún tipo de inconveniente, mientras que otras ni siquiera sospechen que este tipo de alimento no les conviene.

Alimentos
«esponja»

Tal y como hemos visto, cuando algunas sustancias como la sal, el azúcar o las proteínas de gran tamaño (péptidos) no se digieren completamente en el tubo digestivo, se depositan en los tejidos intersticiales, en los que ejercen un efecto «esponja» y retienen agua.

Todos los productos excesivamente salados actúan como alimentos «esponja»: el pan, las *pizzas*, los pescados ahumados, los quesos de pasta cocida, todas las salsas, las conservas, los platos precocinados, los condimentos, las galletas, los cacahuetes, las bebidas gaseosas, los productos de charcutería, las hamburguesas, etc.

La digestión depende de la persona y del alimento

El problema sigue siendo que algunas personas no pueden digerir correctamente todas las proteínas naturales, mientras que a otras les sucede todo lo contrario.

En esta situación pueden verse implicadas algunas proteínas naturales como la leche, por ejemplo, utilizada en forma de yogures o de queso blanco, que en la parte cuajada contiene unas proteínas que reciben el nombre de caseínas, y de otro tipo en el lactosuero, que suelen ser las más beneficiosas, ya que tienen un gran valor biológico. Lamentablemente, hoy en día las tendencias sobre el sabor ya no se inclinan por los alimentos amargos. Así, preferimos mil veces antes la parte cuajada, más dulce pero también más grasa, a pesar de que sus proteínas, en particular las caseínas, poseen un valor biológico menor, y aunque algunos de nosotros no podamos digerirla muy bien. De hecho, una intolerancia a este tipo de proteínas puede ser la causa de un fenómeno de retención de líquidos.

Lo mismo ocurre con las proteínas del trigo. Los actuales tipos de trigo son excelentes desde el punto de vista agroalimentario: permiten sembrar de forma homogénea terrenos muy grandes, y son muy productivos y resistentes a determinadas enfermedades. Sin embargo, algunas personas no pueden digerir bien el gluten, una proteína de estos tipos de trigo modernos, con lo que surgen casos de alergia o de intolerancia alimentaria acompañados de retención de líquidos debido a que no se degradan completamente en nuestro tubo digestivo. Por ello, el trigo puede revelarse como un alimento «esponja» para algunas mujeres y para otras no.

En consecuencia, cada uno de nosotros se encuentra en una posición diferente frente a los alimentos y, por esta razón, en la primera fase de la dieta para contrarrestar la retención de líquidos, debe reconocer los alimentos (o incluso las sustancias químicas) que pueden tener un efecto «esponja» sobre usted. Los productos que se fabrican con trigo o leche como elementos básicos, entre otros, deberán evitarse durante algún tiempo para comprobar si así pueden mejorarse o eliminarse los síntomas de la retención de líquidos.

Identifique
sus alimentos «esponja»

Desafortunadamente, habrá que hablar de dieta, ya que deberán identificarse los alimentos que favorecen la retención de líquidos y los que contienen elementos que faciliten el drenaje de los mismos.

Entre estos elementos se encuentra la vitamina B6 (o piridoxina), que contribuye al transporte de los aminoácidos desde los intestinos hasta la sangre, y cuya insuficiencia puede desembocar en un déficit proteico. Asimismo, favorece el transporte del magnesio. No obstante, varias centenas de reacciones enzimáticas de nuestro cuerpo dependen del magnesio, probablemente uno de los elementos que más escasean en la población, al igual que el cinc o el selenio.

Sin embargo, no nos referimos a auténticas carencias, ya que la falta de vitamina B6 en nuestros países tan sólo se observa en caso de consumo excesivo de alcohol. De lo que hablaremos es de carencias secundarias, que son las causantes de pequeños trastornos como la retención de líquidos que pueden observarse en mujeres que toman la píldora o en las que consumen muy poca cantidad de frutas y verduras.

La dieta para contrarrestar la retención de líquidos comprende una fase de una duración de 15 días, periodo durante el cual habrá que retirar algunos alimentos para, posteriormente, ir incluyéndolos uno a uno, intentando determinar cuáles son los que pueden agravar los indicios de la retención de líquidos.

Supresión del azúcar industrial

Durante 15 días deberán suprimirse totalmente los productos de pastelería, las galletas y los cereales dulces, así como cualquier alimento adquirido en el supermercado en cuya etiqueta aparezca la sacarosa, la dextrosa o la glucosa. Durante dicho periodo, también habrá que evitar los edulcorantes y el azúcar sintético, que, además de contener sal, presenta el mismo riesgo que la glucosa de ejercer un efecto de retención de líquidos en los tejidos.

Reducción o supresión de la sal y de los alimentos salados

Deben suprimirse o reducirse al máximo los alimentos en los que la sal se encuentre en forma muy concentrada, esto es, los pescados ahumados, los quesos, las salsas, las conservas y todos los platos precocinados, los condimentos, las galletas de aperitivo, los cacahuetes, las almendras saladas y determinadas bebidas gaseosas.

Asimismo, debe saber que una barra de pan de tipo baguete, un bocadillo o dos porciones de *pizza* contienen 4 g de sal, es decir, la cantidad diaria recomendada por la Organización Mundial de la Salud, mientras que la cantidad media de sal que consumimos en la actualidad oscila entre los 10 y los 12 g diarios, o sea, entre dos y tres veces más.

Habrá que evitar los aditivos químicos que contienen glutamato monosódico (E621): se trata de un potenciador del sabor muy utilizado, especialmente en la cocina asiática, que está permitido en prácticamente todos los productos alimenticios de venta en cualquier establecimiento.

Deberá prestar especial atención a los medicamentos para el ardor de estómago, ya que contienen bicarbonato sódico, un antiácido muy rico en sodio, sustancia que habrá que limitar.

Reducción o supresión, si es posible, de las grasas saturadas

Durante este periodo de 15 días, deberán reducirse o, si es posible, suprimirse las grasas saturadas, por lo que habrá que evitar los quesos de pasta cocida, la mantequilla, las margarinas, las cremas y la mayonesa, las salsas, los productos de charcutería, las hamburguesas, las carnes grasas, el chocolate y los postres dulces.

Supresión de la harina de trigo blanca

La harina de trigo blanca se encuentra en el pan blanco, el pan de molde, *pizzas*, pasteles, galletas, bollos, etc. En lo que al pan se refiere, habrá que limitarse al pan de centeno o a las galletas de arroz inflado integral. También se permiten los copos de avena y el *muesli* biológico.

Supresión de la leche líquida

Debe suprimirse la leche líquida y también el consumo de quesos de pasta cocida, y reducir el de yogures y el de queso fresco (un yogur al día).

Durante este periodo, lo ideal sería no tomar ningún producto lácteo, ni siquiera un yogur, y en caso contrario, dar preferencia a los yogures de soja o a los fabricados con leche de oveja.

Supresión de algunos tipos de carne

Debe suprimirse el consumo de carnes rojas, aves que no sean de corral y pescados de piscifactoría (salmón, trucha, dorada, robalo y rodaballo).

Supresión, en la medida de lo posible, del café y del alcohol

La mayoría de nosotros tolera bien el café y, además, este posee propiedades lipolíticas (favorece la eliminación de grasas) y diuréticas.

No obstante, en un contexto de retención de líquidos muy ricos en proteínas, cualquier producto de acción diurética favorece la deshidratación e incita al riñón a la fijación del sodio y, en consecuencia, del agua. Por tanto, el café será una bebida totalmente incompatible con algunas personas y no con otras.

Por esta razón, deberá suprimirse durante el periodo de 15 días de prueba y, seguidamente, volver a introducirlo de forma paulatina, a fin de comprobar si estamos dentro del grupo de personas que no lo toleran demasiado bien.

La supresión de todos estos elementos conllevará una auténtica mejora y una pérdida de varios kilos. Al volver a introducir progresivamente los alimentos, se podrá contemplar un aumento del peso o indicios de retención de líquidos, lo que permitirá que cada persona determine cuál es el alimento que debe suprimir en su dieta cotidiana.

¿Qué puede comer
durante estos 15 días?

Ya sabe, el objetivo de esta primera fase es evitar todos los alimentos, incluso en pequeñas cantidades, que puedan tener un efecto «esponja» en una persona en particular y tomar alimentos permitidos en las cantidades que uno desee. Los alimentos permitidos durante esta fase son todas las frutas y verduras, haciendo especial hincapié en los cítricos (naranjas, pomelos y limones), todos los frutos rojos, la uva negra y la blanca, y las verduras al vapor (en particular las zanahorias, el brécol, las espinacas, el apio, la col y la coliflor). También podrá tomar sopas de verduras, aunque tan solo las de elaboración casera, con posibilidad de realizarlas con verduras congeladas.

Durante esta fase, habrá que comer la mayor cantidad posible de plantas leguminosas: lentejas, alubias, guisantes (preferentemente frescos de temporada), habas, etc. Asimismo, podrán tomarse en la cantidad que se desee pollo de corral, pescado salvaje, especias, aceite de oliva y de colza, vinagre de sidra, hierbas aromáticas, tisanas (ocasionalmente) si prefiere las bebidas calientes por la mañana, un sustitutivo del café con achicoria y agua mineral.

Prepare
sus próximas comidas

Una de las claves del éxito para hacer compatibles los 15 días de dieta con la vida cotidiana consiste en dedicar media jornada a preparar los alimentos que tomará los 4 o 5 días siguientes:

— realice una compra de productos frescos;
— prepare una gran cacerola de arroz integral: después de dejarlo en remojo desde la víspera, hiérvalo a fuego lento durante 35 minutos hasta que se hinche (una taza de arroz por 4 de agua);
— prepare una segunda cacerola grande de verduras (zanahoria, puerro, apio, hinojo, cebolla, espinaca, col, coliflor y brécol). Pueden utilizarse para hacer una sopa para la cena o para el trabajo (llevándola en un termo);
— prepare un plato de legumbres (lentejas o alubias), la mejor fuente de magnesio y de selenio;
— compre un pollo de corral entero asado, varios yogures de leche de oveja, de soja o de almendra;
— tenga preparado pan de centeno y galletas de arroz integral, frutos secos para las personas que los toleren, sobre todo ciruelas pasas y albaricoques secos pasteurizados que deberán comprarse en tiendas de dietética, y siempre con preferencia por los frutos secos sin sulfatos (difíciles de encontrar).

Si todavía se encuentra con ánimos, prepare un gran plato de compota de manzana que podrá consumir durante varios días.

Finalmente, acuérdese de los aguacates con diferente grado de madurez, ya que siempre habrá que consumir un alimento graso. Dicho cuerpo graso también puede ser aceite de oliva, de germen de trigo, de colza o de pepitas de uva.

El mejor complemento:
el trigo germinado

• Atención: no nos referimos al germen de trigo, sino al trigo germinado natural, por lo que habrá que comprar en una tienda de productos dietéticos una bolsa de granos de trigo para plantar, que esparciremos en una capa en un plato con un poco de agua.

• Los pequeños brotes salen al cabo de dos días. A partir de ese momento podrá empezar a consumirlos con una cuchara o espolvoreados en legumbres.

Está permitido cualquier tipo de marisco, preferiblemente el fresco comprado en la pescadería. Habrá que tener cuidado con las gambas, las taramás (huevas de pescado) y los cangrejos comprados en grandes superficies, que son ricos en benzoatos (unos conservantes que suelen ser alergénicos) y cantaxantina (el colorante de los huevos y de la carne del pescado).

El hecho de suprimir los productos lácteos durante 15 días no conlleva ningún riesgo de carencias de calcio, ya que las legumbres secas, las nueces y las avellanas frescas, así como las verduras, el pescado y el marisco, son alimentos muy ricos en calcio. Por el contrario, habrá que procurar reservar entre 50 y 60 g de proteínas al día comiendo cereales como el arroz integral o las legumbres, el pescado salvaje, las aves de corral, el marisco o la soja.

Para los entusiastas del azúcar, incluso de manera pulsional para compensar un momento de ansiedad, lo ideal es pasarse a frutas como las manzanas, los cítricos, los kiwis, la piña o los plátanos, así como a la amplia gama de frutas de temporada de las que se disponen en España en verano. Sin embargo, habrá que evitar durante este periodo el azúcar moreno, el jarabe de arce y la miel, ya que estos alimentos presentan una acción sobre la glucemia prácticamente equivalente a la de la glucosa, mientras que la fructosa de la fruta presenta un índice glucémico más bajo, que no provoca un aumento masivo ni de la insulina ni de la glucemia.

A pesar de no poder presentar ningún argumento científico, se recomienda que se evite cualquier edulcorante, sustitutivos del azúcar y sacarinas. Para aquellas personas que no pueden pasar sin el chocolate, una buena solución es comprar cacao en barra como el que encontramos en Sudamérica o en algunos mercados de productos tropicales. El cacao en barra se conserva durante mucho tiempo y puede molerse y tomarse, por ejemplo, con un plátano o con cremas de soja. De esta forma podrá disfrutar del sabor del chocolate sin azúcares ni grasas perjudiciales. Aunque, por supuesto, también puede permitirse degustar lentamente una onza de chocolate negro de excelente calidad. Con todo, debido a la eterna necesidad de placer humano, puede reemplazar el placer de la alimentación grasa, azucarada o salada por otros placeres, cuestión que cada uno deberá dirimir consigo mismo.

En lo que respecta a las comidas sociales y a los restaurantes, en todo momento deberá establecer un razonamiento jerárquico y permitirse algunas transgresiones en aquellos productos que más tolere.

Función del azúcar

• El azúcar industrial se transforma fácilmente en grasa que irá a almacenarse directamente en la parte inferior de nuestro cuerpo. Basta con tomar un poco de azúcar de más al día (20 calorías) con respecto a nuestras necesidades, esto es, aproximadamente el 1 % del consumo energético diario, para llegar a almacenar casi 2,2 g de grasa por día en los muslos, lo que equivaldría a 0,7 kg al año, es decir, 7 kg al cabo de diez años. Conserve esta imagen en la cabeza: un poco de azúcar de más equivale a 7 kg de grasa al cabo de diez años.

• Para reducir peso en la mitad inferior del cuerpo, es absolutamente necesario reducir la cantidad de azúcar industrial que se consume todos los días, por lo que habrá que evitar la sacarosa. En cuanto a los sustitutivos del azúcar, aunque se ha demostrado que estos no se transforman en grasa, pueden producirse, no obstante, intolerancias alimentarias a la sacarina que desembocarían en un fenómeno de retención de líquidos.

• Esa apetencia, ese gusto irrefrenable por el azúcar, se remonta, como máximo, a hace dos siglos, por lo que puede prescindirse del mismo. Antes de que el azúcar refinado se introdujese en nuestra alimentación, la apetencia de nuestros antepasados por los alimentos dulces era mucho menor. Por otra parte, y dejando a un lado el propósito de esta obra, piense que dicha introducción del azúcar se produjo en condiciones tristes, de forma simultánea al desarrollo del fenómeno de la esclavitud. Pero lo que se cuestiona no es únicamente el carácter refinado industrial del azúcar consumido, sino también el aumento de la apetencia por lo dulce. Por ello, el último recurso es sustituir el azúcar blanco por el azúcar moreno, el jarabe de arce o la miel.

Grasas
de calidad

Otra de las nociones importantes es la de la calidad de las grasas, compuestas de ácidos grasos. Uno de los ácidos grasos más célebres en la actualidad es el ácido alfalinoleico, el principal representante de la familia de los omega 3. Sus derivados, denominados EPA y DHA, también son muy apreciados. Dicho ácido suele encontrarse en algunos aceites como el de colza, nuez, lino y germen de maíz; en las verduras como la verdolaga y las espinacas frescas; en los pescados de agua fría como la caballa, el salmón salvaje y el arenque; en el aceite de hígado de bacalao; en la carne de cordero, y en las habas pequeñas.

Otros aceites como el de oliva y el de girasol también son beneficiosos por su contenido en ácidos grasos monoinsaturados, aunque sin la presencia de omega 3. Por ello, los profesionales de la nutrición aconsejan mezclar el aceite de oliva con el de colza, por ejemplo, o consumir trigo germinado. La totalidad de los aceites y de las grasas mono o poliinsaturadas, entre las cuales se encuentran los omega 3, presentan cadenas de ácidos grasos flexibles que forman grasas que pueden eliminarse fácilmente de los muslos, y que participan en la composición de la membrana celular. Por otra parte, las cadenas de ácidos grasos saturados son rígidas y muy resistentes, de ahí que se utilicen preferentemente en la cocción, aunque presentan la desventaja de que suelen almacenarse en los depósitos adiposos de reserva de los muslos, y es muy difícil invertir este proceso.

Incluso los animales de los que nos alimentamos están hechos de lo que ellos mismos comen. Recientemente, un artículo aparecido en el *New England Journal of Medicine* ha demostrado que los huevos de gallinas criadas en batería contienen veinte veces menos cantidad de omega 3 que los de las gallinas que se alimentan libremente en la naturaleza. Por tanto, para hablar propiamente de huevos, cabe tener en cuenta la calidad, aunque considerando tan sólo la cantidad global de lípidos, colesterol y su aportación calórica. Los huevos de buena calidad no dañarán nuestros vasos ni propiciarán el almacenamiento de grasas en los muslos. Sin embargo, no ocurrirá lo mismo con los huevos de las gallinas criadas en batería.

Capítulo 6

Plantas drenantes

A pesar de que plantas como la viña roja o el castaño de Indias eran conocidas desde la Antigüedad por sus virtudes descongestivas, hasta 1930 no nació el concepto de estimulante circulatorio ni el de plantas drenantes.

Algunas plantas han manifestado una acción de protección vascular que se ha puesto de relieve por medio de un angiosterómetro (medición de la resistencia capilar). La mayor parte de las plantas pertenecientes a los flavonoides, la vitamina C (descubierta en 1936) y la vitamina P (descubierta en 1937), también conocida como la vitamina de la permeabilidad de los vasos, son protectores vasculares potentes. Sin embargo, las que más nos interesan son las plantas que presentan una acción drenante.

Flavonoides

- Los flavonoides, un amplio grupo botánico que engloba más de 700 especies, se encuentran en los cítricos, en algunas plantas como el rusco o brusco, y en el *gingko*, el arándano y la grosella negra.

• Los flavonoides deben su nombre al flavedo, que es la parte blanca que se encuentra en la piel de cítricos como la naranja, el limón y el pomelo, y que contiene pequeñas vesículas ricas en sustancia flavonoide como la diosmina y la hesperidina. La mayor parte de los frutos rojos contiene flavonoides: la grosella negra, los arándanos, las moras, las frambuesas, las fresas, las grosellas y la uva negra. Los flavonoides presentes en el arándano se denominan antocianos; los que encontramos en la piel de las manzanas, las cebollas o el té, quercetinas, y, finalmente, los que están en las pepitas de las uvas, oligómeros procianidólicos.

Entre las plantas con acción drenante más conocidas cabe mencionar la centella asiática, el ciprés, el rusco o brusco, el fresno, el guayaco de cayena con cumarina, el hamamelis, el castaño de Indias, el meliloto, el arándano, la ruda, el *gingko* y las pepitas de la uva.

Las sustancias más interesantes de los flavonoides son los citroflavonoides que se encuentran en las cortezas de cítricos como la naranja, el limón o el pomelo.

Otra de las moléculas que encontramos en el rusco, denominado también brusco, es la rutina. Estas moléculas han sido objeto de numerosos estudios en los que se ha plasmado la acción que ejercen sobre la circulación venosa y la permeabilidad de los capilares. Asimismo, podemos encontrar este tipo de moléculas en determinados medicamentos flebotónicos.

La planta drenante más apreciada

La centella asiática, denominada también hidrocotilo, es una de las plantas más interesantes por diferentes motivos: además de su acción de permeabilidad capilar, se trata de la única planta en que se ha podido observar una notable capacidad para aumentar la síntesis de fibras colágenas tanto en la piel como en las paredes de las venas.

Los estudios relativos a dicha acción son particularmente reveladores y constituyen la principal cualidad de esta planta.

No obstante, sus principios activos solamente pueden apreciarse cuando dicha planta se recoge en un entorno silvestre.

Si se cultiva, estos principios, los más potentes descubiertos hasta la fecha, desaparecerán. Es como si, explicado de otra manera, para producir los principios activos que la protegen incluso a ella del exceso de humedad, la planta necesitara las condiciones de vida silvestre; entre estas condiciones, por supuesto, se incluye la tensión de los monzones.

En la actualidad, la mejor combinación de plantas que un médico puede prescribir para favorecer el drenaje del exceso de agua es la asociación de un flavonoide y un producto que tenga como elemento básico la centella asiática.

Sorprendente
centella asiática

• La centella asiática crece en los bosques de Madagascar, que albergan más de 10.000 especies de plantas tropicales, de las cuales algunas tan sólo crecen en la isla, y de ellas solamente unas cuantas se han estudiado. No obstante, con el paso de los siglos, las poblaciones locales han acumulado, por medio de la experiencia, un cierto conocimiento de las propiedades de todas esas plantas salvajes.

• Desde hace varios años, las grandes empresas envían a profesionales de la botánica para recopilar in situ la experiencia ancestral de las poblaciones. A continuación, recogen las plantas que presentan unos efectos especialmente potentes, con lo que se garantiza la calidad de las plantas reunidas, al tiempo que la renovación natural sigue su curso en el bosque.

• Especialmente se ha estudiado la centella asiática. Crece a una altitud de unos 600 m y su descubrimiento por parte de los botánicos modernos se remonta al año 1944. Según la leyenda, los tigres de Bengala usaban la planta para vendarse las heridas, motivo por el cual en India se la conoce como «hierba del tigre». En un primer momento, se utilizó en forma de crema cicatrizante; sin embargo, es la planta con el informe más completo en relación con su capacidad para aumentar la síntesis de colágeno del cuerpo humano y su acción para contrarrestar la retención de líquidos. A pesar de ello, se trata de una molécula antigua, por lo que ya no se ofrece información sobre la misma, ya que las leyes que rigen el *marketing* condenan al sector a fabricar constantemente productos nuevos. A pesar de todo, podemos encontrarla en varios productos de acción drenante, asociada a moléculas menos eficaces pero más recientes utilizadas como argumento de «novedad».

Los mejores cocteles
de vitaminas

Si la agenda alimentaria revela una alimentación insuficiente de productos frescos, vitaminas y minerales, será bastante recomendable añadir a la prescripción de plantas drenantes algún complemento vitamínico que contenga vitamina E (el auténtico protector vascular), vitamina P, vitamina C, vitamina B6, cinc y selenio.

En concreto, la vitamina E, descubierta en 1922, posee una acción de protección vascular. Al principio de su hallazgo, se presentó como la vitamina de la fertilidad. También se la conoce como tocoferol, del griego *tokos* («progenitura») y *pherein* («camada»). Es una vitamina que se ha revelado como indispensable en la reproducción de los animales. En 1938 se consiguió realizar la síntesis y, posteriormente, se descubrieron sus cualidades protectoras para la piel y sus propiedades antioxidantes y antienvejecimiento.

A finales de los ochenta, se descubrió la función de protección de los vasos, arterias y venas. Asimismo, se halló que el consumo regular de la misma reducía el riesgo de infarto y que, por el contrario, un escaso índice de vitamina E en la sangre constituía un verdadero factor de riesgo cardiovascular. En la actualidad, se sabe que protege el conjunto de las paredes vasculares, arteriales y venosas, y que su función es tan eficaz que se la asocia con la vitamina C y el selenio. En nuestros tiempos, se prescribe en caso de mala circulación venosa o linfática, o retención de líquidos, para fortificar las venas y los vasos linfáticos y, al igual que la vitamina D, puede recetarse para fortalecer los huesos.

En la alimentación, encontramos la vitamina E en el trigo germinado (probablemente la fuente alimenticia más rica), nueces, avellanas y almendras naturales (60 mg de vitamina E por 100 g de almendras), pescado de agua fría, olivas, aguacates, huevos, lechuga, zanahoria, manzana y uva (concretamente en las pepitas).

Deberíamos consumir 50 g al día y, sin embargo, diferentes estudios han llegado a la conclusión de que la alimentación moderna que llevamos tan sólo nos aporta entre 7 y 12 mg al día de vitamina E. Por tanto, hay que aumentar la proporción de alimentos que contienen esta vitamina, teniendo en cuenta que esta es sensible a la oxidación, a la luz y al calentamiento de los alimentos; por tanto, debe recurrirse a un aporte mediante suplementos en cápsulas.

Por consiguiente, los suplementos de la dieta para contrarrestar la retención de líquidos se resumen en: una planta drenante del grupo de los flavonoides, centella asiática, vitaminas de los grupos E, C, P y B6, selenio y cinc (muchas mujeres ya consumen bastante magnesio a través de complementos).

Capítulo 7

Fisioterapia

La fisioterapia vascular reagrupa los métodos terapéuticos que utilizan los agentes naturales físicos como el agua, el aire, la luz, la electricidad, el calor, etc. Sus principios y su eficacia se respaldan en recientes estudios que muestran que su acción es beneficiosa para las paredes de los vasos arteriales y venosos.

En lo que respecta a las venas, los métodos de fisioterapia se dividen en técnicas de drenaje (drenaje linfático manual o mecánico y drenaje linfático en agua) y en métodos de refuerzo de los músculos y de las venas, ya sean métodos pasivos como la electricidad, o métodos activos como la GVA.

En cuanto a las arterias, los métodos de fisioterapia pueden ser pasivos como la inyección subcutánea de dióxido de carbono, o activos como la deambulación en pasillo de marcha acuática. Asimismo, pueden practicarse tanto en un contexto de curas termales como de talasoterapia.

Al margen de los anteriores, encontramos los métodos fisioterapéuticos de prevención de trombosis venosas profundas:

• los sistemas de compresión neumática secuencial como el SCD (Tyco, Kendall);

• los sistemas motorizados de reposapiés;

• la contención venosa, que también puede considerarse como un método de fisioterapia vascular debido a su acción de apoyo exterior, que además actúa sobre el drenaje venoso.

Estos últimos años han sido extremadamente pródigos en publicaciones y en estudios en revistas de fisiología y de medicina, que han presentado los mecanismos y han demostrado la eficacia de la actividad física en la prevención y en el tratamiento de las enfermedades vasculares, arteriales y venosas.

Entre ellos, cuatro estudios recientes nos han aportado elementos novedosos:

• Un estudio publicado en 2003 en el *Journal of Physiology* mostró que la práctica regular de ejercicio físico aeróbico, es decir, aquel en el que se produce una contracción muscular activa que provoca un aumento de la frecuencia respiratoria (con lo que se eliminan las técnicas de contracciones musculares pasivas mediante electroterapia), disminuía el riesgo de flebitis asociada al envejecimiento y al estilo de vida sedentario. La práctica periódica de ejercicio aeróbico no sólo reduce los efectos del envejecimiento vascular, sino que, en concreto, este estudio demuestra que incluso puede reestablecer los vasos, lo que hasta ahora no se había demostrado en el mundo de la medicina.

• Varios estudios han puesto de relieve la importancia del óxido nítrico, secretado por las células que recubren las paredes internas de las arterias y de las venas, como un potente regulador del tono arterial y venoso. Uno de estos estudios muestra que el ejercicio físico practicado de forma periódica es uno de los factores esenciales y determinantes para la secreción de óxido nítrico y del factor relajante derivado del endotelio (EDRF, *endothelium dependant relaxing factor*).

• Un estudio japonés publicado en 1999 en la revista americana *Circulation* demostró que la práctica de la marcha rápida (al 50 % del consumo máximo de oxígeno) durante 30 minutos entre 5 y 7 veces por semana durante 12 semanas permitía disminuir la presión arterial y mejorar las arterias de los individuos moderadamente hipertensos que no siguen ningún tipo de tratamiento ni acostumbran a practicar ejercicio.

Los resultados observados con respecto a las arterias se confirman también en lo que respecta a las venas: un estudio publicado en 2001 en el *American Journal of Phisiology* mostró que la práctica de algún tipo de ejercicio regular de resistencia es beneficioso para mejorar el retorno venoso de las extremidades inferiores.

El ejercicio físico disminuye
los riesgos vasculares

Estos estudios recientes confirman que la práctica periódica de actividades físicas en la edad adulta protege del riesgo de sufrir accidentes vasculares cerebrales. Además, un estudio realizado en mujeres con edades comprendidas entre los 37 y los 69 años ha revelado que caminar en torno a los 10 km por semana se asocia a una disminución del 33 % del riesgo de aparición de una enfermedad cardiovascular.

Estudios recientes realizados en medios espaciales y los basados en pasar largos periodos en la cama (estudios *bed-rest*), han demostrado lo beneficioso que es practicar un determinado tipo de ejercicio muscular de las extremidades inferiores para la calidad del retorno venoso. Los estudios llevados a cabo en medios espaciales por el CNES francés en las estaciones MIR e ISS han mostrado el estrecho vínculo existente entre el tono de los músculos posturales y el de las paredes de las venas intramusculares, evaluado mediante una pletismografía por aire. Cuando los músculos posturales adelgazan como consecuencia de pasar varias semanas en ingravidez, las venas situadas en dichos músculos se relajan y se dilatan.

Estudios
bed-rest

• Estas experiencias permitieron evaluar el efecto de una postración prolongada de 3 meses sobre los músculos y el sistema venoso de 19 voluntarios. Diez de ellos conformaron el grupo de control, mientras que los 9 restantes practicaron un programa de ejercicios contra resistencia que hacía trabajar a la vez los músculos posturales de la pantorrilla, del muslo y de la pelvis.

• En ambos grupos, la postración durante 3 meses produjo una amiotrofia de las extremidades inferiores en un 25 %, del mismo modo que si se hubiera colocado una escayola en una pierna rota. Los controles de las contracciones musculares se realizaron gracias a mediciones electromiográficas, al uso de dinamómetros isocinéticos (Cybex 6000) y a biopsias musculares practicadas en la zona de los músculos sóleos de las pantorrillas. Asimismo, se llevaron a cabo controles en las venas con mediciones pletismográficas por aire, volumétricas y ultrasonoras (ecografía y Doppler venoso).

• Los resultados derivados de estos estudios permitieron presentar la GVA y los movimientos Fast Gym propuestos anteriormente.

Métodos
de la fisioterapia

La **fisioterapia vascular** comprende métodos asociados a la red venosa y linfática, así como a la red arterial. En la práctica, la fisioterapia venosa distingue entre los **métodos pasivos**, en los que el paciente permanece inmóvil y «sufre» las manipulaciones del fisioterapeuta o la acción de un aparato externo, y los **métodos acti-**

vos, en los que no sólo entran en juego las manos del fisioterapeuta o el aparato, sino que el propio paciente también participa efectuando contracciones de sus músculos posturales al mismo tiempo que se le aplica un drenaje linfático en agua.

La **fisioterapia venosa y linfática** comprende, por una parte, métodos de drenaje y, por otra, métodos de fortalecimiento muscular y venoso. Los métodos de drenaje pueden ser pasivos o activos (drenaje linfático manual y presoterapia mecánica). Entre los métodos de drenaje activos, el principal es el drenaje linfático en agua (DLA). Los métodos de fortalecimiento muscular y venoso pueden ser pasivos (electroterapia) o activos (GVA).

Los **métodos de fisioterapia arterial** pueden ser pasivos (carboterapia) o activos (marcha de deambulación en piscina o contracciones musculares en resistencia).

Podemos citar otros métodos de fisioterapia vascular para la prevención de la flebitis como, por ejemplo, la compresión secuencial neumática mediante sofisticadas prótesis. Por último, la contención venosa es probablemente el sistema fisioterapéutico vascular más utilizado (con medias de contención, por ejemplo).

Drenaje linfático manual

Este método está indicado especialmente en casos de retención de líquidos y para edemas vasculares. El drenaje linfático manual consiste en drenar los líquidos excedentarios hacia los vasos linfáticos combinando maniobras de reabsorción y de llamada.

Un drenaje linfático manual debe hacerlo un fisioterapeuta que acredite la formación adecuada, y dura, como
mínimo, entre 30 y 40 minutos. El uso de una contención
permitirá continuar con un drenaje activo al caminar.

Los programas de drenaje linfático reforzados con
contención deberán asociarse a programas de rehabilitación muscular adaptados (gimnasia muscular activa). El fisioterapeuta deberá «educar» a su paciente en este aspecto.

Presoterapia

Esta técnica se basa en colocar en las piernas de los pacientes unas botas que van desde los pies hasta las ingles,
equipadas con cámaras de aire hinchables. El aire llega
gracias a unas ondas programadas por un aparato central
que determina la fuerza de la presión, el sentido del movimiento y la duración. El principio se basa en ejercer una
presión decreciente, desde la parte inferior a la superior.

La eficacia de la presoterapia también ha quedado pa-
tente en la prevención de las trombosis venosas profundas.

Drenaje linfático en agua

El drenaje linfático en agua es un nuevo método de drenaje linfático de las extremidades inferiores que se efectúa en una piscina, con el agua a 30 °C. Se trata de un
drenaje activo, puesto que ya no es la mano del fisioterapeuta la que trabaja, sino que es el propio paciente el que

realiza movimientos de gimnasia acuática situado frente a unos chorros que se encuentran en el agua.

La sesión combina una fase de 10 minutos de gimnasia acuática con una de 15 minutos de pedaleo sobre una bicicleta acuática, en la que las piernas se enfrentan a chorros que se encuentran en el agua y que ejercen un auténtico y profundo drenaje activo en los tejidos cutáneos-adiposos de los muslos, de las pantorrillas y de los tobillos. Los movimientos de la gimnasia acuática hacen trabajar principalmente a los músculos posturales, agonistas y antagonistas, durante el trabajo contra resistencia que realizan las extremidades inferiores siempre dentro de un medio acuático.

Métodos de electroestimulación

Los primeros trabajos realizados en torno a la electroterapia se remontan a principios del siglo XX. En la actualidad, los fisioterapeutas pueden elegir entre más de un centenar de aparatos con diferentes indicaciones.

Pueden distinguirse varias aplicaciones:

— La acción antiálgica (disminución del dolor) asociada a la reducción de la velocidad de conducción del influjo nervioso por medio de estimulación eléctrica. La eficacia del bloqueo eléctrico nervioso se acerca a la observada en un tratamiento con medicamentos antiálgicos.

— Las ondas cortas son conocidas por sus efectos terapéuticos: estimulan una vasodilatación capilar y una disminución de los fenómenos dolorosos.

— Los ultrasonidos, definidos como ondas sonoras con una frecuencia superior a 17.000 Hz (inaudibles por el oído humano), se utilizan gracias a su acción térmica y mecánica. La acción térmica es la transformación en calor de la energía ultrasonora asociada a la fricción de las moléculas en vibración.

Más allá de otras aplicaciones de la electroterapia, se utiliza sobre todo para la **estimulación de la contracción muscular**. Los fisioterapeutas emplean numerosos aparatos en contextos de rehabilitación postraumática.

Teniendo en cuenta el estrecho vínculo que une los músculos y las venas, pueden definirse 2 aplicaciones de electroestimulación para el tratamiento de los edemas de las extremidades inferiores:

— La electroestimulación muscular, que permite crear contracciones pasivas al margen de cualquier movimiento en un paciente postrado o en reposo. Asimismo, permite conservar la masa muscular en un sujeto postrado. Sin embargo, no destaca tanto como la contracción muscular generada por una gimnasia que aumenta la ventilación pulmonar. Por tanto, la estimulación eléctrica muscular se reserva para pacientes refractarios a cualquier ejercicio físico o para aquellos de edad avanzada postrados (con artrosis o en periodo posquirúrgico).

— El uso de ondas eléctricas repetitivas de frecuencia muy baja, que favorecen el aumento de la tonicidad de los músculos lisos de las paredes de las venas. El Datavein es un aparato avalado por varios estudios que muestran su acción sobre la reducción de los edemas de las extremidades inferiores, la prevención de las trombosis venosas profundas de los pacientes postrados y la reducción del diámetro de las venas intramusculares asociada al aumento de la tonicidad de los músculos lisos de la pared venosa.

GVA o Fast Gym

Se sabe que una de las principales causas de abandono de la práctica deportiva es la falta de motivación y de tiempo, por lo que este tipo de programa de breve duración puede lograr y conservar un objetivo razonable compatible con el día a día.

Contención

Se trata del tratamiento básico para cualquier edema vascular, cuyo principio consiste en realizar una compresión exterior que compense una presión intravenosa demasiado acusada.

La contención debe ser decreciente, es decir, más intensa en la zona de los tobillos y menos a medida que se acerca a la raíz de la extremidad. La contención ideal debe adaptarse perfectamente a la forma de la pierna, evitando las zonas de estricción (contracción) y teniendo en cuenta los relieves óseos. El médico prescribirá un par de medias de contención.

Las indicaciones de la contención abarcan todas las formas de edemas, insuficiencias venolinfáticas, trastornos funcionales y enfermedades posflebíticas, así como la prevención de la trombosis.

Otros métodos de fisioterapia vascular

Entre ellos, se incluyen:

— Métodos de amasamiento: tienen al Cellu M6 o al LPG como su mejor representante.
— La poleoterapia: entre los equipamientos clásicos utilizados por los fisioterapeutas se encuentran las jaulas de poleoterapia, que permiten realizar un ejercicio muscular orientado. Estas permiten la realización de un gran número de suspensiones y ejercicios contra resistencia, gracias a un sistema de cuerdas, pesas y poleas. Permiten ejercer movimientos con un eje paralelo al de las articulaciones y con una fuerza constante gracias a la resistencia variable aplicada mediante los contrapesos.
— El Fly Wheel: en la actualidad constituye uno de los mejores aparatos para desarrollar los músculos posturales, que son precisamente los que más actividad ejercen sobre el retorno venoso y linfático. Se trata de una especie de sillón deslizable sobre el que se sienta el paciente, con una plataforma delante que deberá empujarse con los pies. La considerable resistencia de esta plataforma está condicionada por un conjunto de pesos variables conectados a un sistema de poleas.

Métodos de hidroterapia

La hidroterapia es particularmente interesante para el retorno venoso: en el medio acuático, el cuerpo humano se vuelve más ligero, aunque los movimientos se realizan en contra de la resistencia del agua; por otra parte, la temperatura tiene la propiedad de descontracturar; el equilibrio es diferente y, asimismo, se estimula el sentido cinestésico.

La rehabilitación en el agua, los masajes subacuáticos y la gimnasia acuática son las novedosas técnicas que imperan en la actualidad en la descontractura y estimulación muscular.

— Los chorros subacuáticos: las corrientes provocadas por los movimientos o los chorros subacuáticos estimulan la circulación cutánea y subcutánea al ejercer un efecto favorable sobre el tejido conjuntivo de la piel. Los pacientes con placas de angiodermitis pigmentaria y purpúrica o de paniculitis crónica en la zona de los tobillos han notado mejora sólo con caminar por los pasillos de deambulación de las piscinas de los balnearios.

— La bicicleta acuática: es el mejor equipo de gimnasia acuática en lo que a drenaje venoso se refiere. Permite un ejercicio que estimula simultáneamente los músculos agonistas y los antagonistas. La bicicleta acuática puede practicarse frente a sistemas de chorros. Durante la realización del ejercicio, el paciente recibe un auténtico masaje hídrico por la pelvis, los muslos y las pantorrillas.

Medicamentos activos:
el último recurso

En materia de retención de líquidos, los medicamentos activos son los denominados **diuréticos**. Estos medicamentos son el resultado de auténticos avances de la medicina. Son extremadamente útiles en los casos en que la retención de líquidos esté asociada a una enfermedad renal, cardiaca o hepática. No obstante, su administración es delicada y pueden tener un efecto incompatible. Todos los medicamentos diuréticos presentan una curva de dosis-respuesta propia, que varía de un paciente a otro en función del caso. Además, el cuerpo se adaptará al medicamento y la respuesta de los riñones en términos de eliminación de exceso de líquido y de sal se regulará en un periodo de entre 1 y 2 semanas a fin de lograr establecer un nuevo estado de equilibrio.

Cabe tener en cuenta que estos medicamentos tan sólo pueden contemplarse a largo plazo en pacientes que hayan perdido su mecanismo de eliminación de agua y sodio con motivo de una enfermedad renal o hepática. Se trata de medicamentos de compensación.

Por el contrario, para las personas que presenten problemas de retención de líquidos asociados a una mala circulación venosa o linfática, a un desequilibrio hormonal o al consumo de alimentos «esponja», los diuréticos no se vislumbrarán realmente como una solución duradera.

Al igual que ocurre con los antibióticos, los diuréticos no pueden utilizarse como medicamentos contra los síntomas sin comprender correctamente el fenómeno de la retención de líquidos.

En definitiva, los medicamentos diuréticos deberán considerarse medicamentos de una calidad excelente si su uso se reserva a la retención de líquidos cuando esta va asociada a enfermedades renales, cardiacas o hepáticas, aunque deberán evitarse en caso de abuso de los mismos, ante la simple aparición de un edema, sin analizar previamente la situación.

Medicamentos...

... que retienen líquidos

• Se debe ser consciente de que algunos medicamentos pueden provocar o agravar el fenómeno de retención de líquidos. Este es el caso de algunos medicamentos utilizados para el corazón o la hipertensión arterial, denominados inhibidores cálcicos, así como los medicamentos corticoides, los derivados nitrados o la amantadina.

• Finalmente, existen casos de retención de líquidos que resisten a cualquier programa de tratamiento bien conducido: por ejemplo, cuando se presenta un síndrome asociado a problemas de tiroides, denominado síndrome de T3 bajo. Efectivamente, un problema de tiroides puede ser la causa de que se formen edemas en las extremidades inferiores. En ocasiones, aunque el tiroides funciona correctamente, al igual que la tirotropina, hormona que lo regula, es la hormona tiroidea periférica la causante. De nuevo, tan sólo un médico con experiencia en materia de equilibrio hormonal podrá sugerir y confirmar el diagnóstico.

Capítulo 8

Un programa antirretención de líquidos

En 2003, un estudio realizado por el Instituto francés de la Salud y de la Investigación Médica (INSERM) a 25.770 personas mayores de 15 años reveló que en Francia más de 14 millones de personas padecían sobrepeso y que 5 millones estaban obesas. Entre 2000 y 2003, la obesidad ha aumentado un 16 % en los hombres y un 18 % en las mujeres. El dato más preocupante es que dicho aumento afecta al 38 % de los franceses con edades comprendidas entre los 35 y los 44 años.

El INSERM identificó dos causas principales: un desequilibrio alimenticio y una falta de actividad física. La novedad es que, en este momento, se piensa que la causa de todo esto ya no es el exceso de calorías, sino la calidad de los alimentos consumidos. En resumen, no se trata de que algunos coman más que otros, sino de que comen peor.

Como es habitual, se acusa a los azúcares rápidos de ser los principales culpables de esta situación, en particular los azúcares industriales, los terrones de azúcar blanco, los alimentos y las bebidas azucaradas, las tabletas de chocolate, los pasteles, los bizcochos, los caramelos, etc.

Lo mismo ocurre con los alimentos con gran cantidad de grasas perjudiciales, es decir, las grasas cocinadas que contienen colesterol y ácidos grasos saturados, pero no omega 3. Los nutricionistas ponen de relieve detalles sorprendentes y desconocidos: por ejemplo, un cruasán contiene casi tantas calorías como un bocadillo de lomo de cerdo, del mismo modo que un gran puñado de cacahuetes o de almendras saladas tienen las mismas calorías que una comida habitual.

Evidentemente, comer entre horas seguirá considerado como el enemigo número uno. En cuanto a la actividad física, los nutricionistas recuerdan que, cuando se consumen azúcares rápidos o grasas perjudiciales y no se practica una actividad física en ese momento, el organismo almacena dichos azúcares y grasas, y las traslada directamente a la celulitis.

Dietas clásicas: insuficientes
de cintura para abajo

En las dietas clásicas se recomienda no consumir azúcares lentos como el pan, el arroz, la pasta y las legumbres. Muchas mujeres aplican estas medidas que, no obstante, no bastan para reducir grasa en la mitad inferior del cuerpo. Como hemos visto, dicha grasa es especial, está concentrada y asociada a un fenómeno de retención de líquidos que puede ser el único responsable de un sobrepeso que oscilaría entre los 4 y los 17 kg. Las medidas que los nutricionistas proponen actualmente están justificadas, aunque no son suficientes, ya que no tienen en cuenta el fenómeno de retención de líquidos.

Asimismo, a estas nociones clásicas hay que añadir la función emocional del cerebro, que es esencial para comprender los comportamientos alimentarios. Para muchos de nosotros resulta complicado identificar y controlar los diferentes estados emocionales. La vida de algunas mujeres, que comienza por la mañana preparando a los niños, yendo en transporte público, asumiendo las obligaciones de una vida profesional activa, y que acaba por la noche ocupándose nuevamente de su familia, descansando únicamente en el momento de acostarse, es una fuente de presión permanente que cuesta controlar. Algunas, recordando antiguas heridas o el estrés de una vida diaria compleja, compensarán todo ello con pulsiones alimentarias, sin poder reconocer la naturaleza de sus verdaderas necesidades.

La sensación de hambre entre comidas suele ser falsa, no se corresponde con una necesidad real de células subalimentadas, sino que es uno de los signos de estos trastornos de comportamiento alimentario, al igual que la necesidad de comer cuando se producen situaciones angustiosas. Cuando el cuerpo pide «un poco de descanso o de felicidad», el cerebro únicamente puede retener una sensación de necesidad, que se traduce por el único producto disponible de forma inmediata: la comida.

Asimismo, nuestro cuerpo alberga unos auténticos centinelas de la regulación que nos permiten, cuando nos encontramos equilibrados, desear los alimentos que necesitamos. Un ejemplo: después de comer muchas frutas o verduras, nuestro cuerpo necesita alimentos más consistentes como proteínas o grasas. Nuevamente, nos arriesgamos a interpretar esta exigencia como un deseo de comer una galleta o un trozo de chocolate, que, aunque son consistentes, no contienen ningún tipo de nutriente positivo. Esta aptitud para identificar y controlar nuestras sensaciones y emociones se denomina habitualmente *inteligencia emocional*.

Función del nutricionista

Uno de los objetivos del nutricionista es el de ayudarnos a reaccionar con normalidad ante la presión de nuestras emociones y crear nuevos reflejos de conducta, volver a descubrir nuestros centinelas de regulación, es decir, el instinto que nos hace desear alimentos beneficiosos.

Para adelgazar de cintura para abajo, no basta con saber que debe limitarse el consumo de azúcares y de grasas perjudiciales, sino que también hay que controlar los impulsos de cada uno por los alimentos grasos, dulces o salados.

Un programa con 3 objetivos

El PCRL se centra en 3 objetivos:

• Actuar contra la grasa con la supresión de los azúcares industriales y las grasas perjudiciales alimentarias, haciendo especial hincapié en aprender a controlar las pulsiones alimentarias por los alimentos dulces, grasos y salados.

• Actuar contra la retención de líquidos con la mejora del retorno venoso y linfático, fortaleciendo nuestros músculos posturales gracias a la práctica de Fast Gym, suprimiendo los alimentos «esponja» (que sólo afectan a un porcentaje de personas que padecen retención de líquidos) y manteniendo un buen equilibrio hormonal.

• Drenar el exceso de líquido mediante plantas y métodos de fisioterapia (drenaje en agua, Cellu M6).

Como puede observar, las dos novedades del PCRL son la eliminación de los alimentos «esponja» y la acción muscular ejercida sobre los músculos más importantes, los posturales. Los 8 minutos diarios de entrenamiento de estos músculos son un requisito mínimo para sostener las venas profundas y limitar la retención de líquidos asociada a una mala circulación venosa.

La Fast Gym no actúa directamente sobre la grasa celulítica, sino que lo hace sobre la retención de líquidos y la circulación sanguínea, lo que permite mejorar la vascularización de las zonas obstruidas por la celulitis. Asimismo, mejora la tonicidad de la piel. La sesión matutina diaria de Fast Gym puede ir precedida de la aplicación de una crema anticelulítica con cafeína, la única sustancia medicamentosa que ha demostrado sus efectos sobre la celulitis. La aplicación de la crema es la oportunidad para efectuar un automasaje con la técnica de amasamiento, que permite suavizar la fibrosis que rodea la grasa celulítica, estimular la microcirculación local, en particular la linfática, y movilizar las grasas.

El PCRL se inicia con un periodo de 15 días y puede prepararse de la siguiente manera:

• Prevea al menos media jornada (¿qué tal el fin de semana?) para comprar productos frescos, y destine, ese mismo día, una hora para preparar por anticipado un determinado número de platos. De esta manera, siempre dispondrá en su nevera de un producto listo para consumir al final de la jornada. Estos momentos son peligrosos, ya que propician la aparición de pulsiones de soluciones fáciles como la comida precocinada industrializada.
• Durante este periodo de 15 días, usted deberá suprimir principalmente todos los alimentos que contengan azúcar industrial y también los sustitutivos del azúcar como el aspartamo, las grasas cocidas, los alimentos demasiado salados, la carne de animales procedentes de crías intensivas, los productos elaborados a partir de harina de trigo blanca y los quesos de pasta cocida.

Desarrollo del tratamiento:
Fast Gym y alimentación

>> Sábado

Por la mañana

• 8 minutos de Fast Gym.
Desde un punto de vista fisiológico, la mañana es el momento más propicio, aunque quizás prefiera esti-

mular los músculos posturales en el trabajo, en su oficina. ¡También es posible!

Complementos alimenticios

Tome en ayunas o durante el desayuno:
- 2 cápsulas de centella asiática,
- entre 10 y 15 mg de vitamina E,
- entre 50 y 100 mg de vitamina C,
- 5 mg de vitamina B6,
- 50 µg de selenio,
- 15 mg de cinc.

Desayuno

- 1 té o 1 café, preferiblemente sin leche, azúcar ni edulcorante,

- 2 o 3 galletas de arroz inflado
  — o 2 o 3 rebanadas de pan de centeno integral,

- 1 alimento graso: preferiblemente medio aguacate
  — o 1 nuez de mantequilla fresca.

No están permitidas la margarina o la mermelada.

Opcional: puede completar el desayuno con un huevo pasado por agua y 1 yogur de leche entera o con *bifidus*, sin azúcar ni edulcorante, de la amplia variedad que se encuentra en el mercado.

A media mañana

Realice las compras de toda la semana

Dedique una hora a comprar los productos frescos que vaya a utilizar durante la semana.

En el mercado

* Compre frutas y verduras: 2 kg de naranjas, 6 pomelos, 1 piña, fruta de temporada (en verano principalmente frutos rojos: moras, fresas, frambuesas, grosellas negras, arándanos, etc.).
* Compre legumbres para consumir todos los días de la semana: lentejas, alubias, guisantes, habas, etc.
* Piense también en las proteínas: pollo de corral asado, pescado fresco para consumir el fin de semana, preferentemente pescado rico en omega 3 como el salmón salvaje y la caballa. De forma ocasional podrá tomar pescado congelado al natural, huevos de gallina criada al aire libre y carne roja de buena calidad para los más aficionados. Cualquier aliño o condimento es beneficioso: ajo, cebollas, hierbas y especias, pero evite los aliños preparados que contienen conservantes, estabilizantes, homogeneizantes y antioxidantes.

En una tienda de dietética

* Acuérdese del arroz integral para hervir, las galletas de arroz inflado, el pan de centeno integral y los zumos de manzana y uva biológicos.

- No olvide los cereales para plantar: trigo, soja, alforfón, etc.
- Estos establecimientos son ideales para comprar aceites prensados en frío y no hidrogenados: aceite de oliva, de colza, de pepitas de uva, etc.

¡A cocinar!

Dedique una hora a preparar las comidas que refrigerará en la nevera durante la semana siguiente:

- Platos de verduras cocidas al vapor (entre 15 y 20 minutos, en función de las verduras) o en la olla exprés (entre 10 y 15 minutos, según las verduras).
- Prepare una parte de las verduras para sopa y refrigérela en la nevera entre 3 y 4 días. Podrá consumir dicha sopa al llegar a casa por la noche, o llevársela al trabajo en un termo.
- Prepare también un gran plato de verduras para consumir entre semana: judías verdes, puerros, zanahorias, brécol... Asimismo, aprenda a cocinarlas de una forma atractiva, ya que, por ejemplo, el brécol puede estar delicioso o soso según cómo se prepare. Asimismo, las verduras deben quedar un poco duras, es decir, no demasiado cocidas. Pueden acompañarse de un alimento graso como, por ejemplo, nueces peladas esparcidas en el plato y un poco de jugo ligeramente salado extraído de un preparado de proteínas o del caldo de las verduras.
- Prepare igualmente una gran cacerola con algún alimento que contenga azúcar lento de buena ca-

lidad: arroz integral (hiérvalo durante 40 minutos como mínimo y después déjelo reposar con un poco de agua para que siga inflándose) o legumbres como las lentejas, ricas en proteínas y hierro, que son deliciosas siempre que se hayan cocinado muy bien.

- Prepare su nevera para los 3 días siguientes: además de la gran cacerola y la reserva de legumbres al vapor, uno o varios alimentos ricos en proteínas (por ejemplo, pollo asado, pescado, huevos o carne roja).

- Los adeptos al pan deben evitar en la medida de lo posible el pan de trigo y priorizar el pan de centeno integral, al menos durante el periodo inicial de 15 días.

Tome el aire

Además de las ocupaciones familiares, el sábado y el domingo son jornadas ideales para oxigenarse, hacer un poco de deporte, dar largos paseos o montar en bicicleta…

Reconcíliese con la fruta

Durante la jornada, no dude en prepararse un pequeño tentempié con fruta o zumo de cítricos recién exprimidos, ya que la fruta entre comidas o al principio de las mismas es ideal. Efectivamente, la mayor parte de la fruta se digiere en el duodeno, detrás del estómago. La combinación con los azúcares lentos, las proteínas y las grasas puede propiciar reacciones de fermentación y putrefacción. No obstante, la flora intestinal varía según la persona: las acostumbradas a comer mucha fruta y verdura no tendrán ningún problema para digerirlas; sin embargo, aquellas cuya flora intestinal ya no esté adaptada a este tipo de alimentación deberán acostumbrarse paulatinamente. A pesar de que podemos vivir muy bien comiendo poca cantidad de fruta y verdura cruda, es recomendable en tal caso aumentar la cantidad de verduras cocidas para ingerir a diario.

Comida

- 1 plato de verduras crudas + 1 cucharada sopera de aceite de oliva,
- 1 pescado fresco,
- verduras en la cantidad deseada,
- 1 yogur de leche entera o con *bifidus*.

Cena

- 1 plato de verduras crudas (ensalada de pepino + salsa de queso fresco, zanahorias ralladas + vinagreta con aceite de oliva...),
- 1 huevo,
- 1 rebanada de pan de centeno integral,
- 1 compota de manzana.

>> **Domingo**

Por la mañana

Tras hacerse la remolona en la cama…
- 8 minutos de Fast Gym.

Complementos alimenticios

Tomar en ayunas o durante el desayuno:
- 2 cápsulas de centella asiática,
- entre 10 y 15 mg de vitamina E,
- entre 50 y 100 mg de vitamina C,
- 5 mg de vitamina B6,
- 50 µg de selenio,
- 15 mg de cinc.

Desayuno

Para las personas a las que les guste comer por las mañanas, el domingo es el día perfecto para regalarse un buen desayuno:

- 1 té o 1 café, preferiblemente sin leche, azúcar ni edulcorante,
- 1 bol de arroz integral,
- jarabe de arce (la cantidad mínima necesaria para endulzar el arroz)
  — o dátiles frescos (también la cantidad mínima necesaria para endulzar el arroz).

Intente siempre combinar un azúcar lento con un alimento graso como:

- 1/2 aguacate fresco
  — o 1 nuez de mantequilla fresca
  — o algunas nueces o almendras frescas.

No está permitida la margarina o la mermelada.

A media mañana

El domingo por la mañana es un momento excelente para convencer a toda la familia de lo saludable que es dar un largo paseo por el campo o ir en bicicleta por la orilla del río más cercano.

Comida al aire libre

También es el mejor momento para activar el sistema de seguridad que le permitirá realizar algunos excesos (relajarse, realizar ejercicio físico, oxigenarse, etc.).

Cena

- 1 ensalada variada + algunos granos de trigo germinado (si es posible),
- 1 pescado,
- verduras,
- 1 ensalada de fruta fresca
  — o un producto lácteo.

Todos los productos «frágiles» como el pescado o las hortalizas crudas deben consumirse preferentemente durante el fin de semana, al igual que los que son un poco más elaborados.

No obstante, podrá refrigerar las hortalizas crudas entre 3 y 4 días en el cajón inferior de la nevera (las hojas de lechuga mojadas pueden envolverse en un paño húmedo).

Para las deportistas

Si durante el fin de semana pudieron practicar 1 o 2 sesiones de deporte, prevea una tercera entre semana.

>> Lunes

Por la mañana

* 8 minutos de Fast Gym.

Desde un punto de vista fisiológico, la mañana es el momento más propicio.

Complementos alimenticios

Tome en ayunas o durante el desayuno:
* 2 cápsulas de centella asiática,
* entre 10 y 15 mg de vitamina E,
* entre 50 y 100 mg de vitamina C,

- 5 mg de vitamina B6,
- 50 μg de selenio,
- 15 mg de cinc.

Desayuno

- 1 té o 1 café, preferiblemente sin leche, azúcar ni edulcorante,
- entre 2 y 4 rebanadas de pan de centeno integral
  — o galletas de arroz inflado
  — o 1 bol de arroz integral, ligeramente endulzado con jarabe de arce,
- 1 alimento graso: preferiblemente medio aguacate
  — o varias nueces
  — o 1 nuez de mantequilla fresca,
  — también puede añadir 1 cucharada sopera de aceite de oliva en el bol de arroz integral,
- 1 yogur de leche entera o con *bifidus*.

No están permitidas la margarina o la mermelada.

A lo largo del día

Si no está pegada a la silla de una oficina, multiplique las ocasiones de caminar, subir las escaleras, etc.; en definitiva, se trata de hacer un poco de ejercicio diario. En caso de que le invadan las ganas, existen algunos ejercicios concebidos para estimular los músculos posturales que pueden efectuarse sentada, en la silla de la oficina.

Comida

- en invierno, 1 sopa (en un termo); en verano, 1 ensalada preparada en casa o comprada en algún lugar cercano,
- algunas rebanadas de pan de centeno integral: siempre se debe evitar el pan de trigo,
- si es posible, un alimento rico en proteínas (carne o pescado).

Cena

- rábanos, de los que se puede tomar la cantidad que se desee,
- queso fresco con un 40 % de materia grasa a las finas hierbas.

Normalmente, el lunes es el día en que se utilizan mucho las reservas, debido al estrés habitual del inicio de semana, el cansancio, la falta de tiempo, etc. Es el momento ideal para calentar lo que preparó el sábado:

- verduras cocidas,
- lentejas
  — o alubias,
  — o pan de centeno integral,
- (opcional) 1 huevo pasado por agua, para el aporte de proteínas,
- para el postre, acabe la compota de días anteriores.

>> Martes

Por la mañana

- 8 minutos de Fast Gym.

Complementos alimenticios

Tome en ayunas o durante el desayuno:
- 2 cápsulas de centella asiática,
- entre 10 y 15 mg de vitamina E,
- entre 50 y 100 mg de vitamina C,
- 5 mg de vitamina B6,
- 50 µg de selenio,
- 15 mg de cinc.

Desayuno

- 1 té o 1 café, preferiblemente sin leche, azúcar ni edulcorante,
- entre 2 y 4 rebanadas de pan de centeno integral
  — o galletas de arroz inflado
  — o 1 bol de arroz integral, ligeramente endulzado con jarabe de arce,
- 1 alimento graso: preferiblemente medio aguacate
  — o varias nueces
  — o 1 nuez de mantequilla fresca
  — también puede añadir 1 cucharada sopera de aceite de oliva en el bol de arroz integral,
- 1 yogur de leche entera o con *bifidus*.

No están permitidas la margarina o la mermelada.

Comida

- 1 ensalada verde
  - — o 1 ensalada de tomate
  - — o 1 ensalada de pepino
  - — o 1 ensalada de zanahoria
  - — o 1 sopa (en termo)
  - — o 1 bol de arroz integral, ligeramente endulzado con jarabe de arce,
- 3 rebanadas de pan de centeno integral,
- si es posible, un alimento rico en proteínas (carne o pescado).

Cena

- 1 ensalada variada
  - — o 1 sopa,
- 1 bol de legumbres (lentejas, alubias, guisantes frescos, habas, etc.),

pescado o pollo.

>> Miércoles

Por la mañana

- 8 minutos de Fast Gym.

Complementos alimenticios

Tome en ayunas o durante el desayuno:
- 2 cápsulas de centella asiática,

- entre 10 y 15 mg de vitamina E,
- entre 50 y 100 mg de vitamina C,
- 5 mg de vitamina B6,
- 50 μg de selenio,
- 15 mg de cinc.

Desayuno

- 1 té o 1 café, preferiblemente sin leche, azúcar ni edulcorante,
- entre 2 y 4 rebanadas de pan de centeno integral
  — o galletas de arroz inflado
  — o 1 bol de arroz integral, ligeramente endulzado con jarabe de arce,
- 1 alimento graso: preferiblemente medio aguacate
  — o varias nueces
  — o 1 nuez de mantequilla fresca
  — también puede añadir 1 cucharada sopera de aceite de oliva en el bol de arroz integral,
- 1 yogur de leche entera o con *bifidus*.
  No están permitidas la margarina o la mermelada.

Comida

Permítase el lujo de comer en un restaurante 1 o 2 veces por semana, preferentemente al mediodía, aunque deberá aprender a controlarse. Da igual que se trate de una comida de negocios o de placer, será difícil apreciar la diferencia. No obstante, cada vez más personas se preocuparán de su conducta alimentaria y, sin duda alguna, sus compañeros comensales también la tendrán en cuenta. En cualquier caso, deberá elegir preferiblemente platos de verduras crudas, pescados, carnes rojas o aves asadas con guarnición de verduras, lo que acompañará con una ensalada de frutas, agua mineral, o para los aficionados al vino, una copa de un buen tinto.

A la hora de pedir, advierta que le preparen los platos sin salsas y con poca sal. Asimismo, y si es posible, pida un limón y aceite de oliva para prepararse usted misma el aliño.

¿Más compras?

Si se lo puede permitir, reserve el miércoles para volver a abastecerse de productos frescos, fruta, verdura y pescado, lo que le permitirá poner un broche final a la semana, el jueves y el viernes.

Cena

La noche del miércoles es el momento ideal para ocuparse de usted misma y de su familia. Si llega a casa cansada, tómese en primer lugar las verduras, las legumbres y los alimentos proteicos que queden y, seguidamente, prepare nuevos platos para los dos próximos días. Si, por el contrario, todavía se encuentra con fuerzas, comience a hervir las provisiones de los próximos días y cocine para la cena un pescado fresco con verduras también frescas.

>> Jueves, viernes, etc.

Se basarán en los mismos modelos de los días anteriores. La variedad puede ser extraordinaria si se sabe jugar con los productos de temporada: espárragos, guisantes, alcachofas, calabacines, tomates, judías, champiñones, etc.; ahí reside la auténtica variedad alimentaria, la verdadera imaginación, y no en la prodigalidad de productos precocinados, que sólo son un espejismo de variedad. Por otro lado, no es necesario saber cocinar para comer sano. Lo que en realidad debe aportar el sabor a los alimentos es la calidad y la frescura de los mismos, y no su transformación ni su aliño excesivo (que, por otra parte, sólo tienen como objetivo enmascarar la ausencia de frescura).

Una de las claves del equilibrio se encuentra en la educación del gusto desde la infancia, desconfiando de la tendencia creciente a consumir alimentos grasos, dulces y salados.

Una naranja, un buen lenguado fresco o un plato de guisantes frescos aportan mucho más placer, y potencia el gusto, que un alimento graso y dulce.

Conclusión

La grasa de la mitad inferior del cuerpo es diferente a la de la mitad superior, ya que está más concentrada y se asocia a la fibrosis y a la retención de líquidos, por lo que es más difícil de eliminar.

El fenómeno de la retención de líquidos puede detectarse y estimarse acudiendo a un médico. Está asociado a una circulación venosa o linfática defectuosa, a un desequilibrio hormonal o a una intolerancia a los alimentos «esponja». Entre los métodos que actúan sobre los trastornos circulatorios (drenaje linfático, Cellu M6, etc.), la GVA o Fast Gym, que puede practicarse en casa y que dura solamente 8 minutos al día, y el drenaje linfático en agua se presentan como novedosos.

Desde el punto de vista alimenticio, la dieta para contrarrestar la retención de líquidos pretende detectar, en una primera fase, una posible intolerancia que provoque la acumulación de péptidos que retienen el agua en los tejidos intersticiales. Sus principios básicos consisten en limitar el consumo de alimentos industriales, grasos, dulces o salados.

Por otra parte, debe tenerse en cuenta la distribución de las comidas: el desayuno es el mejor momento para consumir glúcidos lentos y grasas no cocidas, sin demasiado contenido en colesterol, ricas en omega 3 y en ácidos grasos poliinsaturados; en la comida deberán priorizarse las legumbres y las proteínas (carne o pescado); a media jornada, un tentempié de fruta siempre vendrá bien, y, en cuanto a la cena, esta deberá realizarse temprano y ser también lo más ligera posible.

No obstante, lo más difícil en este tema, sigue siendo la capacidad de identificar los alimentos que no le convienen a una persona en concreto, que favorecen la intolerancia alimentaria y la retención de líquidos, y, al mismo tiempo, controlar las pulsiones alimentarias en los momentos de estrés y de cansancio, y todo ello teniendo en cuenta que nos encontramos en un contexto en el que nuestras costumbres van de la mano de una educación moderna del sabor, que nos induce a consumir alimentos industrializados, refinados, transformados, que son demasiado dulces, grasos o salados.

El conjunto de las investigaciones recientes en nutrición ha demostrado la importancia de la alimentación y del ejercicio físico en la conservación de una silueta armoniosa.

La originalidad de estas nuevas técnicas (GVA, drenaje linfático en agua, dieta para contrarrestar la retención de líquidos) reside en reunir los elementos más eficaces teniendo en cuenta las limitaciones de la vida moderna.

Direcciones útiles

Para realizar una revisión de retención de líquidos

- **Centro de Enfermedades de Venas**
Rda. Universitat, 20, 2.º-1.ª
08007 Barcelona
Tel.: 93 301 11 46
      93 301 17 61
www.centrovenasbarcelona.com
cev@centroenfvenas.com

Para practicar el drenaje linfático en piscina y la bicicleta acuática

- **Balneario de Blancafort**
Mina, 7
08530 La Garriga
(Barcelona)
Tel.: 93 860 56 00
info@balnearioblancafort.com

- **Talasso Antemare Nova Dimensió**

Avda. Mare de Déu de Montserrat, 48-50
08870 Sitges (Barcelona)
Tel.: 93 894 70 00
www.antemare.com

- **Balneario Termaeuropa Arnedillo**

Joaquín Velasco s/n
26589 Arnedillo - La Rioja
Tel.: 901 22 29 02
www.balnearioarnedillo.com

- **Balneario Hespería La Toja**

36991 Isla de La Toja
(Pontevedra)
Tel.: 986 73 00 50
www.hesperia-isladelatoja.com

Para tratar la celulitis

- **Centro de Estética Carmen Navarro**

Sagasta, 21 - 1.º dcha.
28004 Madrid
Tel.: 91 445 52 56

- **Clinique Française**

Almagro, 25 - bajo dcha.
28010 Madrid
Tel.: 91 700 06 94

- **Institut Sagna de Saurina**

Diagonal 611, 3.º
Barcelona
Tel.: 93 419 45 16
www.sagnadesaurina.es

Bibliografía

1. Blanchemaison P. y otros.
    La gymnastique vasculaire active: principes et techniques.
    Angiologie, 2003; 55, 4: 46-51.

2. Stick C. y otros.
    Measurements of volume changes and venous pressure in the human lower leg during walking and running.
    Journal of Applied Physiology, 1992; 72: 2063-8.

3. Guezennec Y., Louisy S.
    Modifications de la compliance veineuse suivant le type d'entraînement physique.
    Phlébologie, 1995; 48, 4: 463-4.

4. Neiwel P.C. y otros.
    Calf blood flow and posture: doppler ultrasound measurements during and after exercice.
    Journal of Applied Physiology, 1992; 72: 1975-80.

5. Elbeze Y. y otros.
   Écho-doppler veineux au repos et à l'effort chez le
   sportif de bon niveau.
   Phlébologie, 1995; 48, 4: 445-50.

6. Blanchemaison P., Guell A.
   Angiologie et espace.
   Angiologie, 2003; 55, 2, 64-67.

7. Chanvallon C.
   Les contraintes physiologiques vasculaires périphéri-
   ques générées par divers types d'activité sportive.
   Phlébologie, 1995; 48, 4: 451-3.

8. Brunner U.
   Cyclisme et saphène externe.
   Phlébologie, 1995; 48, 4: 469-72.

9. Lemaire R.
   La circulation de retour chez le sportif.
   Phlébologie, 1980; 33, 4: 451-9.

10. Larroque P., Clement R. y otros.
    Le syndrome des loges des jambes.
    S T V, 1992; 4: 413-9.

11. Chauveau M.
    Hémodynamique veineuse et exercice musculaire.
    Phlébologie, 1995; 48, 4: 421-5.

12. Joly B. y otros.
    Assistance au retour veineux: flexion dorsale ou fle-
    xion plantaire du pied?
    Ann Kinesit, 1998; 25, 2: 50-4.

13. Blanchemaison P.
L'aquadrainage lymphatique: une nouvelle méthode de traitement de la rétention d'eau et de l'œdème.
Phlébologie, 2004; 57, 1.

Impreso en España por
HUROPE, S. L.
Lima, 3 bis
08030 Barcelona

David Guterson

THE OTHER

David Guterson is the author of the novels *Snow Fall-ing on Cedars, East of the Mountains*, and *Our Lady of the Forest*, as well as a story collection, *The Country Ahead of Us, the Country Behind*. A PEN/Faulkner Award winner, he is a cofounder of Field's End, an organization for writers in Washington State.

THE OTHER

THE OTHER

DAVID GUTERSON

Vintage Contemporaries
VINTAGE BOOKS
A DIVISION OF RANDOM HOUSE, INC.
NEW YORK

FIRST VINTAGE CONTEMPORARIES EDITION, JUNE 2009

The Library of Congress has cataloged the Knopf edition as follows:
Guterson, David.
The other / David Guterson.—1st ed.
p. cm.
1. Male friendship—Fiction. 2. Recluses—Fiction.
3. Washington (State)—Fiction. 4. Psychological fiction. I. Title.
PS3557.U846075 2008
813'.54—dc22 2007041098

Vintage ISBN: 978-0-307-27481-6

Book design by Virginia Tan

www.vintagebooks.com

Printed in the United States of America
10 9 8 7 6 5 4 3 2 1

To A.S.C., A.V.S., and D.W.B.

Je est un autre.

—Rimbaud

CONTENTS

THE OTHER

I

No Escape from the Unhappiness Machine

I ATTENDED ROOSEVELT (the Teddies, Teds, or Roughriders), a public high school in North Seattle, while my friend John William Barry was a student at Lakeside, our city's version of an East Coast private academy like Phillips Exeter or Deerfield. Besides slumping at my desk all day and getting high in Cowen Park at lunch, I also ran the 880—today called the eight-hundred-meter or the half-mile— for the RHS track team. It was a good niche for me. You didn't need to be fast or have the wind of the distance runner. Mostly what you needed was a willingness to sign up. As a sophomore in 1972, I was a good enough half-miler to represent RHS with a time of 2:11.24. To put this in context, the world record in '72 for the half-mile was held by Dave Wottle, with a time of 1:44.30. Roosevelt's best half-miler of all time is Chris Vasquez, '97, at 2:01.23. This is a race that takes runners twice around the red cinder oval found behind many high schools—I say this so you can imagine me losing to Vasquez by about thirty yards, or think of me still rounding the last bend, at the far end of the grandstands, while Wottle is crossing the finish line, arms raised victoriously. Either is a useful picture of me—of someone intimate with the middle of the pack. There's good and bad in that.

I remember one race more vividly than others. It's '72, so Nixon is president, though he and everything else, the world, seem far away from Seattle. I'm sixteen and wear my hair like Peter Frampton's and a mustache like Steve Prefontaine's. (Because of this mustache, I'm sometimes referred to at school as "the Turk," after the guy in the Camel cigarette ads. I'm not Turkish, but my mother's father, whom I never met, was what people call Black Irish, and possibly I inherited his coloring.) I've got on hi-cut satin shorts and a satin jersey emblazoned with *Roughriders*, and I'm at the starting line along with seven other runners, six with better qualifying times than mine. Despite them, I'm a believer that if the ninety-nine-pound mother in the apocryphal story can lift the front end of a Volkswagen off her crushed toddler, I can win today.

I'll dispense with the obligation to describe the weather—whether or not it was a sultry afternoon, with clouds of newly hatched mayflies above the track, or a windless May day smelling of moist turf and mown grass, is beside the point—and cut, literally, to *in medias res:* the eight of us stalwart and tortured young runners rounding the third curve of a high-school track and coming up on 250 yards. It's my usual MO—out front early and counting on adrenaline to keep me there, but with heels nipped and a sinking feeling that's anathema to winning. A race is a conversation with yourself, motivational in quality, until somebody interrupts by pulling away from you, and then it becomes an exercise in fathoming limits. Losing is like knowing that, in the movie scene where a thousand die but the hero lives, you're one of the obliterated.

The right track term is "running in a pack." That's us—a band of runners hardly separated. One keeps exhaling humidly on my shoulders. Another's left forearm hits my right elbow on its backswing. A runner pulls up beside me—the way a freeway driver pulls even in the adjacent lane to take your pulse—and I assess his chances with a panicked glance. Not strictured yet; striding with more ease than I feel; biding his time; relaxed. Working up a freshly adrenalized surge, I gain a quarter-step on him, but purchased with the last of my reserves.

The early leader in a half-mile race rarely finishes first, but he wants to have had the experience of leading—that's part of it—and he's perennially hopeful that, this time, things will be different in the home stretch. I still feel that way entering curve three: that I might have heretofore undiscovered deposits of leg strength and cardiovascular capacity, not to mention will, at my disposal, all this against the grain of my foreboding. It turns out that my foreboding makes sense; at the curve's apogee, I know I'll flag, and with that, the flagging happens. Three runners pass me, going strong.

I'm needled by regret. Why don't I have a better strategy than running as fast as I can from start to finish? I've squandered my energy; I've incurred too large a deficit. But it isn't in me to plan; I just run, as my coach says, on unfocused emotion. These other runners, by the halfway mark—end of lap one, where we're lashed on by friends and exhorted by teammates, a small fire zone of screaming and technical advice—are just stretching out and finding a rhythm, while I'm already in a battle with depletion. I drop to sixth, dragging with me a familiar sense of failure.

Then, on the back stretch, the runner in seventh tries to pass me, too. To anybody watching we're in a pointless and even pathetic battle between losers, but for me what's happening feels critical. Against good tactical judgment—it's a move that slows you—I indulge in another assessment of an opponent: like me, long-haired; like me, in earnest; like me, goaded forward by, the word might be, convictions. In other words, this runner is approximately my doppelgänger.

Ask any track coach. The half-mile is a race for unadulterated masochists. Neither a sprint nor a distance event, it has the worst qualities of both. It's not a glorious race, either. A lot of people can name a sprinter or two—Carl Lewis, for example—or a famous miler like Roger Bannister, but can very many name even a single half-miler? No athletic romance attaches to the half-mile. It's not a legendary or even notable feat to beat other runners over 880 yards. At track meets, the half-mile contest is somehow lost between more compelling competitions, an event that unfolds while fans thumb their programs or use the bathroom. Into this gap of a race, this sideshow, step runners in search of a deeper agony than they can find elsewhere. They want to do battle with suffering itself. It's the trauma they want, the anguished ordeal. It's the approximately two minutes of self-mortification or private crucifixion. All half-milers have a similar love of pain. So this race is an intimation and an opening. In two minutes' time, you get a glimpse.

I do, on the afternoon I'm telling about. There's a kind of synchronicity that can happen in a running race, and it happens now. We run in tandem, my near doppelgänger and I. In running parlance, we match strides. I'm measuring him, as he, no doubt, is measuring me—all the while throwing ourselves forward into fresh pain, so that there are two perceptions, pain and the close presence of another agonized half-miler. In parallel this way, and canceling each other out, we're neither of us ahead or behind for maybe forty-five seconds. That's an unusually long time to run neck and neck in the 880. I'm oxygen-deprived, so everything looks well lit and startling, and from this perspective I see what I probably wouldn't see otherwise. This guy, right here, running next to me, is a version of me. We both feel, romantically, that our running is transcendent. How do I know this? From running alongside him. I also have the benefit of hindsight.

Thirty-four years have passed, but I still remember how, in the final five yards, my double frees himself—like a shadow in a cartoon or a mirror-figure in a dream—and beats me by three-quarters of a stride.

I'm bent over and spent, my hands on my knees after the race, breathing hoarsely and looking at the ground, when he comes over to shake my hand with what I think at first is a grating sincerity. The grip is vigorous. The expression is heartfelt and, post-race, ruddy. The stance is upright, the posture exclamatory. This is gracious victory personified, and for a moment I think—it says *Lakeside* on his jersey—that what I'm seeing is obligatory patrician good manners, a valorous lad with his cursory and vapid Victorian *Well done!* while his heaving breath subsides. But no. He's just fiercely putting forward what he feels—he's honest. There's a sentiment to be noted, life is short, and he doesn't want to just pass by. "Thanks for the push," John William declares, between bouts of sucking wind. "I just about died."

That's how I met the privileged boy who would later become "the hermit of the Hoh"—as he's been called by the Seattle newspapers this spring, in articles mentioning my name, too—that loner who lived in the woods for seven years and who bequeathed me four hundred and forty million dollars.

·   ·   ·

My name's Neil Countryman. I was born in this city of wet, high-tech hubris, which was called, at first, maybe with derision, "New York Alki," meaning "New York Pretty Soon" in Duwamps. Besides me, there are seventeen Countrymans in the Seattle phone book, and all of them are my relatives—my father's two brothers; their sons, grandsons, and unmarried granddaughters; and my two sons. We're close-knit, as we sometimes say about ourselves. Over the years, we've closed ranks around deaths, accidents, follies, and addictions. On the other hand, we shy away from intimacy as if such shyness was a value. We don't ask each other the more difficult questions. I'm generalizing, of course, but a Countryman who wants to go his own way will find, among his relatives—universally on the male side—straight-faced if sometimes dishonest approval. Clannish as we are, we believe in privacy, even when it's obvious that someone you love is making a terrible mistake.

As a boy I enjoyed, with my sister, Carol, *Laugh-In*, *Get Smart*, and *The Man from U.N.C.L.E.* We lived in a ranch house in the northeast part of town, modern for its time and built by my father, with an intercom system my mother used to call Carol and me from the rec room. My family went on summer vacations in-state, sometimes to Ocean Shores, but always to Soap Lake, in the sagebrush interior, where we would join other Cavanaughs—my mother was a Cavanaugh—for an annual rendezvous. At Soap Lake, my mother liked to loll around on a blow-up mattress and drink Tab. Once, I lost a beach ball in the wind, and by the time I noticed, it was a quarter-mile out. My mother brought it back, breathing hard but looking athletic. I remember how surprised I was, when I was eight, to see her so competent on a pair of skis at Alpental. I was under the impression that we'd gone to Alpental so that Carol and I could slide down a hill on inner tubes while our parents stood around with their hands in their pockets, but instead my mother, on rentals, disappeared up a chairlift and materialized much later to spray snow at my father with a stylish hockey stop. My father brushed off the snow as if it was lint on a tuxedo, which was his idea of humor. He was compact, with a recessed hairline and long sideburns, tight-lipped when corrected, and famous among my cousins for his forearms, which bulged like bowling pins. I remember him stretched out on the Cavanaughs' steep roof after it was damaged by a fallen tree, his head downslope, a hammer between his teeth, reaching with his left hand to start a nail by stabbing it into a rafter until it stuck there. My father was a finish carpenter first, but he was also a pack rat. He brought home, from his jobs, used refrigerators and freezers, washers and dryers, coils of plastic pipe, and rolls of scavenged wire, and stored it all in our backyard under an open-air shed he'd built out of salvaged materials. When he got older, he drove a Corolla, but he didn't listen to its radio very much, because, as he said, it was more interesting to listen to its motor. He also felt it was useful to smoke a Camel before heading for the bathroom. When I asked him if he got bored in there, he told me he read the *Post-Intelligencer*, starting with the obits, first to see if anyone he knew had "kicked," second to mull the ages of the deceased in relation to his own years, so that he'd remember not to feel sorry for himself.

For a while, my mother sang with the Merry Mavericks—about a dozen men and women with a Peter, Paul and Mary look but an Up with People sound. They performed at Christmas in the Food Circus at the Seattle Center. My mother was a soloist. Hitting her high notes, she sounded like Judy Garland. I remember her coming off the stage dressed in red-and-green satin and taking Carol and me across the food court for caramel corn. Carol and I were glad when all of this was over, because we only liked pop tunes. In fact, the first album I bought, the summer after eighth grade, was Bread's *On the Waters*, because "Make It with You," sung by David Gates in falsetto, moved me. In wood shop, I built speaker cabinets out of low-grade walnut, then installed tweeters, woofers, and *de rigueur* large woofers from SpeakerLab. I traded a cousin some speakers like this for a battered drum set, and he showed me how to play the opening licks, complete with cowbell, of "Honky Tonk Woman." For two years, I washed dishes at a Mexican restaurant for $2.65 an hour, partly to fund drum lessons from a burned-out but still-hip jazzman. I kept a fish tank in my room, went bowling sporadically, and played hockey on roller skates. I had a normal interest in girls, which I admit is a declaration dispensing with the subject, so I will add that I was the sort of hapless boy who came away from cheap encounters with the blues.

John William and I were of the generation that was slightly late for the zeal of the sixties and slightly early for disco. The most popular song, I think, in '74, was "Takin' Care of Business" by

9

Bachman-Turner Overdrive, though the Doobie Brothers were also esteemed. In Seattle, white guys wore flares, shags, and Pacific Trail jackets; white girls wore sailor pants or 501 jeans and let their hair fall around their faces. We were seven when JFK was killed, twelve when King was killed, and fourteen when four students were killed at Kent State, but by the time we were old enough to fathom "the Zeitgeist" (a term getting play in '74), there was détente, H-bomb drills were quaint, and there was no more draft. Always on the front page of the *Seattle Times* was inexplicable news, for a teen-ager, of tariffs and wage and price controls. Who cared? Gerald Ford became president in '74 and began hitting people with golf balls, apparently, thousands of miles away from Seattle. Everything, in fact, was thousands of miles away from Seattle. It was the portal to the North Pacific. It was where you outfitted to travel in Alaska, gateway to the Last Frontier.

In '74, though, I was the first Countryman to go to college. My father and his brothers were all nail bangers, and most of my male cousins followed suit by working in construction or the trades. They were straight-faced when I opted for college, and they're straight-faced today about the indoor work I've done for twenty-seven years. I'm a high-school English teacher. I'm the sort of high-school English teacher who has an unpublished novel in his desk drawer, and not just one unpublished novel but, in boxes at home, three more in varying stages of disarray. On the upside, I have an agent named Allison Krantz, or Ally, as she signs her e-mails. We've never met, because Ally lives in Manhattan, though now that I'm rich and a little bit famous we're slated to meet next month.

It's been, for me, three decades as an unpublished writer, but I don't mean to cast myself as a failure by saying this, because teaching, at least, has been rewarding. I'm confident I'm good at it. I think that most of my students like me, and that among my peers I have a decent reputation. I feel useful in the classroom, and, most of the time, at peace with my profession. There's something unsurpassed, for me, about a good teaching hour or a good teaching day. So, whatever my shortcomings as a writer of fiction, I do have this— my career as an English teacher—but I will also acknowledge that, like my students, I've been eager for the liberty of summer.

Sometimes, I look across the rows of students—particularly when they're silently taking a test—and tell myself that they're all enigmas. They look enigmatic to me, at least, even though I've listened to their voices and read their essays. Who are they really? is a question that surfaces in me unbidden at these moments. Of course, they come in a wide range. I try to be open to them all, because they're young and tender, but, inevitably, some touch me more than others. Personally, I'm drawn to the young person with a metaphysical complaint, the one upset by the meaninglessness of life who wants to do something about it urgently. Is there something wrong with that obsession? Let me borrow a sappy phrase that's richer for being curtailed—*Oh, to be young*. To still be one's own hero. To still be untainted, and yearning, without anything muddled yet, toward some ostensibly attainable cosmic goal. That, in a way, was my friend John William, which is not to say he was morally irreproachable. Quite the opposite. He stole things. He threw rocks through windows. He damaged what he could. Yet, if I had to sum him up in a way you would recognize, as someone from your own school, a type, I wouldn't use the term "juvenile delinquent." I would call him, instead, the brooder in the back row. The rich kid who hates and loves himself equally. The contrarian who hears his conscience calling in the same way schizophrenics hear voices, so that, for him, there's no not listening.

A week after losing that race to John William, I saw him again, this time at Green Lake. I was doing what I often did on Saturdays in high school—running the promenade, and passing every runner I saw until I found one who wanted to race. I looked forward to these episodes of aggression toward strangers, but what I didn't see was how self-defeating my compulsion was, this looking for someone to lose to. I was doing this when John William ran up alongside me, upright but with hair in his eyes, and said, "Not you again."

We slowed. There were people pushing strollers, kids feeding ducks, joggers, walkers, and bicylists. I said, "Are you a fag?"

"No."

"Just a rich bastard."

"Let's race to the bathhouse."

He picked up his pace, so did I, and we ran grimly, forcing anyone coming toward us out of our way. I lost, and when I'd caught my breath, shortly after he did, I said, "How much did you pay for those shoes?"

We watched girls go by and made comments. We jumped into the lake. John William had dope in his car, which was also full of fast-food wrappers and empty chocolate-milk cartons. We went over to Beth's Cafe, bloodshot and reeking, ate like pigs, and then bought two bottles of MD 20/20 at a place on Ravenna Boulevard that didn't card people. Later that night, John William drove the wrong way down a one-way street. Around two in the morning, we stole onto the grounds of the Seattle Center with the idea of wading in pools there and collecting coins. By day, the center could be crowded with visitors to the Space Needle—that self-consciously futuristic 605-foot tower which, as Seattle's most popular tourist attraction, presides over the north end of its skyline like a moored UFO—the amusement park, the science exhibits, the Flag Pavilion, or the Monorail, but on this night it was rain-racked and so utterly deserted as to feel menacing. John William and I jogged past the locked-down barker booths with their giant pink teddy bear and faux-feather boa prizes, then stopped to toke by the Food Circus. On our left, the three legs of the Needle held up its rotating restaurant, their surfaces lit from below by floodlights. I told John William that the Needle's observation deck reminded me of a mushroom, and his answer was "I hate the Space Needle."

"Me, too."

"I hate this whole place."

"So do I."

We jogged on, passing a closed sno-cone booth and the dark Exhibition Hall, where about twelve years before, at the Century 21 Exposition, I'd taken a simulated space flight in the Spacearium with my parents and Carol. At the pools that John William and I planned to pick clean of change, on the far side of the Flag Pavilion and in the courtyard of the Pacific Science Center, the fountains had all been turned off for the night, but the water surfaces were so roiled by raindrops that the coins below, in wee-hour city light, shimmered like cinematic pirate booty. I have to describe this place not as I think of it now—as a museum I've visited with my sons to enhance their appreciation of science (and, on the way out of the exhibits on dinosaurs or computers, to watch them, with paternal sentiment, make wishes and toss pennies)—but as it appeared to me that night, when I was a teen-ager on the cusp of petty crime. Those pools sat under neo-Gothic arches higher than a lot of downtown buildings, arches reminiscent of the flying buttresses I'd seen in photographs of cathedrals. If you live in a place devoid of much architectural interest, such arches can impress you. They impressed me. They might have been something from M. C. Escher in a slightly less hallucinatory mood than usual. Those vaulting, fretted complications full of latticed interstices, and as delicate and stout as whalebone overhead, gave the courtyard of pools an extraterrestrial ambience, or at least the quality of a dreamworld.

Such as it was and I was. I was also cold, rain-soaked, and paranoid, but with John William I waded in, knee-high, and gathered coins. We stuffed our wet jacket pockets and worked like peasants in rice paddies. If you imagine yourself committing this crime, you'll realize that your field of view is limited to the water immediately below your eyes and to the bottom of the pool, where the coins lie. You don't notice much other than the positions of coins and the movements of your hands underwater to make retrievals. The truth is that in short duration this sort of harvesting is mesmerizing. If you're only at it for twenty minutes or so, your back doesn't hurt and you can enjoy the rhythm, the distorted view through water (and, in this case, the luminous and agitated reflection of those neo-Gothic arches, inverted and foreshortened), and the giddiness of a furtive and illegal act. There's the further pleasure—not everyone enjoys this, and teen-agers enjoy it more often than adults—of surrendering to being soaked on a rainy night.

But I can't explain why we were stealing coins at the Seattle Center. It makes no sense to me now, though it must have made sense to me then. I just don't recall what that logic was, other than to say that, for my part, I was doing something John William wanted to do and, one thing leading to another, I hadn't dropped out along the way. Maybe it was a little like manna from heaven—this scattered, free money in a deserted public place—and so all the more tantalizing. However it was, we had only an aqueous glow to work by, which meant we bent our heads farther than we might have. Intent like this on our underwater misdemeanors, we were discovered by a uniformed security guard, whom we didn't notice until he said, to our backs, "Hey, you little long-haired shits, you're under arrest."

I wanted to run. We had the natural advantage of being young half-milers, and my impulse was to use it. This guard didn't appear particularly fit. I don't remember details other than his muttonchop sideburns and the way he kept his thumbs on his belt like a sheriff in a western, but I do remember feeling he'd have a hard time covering half a mile in two minutes. Granted, we'd be weighed down by watery clothes, but running was still the answer, from my perspective. And so, dropping the coins in my hand, I waded heavily toward a far edge. John William, though, just stood in the pool with a fistful of change while the guard pried open a sheath on his belt, pulled from it one of those giant handheld radios that were state-of-the-art for law enforcement in the seventies, raised it to his lips, and pressed the TALK button. "Base," he said, and that was when John William threw change in his face, lunged for his knees, and, in pulling him into the water, dislocated his hip—although I shouldn't say I'm certain about the injury. I just assume his hip was dislocated because the angle of his leg seemed improbable while he splashed and flailed.

We fled in water-logged shoes, and so loaded down by coins they slowed us and made my jacket bounce. I zipped my pockets along the way so as not to leave a trail of change in my wake and followed John William across the Great Northern tracks at Broad Street, and from there into the brush between Elliott Bay Park—now Myrtle Edwards Park—and the railroad bed with its bull rock and broken glass. A lot of Seattleites stand here to watch the city's Fourth of July fireworks display, but the rest of the year it's frequented by the transient and destitute, who for decades have rolled out their mildewed sleeping bags in the Scotch broom because no one tells them not to. That's where we found ourselves. In the high weeds, we lay on our backs to catch our breath and let the rain pelt us. I didn't feel stoned anymore, and my tide of juvenile adrenaline hadn't crested— instead, I felt washed out and attentive to fresh dangers. John William, though, had his hands over his face. He was clutching his skull, his fingers in his hair, the heels of his palms against his eye sockets, and I realized that he was crying. I was silenced by it, because none of my friends or cousins cried, and neither did I, in front of people.

"I think I hurt that guy," John William said, after a while. "Did he hit his head?"

"I couldn't tell you."

"Did he get out of the water?"

"I don't know."

"We should go back," John William said. "I want to take him to a hospital. I have to apologize."

"Go ahead, then."

He cried more, which I waited out by turning away from him.

"Wishing money," said John William, when he'd composed himself, "is the money little kids throw in the water when they're wishing they'll never have to die and everyone will always be happy."

"I thought of that myself."

"I always wished everyone could be happy when I was a kid blowing out candles. And for no death."

"Me, too."

"Except for my parents. They can be unhappy and die."

It sounded like something a rich kid would say, and since I didn't understand it, I didn't answer.

At the south end of Elliott Bay Park, under a roof overhang on Pier 70, we saw someone sitting against a creosoted timber, wrapped in a sleeping bag and wearing what looked to be one of those synthetic coonskin caps kids used to get for Christmas—an acne-scarred Indian planted between brown plastic garbage sacks and burlap bags—and when he asked if we could spare some change, we both put all the coins we had into his outstretched coffee tin.

JOHN WILLIAM HAD a Chevrolet Impala with cream paint and a vinyl top. His parents bought it new in '67 and drove it for five years before handing him the keys, and it was this Impala that we used, as frequently as we could, to light out for the territories—to light out with all the subtext of escape implied by that phrase from *Huck Finn*. Before we were nineteen, we had already climbed Mount Saint Helens (before it famously blew), Mount Rainier, Mount Baker, and Mount Adams—in short, we were mountaineers at an early and reckless age. We'd hiked beside the ocean from Point of the Arches to the Quillayute Needles, and we'd seen the Pickets in the North Cascades, and the range above the Hoh now known as the Valhallas but back then still called the Pleiades. That Impala served us well. Once, near Yellow Bluff, on State Route 109, along the coast, John William pulled over to face the breaking waves and told me that here, where we were now sitting, looking at the ocean on a summer afternoon, something had happened which he remembered in detail from five years earlier—from the year when his mother, Ginnie Barry, landed in a psych ward.

In the spring John William was telling me about—the spring of '67—she'd become obsessed with Ralph Nader's *Unsafe at Any Speed* and wouldn't eat in restaurants because of DDT and BHC. She kept a copy of *New and Nonofficial Drugs* on her bedside table and became an expert on adrenal glands. She was forty-six, and she'd lost weight to the point where her blouses and jackets hung from her prominent clavicles like sheets. She stayed in bed a lot, with her face sandwiched between fat pillows, worrying, she told John William, that the prevailing winds had driven nuclear radiation toward Seattle from H-bomb test islands in the South Pacific. Examining the Impala one afternoon, she insisted that its windshield appeared pitted by an airborne pollutant no one talked about. The plants in the yard were dying, too—everything looked bleached to the wrong color, in her eye, especially the laurel hedges.

One Saturday night, John William explained, his father decided to weather-treat, in the basement, his sailing sloop's teak hatch covers. Before long, his mother got her car keys, trapped a note under a refrigerator magnet—RAND, YOU'VE POISONED US WITH VARATHANE—and told John William to get his coat.

John William was eleven. His mother drove off after forcing him into the back seat, where he kept a stack of comic books. They made their way south on old 99, and by midnight they'd driven around Puget Sound and were speeding west, toward the true ocean of breakers and swells—the ocean as opposed to the inland sea near Seattle—which his mother believed was cleansing. She told him this. There were mythic overtones to the ocean, she said, that shouldn't be underestimated. John William replied that from his point of view it didn't seem normal to leave for the ocean so late at night without planning and without Dad. His mother struck back with a lecture on Varathane. The entire family of polyurethanes posed a threat to humankind, she told him. They reached the coast in darkness and knew they were there from the din of the surf and the line of white rollers in the Impala's diffuse headlights. "Ah, love," said John William's mother, pressing the button that let down her window and quoting from Matthew Arnold's "Dover Beach," "let us be true to one another," and then she began crying with a hand over her mouth while the ocean air funneled in. Next she sat listening to the waves with her forehead propped against the steering wheel. There was a long spate of nose blowing before she reached into her handbag for a scarf and tied it under her chin. "Well," she said, drying her eyes, "that's the melancholy, long withdrawing roar you've heard tell of, John William, retreating to the breath of the night-wind down the naked shingles of the world."

"I don't understand what you're talking about," John William replied.

"For the world," his mother recited, "which seems to lie before us like a land of dreams, hath really neither joy, nor love, nor light, nor certitude, nor peace, nor help for pain. So now I think I'm going to take that beach walk I came all this way down here for."

"It's dark and it's raining."

"Ever more purifying."

"Why are you doing this?"

"For its cleansing properties."

"You're acting strange," John William pointed out.

"What's strange," answered Ginnie, "is what's normal."

She disappeared then. We have to imagine John William before 911 and cell phones getting out of the Impala every once in a while to lean into the darkness and yell for his mother—his voice disappearing into the Pacific—and honking the horn a lot, which was grating and hard to listen to for long, even switching on the headlights and then coming to believe that in the swirl of white water he could see her like a silkie from an Irish yarn, next calming down enough not to believe it, resorting to his comic books but not distracted by them, as he hoped to be, finally going out onto the beach, where he tripped on driftwood and cut his palm on a shell, though not badly, and got soaked in the dark. She could have gone either way, he knew, and the coast was long. He sat in the car again, in the front seat this time, thinking now of horror stories involving lone parked cars on dark rainy nights, and weaving these phantasms together with the creeping suspicion that his mother had committed suicide in the salty undertow of the ocean. With this intimation came a pang of guilt: Why had he let her stumble off, crying, into this ominous night landscape? And also anger: Why had she included him in her willed death by drowning? Why had she brought him along?

When it was light enough and the rain had tapered off, he went out onto the road and flagged down the first car coming down from Moclips. This was a desolate stretch of coast, so it wasn't until noon that the hunt for his mother was in full swing, involving the Coast Guard, a search-and-rescue team, and volunteers with dogs. John William was given a cheese sandwich and a cup of hot chocolate. His father arrived with family friends, the Mitchells—the Barrys' golf-and-boating partners—and with John William's aunt and uncle, Sis and Walter. John William's father got out of the Mitchells' Lincoln Continental carrying binoculars and his Burberry rain slicker. "I'm sorry, son," he said. "I'm sorry you've had to put up with this."

What followed was a lot of stumbling over driftwood and a lot of talking into handheld radios. It began to get cold; the tide came in. At around six, John William's mother was located, sitting under a tree on Yellow Bluff, and when she was brought down from there, wind-whipped and sea-sprayed, John William heard a search-and-rescue volunteer use the term "fruitcake." At dusk, John William's father put his mother into the back seat of the Lincoln and slid in beside her like a bodyguard. "That's all," he said. "We've all had enough, Ginnie. Just look what you've put John William through."

"Move away, Rand," she answered. "You're poisonous."

I REMEMBER WHERE John William lived with his father. It was a Tudor in Laurelhurst, behind trimmed hedges, from the outside staid, but inside modern. Matched suspension chairs, a tripod table with a smoked-glass top, a stereo console in bleached white birch, a sectional sofa with wedge-shaped cushions—it was the style once known as Contemporary Living, the House of Today from yesterday, the house trumpeted as futuristic at the Seattle World's Fair in '62. Laurelhurst is among our city's most coveted neighborhoods, and the Barrys lived on the water there, with a fine lawn falling to the Lake Washington shore. Yet their Tudor, in its context, didn't look immodest. To get there, you drove on East Laurelhurst Drive, underneath elms and past Spanish-style mission homes and grandly scaled Craftsman mansions. A lot of Laurelhurst is labyrinthine and claustrophobic, chiefly because every square foot of its real estate is worth so much, but from the Barrys' east windows, giving out onto the lake, there was no hint of this urban density. What you saw instead was their L-shaped dock, and Rand's sloop—the *Cornucopia II*—cradled and cleated, with bumpers out. Since Rand was gone a lot on sales trips, John William and I often raided his on-board liquor cabinet. In the house, we uncorked wine bottles and foraged through stainless-steel cupboards, where Rand kept, as I recall, green olives with pimientos and table water crackers. There was also very little in the refrigerator—Brie in crumpled cellophane, a lonely bottle or two of Heineken, herring in cream sauce, maybe a shriveled lime. John William was on the wing-it food program. He ate pot pies or pizza for dinner. I saw Rand maybe half a dozen times in over two years—like most teen-agers, I didn't want to meet parents—because I made it a point to leave the house before he came home from work, or I went there only when I knew he was traveling, when his house was available for a free-for-all. I never saw Ginnie, since she lived in Taos, but I did spend time in her high-ceilinged study, the door to which had apparently been shut since she left for New Mexico and never opened again, at least by Rand. John William and I smoked dope from a waterpipe, sitting cross-legged on her Persian rug, and cranked up the expensive stereo system in her cabinet, which included a tape deck with UV meters and four audiophile's speakers. This study was furnished artiste-style: a divan, a writing table, a small vintage typewriter, rarefied art books, poetry journals, and a fireplace with andirons and tongs. Ginnie's private bathroom, entered from her study, was wallpapered with white-bellied nudes and decorated with half-melted candles in wrought-iron holders. There was a hammered-brass tub for toilet-seat magazines (*Art World*, *The Nation*, *Seattle*), and those nudes making you self-conscious while you tore off toilet paper. They were even on the ceiling, like Michelangelo's Eve. There was also a very rough Georgia O'Keeffe pencil sketch, signed by the artist in a tremulous hand, but was it a man on a horse or an adobe hut?

Ginnie, apparently, was something of a poet. One of her verses had been printed as a broadside on antique parchment paper, and it hung in a frame behind her writing table:

Alki, 1851

They oared ashore through rain,
And though they were egregious in their long-distance purpose,
Kamogwa didn't suck them under in his gyre,
And Thunderbird, on high, watched.

Their friends hanged Bad Jim.
At the Mad House, Sawdust Women plied for coin.
Eskimo Joe cut timber in a union shirt.
Ikt papa ikt sockala Tiee—one pope and one God—or so it was
    proclaimed.

Next came the box-houses and lectures on phrenology,
Faro and Little Egypt, dancing nude,
Bunco, vaudeville, nickelodeons, ragtime,
Pantages, jugglers, graft.

Then donkey engines turned bull teams to beef.
The wool dogs of the Squaxin went quietly extinct.
It rained on the tree farms and on the monuments to loggers,
And the Utopian Socialists surrendered.

The *Minuteman:* they built it.
The engineers in the football stadium:
It's they who dreamed up Dyna-Soar,
Awake beside sleeping wives.

So I cast this prayer on the Ocean of Compassion:
O rising phallus on the plain above the waters,
Be as you are, germ seed of the future,
Help me to count what cannot be counted,
World after world,
And anchor me in Anchorless Mind,
Until I cease.

Virginia Barry
1966
Seattle, Washington

When I asked John William what "Alki, 1851" was about, he said it was about his mother's pretensions, like everything else in her study—the concertos on tape, the Kenneth Callahan landscapes, the framed Barnard diploma, the black-and-white photo of Ginnie with Ansel Adams at Taos Pueblo. To me, she looked alluring standing beside Adams with her Frida Kahlo unibrow and severely parted hair, her taut, exposed arms and undaunted expression, as if Adams was of no significance.

John William's father was a Boeing honcho—first as a project engineer, and later as a vice-president in sales—and early in his career was quoted in the papers on a combination rocket and pilotless airplane, called BOMARC, meant to foil Russian bombers. His family was Irish but not potato-famine Irish, and his ancestors included the John Barry known as the Father of the American Navy. His grandfather, a railroad man, an associate of the financier and robber baron Jay Cooke, had made his fortune floating bonds, then lost it when Cooke closed his bank. His father had been a partner in Diversified Securities, a three-term Washington State legislator, part-owner of the United Exchange Building, a founder of First Seattle Dexter Horton National Bank, and a majority shareholder in the United Pacific Casualty Insurance Company, which underwrote automobile insurance. In other words, the Barrys can be found, consistently, in the lore of our city. The same is true on John William's mother's side, which goes back to the Denny Party—the twenty-two Midwesterners who went ashore in 1851 at Alki Point to start Seattle. A certain Hiram Post was a member of this Denny Party. In 1867, he married Eustacia Case Strong. One of their daughters was Lydia Strong Post—Anglo all the way, but with a Native American name. Lydia Strong Post married H. C. Best—founder of Seattle's Best Trust and Savings Bank, and later of the United Bond & Share Corporation—and their daughter, Dorothy Post Best, married Cyrus Worthington. Moving one more branch down the family tree, we come to Ginnie Barry, née Virginia Best Worthington—in other words, John William's mother. In sum, my friend came from westering pioneers on both sides, and from people with pressing material ambitions who made sure he had every advantage.

They sent him to Lakeside, for example. (His contemporaries

there included Bill Gates, who is sometimes depicted in a '72 photo seated in front of an archaic computer, Lakeside's DEC PDP-10.) In the annual—the *Numidian*—for '74, John William's portrait doesn't appear, and though he's listed with three other seniors as "Not Shown," he's nevertheless visible in a scene on the frontispiece, a figure striding away in the deep background on a path in front of the science-and-math building, his face turned left as if looking at something outside the photo's panoramic frame—a snapshot in search of the idyll of Lakeside's grounds, which does not quite come off because of lowering skies and the not-too-distant hint of a freeway on the modest residential horizon.

Despite the middling nature of its North Seattle precinct, Lakeside itself remains impressive. A year ago, at the beginning of summer, I attended a conference held there for English teachers. Maintenance vans were parked on the circular drive in front of Bliss Hall, most of them with sliding doors open; a small squadron of Seattle firefighters tested the hydrants; contractors in coveralls and earmuffs pressure-washed the brick-lined entry plaza; a landscape team mowed Parsons Field and the Quadrangle and weeded the beds in front of Moore Hall and the Refectory; and the school's clock tower, with its sun-swathed cupola and modest spire, suggested small towns in New England.

So this was John William's alma mater. He had a gifted teacher there named Althea Mastroianni, who's now retired but is known to me—I would go so far as to call her a friend, because we were both active, over the years, in writing curriculum for school districts, and we also once served, simultaneously, consecutive terms on the Washington State Council of Teachers of English. Among the names on Lakeside's faculty list in the seventies, Mastroianni's was the longest and the only one Latin, and among the faculty portraits in the '74 *Numidian*, Mastroianni's is notably subdued. She regards the aperture with no special interest. She's perhaps forty but retains the aura of a lit. doctoral candidate—a lot of listless, frizzy hair tied back and, dominating the picture, outlandishly oversized glasses. This is somebody who looks to know much about something esoteric (as it turns out, her special province was the semiotician Yuri Lotman), though she doesn't seem preoccupied, withdrawn, or owlish. She's been shot with the bony crest of her left shoulder turned forward, but the studio lights are too extreme and cast a sheen across not just this knobby rise—covered by the nap of a ribbed turtleneck shirt—but also across her large, dramatic forehead. One suspects behind this blazing expanse a freighted cranium looming, though this feeling might derive from the Lakeside imprimatur, or from foreknowledge of Mastroianni's densely packed résumé, which includes post-doctoral work at Yale (she once told me she tried to read while there all eight hundred of Lotman's titles and most of the Lotman scholarship), two dozen articles in semiotics journals, and another two dozen in education reviews. Throw in an era of training in Jungian analysis, from 1955 to 1957, at the Carl Jung Institute in Zürich, where all the pedagogy is in German.

You will say that a scholar of this pedigree would seem out of place at even the best prep school, but Lakeside is known, among educators in Seattle, for its faculty of achievers from good Ivy League stock who are brilliant but flawed in some career-breaking fashion and so not trusted to command the podium in a lecture hall full of undergraduates. That's how it was with Althea Mastroianni, who for better or worse had the lovely, trilling voice of a West Texas songbird, and though her mellifluous speech was just the sort of novelty that might briefly entertain an academic interview committee—that soft sagebrush twang on the subject of Lotman and the semiotics of Russian cinema—it was also a death knell when it came time to sign off on a Linguistics Department associate-professor appointment. Mrs. Mastroianni reinflected and modulated as best she could with a view toward losing all trace of El Paso, and while she was able to achieve a rich, mournful timbre that brought to mind Vivien Leigh in *A Streetcar Named Desire*, beyond that she couldn't make her voice go.

Still, that voice was singular. I know it not only from our collegiality, but because I went with John William to Althea's apartment in the early seventies. She lived in the El Monterey Building, on 11th Avenue Northeast—lime-washed stucco, narrow balconies with adjustable canvas awnings, and a high-walled courtyard featuring an algae-tinged pool and a rusting park bench. Very continental, or, more specifically, Iberian—like an ad in the *Times* of London for a villa in San Sebastián that turns out to come complete with motor traffic rumble. She shared a third-floor walk-up with her boyfriend,

Robert, whom I took to be a French intellectual—he had in hand a copy of Roland Barthes's *Sur Racine* when we met—and there she moved seamlessly between the Swiss French she'd honed in her years as a Jungian-in-training (asking Robert—silent "t"—to uncork a bottle of Burgundy) and her Tennessee Williams–tinged teacher's brogue. ("What a pleasant surprise, my goodness, John William. Ro-bear, *c'est le merveilleux et brillant Jacques Guillaume.* Please do, now, come in and sit down.")

We did, on a mohair sofa that smelled of cat fur, and then, with little prelude, Mrs. Mastroianni and John William began to argue about Chomsky's "Notes on Anarchism," which was suggested reading in her class, and this argument went on interminably. Althea wore the tackiest of polyester pants and a Mister Rogers–style button-up sweater for lounging. She tucked her feet under her and stroked her cat, an Abyssinian, as she listened to John William. For a woman in her middle years she had a fine complexion, and in the right light, a dusting of freckles appeared on her milk-white cheekbones. I suppose these things in sum bring to mind this natural question: was there something of the erotic in John William's feeling for Madame M.? I'm going to say no. I don't think my friend felt a physical desire for his English teacher. On the other hand, there might be something like Platonic Eros, and if there is, I would say this was present. Indeed, there had to have been some kind of yearning here, or why would John William have knocked on her door? Merely to talk about Chomsky?

In February of '73, Althea once told me, she assigned the eighteen students in her Identity Crisis class to write papers of fifteen to twenty pages on Erik Erikson, Malcolm X, or *As You Like It.* There was enough range in that triumvirate to provide substance for everybody, she supposed—psychosocial, political, or literary. There was the expectation of outside reading and of documentation complying with the *MLA Handbook for Writers of Research Papers.* There should be footnotes and a bibliography but no title page, because a title page was too grandiose—it was sufficient, she stressed, to put the title at the top of page 1, centered but not underlined, with one's name and the date just above, flush left with the text margin. None of this was new to Lakeside students, who were well steeped in the fussy mechanics of the academic essay, though the minimum of fifteen pages was more than they were accustomed to. Aware that such a minimum might seem daunting, Mrs. Mastroianni used the term "term paper" to describe what she envisioned, and gave her charges a due date ten weeks hence.

John William's paper, "Cosmology of the Gnostics: Penetrating God's Illusion," consisted of forty-seven double-spaced pages. Mrs. Mastroianni was impressed by its scholarship but disturbed by John William's obvious affinity for these early Christian heretics, with their dark take on God as a sinister deity who can only be transcended by defiance of his commandments: God as the devil, reality as a ruse, and life as a form of entrapment. In the courtyard of the El Monterey, throwing up her hands, she exclaimed, "All this gnosis, this very disturbing gnosis, this darkness and pessimism, this spiritual dread," and I assured her I knew what she was talking about, that gnosticism was something he'd disturbed me with, too, and that I remembered him saying, many times, with urgency and self-regard, that the world's a prison for our souls.

Althea recalled the comment she'd written after John William's last bibliographic entry, because it was such a handy, stock essay-criticism: "While this is well done, you haven't followed the assignment," followed by a grade of F. As a teacher, I'm familiar with her quandary. Here's a worthy exhibition of skills, a demonstration of learning and active intelligence, an essay she feels inclined to celebrate, but one that at the same time gives her deep pause because it brazenly ignores her instructions. I also know that, when a teacher comes across this sort of thing in a stack of papers, much depends on her mood of the moment, which might be colored by, for example, how much the obligation to read and comment on student work stands in the way of other things she wants to do, or whether this is the seventeenth paper she's read in one sitting or the second.

Possibly this is the crux of the matter: that Althea Mastroianni had a life to live outside of Lakeside, and that, however committed she was to her students—to their education and to their developing psyches—she naturally put herself first at times. She put herself first when John William needed her to put herself second. Maybe Althea resented the English teacher's burden by the time she came across John William on gnosticism in the stack of papers otherwise on Erik Erikson, Malcolm X, and *As You Like It*. Forty-seven pages on gnosticism—she would have flipped forward to that number, 47—and her first response, we might easily guess, was that John William had given this essay to the wrong teacher; it was meant for some other Lakeside course.

She'd been fond of John William—Althea stressed this to me. She'd sat across from him on a number of occasions, both after school in her Lakeside office and in her apartment at the El Monterey, and each time she'd made herself attuned to his presence, listening closely and responding in ways that let him know she understood who he was and what he meant as he rambled across subjects that interested him, from the Port Huron Statement of the SDS to the optical fundamentals of the phase microscope. In all her years as a teacher, she'd known no student whose mind was as overwrought. He reminded her of a boiling pot—hot water always about to spill over, and the perpetual manufacture of distillate. It did occur to Mastroianni, when she found him as much as an hour after school still waiting for her by her office door, that his need for her, though not necessarily unhealthy, was suggestive of a wounded psyche. As a trained Jungian, she had theories about this young man so earnestly moral and consistently distraught about the shape of the world, and, having met his father at an open-house, and having noted that John William was an only child whose mother was living in New Mexico, she had the sort of fodder for conjecture—including the dream journal he'd kept for Dreams and Literature—that Jungians, by definition, require. "What a terrifying loneliness he lived with," she told me. "I suppose I must have offered the attentiveness he'd been waiting for all his life."

After the paper on gnosticism, though, John William stopped visiting at the El Monterey and became stiffly cordial in her presence. In other words, after her F, their special relationship was over. I commiserated with Althea about this result and said I understood her regrets. I told her I'd had my own bad moments. I said I'd had young people attach themselves to me and in one way or another hadn't been what they desired. "While this is well done, you haven't followed the assignment," followed by an F—I assured her I'd written approximately the same, similarly alienated students. But isn't such terseness, finally, just the shortcut of the tired English teacher with her stack of student essays on a Saturday, naturally exasperated by forty-seven pages? Just that and not a personal betrayal? Althea Mastroianni in the courtyard of the El Monterey, retired now and wearing summer sandals: "In the end, I wasn't a good mother surrogate, and I suppose I made things worse for John William by taking our relationship as far as I did, by letting him in the door of my apartment and then spurning him at the very moment when he was trying to tell me about gnosticism."

WHY WERE WE FRIENDLY, John William and I? I had more than an inkling of his disturbance, after all, and from the beginning he derided and provoked me. Nevertheless, about a month after our adventure at the Seattle Center, I followed him up Mount Anderson, my first glaciated peak. We made it up on the wings of youth, but thereafter got confused in the clouds, and, coming off the summit, missed Flypaper Pass, and so ended up on the Linsley Glacier, which not only terminates in vertical wet rock but is impassable when its crevasses are open, unless you're a technical climber and properly equipped, but we were just two sixteen-year-olds carrying candy bars and a hash pipe. Down we went, I would have to say merrily, leaping cracks and circumventing chasms as if our lives were charmed, progressively brazen until, near twilight, we came to an ice canyon broader than a city street. "What now?" I asked.

John William got down on one knee. The gap in front of us was like something from a fable, with no light in it after the first twenty feet—a maw, then nothing but a chill. "Screw it," John William said. "Let's die young."

"Great solution."

John William put his head and arms in the canyon and dug the toes of his boots into the snow. "Come on," he said. "If we make it, good. If we don't, we're out of here—absconded."

"Here's where we go separate ways, rich boy."

"We're not going separate ways," he answered.

His head was still hung over the abyss, which made me nervous. It muffled his voice. "What if I'd rather be dead than not jump?" he said. "What would be the point of living?"

"You tell me."

"There wouldn't be any point."

He backed out. We sat on our packs and put our hats on. John William went on arguing for a glorious suicide in the slow June twilight until I told him my plan was to build a snow cave on the glacier and in the morning go up the mountain again, to look for Flypaper Pass.

"Have you ever built a snow cave?"

"No."

"Well, you don't have a snow shovel, a snow saw, or an ice ax. And this is ice, not snow."

"I'm going back up the mountain in the morning."

"Let's jump," he pleaded.

"You go ahead."

"Not without you," he said.

Looking back, I give him credit for keeping his death wish to himself on Mount Anderson. He didn't leave me there, and he knew what to do. This was before internal-frame packs were widely used, but John William had one, and on Mount Anderson he removed its aluminum stays, which could be bent to conform to the backs of different climbers, and with them we excavated ice blocks. We worked up a sweat while, in the northwest, the last light played out across the high country. I'm not going to call what we built an igloo, but it did have an igloo's curve, and, rudimentary as it was, we passed the night in it, sitting on our packs, smoking hash, and eating candy bars by candlelight, laughing but cotton-mouthed, heating the place ourselves until the sidewall nearest John William's candle began to drip into a water bottle. This is vivid to me still. We drew on that pipe until the drip of melting snow was more than just interesting— it and the candle flame, both so elemental, became deep entertainments, and not just edifying but revelatory icons. I carried a journal in those days, and that night, when John William saw me scribbling in it by candlelight, taking notes on "the blue concave sheen of our icehouse," for example, he said he couldn't think of anything better than being a writer, but I'd also heard him say otherwise when I pulled out that journal or reminded him, in some fashion, that I wanted to publish one day. "Lackey," he would say, about half sardonically. "Fame and money for prostituting your soul. Minister of Information for the master class." But not tonight. Tonight he sat back in his dope-induced acquiescence and quoted Muir from a popular mountaineering poster: "In the gardens and forests of this wonderful moraine one might spend a whole joyful life." And Robinson Jeffers, whom he'd read with Althea: "When the cities lie at the monster's feet there are left the mountains." I took my notes while he passed into reverie, then crawled through the low entry John William had crafted and, outside to piss at ten degrees, saw not only constellations but the wheel of the Milky Way—the lit disk of our galaxy—harbingers of the clear morning I desired.

SINCE THOSE DAYS, I've become a trail hiker, someone who takes no chances in the woods but goes to them frequently, in all weathers. I walk with my wife sometimes, or with my sons or with a friend, but mostly I walk by myself. It's admittedly a questionable hobby, this putting one foot in front of the other for long hours— questionable enough that sometimes, while walking, I can't quite endorse or justify my wish to put these miles between myself and others. Why do it when I could do something else? Why this intentional and self-imposed loneliness? "So might I, standing on this pleasant lea, / Have glimpses that would make me less forlorn," wrote Wordsworth, which is something I know because I teach him. Yet in one of my classes—Nature in Literature—I'm prone to overstating, in small fits of passion, a parallel reinforced by my own experience: that poetry and nature are occasions for introspection, but not necessarily for happiness.

As a teen-ager, I never traveled by myself in the woods or mountains. I went with John William. What we liked best was to walk where there were no roads or trails for as many days as possible, or to walk in country little visited and unmentioned in guidebooks, like the drainage of Depot Creek, northeast of Mount Redoubt, or the valley of Luna Creek on the north side of the Picket Range—those were the places we sought. A lot of hikers like off-trail travel where they can see across open slopes into the distance, but our preference was for forests without spacious views, for "the deep and gloomy wood" that made Wordsworth mushy above Tintern Abbey. I followed John William into this terrain—I followed him because he wanted to go—and gradually I came to like dark forests, too, forests no one went to because, in essence, nothing was there, no lake to camp at or mountain to climb, just trees and a lot of them, so that wherever you went it looked like all the rest: woods in all directions in an unbroken density, and no points of reference. A premium is placed on orienteering where the grid of things is all the same, so my journals from that era are full of terse waypoints we could follow in reverse, though the objects I listed had little to distinguish them—"pecker damaged snag (216)," "rootwad (221)," etc. It wasn't exactly my calling to navigate, but from anxiety I navigated anyway until it became a pleasure, this sort of knowing where I was at all times, to a fault and neurotically. I didn't want to be lost, and rigorously took bearings at every turn, never losing sight of what was behind us without noting something abreast or just ahead—though in the end I did get lost, along with John William and a boy named Pete Jenkins.

To really understand "lost" in this context, you have to understand the North Cascades, which in '73 was the largest roadless wilderness in the lower forty-eight—and not even that gets to the sense of being lost there, since the border between the U.S. and Canada is meaningless to anybody wandering without a map in this region. You have to throw in the contiguous roadless area in Canada, too, and then the wilderness of our confusion jumps from 3 million to 8.5 million acres, or 13,281 square miles, which is about like Massachusetts and Connecticut put together, or larger than Belgium. Granted, some of that was above timberline, but a region as large as New Jersey was "primeval American forest," a terrain that by '73 had become, for the most part, a history-class concept, even though it wasn't all gone yet.

Now I'm in my garret—my older son's former bedroom—with a map out as a goad to memory. It's a U.S. Geographical Survey Map prepared by the Army Map Service, in '55, so there's no North Cascades Highway and no North Cascades National Park; the place we got lost in was then called the "North Cascade Primitive Area," which means no one knew much about it; that's why we went there. We also went because of Pete Jenkins' interest in getting into the country Kerouac had celebrated from his fire lookout on Desolation Peak during the summer of '56—Pete, the Lakeside linebacker who liked the Beats; Pete, who appeared to have footballs in his calves as I walked behind him in the woods up there; Pete, who read Kerouac's *Desolation Angels* three times during our escapade while tightly cinched in his sleeping bag. Pete's father had been to Everest as an expedition physician, and Pete himself had climbed, with his dad, his uncle, and a mountaineering celebrity whose name I forget, in the Himalayas and Patagonia. Like John William, he couldn't quite arrange enough personal disarray to dispel his birthright, and, like John William, he had with him good gear and that air of intrepidness certain upper-class adventurers bring to the woods. To me he looked like Jethro from *The Beverly Hillbillies*—if Jethro had been born into wealth—with the same more than slightly gullible expression and the same good shoulders. When we rested, he sat with his hands behind his head and his legs crossed, like a big rube on a picnic, and tried to drum up a conversation. For example, he wanted to know about "Roosevelt girls." He wanted me to sum them up for him. Or he sat with a chunk of rock in his hand and delivered a geology lecture. I didn't know what a liverwort was until Pete explained it, and I didn't know rock tripe. I'd also never heard anyone use the word "stamen" until Pete did. On our first day out, he told me, covertly, that at Lakeside the consensus was that "JB," as he called John William, was "a complete asshole." Pete had the sort of humor and intelligence that homed in on the logic of language, and so he couldn't help adding, "As opposed to a partial sphincter." Like John William, and like me, he was on his own—his parents were divorced, and his father, that summer, was climbing in the Caucasus, which was "far more accessible to the West now," Pete told us, "because of détente."

Our plan was simple. We were going to stay off trails for two weeks, penetrating wilderness northward for seven days before following carefully kept waypoints back, but instead—blame me—my waypoints stopped making sense under the influence of marijuana and, as we found out on day eight, backtracking was impossible. One minute my orienteering notes made sense, the next they bore no relationship to the landscape, as if while our backs were turned things moved. I remember us sitting on our packs and laughing about this. We were lost, so it was time to smoke reefer. Pete said I should be "summarily shot for a failure of duty" and then got a map out and started turning it in circles. He took over, and we lost track of things completely. Time, once again, for dope.

Devils Park, Devils Pass, Devils Dome, Devil's Staircase, Joker Mountain, Hell's Basin, Nightmare Camp, Freeze-Out Peak—there'd obviously been a lot of desolation in that region, desolation and mental-health crises in those recent days of yore, when landmarks were named by starving surveyors and prospectors with syphilis. Again, no claims to symbolism, but it does seem at least close to appropriate that John William, Pete Jenkins, and I got lost in the vicinity of Three Fools Creek—evident now as I look down on the contours of my map, though at the time we all gauged it 50–50 as to which country we were in, the U.S. or Canada. Imagine such limbo, international in scope and vastly suffocating. There's nothing to compare it to except maybe amnesia, because, no matter where we went, we didn't know where we were—we could right now be in the same place we were yesterday and not guess that, or we could guess it without our guessing mattering. After a few days in this situation, you can come unmoored without knowing it. A man astray for five days in Colorado was found wearing only his wristwatch, for example. How do you explain that? But I know the feeling. When your mind has no reference points, it can't bounce off anything, and then it stops knowing where its borders are. That's when you start bending your map to make it fit inside your head, or smash your compass with a rock because it's lying to you. So there we were in our claustrophobic wood, needles in our hair, sweaty and rank, hunkered in the gloom, bug-addled, parched, trying to fix our position by sun bearings where there was no sun, taking resections with no landmarks, and dead reckoning from no starting place except where we were—in short, orienteering in a void of sheer relativism: a little like the math question asking *What is x?* when nothing is known. The ancient sailors with their astrolabes, on seas no human eye had seen before, at least had the North Star, but what did we have where we were? In our matrix of trees, under shrouded skies? In this world of bark, bad light, and silence? This territory of thick brush and steep ravines? We kept spinning our map around and rereading its contours, but so what? There was no way to make its symbols correspond to the world. Always this pattern—the three of us huddled over our map and deliberating on emptiness, then coming up empty. Was there something, somewhere, we could anchor to? The answer was no for a week.

I'm making it sound bad, like derangement. Actually, our being lost was in some ways a lark, if you subtract my private panic in that forest of no return, our days of painful hunger, our battle with heavy rain, and our running out of dope on our third day in limbo, when we nose-toked the last roaches in Pete's snuff tin. (It was just as well, our dopelessness, because stoned we'd scarfed all our food.) That evening, potless and tent-bound, we boiled some greens John William thought were edible, then passed the night bent double and convulsed. But the next afternoon, having chanced on a beaver pond, we hand-caught red-legged frogs, which we skinned, skewered, and cooked over flames—two of them, about two inches each—and that was what we ate that day, other than a few beetle larvae from under the bark of a snag (we'd followed the hammering of a woodpecker to them, on the assumption it wasn't hammering for nothing). In the morning, we saw fingerling trout in a creek pool but couldn't catch any, though we tried with twine and a safety pin festooned, Pete thought laughably, with a poisonous baneberry, which John William said resembled a salmon egg. I took a turn, swearing at these fish no more than an inch in length for not taking my bait, and, finally consummately frustrated, I tried to grab one from the water with a bare hand. No food that day, other than a few unripened kinnikinnick fruits bitterly chewed in passing.

By the midpoint of our limbo—by our third day of being lost—our hunger was constant and all-consuming. We spent our waking hours addressing it, or, if not addressing it, aware of it, and still we got hungrier, until everything seemed potentially food, even the inner surface of tree bark, which I scraped toward my palate on the edges of my incisors. We bickered about what was edible or inedible. We began, in earnest, to blame each other. "Fricking JB," Pete muttered to me. "I should have known better."

Later, we ate raw glacier-lily leaves, grazing for them like mountain goats; they gave us all the runs again and made us freshly leery of greens, but still we foraged, because we had no choice, and got thinner. Hunger made us shrewdly primitive. A gray jay lit on a nearby branch, and after Pete suckered it in with pieces of *Desolation Angels'* end page torn and crumpled to resemble bread crumbs, John William trapped it under a tossed parka. There was a little bit of breast meat, which we cut out and savored, but everything else, feathers and all, we brought to a boil that made us impatient—all three of us lowered our faces to the high smell of that small bird percolating. It was fatless, so the broth was thin; nevertheless, we felt some vindication as we tore its paltry carcass apart and sucked its sweetmeats. Girded by the taste of blood, we next did battle with a restless ground squirrel, whose manic spirals over fir bark we noted while traversing a ridge; down it went after our strategy of a pincer proved effective—we moved in on it, each with his rock, and, letting fly while it scrambled and made defiant noises, snuffed it by virtue of Pete's good aim. This animal, too, went into our pot, skinned and gutted, whole but for the strips of meat we skewered and broiled in flames.

A rain close to snow, sleety, pebblelike, fell unremittingly one full night and day. We holed up and took turns reading *Desolation Angels*, and poring over a manual John William carried in his pack called *Outdoor Survival*—really a pamphlet, with diagrams of fishhooks improvised from thorns, clever snares, snow goggles crafted from strips of wood in which slits had been cut, the northern sky at night, etc.; these rough drawings were coupled with commentary on survival and with the divulging of lore. Being hungry hurt, but if you didn't move around too much you could take it. We sat around, tent-bound and morose. It was during this torpor that Pete openly rebelled—"JB," he said, "say more about gnosticism. You haven't bored us for a while."

"Okay," John William answered. "You have a piece missing, Pete. According to the Gnostics. Something's not right, but you don't notice."

"Right," Pete said.

They squabbled until it got old, and then—tent silence. Our languishing and reading were hypnotic but boring—comparatively warm, dulled by hunger, I heard the call of hibernation, though it was also necessary to take turns gathering firewood, keeping enough on hand at all times so that some was always drying by the flames. In our womb of nylon, we cut cedar shavings with Swiss Army knives, fluffy firestarter we slept with so as to warm and dry it overnight— all this so we could heat our boots beneath the tarp lean-to we'd raised and boil what we were throwing in our pot, from watercress to the hedgehog mushrooms Pete said were edible (he was right).

Dire as things were the next day—us with the runs, wet beneath our clothes, and hunting grubs and night crawlers as we stumbled through the forest—we could always count on being resilient, favorably dumb, and braced by the optimism of teen-age hubris. We traveled north—and were turned aside from our zero compass heading daily by cliffs—on the hunch that the southmost road in Canada was closer than the northmost road in the United States, and one night we heard wolves, since this was before wolves ceased to haunt that region—a howling more like the slow, simultaneous closing of rusty screen doors than anything else, and from so far off we couldn't be sure it was wolves until the wind died down enough to halt the stirring trees and our fire stopped hissing. Even then we didn't know what it was for sure, but what else could it be, because what else sounds like that? At 2 a.m.? In the "North Cascades Primitive Area"? All sound in the woods is disorienting and confusing, but this sound was clear enough, eventually, to be chilling. Tent flap open, ears pricked, I thought that distant howling through, and it was a very short stretch from my own mean hunger to the perpetual, rapacious drive of wolves—but in the end we never saw any, though we did once get downwind of a black bear who, busy with an ant nest, treed itself at our approach. All three of us yearned to eat this bear, but none of us knew how to slay it. It must have discerned our shortcomings in this department, because when we dropped our packs and knelt to eat ants it scrabbled down, and we left, fecklessly.

On our fourteenth day, in light rain, we re-emerged with no fanfare south of Hope, British Columbia. You can imagine our reaction to the four drivers who ignored our thumbs; for the fifth, we stood mid-road like highwaymen and explained ourselves. Though there was sympathy in that car despite our rankness, we were nevertheless dumped at the first service station, where we sat on a concrete apron beside the gas pumps slamming cheese and chocolate milk, and feeling grateful to the cashier who took pity on us by accepting American coins against her boss's dictum (we were eating before her till opened, that was a big part of it) but not without a handkerchief across her nostrils. After a journey like ours, people in the "real" world seem misguided and innocent of reality, and this was true not only of the travelers I saw pumping liters of fossil fuel but of everyone around me for a week or more afterward; and even well after a week, there was a residue of this lonely and acute perception of the organized social world as a pathetic illusion, and moments of re-embracing that perception in much of its original intensity (this happened to me while watching diners through the window of a restaurant one night in the University District, where I'd gone to meet cousins at a tavern that didn't card). Yet, when my blisters had healed, and I'd eaten myself, once more, into arrogance, I happily recovered my old manner of being, though not without adding what I thought was a new layer of wisdom, and not without talking about those woods so much they palled at the same rate at which words about them formed in my mouth. I mangled and then annihilated our whole passage through the North Cascades by engaging in braggadocio about it for hammer-swinging Countrymans, and my sensation of loss was immediate and visceral and left me wistful for what I'd had before. When I mentioned this to John William a month after our deliverance, he said he knew what I was talking about because he'd tainted our journey in something of the same way by writing about it at school. Then he asked me if I wanted to go on another expedition, under similar circumstances, immediately after graduating, this time without a map or matches, relying instead on memorizing our path and making use of a flint and steel. I said yes. Pete Jenkins declined.

John William and I celebrated our release from high school by dropping, each, a tab of acid. Things went well, for me at least, as we wandered on foot through downtown Seattle, with cars passing us or coming toward us in the early-film-era style of moving objects in a stereopticon, and with every citizen on the sidewalks emotionally transparent. I had a mental battle with an alley cat—an eye-to-eye contest of wills I won with my third eye—and stopped a bus with a spread hand. All sound approached slowly and in increments, then left the same way. I knew who was dangerous and who wasn't, effort-lessly. However it was—and not to make too much of the experience of psychedelia—at some point John William's sobbing registered with me as something not to be absorbed any longer. I'd watched his tears, even gathered a drop from his cheek on a scrap of paper so as to examine its stain; nevertheless, his crying had seemed not only distant but, however unhappy, required. With every wail, more grief passed out of him, permanently expunged, I felt—in fact, for me this was tangible, and his escaping sorrow had a color, a darkly burnished orange, that I perceived as an emanation. I saw his sadness as a bloodletting, and I was happy for my friend. But then things changed. The working of lysergic acid in the brain can produce dramatic shifts, and I came into an awareness of John William's nightmare. A shroud descended, and the cast of things altered. I found myself beneath the glass roof of the iron pergola in Pioneer Square, with my back against a stanchion, looking north toward the Seattle First National Bank Building at Fourth and Madison—Seattle's first skyscraper, and at that point its only one—and it terrified me, this dark monolith. All night, John William had been mumbling something under his tears, and now I finally homed in on his mantra as he curled on the cobblestones a few yards away from me with his hands clutching his face, as if in so doing he could hide from the truth of things—"No escape from the unhappiness machine . . . No escape from the unhappiness machine . . . No escape from the unhappiness machine . . . No escape from the unhappiness machine . . ." I started chanting that, too.

2

Now They Would Have the Run Home Together

Earlier this summer, for the first time in eleven years, I hiked in the valley of the South Fork Hoh, where John William and I went without a compass or matches two days after our acid trip, and where John William spent seven years living alone. The trail passes under Sitka spruces, some more than five hundred years old, and under bigleaf maples hung with club moss. You would have to say that, given the presence of these maples, this isn't quite your classic rain forest but a variation, with the maples thriving amid cobbles and rockslides and in the glacial till of the river bottom. Rain on the South Fork Hoh is common, but on my recent walk there was no sign of rain—instead, it was warm, and a little dusty where the silt had baked in the sun on the north bank. Still, rain remains this region's most obvious feature in any season but summer. Notable, too, is the silence here, broken infrequently by the winter wren's trill—reminiscent of a hysterically played flute—at other times by the ventriloquy of ravens. Then there's the din of the river, fed by snow in the Valhallas and glaciers on Mount Olympus. In June, the South Fork Hoh runs gray and milky. It's in places slow enough to suggest tranquillity, but elsewhere it's extreme in its energy and character. So this is a hike of disparate feeling, unfolding under a dense forest canopy broken by glades of arcadian maples. It's also a hike through lonely country, four and a half hours by car from Seattle, infrequently visited not only for this reason but because the main fork, a few miles to the north, has a better road and a visitors' center near its bank. More, the main-fork trail takes climbers to Mount Olympus, whereas the South Fork Trail just leads to deeper gloom and, eventually, into a canyon. Sometimes anglers will try the South Fork's upper stretches; even more rarely, a party of climbers will pass through on its way to the Valhallas, though I should point out that the first ascents of those peaks were mostly made in 1978, and none earlier than 1966, which should give you some idea of their remoteness. When John William and I first went there, in '74, wandering into Valkyrie Creek Basin and making camp on Valhalla Ridge, the pinnacles of Bragi, Mimir, Vili, Sleipnir, and Vidar North and South had not yet been climbed, and this wasn't because of their difficulties but because few climbers had gotten to them. They might have been busy with more accessible mountains, or maybe they hadn't noticed this part of the map yet, southeast of the town of Forks.

This June, I walked alone on the South Fork Hoh Trail, three days after the end of the school year, one day after the graduation ceremony held, because of foreboding skies, in our remodeled gym, where students hooted as I strode to the podium in order to recite, into all that space, underneath a raised basketball hoop, "The Road Not Taken." I have an annual date with Frost at this ceremony, and in the past have read the poem's well-known final lines with embarrassed misgivings: "Two roads diverged in a wood, and I— / I took the one less traveled by, / And that has made all the difference." Will the narrator's apparent self-regard accrue to me? Will the convocation, seeing Frost's narrator as superior, see me as superior by association? This year, after I cleared my throat, a student yelled, "C's all filthy!," meaning "Mr. Countryman's rich," and after everyone twittered, I delivered the Frost. The following day—the first of vacation—I got up early, filled my thermos with coffee, made a sandwich, and drove away before first light, and, frankly, despite the things I like about my work, felt glad I was free to walk along the South Fork Hoh instead of teach. It's an easy journey in its lower reaches; in three miles a hiker gains five hundred feet, and after that, where the trail fades to moss, it's a matter of meandering across soft green flats or treading on gravel bars near the current. I found myself preferring moss to gravel, even though there's less gloom beside the water, because recently I've developed a Morton's neuroma where the third and fourth toes on my right foot meet, and this makes me wince if I walk too many hours on unforgiving surfaces like river stones. Pain gives me reason to stop more often than I once did. I take off my boots. I eat a little something, or shut my eyes for a few minutes. Sometimes I lie in the fetal position and try, unsuccessfully, to sleep in the forest. It was in this posture, in June, that I heard a trilling winter wren and, later, a raven. The raven's call was like water dripping loudly—like large drops of water striking a pool. It seemed to have nothing to do with nature; instead, it sounded like a plumbing problem. I wouldn't have thought it was made by a bird at all except that on other occasions I'd watched ravens make this noise, though even with such clear verification it's a note that still seems improbable and dreamlike. As does the past, sometimes.

John William and I, finished with high school, came at the South Fork Hoh from its headwaters, entering the woods at Boulder Creek Campground, and traversing the Bailey Range over four cloudless days, finally departing from published routes beneath Mount Olympus, where at close to eight thousand feet you can smell salt water on the wind. From there we found our way to the South Fork Hoh—which we didn't know was the South Fork Hoh, because we didn't have a map or compass, by intention—or, rather, to where it gathers in a moraine of icy water and wind-blasted scree, and then, walking in the river itself while the current wrapped around our legs, and using a climbing rope in watery belays, we came down from the high country in a canyon. Between rock walls, the falling water was so loud we couldn't speak to each other. Trees grew from clefts in the cliffs or lay askew in the current. It seemed to me our purpose was to drown. Climbing down vertical walls in a river was something you had to be young to try, a form of lunacy, and yet my friend's face was animated by happiness. Water dripped from his well-made chin. He'd come all this way committing landmarks to memory, so that we might, if necessary, reverse our course, and there was something in this epic mental effort, I saw, that appealed to him as an adjunct to danger.

Finally, things calmed. At midday, we sat by a pool under high slopes, taking the brief sunlight there and tossing stones competitively. We built a rock cairn, too, on a flat boulder in midstream. We were buzzed by a kingfisher, which we saw as a good omen, that the canyon might soon open into more passable country, which it did in the afternoon. Through the long twilight we walked along a tributary into deeper forest. The cedars here looked especially hoary because of their bare withes, which hung like deadwood. Later, we needed a drying fire and tried John William's flint, steel, and char cloth, and though we did eventually produce sparks and smoke, in the end we used up the last of his char cloth without conjuring flames. It's difficult, making fire this way. It's an effort that makes you appreciate the achievement in a match. But it was warm in the June woods, and we slept on moss that night, with our boots and socks drying in our sleeping bags. The next morning, our tributary became dispersed and transient, and we left it in favor of keeping ramparts on our right. I remember sitting in dense woods, playing chess with John William on the type of miniature board air travelers used before the advent of laptops, my friend lying back on one elbow and crossing his ankles like a country squire at leisure, but shirtless and in baggy wool pants. Hair in his eyes, he made his moves with an anticlimactic nudge, then scratched his mosquito bites, teeth set in an impatient overbite, while I contemplated. As I recall, we played to a stalemate. It's hard to understand why we wanted to spend so many days in the back country with little food, no fire, no map, and no compass, but maybe it was partly for that interlude of chess, for the disparity between chess and where we found ourselves. John William and I played a match of attrition while reveling in our isolation and eating the last of our raisins. Finally, we were only pushing lonely kings and pawns around the board, and the space between two moves became, for both of us, a nap. I felt languid after so much time in the high country and after banging against the boulders in the river, and to loll there in the warm breeze of the forest, my limbs at rest, was a luxury. I slept deeply, rare for me in daylight. When I woke, John William was reading *Outdoor Survival*—the manual he'd brought for our North Cascades debacle, too—with his head propped on his pack. He wanted to look for yew wood now, as appropriate material for a fire drill. Fire, he said, was "the key to everything." I didn't ask what he meant—what "everything" included—and after a while we pushed ahead into more gradual terrain, where the trees were widely spaced and so uniform around that the girth of each rose like the shadow of the next. On exposed stones, we crossed a stream; beyond that the land flattened. Through the branches overhead, a rock wall rose higher than we could see, disappearing into the canopy. This was a country of easy walking: no thrashing through swales of devil's club and slide alder. We stopped to make camp in the early evening, and I sat on a log, wrapped in my sleeping bag, while John William tried again to conjure fire. He had a yew-wood drill and a cedar fire board now. He would drill for a while, then alter something—push tinder around, carve a fresh notch—or scrutinize the diagram in *Outdoor Survival*. I helped a little by prodding at the tinder; once, I put my cheek to the ground in order to blow softly on an ember, which went out. At that moment, I thought I was responsible for our failure. Maybe if someone else had done the blowing. But still we persisted, taking turns with the drill, which tired our shoulders. Yet our most energetic attempts produced no more smoke than a blown-out candle. The friction of the yew turned the cedar to black powder, warm but never combustible.

In the morning, about a half-mile away, at the base of a limestone cliff, we found a seep, which at first was nothing more than a sulfurous vapor we noticed while looking for denser yew wood. Seeing algae crusting a few nearby rocks, we clawed with our ice axes until a small, warm pool gathered. It was like finding a vent on the sea floor, so rare and unexpected is a hot spring in the Olympics. (Counting ours, there are only three.) John William and I went on picking at the limestone; for much of that day we excavated, until our pool was approximately on the order of a bathtub. Then we stripped, stepped in, and crouched there for a while, but the water hadn't settled yet, so this was a little like soaking in hot mud. We had to pour creek water over our limbs to rinse the stain out.

That evening, we stayed near our handiwork for its warmth, and as time wore on—we had nothing left to eat—it began to look less roiled. We sat wearing our sleeping bags like capes, with the pool producing its mineral effluvium, and our bare feet propped on rocks near its waters so as to warm our soles. I remember reading the first-aid pamphlet inside my kit as an antidote for boredom while John

William carved a fresh fire drill from a length of yew. He wanted an abrupt transition, he said, between two diameters, as suggested in *Outdoor Survival*, so that a disk of pine with a hole at its center could be slipped partway down the shaft as a rest for his drilling hands. After a while, this ancient device was ready. We threw off our sleeping bags and knelt by the fire board. The twilight in June is long, and we used about all of it, working in near darkness. At the edge of the pool, with the kind of humorless diligence John William was prone to—me, too—we finally made the flash point for cedar tinder. The powder churning at the point of the drill turned briefly orange and then rolled into our pile of deliberately arranged shavings, where John William blew it into flames.

Six years before, in '68, there'd been a band called The Crazy World of Arthur Brown, known almost exclusively for its song "Fire," which was on the charts for a while, so that you heard it often on the radio, and it was this that John William quoted at that moment—"I am the god of hell fire and I bring you: fire!"—which made us both laugh. We fed the flames, throwing our shadows against the cliff wall—where their skewed shapes formed a backdrop for lofting sparks—and celebrated not only fire but ourselves. John William said, "We can't tell anyone about this place. I mean it. We have to have a blood pact. We have to cut our palms and shake hands."

I said, "That's some corny bullshit."

John William dug his knife from his pocket. "Neil," he said, "don't wimp out."

It hurt. But the hard part was doing it, not the pain. As you might expect, every time you move the blade toward your hand your brain stops you. John William got it done after one false start, but I pulled back three times while he bled. "Pretend it's not your hand," he advised.

I finally opened my palm down the center. I'd cut myself before, but only accidentally. This was different; I didn't feel damaged.

John William and I opted for the soul shake. It didn't start with white guys, but white guys can understand at least part of it, and since it seemed right for this occasion, a deeply solid contact, thumbs clamped, arms crooked, the weight of each brother in a fleeting, felt balance, we mingled our blood that way.

My mother died when she was thirty-nine, a month before I turned thirteen. She had a Grade 4 astrocytoma—an aggressive brain tumor—that didn't take long to blind and kill her. What I remember best is that her singing voice still moved me right up until a few weeks before the end. I remember her singing "The Maid of Llanwellyn" in a lilting a cappella, even after she'd gone cross-eyed. Of course, she knew that my sister and I, and my father if he was home, could hear her singing from elsewhere in the house, and she also knew, I'm sure, that it got to us. I used to stop what I was doing when she sang. I guess I poised myself to ponder more clearly, with the evidence for it plainly in my ears, the trajectory of her last days. A few times, I sat in a closet and plugged my ears, because listening made me angry. Even at twelve, I understood that my mother sang in an emotional register no listener could easily ignore. One day, seeing her at the piano with only a little hair on her head, I realized I hadn't heard her sing for a while, and after that she didn't sing anymore, and then she didn't play the piano, either. I'm not sure, but I think she chose not to sing, late in the game, because she didn't care for what she heard.

It was July, and we skipped the Cavanaugh reunion. My father went on working, but he lost weight. He owned a battery-operated shortwave radio, and I walked the streets carrying that on my shoulder, the way kids carried boomboxes in the eighties. It was '69, so there was good music on FM. One place I liked to go was a half-lot with a transformer station behind a chain-link fence, where I'd loll in the shade with the radio beside me. I also walked railroad tracks, breaking every bottle I could find.

People, it's said, die in character. After she was told about the astrocytoma, my mother, for a while, tried to learn Gaelic and got interested in the Book of Kells. She bought a book of Irish tales, which I inherited by default—"Oisin in Tir Na nOg," by P. W. Joyce; "The Legend of Knockgrafton," by T. Crofton Croker; and so on. Wraiths, corpses, coffins, graveyards, solitary ruins, sorrow on the wind, and landscapes of gray loneliness. Characters are hounded toward death, or wither, or freeze, or slide into the sea, and in the end the storyteller will say something like "The blessing of

God on the souls of the dead!" or "Thus did the hermit lay the four children of Lir to rest at last."

At the funeral, Carol refused to look at our mother, but I went up and saw that her face had been arranged in approximately the expression I'd seen at Alpental when she snow-sprayed my father with rental skis. My mother in death had a mischievous regard. As the coffin was lowered, Carol laid flowers. At the same moment, my father took off his sunglasses and put his carpenter's hand on my biceps. It stayed there until the coffin was in the ground, and then my father slid his sunglasses on and, done holding himself up, removed his hand.

My father did two things shortly thereafter. He started paying Carol to look after me, and he split between us the $10,000 from our mother's life-insurance policy. He didn't turn us over to our grand-mothers or aunts for the same reason he didn't remarry—to his way of thinking, the love we needed was just across death's divide, and to try to replace it would be to adulterate our mother's presence and prompt it to wane. That's a sword with a double edge, of course, well intentioned but inherently dangerous, even for a man who didn't believe in ghosts or an afterlife.

Mourning took me a while. I remember going to baseball prac-tice early so I could sit in a plum tree before anyone else showed up. In this period of what probably looked like obtuseness, I felt there was something hallowed about my $5,000 in life-insurance money, which I left in a bank and didn't touch. Five thousand dollars wasn't much, but it was my version, if wan and proletariat, of John William's muscular trust fund. When I told him about it, he asked if there were strings attached, because—he added—he had strings attached: he had to enroll at a college, he said, to get his first $50,000. Bowing to this, he was going to Reed, a liberal-arts school in Portland, Oregon, family-approved but not on the East Coast, home to Rhodes Scholars but not far from mountains. I was going to the University of Washington, about a mile from where I'd grown up, partly because you could get in with a 2.8, but mostly because the tuition there was $540.

We had different plans for the summer months, too, following our mineral-spa blood pact. My hand had healed pretty well, but there was a raised white scar across my palm that looked like a crescent moon. John William had one, too, but his was straighter. He was now bent on solo beach-hiking, in Oregon, whereas I was using my inheritance, or some of it, at least, to shift about in Europe among the horde of young Americans who descend on Europe every summer with Eurail Passes, guidebooks listing the addresses of hostels, and overstuffed, filthy backpacks. My aim was to have experiences. I had no other purpose in going. I thought that if I was to be a writer I would need to travel in foreign places and take notes on how things looked, sounded, and smelled. When I told John William this, he snorted. He said that my orientation was backward, and that if I felt so dire about seeing the world I should go to the Andes or Mongolia. I ignored that and told him to write me at some hostels I was set on inhabiting—Avignon, Barcelona, Grenoble, Brunico—Brunico because I was planning on soloing myself, in the high country of the Dolomites.

On my own, I flew to Amsterdam and spent my first night abroad at the Seamen's House, a salty fleabag open to anyone with a few guilders. The next day, I sat by the Herengracht with a packet of *frites* in my hand, crying, because this is what had become of my mother. She'd been transmuted into an experience I was having— me beneath a patinaed lamp, looking at windows framed by pilasters and listening to bicyclists bumping over cobblestones while ringing their quaint little bells. I did the things you do when you are eighteen and alone in Amsterdam, which is to say I milled on the Damrak in a surfeit of melancholy, pinching my pennies and taking notes on the pigeons, distrustful of all comers. I found other streets more lived in, more personable, where the lights in the windows at dusk looked familial, but the canals, the cartouches, the towers, the churches, the black bicycles, the gilded shops—all of it only left me more lonely or, to put it a different way, exposed to myself. By those old and fetid European waters, black as they were with commerce and fever, I felt saddened and stripped. This kind of glum interiority is often the province of solitary travelers, but I was feeling plowed under by my mother's presence wherever I went, and when parting with every guilder I spent. I was trading her for this—for the Oude Kerk and its carillon chimes and for herring sandwiches.

One morning, I walked over to the train station with my pack, a bag of rolls, my journal, and *Swann's Way*. I must have looked like hundreds of young travelers who pass through there each summer—all wearing intrepid expressions as shields against the world and, I would have to guess, pretending to an experience of life they don't possess. I took a train that went through Antwerp and in Brussels transferred to a different train, antique and slower, with scarred wooden seats, and this one went to Liège and eventually to Trier, where I got off and walked around noticing things, stopping now and then to write down impressions of the Porta Nigra, Trier's Basilica, the hue of the Moselle, and so on. I was face to face with my own vagrancy after that, and got more comfortable adrift. I became attached to train travel—to seeing the grimy backs of the buildings along train lines, the fenced industry and hung laundry. I slept in train seats. I learned to opt for the rear car, so that in long bends, in open country, I could look ahead and watch the engine pass particulars of the landscape. And in the interim between the engine's passing of, say, a half-fallen brick pumping station and my own passing of it, happiness inhabited my journey. It was like the feeling I had on station platforms sometimes just after sunrise, when no one else was around and no train was expected for an hour or more, and an express had just gone through at high speed a minute or so before, the passengers in it flashing past like the kings, queens, and jacks in a thumbed deck of cards, ephemeral as thoughts. I put down my reading when that happened and enjoyed the absence of the train's noise, the silence of a station in the countryside. To be awake in the cool of morning on a bench near train tracks, hungry, with a little breeze blowing, and whatever book you were reading open in your lap, was a little like listening for something you thought you might have heard a moment before. I suppose you could say I felt the sweetness, then, of being alive and in good health. At the same time, my romantic spells were curtailed by the sight of garbage near the rails, or by a wandering dog raising a leg at the corner of a building. I just didn't have the psychic wherewithal to incorporate these images into my affection for living; I let them dispirit me, as the heat of the day and the crowds on the trains dispirited me, most days, during the afternoon. And then, for no reason, my interest in this brand of transience waned, and I took to foot travel. In San Sebastián I bought a tent, sleeping bag, ground pad, cartridge stove, and cooking pot, and set out toward the Pyrenees with a long

French loaf strapped to my pack and an English-language edition of *The Wings of the Dove* stuffed in a side pocket alongside my journal. It was what I expected: the smell of goat dung desiccating in the dry heat of the plain, and the dust lifted even by the passage of a bicycle as someone rode toward me out of the mountains. I stopped frequently, in whatever cool, furtive place offered privacy. I spent half a day beneath a stone bridge reading James, until some sheep came down through the cork oaks behind me to drink from the stream there. I'm making my solitude and the liberty I had abroad sound pleasant and pastoral now, but the truth is, I felt abysmal most of the time, especially in my tent after dark. Once, in some Navarran village or another, I sat at an outdoor table writing postcards and reading the *International Herald-Tribune*, and just the act of putting down my home address agitated my loneliness.

In August, I took a train over Brenner Pass and came down into the Alto Adige. I had a beard now, dark and dense, and a pair of used boots from a secondhand store in Innsbruck. They didn't fit right, and I was reliant on moleskin, which I cut with a pair of dull tailoring scissors. With these same scissors I cut my hair one night, while sitting cross-legged in front of my cartridge stove waiting for some orzo to boil. I was ill-prepared for the August weather at night in northern Italy, and in San Vigilio bought a surplus Austrian military ragg sweater, a cap with padded earmuffs and a chin strap, and a pair of fingerless wool gloves. I was sitting beside a trail the next day with this getup on, as well as my glacier glasses with their sweat-stained leather side shields, taking my incessant and obligatory travel notes and comparing the Dolomites with the North Cascades, when I heard faint voices. There was a conversation going on in American English among the spruces and pines on the ridge below—I could pick out a few words and phrases of it coming toward me on the wind. While listening, I wrote about the view from there: San Vigilio in its valley with its larches, lindens, and broad Ladin roofs; immediately above it, hayfields and poppies; and above that, closer to me, white cows grazing on bits of grass growing between barren rock. The trails in the Alto Adige all look rutted by centuries of use and sometimes pass by rustic chapels, situated in the lee of the wind, in which are gathered pots, cans, nails, worn shoes, bits of wire, even lost handkerchiefs, and I was sitting beside one of these, which had in it, besides the usual debris, a number of rusted iron spikes and some small pharmaceutical vials of thick glass, with stoppers. I took notes on these things, too, of course. Then the loud hikers came into view against a backdrop of scree. Silent now, saving their breath and leaning forward under their packs, they came up the hill. They were still small, and mostly what I saw of them was the tops of their heads and some bright-red pack fabric. I hadn't spoken in English to anybody for some time and was eager for that suddenly, after all the pidgin talk and hand signals with continentals. On the other hand, I also felt antagonized, because of all of the work I'd done to come to grips with lonely travel. However it was, my compatriots passed beneath striated rock faces, white rock ribbed or marbled with black, and, in making the ridge, began to walk more upright. I could see that they were women after that, two tall women in hiking shorts. This was early in the day, and because the sun was behind them on a bright, cloudless morning, I had to leave my glacier glasses on as they approached in order to see very much. Between the glasses, my chin-strapped cap with its padded earmuffs, my beard, and my fingerless gloves, I must have looked ridiculous to the two women coming up the trail. In fact, I know I did, because one is now my wife and she's told me how I looked, how she made a ridge in the Dolomiti and found a guy there with a journal in his lap, suggesting, maybe, as she once put it, an explorer who'd stopped taking care of himself. Her name is Jamie Shaw. There was no love at first sight, a thing some people claim is real but, frankly, a concept foreign to both of us. I did think she was pretty, with her knobby knees and pointed elbows as she pulled on her wind pants, and I liked the look on her face right away, which was openly skeptical. She kept covering her mouth with her thin fingers and pushing a lock of hair behind an ear, and I was drawn to these gestures and to her outdoorish athleticism, but not especially drawn to them, not at first.

WHILE I WAS WANDERING in Europe, John William—according to aerogrammes I got in Avignon, Barcelona, Grenoble, and Brunico—was hiking in Oregon. His long-winded letters were scrawled in a cramped hand. He wrote to say that he'd hitchhiked to Portland and then walked toward the ocean on the south bank of the

Columbia—on railroad right-of-ways, the verges of marsh, and trails used by anglers and goose hunters. He ate a dead carp washed up in a side water and got the runs and a fever. Curled up in a duck blind, sick but sheltered, he nearly abandoned his plan to hike to the salt water. But then, in a Dumpster behind a tavern, he found some fish and chips, and that got him going again. I was in Avignon eating a *pêche Melba* while reading about this, and it seemed, under those circumstances, more than a little hard to understand.

John William unsettled a trio of late-winter birders launching their skiff in a slough by walking past them at first light. He also came on two sturgeon-fishers, with their rod butts anchored between stones, who'd built a lean-to out of plastic and saplings and sat in it nursing a blaze while boozing. John William stayed in the woods downstream, hunting crawdads, until they reeled up and left, and then he occupied their lean-to for the night, encouraging the coals of their fire. The next day, he walked in rain and watched mew gulls. Eventually, the country became estuarial, and, beside the channels of the river, his boots filled with mud. At a boat launch, he found an oily sardine tin and a poorly cleaned salmon carcass in a garbage can, and at Astoria he gathered enough coins to buy, at a corner market, a banana and a day-old ham sandwich. Fortified, he walked through the night past Warrenton, and from there to the coast, where he slept in brush. There were gulls, he wrote, with their heads down.

John William walked to Seaside, where he stood outside the arcade collecting coins from late-night pinball addicts. Later, foraging in garbage bins, he found a lode of canned goods, and after smashing open cans with a rock, ate a lot of fruit cocktail. This was the first night of visible stars since he'd left Portland, and, walking under them with the beach well lit, he gathered driftwood, and, later, above some dunes, scraps of lumber from a development where view homes were going up. John William built a high-mounded blaze, and when it died to coals he spread them out, dressed them with sand, and slept.

His aerogramme read: "I was arrested at dawn and handcuffed. 'Suspect is a vagrant, age 20, 6', 180 lbs., brown eyes, brown hair, carrying no ID but giving his name as Gempler, (nmn), Ivan'—that's what they got from me. In jail I met this Pete Moss—like Gempler, supposedly an arsonist who'd crisped a beach house. They thought I was an ecoteur with a *nom de guerre*, like Moss, even though the handle I gave them sounded Amish. Fortunately, I was liberated the next day by a lawyer who came for Moss and two other hippies, so I got a ride to Eugene in a lawyer-Volvo. Maybe it's another *nom de guerre*, but my pro-bono savior gave me his card, which I'm looking at right now—'Mark Sides'—actually a smart guy, pissed about the right stuff. He got me some work, or got Ivan Gempler work—counting standing deadwood today and tomorrow. No pay, but I'm domiciled for nothing in this mail-order tepee with Moss and some other freaks. I showed these potheads what's up with a fire drill. They think I'm God because I make fire with sticks and catch mice with my Paiute rock-fall trick. Even Mark Sides is impressed."

"Hey. Countryman," John William wrote, at the end of his last aerogramme, "don't forget to write me back. Drop me a line. Don't be a stranger. And don't get lost, blood brother."

IN THE DOLOMITI, I sat by the chapel with the American women and brewed tea on my cartridge stove. They were sisters. They both had the look of collegiate basketball players, but the younger one, my wife's sister—Erin—a little less so. She kept calling Jamie "James." For example: "James." Jamie looks up. "Toss me your water." A little later, describing a chamois seen the day before, Erin thinks I'm dubious about sixteen-inch horns. "James." Jamie took her hand from her mouth. "Back me up already on this." We drank tea. I felt awkward. I'd been glad, until then, for the details of tea-making, but now there was nothing between myself and my reticence. Traveling, I suppose, I'd lost the hang of speech. Erin sat cross-legged and warmed her hands around her cup, but Jamie sat with her arms roped around her knees and watched me, I would have to say, with not-quite-completely concealed suspicion. Her front teeth were slightly gapped. There was something coercive in her manner of observation, I think, because, in the face of it, I took off my glacier glasses with their leather eyecups and my cap with its curled, weathered chin strap. I had that haircut, self-administered a few days before with the dull tailoring scissors, and the naked, convalescing look around the eyes you see in a lot of summer alpinists who, because they rarely remove their sunglasses, are tanned or sun-burned and yet owlish. I must have looked like a pilot who has bailed out in mountains and wandered for a week across blinding snow-fields, though this isn't an image my wife has used in recalling my appearance. She remembers instead my formality—my getting the tea right—and how she decided, after twenty minutes, that my inse-curity wasn't cultivated. She remembers that the presence of my journal, really just a cheap spiral notebook, put her at ease. A person who takes notes, an observer who wants to turn the world into words—this is probably not someone inclined to steal your pass-port, in her way of seeing it. I stress "probably," because Jamie has never been naïve about people. She looks at them the way she looks at herself, with the same full measure. She's able to do this without being defensive, without assuming the worst, and without rose-colored glasses. I think she strikes a balance between curiosity and wariness that works in her favor, because she's rarely intimidated. On the other hand, if you didn't know her—as I didn't know her yet in Italy—you could easily misread her quiet scrutiny. You could miss the fundamental neutrality in her watchfulness. There's a strong element in Jamie of self-preservation, but she's not averse to the occasional gamble when most of the signs look promising. Though you wouldn't have known that, either, above San Vigilio, where we sat by the chapel with her sister.

I didn't ask for their names or their story. But we did look at a map they carried, which Erin unfolded and spread on the ground, and which Jamie held down with her fingers and some stones, and so I heard about their travels. They'd come up from Rome. They'd come because it was too hot in Rome, and too hot to go to Venice, as they'd intended, and because they'd been told, by some Romans, that in the Dolomiti their money would go far if they traveled on foot and stayed in *rifugi*. In Rome the heat and the crowds got to them—the long lines, underneath the sun, in order to get into the famous basilicas—and so they'd taken trains to Bolzano and from there caught the bus to Cortina d'Ampezzo, which was in the east on the map they held open. That map was well creased; along some of its folds, it had been rubbed white until its symbols disappeared; it had been abraded by damp weather and constant reference. Yet they were still able to show me, both of them using their little fingers and keeping the bulk of their hands out of the way, the trails they'd followed, the valleys they'd descended into, the *rifugi* they'd passed nights in, the chairlifts and funiculars they'd used between Cortina and the Tofana di Mezzo, and the places where they'd gained or lost elevation on old ladders, left over from the Great War, bolted to rock faces.

I remember the look on Erin's face when it became clear that I was abroad without a map of my own—I think she saw me as foolhardy after that, as romantic to the point of a dangerous narcissism. I recall that while I was putting things away—my journal and my stove—and while Erin deliberated over landmarks and trails, Jamie made a survey of the chapel's dirt floor, picking up the spikes and the stoppered vials, turning them around meditatively in her hands, and putting them back exactly where she'd found them, all without making any noise. She knelt there, scrunching her hair behind an ear, and wiped her nose on the inside of her shirtsleeve.

WE LEFT FROM THERE together because it was unavoidable—because we were going in the same direction, and because we were part of the same generation, and because we were Americans hiking in Italy—and because we all wanted to, finally. Of course, I might have gone on sitting on my rock when they began to gather up their things—I could have stayed by myself, since all that took was inertia—but instead I rose when they did, and the three of us went on, with no discussion of this arrangement. We passed some hikers so well dressed that Erin surmised they were Romans on vacation. We passed some Ladins with long-handled scythes who Erin proposed had been paid to be there by the Associazione Turistica. I suppose it was an element of my European mood to avoid replying with a witticism of my own, even while mulling some, but I can see now how Jamie was prominently responsible for my general muteness that day. I didn't want her to disapprove of how I saw the world, though I knew there was an equal jeopardy in remaining tongue-tied. We stopped once and stepped off the trail to let eight cows come up, their bells tinkling, and because I was so self-conscious suddenly, I didn't get out my journal. I'd been keeping it handy up to that juncture, walking with it in my left hand and my pencil in my right, but not now. I asked Jamie, that night, at a table in the bar at the Rifugio Lavarella, how many cows there'd been, because by then I was more comfortable around her, but at the moment, on the trail, I didn't write or say anything. It had grown cold again, and windy, and while we waited there for the cows to pass I took mental notes on the languor in their progress, on how obliviously they shat, on the ivory complexion of their late-summer hides, on their bovine odor, their lowing, the action of their tails, but this relentless, even obstinate, gathering of impressions, to date so central to my continental travels, was now not only left unrecorded but undertaken in the context of the Shaw sisters. The Shaw sisters were robust walkers, though without forced enthusiasm, and with the white dust of the region in the leather of their boots, and both wore red wool socks. There was a gash in the knee of Jamie's wind pants, and her palms looked wind-chafed. All this is what I noticed now, and also that I felt ancillary to them during their sisterly exchanges, a male third wheel and not a Shaw, instead of noticing the water in the streams, the carpeted meadows, and the crags.

Late in the day we passed, according to the Shaw sisters' map, underneath Monte Sella di Fanes, and came into barren and colder country. In a saddle to the southeast was another rustic chapel, this one of unmortared stone, and below that was a slope cut by bands of rock and broken by rivulets, near the bottom of which we could see the Rifugio Lavarella, or the smoke from its chimney and the late sun against its west-facing façade, and beyond that was Lago Verde and a road snaking up from a valley of trees and pastures. I remember all of this because when we paused to take it in there was pink light against the stone pillars to the east of the *rifugio*, which prompted Erin to say "coffee-table-book-ish." We stood a moment longer, and then Jamie intoned, "Now they would have the run home together," but I was too embarrassed to ask her what she meant.

WE DRANK GRAPPA that evening. It's made from grape skins and whatever else is left, the seeds and pulp, after a wine pressing. These dregs are distilled until a clear liquid results that retains, supposedly, the vapors left behind by the grapes gone to the vintner. I say "supposedly" since this was all explained to us, in English, by the *rifugio's* bartender, who may not have been reliable as a source on this after-dinner drink, and who also warned that the grappa he was serving might sting our palates and taste a little flammable. Erin, after drinking hers as if it came in a shotglass, employed the term "solvent" before switching to German lager. The bar was full of smoke, from cigarettes and from the woodstove and from a few jaunty Tyrolean briar pipes. Its low ceiling was black, and its floorboards were warped. The windows were fitted with wooden shutters, but on this night they were open, so stars were visible. We had to lean on the bar for half an hour until a table cleared, and then we sat down and started a round of Hearts, with me keeping score on the inside back cover of my journal. I was happy to be there, drinking grappa and playing cards. The light was low, but there was a lit candle on a nearby sill by which we could see our hands, the abuse the tabletop had taken through the years from Alpine travelers—people had put ice axes and crampons on it—and each other's faces. After a while, Erin went to the bathroom, so Jamie and I put down our cards, and I said that I would take a few notes if she didn't mind. This is when she remembered that there'd been eight cows that day on the trail underneath the Sasso delle Nove.

Something else from my journal. When you're feeling good about somebody there comes a moment when his or her appearance improves, and that's what happened with Jamie that night in the *rifugio* bar. I'd thought until then that her green eyes were conspicuously too far apart, but from then on it hasn't seemed so to me. "You might be wondering," said Jamie, "why Erin is constantly trying to shoot the moon, even when she doesn't have the right cards."

"Some people play like that."

"So far she's losing by something like two hundred."

"We can quit if you want."

"My sister's up and down," said Jamie. "She's had a good day, but tonight is bad, with the beer and the way she's playing Hearts."

I don't want to hold forth, or write the way a teacher talks while standing at the front of a class, but I have to say that things are rarely simple. You don't get to come across two sisters in the Dolomites, young and long-legged, both fair, and walk with them in the pink light and drink grappa beside them, without sooner or later coming to see that they don't just embody your romantic fantasies. They're themselves, too, with all that implies: in Erin's case, a bipolar disorder. Her illness is now controlled by lithium, but not in '74, in Italy, when her symptoms first came to light.

But I didn't ask, in the *rifugio* bar, what Jamie meant by "My sister's up and down," and changed the subject to something I'd just written in my journal: "Now they would have the run home together." "Erin and I've been cracking up over that line since high school," said Jamie. "Since Mr. Cheadle's class. Since Cheadle and his Hemingway stories. 'Now they would have the run home together' is the last line of 'Cross-Country Snow.' Nick Adams is skiing in Switzerland with George, only now he has to go back to the States because his girlfriend's pregnant."

"George?"

"His skiing buddy."

"I don't know it."

"Well, it's one of Hemingway's poor-Nick stories," answered Jamie. "Nicky doesn't get to play anymore. He has to go home and face the music."

IN THE MORNING, around five, I was awake and had my pack ready and wanted to go, partly because I always want to go, but instead I sat in the bar eating breadsticks left on a counter overnight, reading my notes, staring out the window, and nodding at other hikers who came in to have cigarettes and coffee for breakfast, and to look at maps together and talk in Italian or German, probably about the trails and the weather. Then I had coffee, too, with a *cornetto*, which I ate slowly while taking notes on the changes in the light outside the window as the minutes wore on, and more hikers came into the bar, where by now there was muesli and warm milk on the counter, and hard-boiled eggs, bottled water, and almonds and apricots for the trail, and I realized after a while that some of the hikers were ordering lunches, which came to them out of the kitchen in small cartons. I ate some muesli. I ate an egg and had more coffee. All the while, I thought of leaving but didn't get up. I nearly left on a couple of occasions, thinking that, all things considered, I still wanted to walk on my own, but instead I looked out the window.

Other hikers, in groups, were on the trail already, disappearing around a bend to the southwest, and I took notes on how the details of their clothing faded gradually as they moved into the distance. My chair was uncomfortable, and I wrote about that as well. Then the Shaw sisters came into the bar at seven-thirty, and Erin, with a demitasse in front of her, asked me to look at the back page of my journal regarding her final Hearts score, and Jamie pursed her lips to stifle a laugh. I noticed that the color of Jamie's eyes was variable, though since then I've come to see that most people's are, according to the light: in the morning pallor of the bar, her eyes were gray instead of the green I'd noticed the day before.

The Shaw sisters didn't seem to share my impatience. We sat with their battered map spread, and Erin said, "Hey, James, remember Tim Football? He used to have this phrase 'cumulatively tired.' That's kind of perfect."

"Eat something."

"Neil," said Erin, "do you have a car?"

"Have muesli," said Jamie.

Erin put her head on the map and looked out the window. "Tim Football. Touchdown. Extra point. Third down. 'Cumulatively' was a huge word for that . . ." She didn't finish.

"Understood," said Jamie. "Let's walk to San Vigilio."

"We could also split cab fare."

Jamie sighed, and Erin said, still staring out the window, "James, but what would Mom do?"

"What's your call?" asked Jamie. "What are we doing today?"

Erin said, "I say languish. Minus the 'l.'" She lifted her head and regarded me now as if my appearance in the bar surprised her. "We're slowing you down," she said.

"No, you're not."

"Yes, we are."

When I didn't answer she said, "*Buongiorno*, Neil. *Grazie*. Sorry. Now, James—could you bring me an egg?"

WE WALKED TOWARD San Vigilio together only partly because I'd said "No, you're not," and, starting that morning, I was complicit with Jamie in the coddling that was going on. Toward the middle of the day, we were passed on a road of white sand by trucks taking farmers up to cut summer hay, and we spoke with some hikers eating fruit and cheese on spread blankets who were Romans interested in the mushrooms of the region, in particular some rare truffles they pointed out in a guidebook, Erin supplying some Italian phrases to a conversation for the most part conducted in rudimentary English. We sat down there, and Jamie said to me, while Erin was preoccupied with being upbeat and charming, that there was no reason for me to feel obligated just because we'd met on the trail. I said I didn't feel that—the kind of thing you try to say with as much neutrality as possible, so that your implied meaning remains ambiguous.

Later in the afternoon, we stopped near racks of firewood, near some axes leaning against a tree, in lower country, where the air was warm, and while Erin snored, Jamie and I sprawled with our heads against our packs watching finches flit among the spruces. I noticed that she had a small scab on her knee. One summer, my sister spent a lot of hours in the sun, lightening her hair with lemon juice, thinking this would make her look like a Californian, and that was the suggestion of Jamie's hair, too, so that I wondered if she'd used the same technique. "So you don't feel obligated," she said.

"No."

"Were you going to San Vigilio?"

"I wasn't going anywhere."

Later, another group of hikers came along, including a very small dog, an old man with two walking sticks, and a girl in gaudy orange bellbottoms. They hailed us, and we hailed them back. A man in felt knickers and high stockings, a feather in his cap, did the talking. There was some discussion, in English and Italian both, about the beauty of things. I heard the word *splendidamente* repeated. When they were gone, we stood up and got on our packs. "I'm officially OD'd on Italy now," said Erin. "I can't take any more great scenery."

IN SAN VIGILIO, we booked rooms at the Hotel Monte Sella— expensive, but one night seemed justified. At dinner, two men in lederhosen sang folk songs, one with an accordion, the other with a guitar. We ate gnocchi, barley soup, and spinach pies, in that order, and then the waiters came in while the entertainers played what you might call a Tyrolean fanfare, and these waiters were carrying, by their heads, platters of beef haunch surrounded by pineapple and watermelon slices, lit sparklers stuck in the fruit throwing sparks across the meat and onto the floor tiles. The waiters had no English but leaned in and smiled and with their tongs put small potato balls or broiled tomatoes on our plates. "I don't think we're in Kansas anymore," Erin said when the entertainers started yodeling. She pretended to an appetite but, claiming an attraction to down comforters, and to wood shutters thrown open to Alpine air, began to move toward bed: during the intermission before the final act of dessert, she dropped her napkin on the table and yawned theatrically, patting her mouth. "Please," she said, on getting up to leave, "you don't have to tuck me in, James."

"I wasn't going to."

"Oh yes, you were."

Erin added, sliding in her chair, "You and Neil can just sit here without me and, I don't know, fall in love."

WE WENT TO the bar. A lot of the hotel guests had moved into the bar to smoke cigarettes and drink thimbles of coffee. There were children in the foyer fighting in a mild way—a little boy in suspenders kicking a little girl—and outside our window other guests played table tennis. There was an elaborate armoire at one wall of the bar, a two-tiered cupboard with its upper doors left open, inside of which, on a silver tray, were bottles of complimentary port, brandy, and sherry. Jamie and I, across from each other in a booth, drank brandy out of snifters and played Kings in the Corner. For whatever reason, it was sometimes difficult to pick the cards up off that table, so Jamie would use a fingernail to get them started. She shuffled cards by aiming the close corners of the split deck at each other while throwing forward the flats of her elbows, and she dealt with small tosses. When you're playing cards with people you watch their hands a lot and the way they use their fingers—it's hard not to—so I noticed that Jamie would sometimes manipulate a card by pincering it between the pad of her middle finger and the nail of her forefinger, which seemed unusual to me. I also became self-conscious about my own hands, which are blunt. They're the Countryman hands, good for squaring lumber and durable in cold weather, but decidedly inelegant carpenter's mitts, right down to the broad nails and deeply dimpled joints, the wrists with their bony outside protuberances and the thick metacarpals with valleys between them. My hands are pawlike, and when I gesture with them in front of my students, employing them for emphasis as I talk, I'm sometimes conscious that they're lacking in grace, and that was what I felt in the Monte Sella bar playing Kings in the Corner with Jamie.

We lingered. There were two things that mattered, from my point of view. The first was that Jamie went to Portland State University, which is only 172 miles from Seattle. The second was that she was saddened, nearly to the point of tears, by the fact that she didn't know what to do with her life. "I take classes to take classes," Jamie said. Yet she wasn't being melodramatic—she was just being serious about her future in a way that got to me. Although, looking back, it's probably even simpler. Taking nothing away from Jamie, her attractions, I was always ready, from the time I was thirteen, to marry the first girl who came along.

THAT NIGHT, WE DRANK a lot of brandy. Erin, said Jamie, had come to Rome in June on a student visa to take twelve credits of art history. In July, an art-history administrator called Jamie and, in a calm, even assiduous voice, explained that Erin was having psychological difficulties, which at the moment consisted of lying despondently in bed, so now he was making use of the emergency number she'd provided. Jamie understood then that this administrator assumed he was talking to Erin's mother. She didn't tell him otherwise. She listened to him explain that the program had a good relationship with a clinic, and that Erin would get care, even on a Sunday. Rome on Sunday was generally quiet, but this clinic was responsive to the program's requests. Failing that, there was a private home number the administrator could call in order to get around-the-clock attention. This ought to get results, but if it didn't, he would try a second and a third number. Someone would help Erin, of this he was certain. Rome worked in strange ways, he said, but ultimately Rome worked. It was these protests, Jamie told me in the bar, that tipped the scales in favor of her going to Rome—

say all of this hadn't happened on a Sunday, maybe she would have stayed in Portland and not come to Italy. But it was on a Sunday. Jamie worked in the gift shop of a hotel—on evenings during the school year and for eight-hour shifts since the start of summer—but on Monday she told her manager that she had to quit because of a medical emergency in her family, and on Tuesday she went to a travel agent who helped her get a discounted fare which was nonetheless exorbitant because of short notice. I said I wondered what she'd told her parents.

"That Erin invited me to Rome."

"That's all?"

"It was kind of true."

"How much was your plane ticket?"

"All my savings."

I told her about my life-insurance money then. I was effusive, in part because I'd been drinking the Monte Sella's brandy, but I suppose the gates opened for other reasons as well. In the end, I talked too much about myself. I told Jamie that I was going to be a writer. I celebrated train travel. The next day, on the trail—because a trail is good for privacy of thought, even when you're with other hikers—I felt ashamed of my garrulousness. I was then and am now a believer in reserve, in brevity, and in the value of silence. I once saw a book called *Mouth Open Already a Mistake*, written by someone described on the flap as a Zen master, and though I didn't thumb its pages, it did seem to me a title describing something I've known to be true—*Mouth Open Already a Mistake*. That's the sort of thing that's sometimes in advice columns. Even so, my mouth's been open, at length, every day in my classroom. I've made my living opening my mouth. The bell has rung, as a bell rings to start and end the rounds of a boxing match, and I've come out with my mouth open. And all the while I've privately preferred silence. "The new year's first snow: / how lucky to remain alone / at my hermitage" is from Basho, who for the most part has bored my World Literature students. That's a class where we sit on old sofas and discuss, for example, Chinua Achebe. I like these conversations, most of the time, but nevertheless, I often see my life as an effort to thwart dialogue, and just about everything else, so I can be by myself, either by myself or taking, for better or worse, a kind of refuge in Jamie. This may or may not be the best sort of marriage, but it's partly how ours has unfolded anyway. And I know, because she's told me, that Jamie takes refuge in me, too, though she doesn't incline, as I do, toward solitude. If she had her way, our two grown sons would come for dinner every night, and nothing would ever change.

LAST NIGHT WE BOTH depressed ourselves a little by renting, and watching, a forgettable movie, one we should have turned off after half an hour in favor of doing something else. A movie like this makes you feel you're wasting your life watching it, and that's what happened to us. And yet we watched anyway. Then it was over, and we both felt self-conscious about how we'd spent our evening. Jamie said, "Let's not do that again; if it's bad, let's turn it off next time," and I agreed with her, though we both knew no principle would guide us in the future. I went up to my garret and checked my e-mail— hoping, I confess, to hear from my agent, Ally Krantz—and then sat in an old club chair, napping. It was the kind of napping where you argue with yourself, for a long time, about getting up to go to bed. Images come in curious procession, punctuated by inter- ludes of clarity, like rising to the surface after being underwater. At last I stood up. I keep a few artifacts and totems on my desk: a spoon one of my sons carved for me in a wood-shop class; a figurine of the see-no-evil, hear-no-evil, speak-no-evil monkeys; a fire-drill set— a charred cedar board and a carved yew-wood stick—that was once John William's; and a postcard of E. B. White at his typewriter in a shed. These, for whatever reason, caught my late-night attention, and I was struck by how little I noticed them for months on end, despite all the time I spend in this room—these things that are there because they have a private meaning or because they're meant to induce aesthetic pleasure, all of them only inches away but largely ignored.

I went to bed. But now it was hard to sleep—that's the problem with late reveries in my club chair—so I thought about the past to pass the time. Around three in the morning, Jamie asked, out of the blue, though it didn't entirely surprise me, "So what are we going to do with the money?" We talked about that for a long time without deciding. It got light, and after my morning routine—feeding the

dog, brewing coffee, stretching a little, and staring out the window—
I returned to my garret. At eight, Jamie turned on the water in the
shower. I could hear her—even though we were on different floors—
hawking spit in the stall and singing with parodic intent. We sat in
the kitchen drinking coffee and eating toast. I thought Jamie looked
good in her outfit—just a simple cotton V-neck shirt, short-sleeved,
with a wrap skirt and sandals. She's past fifty; even so, I think she
moves through the world looking good to other people, too. Until
recently, Jamie had a job appraising real estate, which she didn't particularly like, but we needed the money. The boys were gone, but we
still needed her paycheck. One thing: Jamie and I never argued
about money. I'm frugal to a fault and so is she.

Our wedding, twenty-eight years ago, was an agnostic affair, held
in a gazebo with our families present and a judge presiding, near
formal specimen trees in the Washington Park Arboretum, just a
few miles from where we live now. Sometimes, on walks, Jamie and
I sit in this gazebo to get out of the rain, maybe looking at a small
tree-handbook we carry, with its descriptions of leaves and needles,
its pencil drawings and index of Latin names, or warming our hands
in our pockets and reading the graffiti penned on the posts; or, at
some point, I'll mention the neuroma in my foot or Jamie the arthritis in her fingers, or, most likely, the two of us will add another seg-
ment to our dialogue on how our grown-up sons are faring. You
would think that sitting sheltered from the rain in the gazebo where
you were married would feel romantic, and it does, but the fact that
it feels romantic no longer seems, to either of us, important. We
leave that feeling in the background, so—for example—if you were
to see us deliberating over jars of pasta sauce at our regular grocery
store, the Trader Joe's at Roosevelt Way and 45th, it wouldn't occur
to you that romance is part of our relationship, and in the same way,
it wouldn't occur to you if you saw us in that gazebo. You would just
see a couple at midlife, identifying trees together or talking quietly.
You would, I think, barely register our existence on your way to
wherever you're going, just as we hardly noticed other people when
we were walking, thirty-two years ago, in the Dolomites.

3

GODDESS OF THE MOON

ON A SUNDAY this April, the *Seattle Times* ran a front-page feature, continued, densely, on two inside pages, about me and the hermit of the Hoh. It included a photo, lifted from the '74 Roosevelt High School annual, in which I'm wearing a black bow tie and a white dinner jacket, a shag haircut, and a mustache, and another of me taken this April on the South Fork of the Hoh, sitting with one leg over the other and gesturing toward the water. I'm described as, among other things, the hermit's only friend, and it was this, apparently, that prompted a call I got shortly afterward from a Cindy Saperstein.

I didn't know what to make of her at first. The sentences emitting from the other end of the line were so pell-mell they put me off balance. Was I really John William's friend? she asked. If so, she wanted to sit down with me, because years ago, she said, she'd been his "flame."

I said John William had never mentioned any "flame."

"Okay," she said. "You've been getting weird phone calls since the newspaper thing."

"No," I said. "Well, one."

"This isn't a weird call. I went with him at Reed. My name's Cindy Saperstein. Houghton then. I was his girlfriend."

I considered hanging up. "Come on," Cindy pleaded, "I *went* with him at Reed. Gnosticism, right? Always talking about the Gnostics? Did he go off with you constantly about the Gnostics?"

"Constantly."

"So let's meet."

We converged, three days later, on a Starbucks halfway between Seattle and Portland. Since I was unsure about traffic, I beat her there by fifteen minutes, an interval I partly spent watching drivers maneuver to park in an undersized lot, including Cindy in her unwashed Volvo station wagon with its barricading dog-screen and defiant, if moot, kerry/edwards bumper sticker. Why did I dismiss the woman who struggled out of this iconic vehicle with a large sisal handbag and a practical sunhat as not the person I was waiting for? The politics were apropos if I extrapolated forward from Reed in the mid-seventies, and the woman herself was of the right vintage, but it still seemed impossible that this gray-haired Democrat—who'd advised me to look for "a past-her-prime earth mother"—had once been John William's "flame."

It was 2 p.m., and Cindy wanted a midsized iced Mocha Frappuccino made with skim milk. I wanted one, too. I think we both enjoyed watching the barista because of the federal case this young woman with a tiny tarnished nose-ring made out of preparing our concoctions—Cindy and I shared middle-aged amusement and middle-aged forbearance, bonding, I thought, by virtue of a generational contrast. At our table, Cindy sipped through her straw, then removed her sunhat with a sweaty flourish. She told me that for years she'd had a landscaping business and still did occasional landscape design, but right now she was writing screenplays. She'd written one, in fact, that had recently been optioned, about an eighteenth-century explorer in Florida "taken in by natives." Her husband was a CPA and blues pianist. Her college-senior son was working with an NYU chemistry professor on . . . Cindy didn't understand it, but it had to do with nanobots. Her college-sophomore son was an exchange student "studying snowboarding" in New Zealand, and her high-school-sophomore daughter, in a humbling surprise of parenthood, was now at cheerleader camp in Idaho.

With this mention of her daughter, Cindy did something girlish—

she reached back and laid her hair on her shoulder. When she turned her face to the side, I saw her as she might have been at Reed: as an ingénue painted by Vermeer, maybe with an earlobe poking out of her tresses. "To be frank," she said, "I called you for a reason. The reason being that after seeing you in the paper I thought we should talk about a screenplay."

"What?"

"Between the two of us," she said, "we've got a story with juice."

"No one's going to make a film about a hermit."

"Yes, they are," said Cindy.

SHE WAS HARD to stop. And I'd driven for close to two hours. So I sat there while she told me how she'd met John William at a Reed dorm dance and how, in the semidarkness, she'd noticed him long before he asked her to the floor, because he was the type that attracted her—"the boy next door with a dark side." They danced to "Long Ago and Far Away," by James Taylor, which in blunt despondency asks, "Where do those golden rainbows end?" and "Why is this song so sad?" and which is so languid it left them, Cindy told me, with no alternative to the "slow dance" mode of the era. This meant dancing very little, or for that matter hardly moving while in one another's clutches, but it was also, or could be, an intensely pleasant exchange of scents, pressures, hot breath, adjustments of hands, small turns of the head, and noses brushing hair, all of which she experienced while dancing with this handsome, clearly well-bred, but rough-around-the-edges guy who so far had no name and whom she couldn't remember having seen on campus; but it was only early October of her freshman year, and she hadn't met a lot of people yet; she had so far, mostly, done a lot of apologizing for being from Aurora, Illinois.

"Long Ago and Far Away" ended. They uncoupled, Cindy with reluctance. The guy she'd danced with didn't say his name or ask for hers, but he did say, as he stepped back, "Marry me."

"Okay," answered Cindy. But she also felt that if this was irony her dance partner had an excellent poker face.

They went for a walk. A fall night, with all the silvery edges trees have on a fall night because of moonlight and dry air, all the little campus bushes looking lit and still, and (Cindy, at Starbucks, thinking screenplay) no dialogue. Cindy couldn't tell if she was headed toward the college-library roof or going out for ice cream. She was aware that October moonlight showed her face to good effect; she was also aware that October moonlight was a romantic cliché associated with the heartland of America, from which she'd sprung. They walked without saying anything, leaving campus, and as their silence deepened she began to wonder, with burgeoning alarm, what it meant, this intense atmosphere of no words between people who'd just met. "Where are we going?" she finally asked.

"Please," he answered. It sounded like pleading.

They were standing in front of a well-maintained Craftsman house where a golden retriever watched them from the porch. Or that's the gist of it—what Cindy called "the ultimate statistically correct family domicile." She remembered it because it was what she was looking at when John William kissed her. His eyes were shut, but hers were open. He was a tender kisser, interposing his lips between hers without insistence or pressure. When he came up for air—"Well, this is always an awkward moment, isn't it, when you've just shared a kiss with a person for the first time and there's the question next of what to do with your eyes. But most of the time you work that out, right? Kiss again, or act casual about it? John William, when he got done kissing, he turned around and *split*. Like that. The guy turned around and walked away."

Cindy Houghton slid her hands into her jeans pockets and watched this strange boy retreat. "Hey," she called. "What's your name?"

At Starbucks: "He gives me all three names. Like I was asking for his middle name, too. I mean, this is what I'm talking about. He kissed me and told me his weird, scary name, and then he just walked away."

HE WROTE HER a letter in an intense, slanted script, dutifully cursive but inelegant. "I found out your name," it began. "I got your dorm room number." That same day, when she emerged from her last class at three-twenty, there he was, falling into step beside her out of nowhere. "I wrote to you," he said. "Did you get the letter I sent?" He was wearing hiking boots recently treated with a water-proofing wax and, despite the cold, he had no coat, just a gray flannel union shirt with its buttons open, its flaps revealing a V-shaped swatch of hairless chest. His sleeves were pulled to the elbows, and the cold emphasized the blood vessels in his forearms. She kept asking herself whom he looked like until she remembered a painting she'd seen in a Chicago museum of the death of Robespierre, which was mostly about Robespierre's unbridled hair and blousy, unlaced *chemise d'homme*, and the fact that he'd shot himself ineptly in the jaw in a stab at suicide before his date with the guillotine. "Yes," she said. "I got your letter."

"You didn't write back."

"Not yet I didn't."

"What does that mean?"

"I didn't have time."

John William put a hand to his forehead. "Please don't say that," he pleaded.

What? He was nimble and tense, an overanxious strider, but she wanted to keep up with him, because she felt his adoration, and to be adored was the point of her life, the state of things she'd yearned for dating boys in Aurora and still yearned for at the moment, as a college student on the West Coast mulling majoring in botany; now all of this intensity aimed in her direction made her feel a lot at once. "Your name means 'woman of Kynthos,' " he'd written, "the mountain on Delos where Artemis and Apollo were born. Cynthia, another name for Artemis, goddess of the moon, of the wilderness, the hunt, wild animals, and fertility. A virgin goddess, armed with a bow, guardian of children, patron of women in childbirth . . ." The notes she'd gotten from other boys, in high school, had said things like "kegger on Fri. at Tommy's" and "let's do a doobee after 3rd." So she held her books to her chest and made no effort to widen the space, which John William had made intimate, between their shoulders. ("Of course, back then one of the givens in life was that you were aware of feminism," Cindy mentioned at Starbucks. "But I still wanted adoration.")

They walked in an ellipse, in an intentional and hard-driving aimlessness, which for her was evidence of something she couldn't discern; that they were hardly talking must imply something, too, but what? The trees were aflame, as in poetry about October—the sycamore maples in front of Psychology, and the European beeches on the walkway toward Art—and the grotesques staring down from the walls of the library didn't look threatening or disturbing. Cindy was wearing a blue parka, unzipped; the tips of her ears felt hot pink with cold. The boy beside her, meanwhile, seemed top-heavy in the shoulders. His best feature was his goat-boy's mane of hair, not washed recently and sexually evocative—as though in his potent urgency about everything there was no spare moment to brush it away: his hair formed a dark scrim across his eyes. Clearly, though, he was a blue-blood. Cindy could tell the boys from good families by the envelope of fundamental neatness that traveled with them, but she also, normally, found them boring in their narcissism. Maybe this is what this "John William" was, but in a new permutation, so advanced in his self-absorption he'd come out the other side, as if his adoration of her was self-absorption inverted. This light he shone on her was—maybe—as much about its source as about its object—like the moon, she was brightly lit by it but still devoid of her own atmosphere. "I don't understand you," she said to him.

"I don't understand you, either."

"I don't understand what's going on."

"Neither do I."

"Where are we going?"

"I don't know."

"Why did you run off the other night?"

He sighed—a graphic heave from the solar plexus up—as if completely aghast.

They ended up making out while standing in the trees by an amphitheater. He was standoffish from the waist down, explicitly prudish about contact below the belt, and stopped the proceedings at frequent intervals to hug her in a platonic way or to look into her face from an intimate proximity. When she cupped his cheeks in her hands during one of these presbyopic stare-downs, he whispered, "Thank you."

"See what I mean?" Cindy tapped the plastic lid of her Frappuccino. "Between your hermit stuff and my tale of bizarreness, we've got a screenplay."

"The barista has a screenplay."

"Not as good as ours."

"So what exactly do you mean by bizarreness?"

"Listen," said Cindy. "It's probably hard to believe this now, but when I was younger I had a super body, and guys would go from a first kiss to unzipping their pants in about half a second, so talk about weird and a big relief, the way John William treated me— I never felt urged, is the way I'd put it, to do something against my will, okay? And for a guy, that's bizarreness."

He was, she added, endlessly attentive, punctual to a fault, and an idealist, which she respected. He'd salvaged a broken mimeograph from a Dumpster and was repairing it, which to Cindy seemed novel—he had the idea of mass-producing political broadsides once this hand-cranked machine was in order. From the campus treasurer's office, John William procured a copy of Reed's financial report, and while she studied Plato at his side, he marked it up with a highlighter. In the cafeteria, he ate mostly raw vegetables. He had a peculiar sense of what constituted a date—for example, he asked her if she wanted to get up at 4 a.m. on a Saturday and walk until dusk, the idea being to follow the Willamette to its confluence with the Columbia. She agreed and got blisters. When it rained, they huddled in a railroad car inundated by blackberry creepers, and even though this felt dangerous and tawdry, she also felt enamored of the industrial sound of the storm beating on their rusted hideaway, and of the idea of what they were doing. She noted again that John William was conspicuously less horny than other boys she'd known, who surely would have pounced on her in such an opportune setting. No thrusting loins, no poking fingers. He had a lot of ideas, though, and despite his post-dance prologue of tormented silence, he now proved to be an insatiable promulgator, for his audience of one, of heartfelt positions. He had a way of animatedly twisting up the political with the metaphysical that made him impossible to follow, but Cindy didn't care. She was his fond, confused listener. If Buddhism, existentialism, and anarchism went together, that was all right with Cindy. Instead of pinning her and clawing at her bra, like other boys, John William sat with his knees up and rambled effusively, saying that Pol Pot's education in Paris subverted the ideal of a liberal-arts education, or questioning the New Deal. Other smart boys had liked her, but this boy's brain was on fire. Plus, here in the

Oregon country the midday light was soft and broad beyond the frame of their boxcar door, and there was wind riffling a field of high weeds and woody Scotch broom. An alluvial fertility could still be felt transpiring in the earth in the week before Halloween. The color of the sky was like a length of white chalk turned on its side and rubbed into asphalt. Sanded—that was how the world looked, worked slowly down to no rough edges. All of this wasn't sweltering cornfields, and it wasn't a plate of salty French fries at Big Larry's Drive-In on the road between Aurora and Sugar Grove, where she used to go with a senior named Ted Lynch when she was a sophomore at East Aurora High School—Ted Lynch, who drove a two-tone Plymouth Duster 340 and played second-string free safety on the football team. Now she and John William walked the Willamette with their arms around each other, and when they came to the Columbia at Kelley Point, in the wet haze of this October afternoon, John William regaled her with stray information: Lewis and Clark had camped here; they'd also employed elk brains to soften hides while wintering at Fort Clatsop; in Montana, the Corps of Discovery had fallen so hungry some members ate their candles. No matter. She preferred his agitated brain—its speed, heat, and recall—to anything she'd come across so far in suitors, and his frenzied chivalry also had an appeal: when she observed offhandedly that it was cold, he splintered discarded apple-crates with his boots and built a fire on the riverbank, inducing high flames until she asked him to stop, whereupon John William desisted immediately, and with the obeisance of a knight. And so she came back to campus that evening happily disheveled, her hair smelling like smoke and rain, mud in her shoes, drawn tight and light-headed from not having eaten (he'd insisted that fasting would enhance the day, and she had to admit there was truth to that, even though, for most of the afternoon, she'd felt preoccupied with the idea of finding a tuna sandwich), and the coppery taste of his mouth in hers, because, by her dorm door, she'd slugged him once in the gut playfully, then pushed him against the foyer wall and, with her forearms against his chest, slid her tongue between his teeth while she had his lips parted. He didn't flinch, but, as she said, "he had a hard time admitting to his body." Afterward, he said that the day behind them already wounded him in memory. "You're weird," she answered, and slugged him again with the tomboyish coquetry she'd developed for use with her boyfriends in Aurora. This cool and different West Coast guy—it was time to write home to her friends about him, because he was such a trip.

"HE TOOK ME to Seattle on the Union Pacific in a boxcar. I remember waiting under the Forty-second Street bridge and making our jump when they changed engine crews. You have to understand, I'd grown up getting excited about cotton candy at the county fair and rolling my dolls up and down the street in a baby carriage, so hopping a train out here on the West Coast and doing reefer, hanging out with this intense, strange guy . . . Talk about sudden— I went from being Daddy's little girl to dodging bulls and riding a freight north, all in about fifteen minutes—well, okay, with an interlude of Schlitz and back-seat car sex in between." She laughed. "Cold," she said. "It's freezing in a boxcar. We finally hopped off around midnight on a Friday. I remember being really impressed by the shopwindows in Seattle—like at Jay Jacobs, where there was a Roman fleece robe in shocking pink for sale, and thinking how nice it would be to flounce around in one of those while drinking— I don't know—Taittinger? John William wanted to put a rock through that window. Oh yeah, we went into a Steve's Broiler on Fourth Avenue. I doubt it's there anymore. Are there still places in Seattle where people smoke? I noticed something," said Cindy. "When he was stoned he was definitely more amorous and sensual. It would be so unlike him to volunteer a kiss, but when he got a little weed in him, that changed. So we were sitting in this Steve's, stuffing food into each other's mouths and kissing in between. And talking about school. Or he was talking about school. Whatever he was reading. I don't know. He'd go from Francis Bacon to Euripides in half a sentence. Then he'd kiss me. Then we'd eat some more. It was incredibly sexy. And it was so romantic. I felt like I was dating Byron. I was really a sucker for the Romantic poets when I was nineteen. Later, we hung out at the Greyhound station. You know, like in Simon and Garfunkel—I've got my head in his lap, and he's reading a paperback with his hair in his eyes and with this sexy stubble on his jawline. I remember. This is the kind of thing you remember.

I had my nose sort of up against his belly, which smelled like, I don't know, you'll have to supply your own simile—it smelled like a guy, is all I can say. I admit it, I was sort of in love. But—we were just sitting around in the Greyhound station, and he says to me, 'What do you think of *Romeo and Juliet*?' What? Was this a Shakespeare question? I think I made a joke like 'Too much doo-wop,' and then hummed a few bars of . . ." She hummed the refrain from "Just Like Romeo and Juliet," by the Reflections. "John William said, 'No—I mean killing yourself.' He's like 'Could you do that? Because I'm looking for somebody who can do that.'

"Wait," said Cindy Saperstein. "I guess I should have gotten on a bus right then instead of pretending I was into it the same way he was, but the way it lays, you're nineteen, you're stoned, it's four in the morning, you've been slumming all night and running around with this good-looking guy, and so I guess it was too late for both of us. I mean, for a half-second, as a game with myself, I bought into this Romeo-and-Juliet myth. I said yes, because about ten percent of me yearned toward this romantic fatalism that was so entertaining, so I said yes, I'd kill myself, but it was strictly an act—the other ninety percent was just this normal college girl who was hanging out and having fun."

"An act."

"I wasn't going to kill myself, obviously."

She reached back and again laid her hair on her shoulder. The more time you spend with someone in her middle years, the more you penetrate to her salad days—I couldn't be certain, but was there some modicum of regret in the way she absentmindedly, and fleetingly, inspected her split ends? In that Madonna-like leftward, downward glance, so briefly ruminative about this moment from over thirty years before? So girlishly retiring and mutely sad? Cindy rolled a strand between her thumb and forefinger while I noted the long curve of her ear flange, and also the grace of her hand in repose. There were the bony protuberances and calluses of age and work. But have you seen, perhaps in a painting, a wool spinner drawing strands from a spindle gently, as if by calm sleight-of-hand? I was reminded of that—Cindy touched her hair in just such a light, artful way. At the same time, I was looking at the crown of her head. For some reason, up top she was salt-and-pepper instead of gray.

Cindy said, "I mean, I wasn't even going to kill myself in *metaphor*, okay? And I should have told him that instead of saying I was Juliet."

BY LATE NOVEMBER, at Reed, Cindy had misgivings—she felt John William's anguish over their Thanksgiving parting was incommensurate with the duration involved, a mere four days. When she embraced him again, back at school from Aurora, he gave her a puka-shell necklace with pink bead spacers. His other gift was a photocopied essay on Penthesilea, whom Achilles slew on the plain at Troy but fell in love with as she drew her final breath—John William had underlined passages Cindy didn't think were special and had written indecipherable notes in the margins. One December night, they walked up Market Street to Washington Park and climbed wide steps to Portland's formal rose gardens, sterile and bloomless in early-winter weather yet still brandishing, on this night, luminous thorns. There were stark canes mulched in the city's sleeping glow, but John William was heedless of the invitation in such a scene, busy as he was delivering, for Cindy's benefit, a lecture on the medieval troubadours of southern France. Enough already. She couldn't make him notice the view of downtown lights through a lane between trees, or the way the mulch had hardened beneath crystalline frost so as to fracture, gently, underfoot. He didn't see any of this, because in his brain fever, the real world didn't exist.

He gave her, that December, in swift succession, a choker of quartz-and-amber flowers, a twisted leather bracelet, a sailor's-knot bracelet, a pair of powder-blue butterfly-crystal drop earrings, and a sterling-silver toe ring, none of them wrapped or boxed but just handed over with terrible impatience and an eagerness that, each time she felt its acquisitive gravity, increased her unease about the charade she was engaged in. All these cobbled-together trinkets and street-market baubles, made by hippies or Taiwanese, weighed her down and made her feel collared—especially the choker, with its poorly shaped flowers, which strangled her when she turned her head.

Christmas approached, with what Cindy had begun to see—for the first time in her life, while removed from home, with her old sensibility swamped by her new education—as a forced gaiety and a mass hysteria about excess. "Well-decorated consumption," as John William called it, "bearing every relation to the dark triumph of capital." Some of her dorm-mates strung lights in their dorm rooms or displayed holiday kitsch. A lighter mood prevailed on campus even as the sun grew lesser; one evening she even heard Bing Crosby from a turntable down the hall, crooning "Here Comes Santa Claus" alongside the Andrews Sisters. Despite herself, Cindy felt a warm indulgence and domestic pleasure, a resurgence of her already receding Midwest, and joined the circle of rum-eggnog drinkers and holiday pot smokers sitting on parallel dorm-room beds and yogi-style on the parquet, who soon opted for another seasonally appropriate LP track, Cheech and Chong's "Santa Claus and His Old Lady." All a crack-up, but not for John William, who was jealous of her friendships and wanted to consume her, who denounced in a fell swoop every student on campus as infantile and dependent, with the college as parent surrogate and the institutional dorm beds in their lifeless cubicles a humiliation and a death to the spirit. When she asked him in a parry about his dorm room—which she'd never visited—he said that after one night there, listening to his freckled Bostonian roommate argue for the profundity of lyrics by the Eagles, watching him tack up a poster of Grand Funk in concert, seeing him sharpen two pencils in preparation for his first day of classes, noting how new his toiletries kit looked—split-grain leather, pop-topped, unstained—he'd opted out. He slept on couches in lounges, he told her. The campus, so poorly secured and inherently optimistic, set in its mild and friendly community and admitting into its fold only scholars to be trusted, had many furtive and unlocked corners, overheated all night by central boilers; he'd even gone underground, into the labyrinth of ducts there, and slept beneath the frosted greens and darkened buildings in mechanical bunkers. Showers? The question occasioned a diatribe on water usage. The cleaning of a human body required no more than two quarts of water every forty-eight hours if the bather was wise and responsible, whereas the cultural norm in the modern world was to send gallons down the drain daily for no sanctionable reason. In this case, said John William, there ought to be a law—as long as we were living in a society of laws instead of in a state of consensus—a law sharply limiting the high water usage Americans viewed as their birthright. And what was more wasteful than the metal trays, under heat lamps, in the school cafeteria, each with its baleful, glistening load of food-industry proteins and hybridized grains, some percentage of which was slated three times a day for the college disposal bins, a measure of excess always in reserve so as to slake all possible young appetites? An unconscionable food status quo, as unquestioned as air and paid for by tuition moneys, which obligated every student at Reed, said John William adamantly, to do something about such sickening extravagance—to do something about it as opposed to shopping at Kmart after classes for ironic Christmas elves.

John William, Cindy told me, had a policy of no Christmas gifts, but she didn't and gave him one, wrapped in pages of *The Oregonian* with big felt-penned hearts penetrated by Cupid's arrows drawn over text—George Harrison's Hindu-inflected triple-album set, *All Things Must Pass.* They were out on one of the campus commons, on a bench beneath a bare Oregon myrtle, a few hours before she was catching an O'Hare-bound plane. Cindy watched John William scrutinize, with what looked like perplexity, the album's moody black-and-white cover—the enigmatic Harrison, in tall rubber boots, slumped on a stool and surrounded by garden gnomes. "I can't accept this," he said.

"Why not?"

"It's a Christmas gift."

"Big deal."

"Don't say that."

This common phrase of his, "Don't say that," was condescending and censorious, producing in Cindy a moment's frustration, but she decided she would say "I'm sorry" to her boyfriend in the most genuine tone she could rouse. It was a mid-December afternoon, and the word was carried away from her lips as vapor. "But," she added, "couldn't you just think of it as something else?"

"That's dishonest."

"It's recycled. It's from a used-record shop."

"I still don't want it."

He rode the bus with her to the airport. He shouldered her bag; he escorted her to her gate. They sat together, John William with his arms around her, so that she felt penned in. Outside, beyond the tall windows, against the planes at the jetways and on the tarmac expanse, sleet fell at a windblown angle, and Cindy missed home. In the winter wind from off the plains, her skin would demand emollient, but, on the other hand, a person could actually dress for mid-American weather; here, no matter what you did, you felt clammy from the inside. She pointed this out to John William, who shrugged and pulled her closer. Worse, he replied, was this antiseptic terminal, devoid of weather altogether; artificial environments, he added, were designed to induce malaise. Immediately Cindy regretted having spoken about the weather, but what was more banal—what ought to be safer—than meteorology? And what subject didn't instigate, in this boyfriend of hers, so muscular and earnest, so angry at the world, a rant or complaint? On he went against their backdrop of slanting sleet outside and a benign seventy degrees inside, explaining to her that the point of obliterating the natural world was to deaden the senses; once the senses were deadened, a human being became an automaton; at Reed, as elsewhere, the experiments in the Psychology Department were funded by corporations; if Pavlov's dogs could be made to salivate at the ringing of a bell, it followed that human beings could be made to buy what they didn't need. "And meanwhile we're just sitting here," he said, as if that was the final word.

He stood in line with her. As they approached the boarding ramp, in the restless pack of holiday travelers with their carry-on bags and airplane books, John William asked her not to go. At the last moment, abruptly, he kissed her with a flagrant and overwhelming suction—the kind of public farewell kiss that evokes in its observers a jealous wish for equal passion in their own lives, even as it amuses and embarrasses them. *This sort of thing can't last* is the common reaction: these young lovers will either part or mature into something less dramatic. But what does a watcher know? Cindy, decamped at last with *All Things Must Pass* in her arms, queued for boarding in the jetway, felt mainly relief that John William was behind her. Relief and the prospect of a Midwestern Christmas, as opposed to the sorrow of a sojourning lover. So the parting a watcher might predict at the touch of their lips was already present, although she'd thrown herself into that lovers' adieu like the fair young Capulet herself.

At home, she took the hayride down Candy Cane Lane and the wagon ride through the Sinnissippi Forest that were Houghton family traditions. Cinched into an apron, flour on her T-shirt, she made apple-cider donuts and watched the black-and-white television her mother kept on the kitchen counter. For gifts, she went shopping at West Aurora Plaza. She drank Pabst with high-school friends and got modestly inebriated, enough to make her talkative about her West Coast boyfriend. There was an evening of hash and of vermouth something-or-others with a friend home from Bowling Green. But here was the problem: about three times a day, John William called, urgent, pining, and distraught John William, calling to underscore and emphatically reiterate the depth of his feelings, cross-examine her about her activities during the hours since he last rang, and deplore Christmas. "On with the performance," said Cindy. "But now my motivation was different—not to make him happy, but to get him off the phone—or both, if possible, because he was calling ad nauseam. And there was this serious disconnect between the sound of his voice and me in my old bedroom, where I used to lay around at Christmastime with the radio on and a Whitman Sampler box. Sort of ironic—me eating caramels with my legs crossed and my head on fluffy pillows while he's talking about saving the world."

"What about your parents?"

"I told them yes, I had this new boyfriend, who was very enamored of the telephone."

She sipped her Frappuccino. "Being hounded is flattering," she admitted. "It's obnoxious but flattering. Really, as much as I felt invaded by his phone calls, there was something great about my mother raising her eyebrows suggestively every time the phone rang. I ended every conversation with 'I love you' and 'I miss you'— phony on my part, but I enjoyed the role. That's the advantage of a phone romance: hang up and it disappears. You don't have to deal with it. It's back to baking pies and listening to Perry Como. Although I didn't enjoy Christmas that year. There was this nagging feeling I had that something was askew in my life. I mean, John William never once wished me a Merry Christmas. Not even when he called me on Christmas morning. I'm sitting there in my bathrobe, a little urgent to get into the shower because we're leaving for my uncle's house in Elgin pretty soon, and John William is talking, for some reason, about gnosticism instead of wishing me a Merry Christmas. Gnosticism! What the hell? To me, it sounded like devil worship. I could have gone with a normal guy, I guess, but this is what I'd chosen—or, should I say, this is what happened to me. Personally, I think I went brain-numb that fall at Reed because I was fresh from Aurora. This guy, he couldn't deliver a 'Season's Greetings.' Everything—everything—was an ethical question, in his head. I mean, how paralyzing is that?" Cindy sighed.

"John William and I did the one thing we were good at in January: we took walks. He ranted and raved while I checked out the scenery and, quite frankly, brooded kind of darkly about my situation, my conundrum. How am I going to extricate myself? was a question that made me ridiculously gloomy. If you've declared your undying love for a guy and then break up with him—blah. How do you keep from feeling just blah? And that's just the selfish side of the equation—obviously, there's the other person's pain to worry about, too. The other person's reaction. But I had to get out. I was on the verge of a panic attack. Here I am strolling the riverfront with John William, where I ought to be peaceful, and instead I'm sunk in dread, even while I've got my arm around his waist, even while we're stopping to kiss. Like I said, he was a good kisser. It still felt great to just sort of tuck into his warmth on one of those cold January walks and drown out whatever he was talking about. I remember sitting on a bench with him at Johnson Creek Park and, being nineteen and romantic, thinking how we'd met slow-dancing to that syrupy James Taylor song, and how appropriate that seemed right then, when I needed to break up with him. Born in sadness," said Cindy, "and ended in sadness, like all my other relationships until I met Bill, because Bill doesn't need a mother. Bill's the one guy I've met in my life who doesn't seem to need a mother."

She reached into her handbag then for a slim pair of reading glasses tucked into a leather case. "Plus-threes," she said. "Nonprescription. I use them for needlework and the *TV Guide*. Bill has about ten of these. They're all over the house." She slid them on and inspected her nails. "Garden dirt," she said. "I was pulling weeds this morning. There's something to be said for meditative gardening, for solo gardening—just you and your weeds. In fact, this morning, while I was weeding, I had a chance to get focused on what I was going to say. How much I was going to tell you."

"How much?"

"Some things are really private," said Cindy. "But now that we're here, let me tell you what happened. Even though I can't believe I'm doing it."

"Doing what?"

"Talking about my sex life as raw material for a screenplay. You know what? Maybe I should skip this."

But she didn't skip it. Instead, she reminded me that this boyfriend of hers, so manic about issues, so upset about the universe, so voracious in his reading, so frenetic in his walking style, seemed to lack normal sexual intensity. She had a number of theories—he was gay, nervous, preoccupied, had an ethical problem, or, most likely, he'd been emasculated by his gnosticism, within which he frowned on "depravity." He sometimes talked about an Epiphanius, who'd castigated nudity, love feasts, and orgies—Epiphanius, John William droned on, who joined with Jerome to denounce Origen as a heretic; Origen who, in accordance with Matthew 19:12, castrated himself; who nevertheless seemed sound to John William in his espousal not only of reincarnation but of "apocatastasis, the salvation of everybody." But what was John William talking about? Instead of trying to unbutton her pants? Sitting on a log in Reed's wet canyon with its vista of a marsh full of rotting alders, he argued, aloud, with long-forgotten Carpocratians instead of making normal young-male advances. His kisses were pleasurable, but he wouldn't move beyond them; he never made a search inside her clothing.

It was late January. Her inability to break up with him had gotten critical. There seemed no way to do it. The rain in Portland had reached what she hoped was a wintry crescendo, true downpours driven on a south wind that overwhelmed the storm drains and the campus buildings' quaint copper downspouts. The sky hovered not far overhead, dense and in motion, as if churned by this malicious Jehovah John William talked about. She didn't like it, but she and John William kept perambulating like lovers and striding intently through canvassing expeditions, since she was now a foot soldier in his "Restructure Reed" campaign, which entailed just the two of them. They would be walking through a neighborhood, and he would point out how the roots of the elms had reared up the pavements as if insisting on their rights, and Cindy would fight the urge to push him up against a telephone pole and reach into his under-wear. Then, one day, it occurred to her: sex might be the way out.

The following Saturday was propitiously sunny; the sky cleared for her spicy if lugubrious plan. Their idea—her idea—was to take a blanket and go into Oaks Park to look for butterflies awakened briefly by this unseasonable warmth. She lied. She said her biology professor had mentioned a bloom of California tortoiseshells that might show up on a sudden sunny day in winter. So they went, she and John William, with the thin blanket from her dorm-room bed in the day-hiker's backpack she'd gotten from her parents for Christ-mas, and with a box of Chilean cherries from a roadside market. In a stand of cottonwoods above the river, they spread out the blanket and ate their fruit. The spot was lonely. Winter sunlight penetrated the forest whitely and lit the lichens spackling the trees. Cindy wore a ribbed sweater, a black moleskin skirt, and a utility jacket—all Goodwill finds—with mid-calf woolen socks, tan patrol boots, and—a final touch—her Patty Hearst beret. Her pink legs had purposely not been stuffed into winter hose for this occasion; she sat on them spitting cherry pits by folding her tongue around them and, with her lips shaped like a small O, blowing. Then she brought out rolling papers and a film can of dope.

For a while, they passed cherries between their mouths and smoked. He didn't entirely lose himself in it, but she did feel that he'd been slowed enough to enjoy what they were doing. Cindy licked a fruity excrescence from the corners of his lips until, in his bravest moment yet, he tried to reciprocate, lapping at her face with a hint of vulgarity, although primarily politely, as if cleaning up a child's mess. She felt hopeful until John William stopped their lin-gual lovefest to keep the empty cherry bag from blowing away on a gust of wind. Freshly determined, she stuck a second joint between his lips and lit it. ("The original date-rape drug," she said at Star-bucks.) Miraculously, a few butterflies made their appearance; one fell into the coarse nap of their blanket, where they inspected it, Cindy on her hands and knees. In short, she was doing everything in her power to direct her own porn film. All the elements were in place for outdoor sex. A blonde coed on a blanket in the forest rearing up in feigned innocence to note a butterfly, her throat stained by cherry juice, her ears red and labial, her shiny hair cascading, her beret a little militant, and her patrol boots untied. And beside her the handsome but clueless young buck, in need of initiation.

They stood. She worked on him to kiss more lewdly. At first he seemed repulsed, but she held his tongue against the floor of his mouth in an intimation of dominance, and his reaction was to seize her by the shoulders more forcefully, which she thought was promising, which she thought intimated a quelled sadism and contained the spark of a truly libidinous response. Cindy pressed herself to him from knees to sternum. This time, he didn't pull away. She threw off her beret and opened her jacket. ("So embarrassing, but I knew my good features.") The pull-chain zipper on her ribbed sweater caught sunlight. She locked her hands in the small of his back so as to gain purchase should he attempt a retreat. All freshly erotic to her—a boy who smelled good and wanted to get away must be snared by all possible wiles, and the use of those wiles, in league with the spur of her anticipated betrayal, propelled her enjoyment.

"What was it I wanted? I thought that if I did something coarse he might be appalled enough to drop me, although I just plain wanted him, too. Admittedly a confused strategy, but, then, I was dealing with a confused person, a guy who, I hate to say this, was a prig, which is a term I use with hesitation, because I don't want to denigrate his moralism, I really don't—I didn't sit down with you to do that. But you know what? I also wanted passion. He'd sort of driven me nuts for three or four months with his tender kisses followed by nothing. I'd done two things that morning," said Cindy. "Number one, I'd put on a clean and soapy-smelling floral-embossed bra; and, number two, I'd doused my cleavage with some Chanel N⁰ 5 I'd gotten in a free-sample mister. Anyway, I hooked his finger in my zipper ring and sort of worked up onto my tiptoes until the zipper went down and the point of his finger was where I'd spritzed the Chanel. And finally John William had his hands on my boobs. After all that time we'd gone together, he was finally doing what a normal guy would have done in ten seconds."

Cindy shook the last ice in her Frappuccino. "Every girl knows that the way to really own a guy—here I go with something really humiliating—is to get on your knees in front of him. I'm not going to be explicit about this, and I feel ridiculous talking about it, but you know what I mean. You know what I'm getting at. Guys have all kinds of terms for it. 'Play the clarinet' or 'go French the hard way' or whatever you guys say between yourselves in the locker room. I was going to, you know, *gam*, as the English put it, except I assumed he'd wake up from the spell I had him under in time to stop me. So this is very strange. I was at that moment men put so much stock in: about to unbuckle his belt and— I'm not going to flesh this out because it's totally embarrassing. I'll just say—you know what?—it didn't work. If you catch my drift. And skipping the mechanics of whatever you want to call it. Because he let me go ahead. That's right, buried inside of him was a guy like any other guy who wanted to be worked on in the way I keep talking around. I hate details, but I did have his jeans and his underwear down, and, no matter the guy, there's something really pathetic and vulnerable about that, the legs with the underwear wrapped around them—like I said, I hate details; the light of day is painful. How am I going to say this? The whole aura of what we'd been doing with the cherries and my sweater zipper and so on just evaporated; that's the easy way to describe it. I mean, suddenly it was winter in Portland in some clammy, dirty woods, and I couldn't make it happen for him no matter my efforts. I tried, but it was sad and futile. He was so uptight. He had his head turned to one side and his eyes squeezed shut, like I was about to light a firecracker in his face or something, or shoot him with a pistol. He was holding his breath. It was like he was in pain. It just didn't happen for him, and after a while I gave up. And this is typical—I felt terrible about myself. Can you believe that? I thought it was my fault instead of a problem he had—unbelievable. But here's the weird part," said Cindy. "He wasn't embarrassed. I've seen other guys go through this; they're so humiliated they don't know what to do next, how to handle it; they're freaking out. But not John William. John William *proposed* to me. He proposed when other guys would be endlessly apologizing. He got down on one knee and made this solemn speech, that he was ready to 'throw it all over,' whatever that meant, in the name of love, that we would 'from this day forward,' et cetera, whatever, the reunification of the duad or something—it was that type of elocution, like he was reading a proclamation just before the tooting of a herald's little trumpet. He said we should drop out of Reed and find a place where we could build a cabin and grow vegetables and procreate; have I gone on long enough sarcastically about him for you to get the picture? I told him, 'Look, you're stoned right now, and things just got sort of weird between us,' and that's when he freaked out."

She'd spoken for an hour and forty-five minutes with no hint of sorrow, but now that changed. This woman with three children and a twenty-four-year marriage was remembering being nineteen in the woods near Oaks Park with burgeoning pain. Her voice trembled while she told me how John William reacted to this answer of hers—"Look, you're stoned right now, and things just got sort of weird between us"—this casual and pragmatic answer that was not an immediate yes. "There was the longest silence. I guess I'd made the wrong reply. I hadn't passed the test; the slipper didn't fit. He couldn't process that. He just stayed there on one knee staring at me, and finally he said my name, Cynthia—'Cynthia' instead of 'Cindy.' He said it twice while a couple of really huge tears rolled romantically down his face." Cindy tried to laugh. "He wasn't urging me toward anything," she said, "and there was no inflection of a question in the way he said my name; instead, I felt damned, judged, condemned, blamed—to go back to Juliet, what's in a name when it's said twice that way by a lover who feels metaphysically rejected? You know what? John William was serious. He was asking me to spend my life with him, and to this day I'm certain he meant it. But here's me: I told him, look, I like you a lot, but I'm not going to leave school and go live in the mountains. Well—bam. He got up and made tracks. The rapid exit as the solution to everything. And there's some symmetry to that. It was the same thing that happened after our first kiss. Retreat."

Cindy rotated in her chair to take in more of Starbucks—as if checking to see whether she was indeed free to speak—and then said, in a whisper, leaning toward me across her empty Frappuccino cup, "I actually really liked him. I even still think about him, the boy I knew at Reed who smelled so good and loved me like an idiot. And I'm not putting Bill down by saying that, you know. But it was just . . . a different kind of thing. One of those very rich moments in your life. Where do those golden rainbows end? Why is this song so sad? One of those kind of moments."

I LET HER RECOVER: I said I had to use the bathroom. There was a poster in there of a man in a bowler and spats riding an old-fashioned bicycle with a looming front wheel along the

Champs-Elysées while fair but faceless mademoiselles under parasols promenaded in the background. There was another of Monet as a shriveled old dwarf with a silver beard seated contemplatively on a wicker bench in his garden at Giverny. I passed a little time contemplating the shadow on Monet's face and admiring the climbing roses. Both posters were clichéd. They would achieve the status of kitsch among a future generation—assuming there is a future generation. In the Starbucks bathroom, I doubted there would be. I suppose I was in John William's frame of mind right then—everything seemed proof of something wrong with the world as it was currently configured. Yes, the paper towels were an 80-percent postconsumer-waste product, but what about the other 20 percent? Could humanity sustain that? When a question of this sort travels with you to the bathroom, life's unpleasant. You aren't going about with the necessary blinders on; your mind sees, in every scene and object, some harbinger of retribution and apocalypse. There's then some logic in seeking a breast to rest on, just as there's logic in abjuring social action. Why put yourself in the way? Why struggle against Jehovah? Embracing impermanence, the soul finds something that feels like rest, or at least a sustainable modicum of acceptance. Then the solitary searcher, like a climbing rose, is domesticated, and wants only a corner of the garden in which to thrive while twining, sunnily, with a complementing blossom.

She seemed better. She seemed composed. There was some denouement to share—that John William spoke to her only one more time, to demand the return of all the street-fair baubles and bangles he'd presented her with that fall ("I'm leaving no part of myself with you, Cynthia"); that she returned them; that he rigorously disdained her subsequently; that in February he was in the student paper for chaining himself to the radiator in the school president's office while brandishing a petition; that she saw him more than once, with a nascent beard, standing under the branches of a plane tree in a campus courtyard, calling for the shutdown of the college, and distributing broadsides. That she disavowed, or at least diminished, her past intimacy with him when the subject was broached by friends ("We went out a few times, but the guy was too intense"); that she came on him once watching wood ducks in the canyon and assayed a rapprochement ("I love watching wood ducks");

that in March she overheard someone in the cafeteria say that "the barefoot speechifier" had departed campus—and that all this happened while she also took up skiing, led craft activities for disadvantaged children, experimented with acid, and worked at the Hauser Library. "John William basically went downhill very quickly. Everyone saw it—Reed's a small place. Privately, I felt criminal about it, but isn't that kind of self-inflating? To think that by spurning him I pushed him down a hole? In my saner and more lucid moments, I knew I had nothing to do with his strangeness—it was there before me and it was still there after me. If not me, someone else; if not someone else, then something else."

Cindy brushed nonexistent crumbs from her smock. "I have a confession to make," she said, sounding furtive. "Yes, I'm very, very interested in a screenplay collaboration. I'm hoping we can at least exchange contact information. I'd like to see us go forward with a dialogue. It's not completely a harebrained plan. But the fact of the matter is that talking about John William has, until now, been an obstacle for me. I've had a terrible resistance to talking about him. What's interesting to my therapist is this constant resistance. He—"

She was crying, so I went for napkins.

4

COUNTRYMAN—GET OUT HERE
BEFORE IT'S TOO LATE

ALMOST ALL OF MY STUDENTS noticed me in the papers. Mainly, they celebrated my dark-horse celebrity, treated me as if I'd won the state lottery, or commented critically on my annual photo, but in Nature in Literature, an elective for students who view themselves as college-bound, someone asked if John William was like Thoreau, probably because we'd read *Walden* together, and I answered that I didn't think we could put Thoreau above Dickinson when it comes to hermitry. There were, after all, Thoreau's visitors at Walden and his excursions to Concord for meals with his mother, whereas Dickinson, I told my class, was truly hermitic, and didn't leave the grounds of her family's estate for a quarter-century. As it turned out, one of my students had written on Dickinson in American Studies the previous semester, and told us that the Belle of Amherst, unwilling to leave the second floor of her house for about seven years, had been known to lower, from her bedroom window, baskets of gingerbread, tied to a rope, into the arms of neighborhood children, but this didn't mean she was a hermit by choice, only that, most probably, she suffered from an anxiety disorder called agoraphobia, or fear of public places. Which came first, I wanted privately to know, the mental chaos or the retiring?

AFTER TOURING EUROPE, I flew home with Jamie Shaw's phone
number not only in my wallet but in one of my journals, too. I was
keeping them apart, in case I lost one. In my bedroom, I emptied my
pack onto the rug—the dirty laundry, the camping gear from San
Sebastián, the cold-weather gear from San Vigilio, the used boots
from Innsbruck—and already these things looked archival. I started
the laundry and put the gear in the basement. With my French tailoring scissors, I trimmed my beard as closely as I could and shaved
the rest, cleaning up afterward with a broom and a vacuum, and then
I lay down and read passages in my journals until my father came
home. He said he'd fallen off some scaffolding in July, and that this
misstep had slowed him, and then, in the kitchen, we talked about
my trip—all of it but Jamie—while eating egg sandwiches. My
father said that Carol had a new apartment but still worked at Bar
Mart, a restaurant-supply company, and that my cousin Keith, it had
come to light that summer, was diabetic, and had to sit down on the
job sometimes to eat a pan of brownies. I asked if there were phone
messages or mail for me, and my father produced a folder on which
he'd written my name. Patiently, he ate Fritos from the bag while I
looked at my messages. No one had called from Portland.

After washing the dishes, we settled into *Hawaii Five-O*. This is
how it was before I left—the widower in the evening with his only
son, lights off, television on. When he fell asleep in his chair, I
looked at my mail, which included a bank statement indicating a
depleted account, my college schedule and tuition bill, and a postcard showing a logging truck hauling a single enormous log toward
a mill. On the back, in inelegant capitals, it read:

COUNTRYMAN—

AT BADEN-BADEN THROUGH 9/4 THEN GOIN'
TO GIT EJUKATID.
GET OUT HERE BEFORE IT'S TOO LATE.

BLOOD,

SIMON MAGUS

I went to the bookshelf and looked up Baden-Baden in the '64 *World Book Encyclopedia* my mother had worn down my father about buying, because, worldly as I was after my turn on the Continent, I didn't know about those famous German thermal baths. I also looked up Simon Magus, but there was no entry for anyone by that name. COUNTRYMAN—GET OUT HERE BEFORE IT'S TOO LATE. Too late literally, as in a date on a calendar, or too late in some deeper, more ambiguous fashion? COUNTRYMAN—GET OUT HERE BEFORE IT'S TOO LATE: I saw it as a directive and a warning both, urgent, dramatic, ambiguous, comic, friendly, condescending, and grave. I see now that I parsed it incorrectly by deciding to focus on its possible humor, by deciphering it as a parody of something I couldn't put my finger on. I also read it, or misread it, as a fresh call to danger in the woods. I thought he was saying we ought to get lost again. I thought I was invited to punish myself in hidden places for the pleasure of it one more time. I thought he wanted to get me killed amid great exhiliration. But, as I said, I was wrong in translating John William's note, missing my friend's tone and misconstruing his content. COUNTRYMAN—GET OUT HERE BEFORE IT'S TOO LATE: part of its presumption, if you didn't read in humor, was its dismissal of my summer—though "Baden-Baden," I should have understood, paid it oblique homage—or its dismissal of me, more broadly speaking, as if everything I did, or was doing, or would do was in the way of something under John William's auspices that mattered more.

Around midnight, when my father went to bed, I called Jamie. I said I was sorry to call her so late, and she answered, "I'm a night owl." I said I didn't have a reason for calling other than curiosity about Erin, and Jamie said that Erin had quit school and was getting treatment from a psychiatrist in Pocatello, adding, "My dad doesn't want to pay for it, but my mom does," and then immediately asking if I'd read *The Bell Jar*. I remember feeling grateful to Jamie for directing our conversation onto open ground, where the point of a topic was its discussion. So that was a long phone call. We talked like friends, easily, although I'd gotten to the point, after parting with her in Rome, where I felt sick to my stomach about Jamie. Near the end of our conversation she said, "Hey, if you're ever coming through Portland, check in with me." I said I would call in that circumstance, and I did call, thirty-six hours later, and said I was coming through in a few days, but I lied, of course, because I wasn't coming through, Portland was where I was going.

The day after I flew home from Europe, I went to the Barry house on East Laurelhurst Drive; my idea being to requisition some scotch, vodka, or bourbon from the *Cornucopia II* in preparation for an afternoon with some Countrymen cousins. Instead, I found John William's father, after jogging down a flagstoned side path, and having rung the front doorbell and getting what the burglar hopes for: no answer. It was a late-summer Saturday, and he was on his patio, not far from the lake, in view of his sloop, reading a newspaper in shorts, a polo shirt, white socks, and deck shoes. Under the shade of a tilted umbrella, on a wrought-iron chaise longue with wheels and cushions, Mr. Barry wore black plastic glasses. Over the years, this style of glasses—Buddy Holly's style—has waxed and waned, but mostly they've functioned as a comic prop or as a prosthetic for the elderly urbane, sometimes appearing on the faces of mods or dissonantly on generals hauled before the press. But what I want to say is that, on his patio, reading in the breeze from off Lake Washington and before he became aware of me, Mr. Barry didn't look tranquil. In this naturally tranquil scene, behind the house in Laurelhurst, with lake water lapping, beside the backyard lawn and the brick walkway in a herringbone pattern, by the planting beds in late summer, not far from the dock, the boat, and the semi-dwarf plum trees, and near some wisteria twining on an arbor, Mr. Barry read, I would have to say, as if it was burdensome. There was no radio, no drinking glass, no garden tools in the scene, or on the scene's periphery as if waiting for him—just newspaper sections stacked on the side table and, on top of them, acting as a paperweight, his glasses case.

John William's father, in the summer of '74, was the age I am now—fifty. I'd seen, in the house, displayed in a hall, framed photos, with captions, from his younger years—one at Cape Canaveral; a second in the cockpit of a Dash 80, shaking hands with a pilot; a third with Boeing brass at a party, holding a highball glass; a fourth on the tarmac at Boeing Field, standing on risers with a group of Japanese businessmen—and in each he wore the same nervous expression etching his face on that August Saturday morning when I startled him by appearing, unannounced, behind his house. In fact, I had the impression he thought I was going to rob or attack him; then quickly he understood it was just me, a friend of his son's, and that his luck had held. Mr. Barry's legs were already to one side, probably to keep his shoe soles off the chaise-longue cushions, so he was able to swivel up, defensively, not to his feet but to a seated position, with his newspaper section tucked in his lap, and there he removed his glasses. "It's considerate to make some noise," he said, "unless you're the advance scouting party."

"Okay."

"Do you have our phone number?" But the question was rhetorical, in the sense that he was asking me not to surprise him in the future by coming around to the patio. On went Mr. Barry—"You're weary of advice from adults, but clear your throat next time"—and he showed me how to do it, clearing his own against a muffling fist, as though this was a lesson in etiquette. I tried but could see no humor in him. I'm not going to say it was a sense of entitlement that governed Mr. Barry's tone as he spoke to me, but, on the other hand, it might have been that, or partially that, there on the patio, where he was taking his lonely leisure so stringently in the breeze from off the lake.

Mr. Barry made small talk with me. On hearing that I'd gone to Europe, he was moved to say that a stint on Munda, where he'd served with the 73rd Seabees Battalion, was what he'd done in lieu of the grand tour I'd taken. On hearing that I would shortly begin freshman classes at the University of Washington, he named two regents he knew. Mr. Barry said that he'd forgotten my name, and when I reminded him of it he told me that a Countryman, years ago, had refurbished his master bathroom. Then, a little strenuously, he committed me to memory. "Neil Countryman," he said. "*Neil*. Have you heard from John William? He hasn't called or written since June."

Our younger son, when he was twenty, disappeared like this, too. He thought surfing was the greatest thing in life and, with $80 in his pocket earned sanding for a painter, went, by himself, on a freighter, with his surfboard, to the Andaman Islands in the Bay of Bengal. I say this to underscore that I understand, retrospectively, Mr. Barry's feelings that morning on the patio. During the summer our son was gone, I saw two of his friends in Ravenna Park, and under the no-doubt transparent guise of small talk asked them what they'd heard from him—as if that was just another question, equal in weight to my questions about their jobs and warm-weather recreations. In other words, I know about these preludes—so falsely unalarmed—to a parent's actual subject, though I didn't grasp the matter back then, on the patio, when John William's father asked me, barely hiding his urgency, if I'd heard lately from his son.

"No."

Mr. Barry, in response, straightened the newspaper on his thighs, put his glasses in their case, rose off his chaise longue, and checked the *Cornucopia II* as a passing speedboat, hauling a water-skier, caused its mooring lines to creak and its hull to rise and fall with the water. He seemed frozen by this daredevil's antics and the rippling of Lake Washington under his sloop, and that seemed to me an opening, or a momentary liberation, and I said, "I think I better go."

"You think you better go."

Once again, his tone suggested humorlessness, and so, taking the easy way out, I said "Thanks," that serviceable and meaningless conclusion to dialogue employed by teen-agers as an exit strategy. I've had students who do this, thanking me when no thanks are due, just so they can get out of the room.

I BORROWED my sister's car and went to Portland. I found out there, while browsing with Jamie at a used-book store, that Simon Magus was "the father of Christian gnosticism." In the religion-and-philosophy section, between high shelves, Jamie told me that without my beard I no longer reminded her of Al Pacino in *Serpico*, and that I now looked more like Pete Maravich, the NBA basketball player well known then for his behind-the-back passes and floppy socks. We walked around Portland for a long time with no destination, and then bought, at a corner store, two apples, some rolls, a block of cheese, and a bottle of wine, and took this meal up to Jamie's apartment, where she lived with another PSU student named Gail Thornton.

In the kitchen this morning, I asked Jamie if she remembered this small dinner in Portland. She'd forgotten it. She said that, for her, "things blur together." Then we searched through photo albums until we found what we were looking for—a photo of Jamie's apartment building in Portland, the Casablanca, which was faced with what looked like white fish-tank gravel. Most of its tenants were students, so there were a lot of bicycles locked to the railings, and, by the trash bin in the alley, damp pieces of jettisoned furniture. In the photo, Gail and Jamie are moving in, muscling a sofa up outdoor stairs. There's another of Jamie wearing a red bandanna and, with a nylon brush, scrubbing her toilet. There's a third of her standing inside the open door of her refrigerator, guzzling from a wine bottle and, it's clear from her expression, trying not to laugh. None of this helped—Jamie, this morning, still couldn't remember the rolls, cheese, apples, and wine, or sitting on the sofa during dinner listening to an Aretha Franklin album, or going to see *Lacombe, Lucien* later that night in a run-down theater, or that there were panhandlers on the street as we walked back to the Casablanca. I remember all these things, as arbitrary as they sound, as well as sleeping on the sofa after four or five glasses of Chianti poured from a gallon jug and, because it was kept in a broom closet, warm. Jamie is blank on these details, but she does recall that, at some point before dinner, we walked along streets in the Kings Heights neighborhood, noting trees and bushes we liked in yards, and noting, too, houses we admired and—this is what Jamie sees as important—we both responded to simple, clean lines and to façades pleasing in their symmetries. I have no doubt this happened, if she says it did, but I don't remember the streets or the conversation. I do remember that, as I lay there on the sofa, with my Chianti glass—a jam jar—on the floor beside me, I thought about getting up and going into Jamie's bedroom, fully dressed as I was, and curling against her back without saying anything about it, but I didn't do that. I just lay there thinking of it apprehensively. There was a lot of noise from an adjacent apartment, male and female voices and a stereo with the bass turned up, and around two, Jamie went past me barefoot, wrapped in a blanket, and took care of the problem, and then we sat in the living room—me on the sofa and Jamie in a chair—and talked in soft voices, in the dark, about the tenants next door and their propensity to throw parties, and about *Lacombe, Lucien,* how we felt about it these hours later and whether its emotional weather remained with us. Finally, I said, "What should we do tomorrow?"

Jamie, still wrapped in her blanket, said, "What should we do right now?"

Our bungalow is empty, on a lot of days, except for me, and I admit to liking this as long as it's fruitful, a category that is, in my view, expansive, and includes, among other things that might appear idle, the exertion of memory. I have a tendency, in fact, to place events in memory while they're happening, which might be construed as detachment from experience, although in the end this simultaneity is, instead of something else, the experience I'm having. I remember telling myself, that first time with Jamie on my first night in Portland, not to forget what was happening as it happened, and now having told myself not to forget is bound up with the rest of that memory.

The next day, in a shop housing clutter, Jamie bought a cheap pair of Ph.D. spectacles, granny glasses with no magnification. I've failed to mention that she's three years older than me, which in the beginning was something we both liked. Those glasses, so owlishly large, were a sham, because her eyesight was perfect; they'd been discarded, and she'd retrieved them as a potentially useful prop. Gail Thornton had something of this self-parodic air, too—she used a pencil to lock her hair bun together before going out at night— and it was a joke between them. But mostly Gail wasn't in the picture. Mostly, in her apartment at the Casablanca, Jamie and I drank warm Chianti and listened to used LPs. In '74, we were retro, largely because music was cheaper that way. I can call up Coltrane, Quicksilver Messenger Service, the Seeds, and *Cheap Thrills.* Jamie had a record player in her room that could deliver five album sides successively, each new one dropping while the stylus rotated out of the way, so that you didn't have to think about anything.

We walked up Nob Hill on the day after Jamie got her glasses. I bought a copy of the *Kalevala*—the national epic of the Finns—since a used illustrated copy of it was on sale for next to nothing and both Jamie and I were enamored of the pictures. Later, we lay on Jamie's bed admiring these, and eventually my eyes closed. When I woke up, Jamie was sitting against two pillows with her glasses on, read-

THE OTHER

ing the *Kalevala* studiously. "Hey," she said, "I have a question for you. 'Shall I open up the casket, / Treasure box of magic sayings, / Strip the end off from the yarnball, / And undo the knot entirely?' " I said, "Those are beautiful lines," and she answered, "It must be cold in Finland," and put the book on the side table.

Blissful day the fourth in the City of Roses. We bought the Sunday *Seattle Times* and *The Sunday Oregonian* at the Magazine Emporium on Broadway. We went to bed in the late afternoon, and when I woke I heard rain, heavily, in the courtyard of the Casablanca. As before, Jamie was sitting up against pillows with an exaggerated straight face, peering over the top of her glasses, but this time with a pencil pressed against her lower lip while she worked on a crossword. "You're good," I said, and she immediately replied, "I could use a clipboard and a lab coat."

Into this Eden some gloom was interjected when I read on the page of *Seattle Times* obituaries about the death of John William's grandmother. "Dorothy Worthington, 77, Granddaughter of City Founder." Among the stories about the dead that day, hers led, and it began with "Heiress to a considerable fortune, Dorothy Best Worthington was well known in Seattle for her collection of antiquities and for her lifelong devotion to the Cornish School."

Mrs. Worthington was the daughter of Lydia Strong Post—whose father, Hiram Post, was a member of the Denny Party—and of Henry Carter Best, founder of Seattle's Best Trust and Savings Bank.

Traveling to the Near East on numerous occasions, Mrs. Worthington gradually amassed what is widely considered the city's most significant private collection of antiquities. A patron not only of the Cornish School but of Northwest painters, Mrs. Worthington was a leading light in Seattle's art community for many years.

"She liked to travel in the grand style," said her assistant, Lucy Hatch. "She was a dedicated amateur Hellenist who was generous in sharing her collection with the public."

Mrs. Worthington, a woman of many talents, died at her Madison Park home August 29 of kidney failure. She was 77.

Besides her interest in antiquities and Northwest art, Mrs. Worthington was a devoted and knowledgeable gardener. During World War II she funded the removal of Himalayan rhododendrons to the Pacific Northwest for cultivation and research.

She also made numerous gifts to the Cornish School and was

instrumental in inspiring other benefactors. "Our music program in particular is indebted to Dorothy Worthington," said Phyllis Wood, a fund-raiser for Cornish. "In recent years she came to every recital and was a gracious and welcome presence."

Born Dorothy Post Best in Seattle in 1897, Mrs. Worthington attended Mount Holyoke College in South Hadley, Massachusetts. In 1922, she married Cyrus Worthington, president of Worthington Timber from 1932 to 1967. With her husband and daughter she lived for many years in Madison Park and in a second home in the Highlands, where her antiquities were often on display.

Family and friends remember Mrs. Worthington as erudite and serious, but also capable of humor. "Dorothy had written instructions for the annual installation of the family Christmas tree," recalls Lucy Hatch. "Yet she was able to laugh one year when it tipped over during a Yule party."

In her later years, Mrs. Worthington took up the piano. According to Ms. Hatch, she read avidly during prolonged sessions of kidney dialysis over the final nine months of her life.

Mrs. Worthington is survived by her only child, Virginia Barry, of Taos and Seattle, and by one grandchild, John William Barry. She was preceded in death by her husband, Cyrus, in 1971.

A graveside memorial will be held at . . .

This all struck a chord with me because in the winter of '73 I'd helped John William move a piano for Dorothy Worthington. One afternoon, we went to her home in Madison Park, a mansion better suited, I thought, to a plantation in the South, because it had tall columns and a widow's walk. Inside, the furniture looked monumental, with shells, eagles, and leaves for touches, and the foyer smelled like tarnish paste. It was dark in there, and drafty even with the radiators percolating. We were led by Mrs. Worthington's assistant— a woman with a lustrous silver pageboy, in jeans—into a conservatory: white wicker, a small television, and a view of rhododendron bushes seized by frost. There was also a space heater on wheels, and a folded-back *TV Guide*. After ten or fifteen minutes, Mrs. Worthington shuffled in, announced, "The punctual piano-movers have arrived on *shed-ule*," and kissed John William on both cheeks. There was lipstick on her teeth. She wore a cardigan cable-stitch sweater and brandished a glass-handled cane. She had a man's jaw and looked a little pop-eyed, plain like Eleanor Roosevelt but with the rimless glasses of Harry Truman. "Tell me," she said, sitting down in a wicker rocker. "How are you enjoying the Lakeside School?"

"It's great," said John William.

"Dexter Strong, you know, was a good friend of your grandfather's."

John William scratched his head.

"We knew Bob Adams, too."

"I don't know Bob Adams."

"Bob Adams was headmaster," said Mrs. Worthington. "You're looking so virile these days, John William, with your wonderful, poetic head of hair."

To me, she sounded like Katharine Hepburn—like somebody from the horsy set as it might have existed before color television. The tremulous tone of her patter was benign and scary at the same time. I noticed that her shoes were orthopedic, and that she kept her chin tilted, as she spoke, to good advantage. Her gaze was aggressive, and her cane could have been a prop. John William said, "This is Neil Countryman. He's moved a lot of pianos in his time, and I thought he might be useful."

Mrs. Worthington smiled. "Neil Countryman," she said. "I like the sound of that. Are you interested in painting?"

"Yes."

"Behind me here, in the next room, is an Ambrose Patterson worth a little of your time."

I'd thought she meant house painting. I'd thought she might have had a job for me painting a room or a wall. "Okay," I said.

"There are also some wonderful Tobey murals in the house, and a Clayton Price which you'll see when, I suppose the phrase is, we tackle the piano. Are you Punctual Petes ready to tackle the piano?"

We made a long, slow trip behind her through dark rooms. Around a corner, the silver-haired assistant was waiting for us, standing with her hands clasped in the doorway of a study where a fire burned. "Lucy," said Mrs. Worthington, "Lucy, this is Neil Countryman. Don't you think 'Countryman' is a wonderful name?"

"I do think so."

"And my grandson, John William."

"Hail," said Lucy.

We traveled on—Lucy, as it turned out, was just acknowledging our passing, and returned to her desk work and fire. Then we came to what I think you would call a drawing room. That's of course an antiquated term, "drawing room," but it wasn't hard to imagine that here, in the past, the Worthingtons had entertained guests. Now this drawing room was a music studio smelling humidly of Turkish rugs. It was lined with books, and it housed a few of Mrs. Worthington's antiquities—for example, a fragment of a black jar, a jug, and a bronze warrior on horseback. To me it felt cryptlike, with its drawn shades and ancient knickknacks. "Your adversary," said Mrs. Worthington, meaning her piano. "And you thought this would be easy."

It was a Bösendorfer grand with an ebony finish. For a moment we stood admiring its strings and hammers; then John William, unsolicited, swung a rod out of the way and closed the top. "Where to?" he said.

"Darling," said Mrs. Worthington.

She called our attention to some rug scraps on the piano bench by prodding them with the rubber tip of her cane. "Look down," she said. "Those are some very unfortunate fir floorboards Grandfather Cyrus coerced me into in 1957. So I asked Lucy to bring up four scraps. The idea is that one of you strong young men will *carefully* lift a corner of the piano, and the other will slip a scrap under the wheel. You will notice that my scraps have a top and a bottom. I want the soft side down, of course. We'll coddle these floorboards." She tapped an orthopedic shoe, as if in a test. "I have Palladian furnishings," she said. "Strong, solid pieces. Underneath some of my carpets, there's damage. Men who worry their hair about, to hide their bald spots—I'm like that with my Douglas-fir floors. Do you remember the Highlands?"

"Yes," said John William.

"Very hard, very nice oak floors."

"I recall."

"When were you there?"

"Christmas. Three weeks ago."

Mrs. Worthington said, "Oh dear."

We moved her piano. She only wanted it rotated, really, so that while playing she was closer to the radiator.

In the conservatory once more, we each drank a glass of water. Lucy joined us for this restorative, and I was made to divulge that I lived in North Seattle and attended Roosevelt. "The Teddies," said Mrs. Worthington. "But how, then, did you boys meet?"

John William, with his forefingers, trapped his forelocks behind his ears. "Not everyone I know goes to Lakeside," he told her.

"Of course not," replied Mrs. Worthington.

"Countryman's not a sellout," John William said. "He wants to be a writer—a novelist."

Lucy seemed interested in this piece of news and turned in my direction. Since she looked intelligent and fit nicely in her jeans, I found her gaze embarrassing and tried not to redden, which made it happen. Lucy said Gary Snyder had grown up in Lake City, and Mary McCarthy had grown up in Madrona; also, that Alice B. Toklas had attended Seattle University at the turn of the century. Mrs. Worthington added that the vaudeville impresario Alexander Pantages had once lived around the corner. We finished our water and looked at the Ambrose Patterson in the next room—it was called *Rocky Landscape*—at the Tobey murals—which to me looked like scribbling—and finally at the Clayton Price, which Mrs. Worthington said had "a scumbled surface and somber, earthy tones." Then, at the door, she took John William's hand in her own and said, "Tell me, how is your mother doing?"

"She's in Taos."

"You're fending for yourself?"

"Always."

"You're not in need?"

"I'm not in need."

"Do you hear from her?"

"No."

Mrs. Worthington's fingers twisted around her cane handle. "Oh dear," she said. "Oh, Virginia."

She kissed John William's cheek. She patted his head. My friend put his arms, for a moment, around his grandmother. "Never you mind," she said. "None of it's your fault, love—none of it."

"I feel like it is."

"Tsk," said Mrs. Worthington. "There, now."

John William and I went to the curb and got in the Impala. "Sorry," he said to me, while waving to his grandmother.

"We moved her piano two inches."

"I've met Lucy a hundred times—two hundred times."

"Dahling," I said. "You *must* see the Clayton Price."

"My grandfather cut down all the trees in five counties," John William replied, "so my grandmother could buy all those finger-paintings."

I STAYED TOO LONG in Portland. The "9/4" deadline named on John William's postcard came and went without my noticing. In fact, I was parked at a rest stop between Portland and Seattle, on my way home, when I remembered it, and I only remembered it because the postcard fell into my lap when I pulled the visor down so I could take a nap without the sun in my eyes. COUNTRYMAN—AT BADEN-BADEN THROUGH 9/4 THEN GOIN' TO GET EJUKATID. GET OUT HERE BEFORE IT'S TOO LATE. BLOOD, SIMON MAGUS. It was 9/5, and John William was at Reed.

I had two weeks before my own classes started, so I bought a one-ton stakebed from my uncle Lynn for $200, in the full knowledge that its steering was perilously loose, and went to work cutting firewood with his son Keith, the diabetic. At first, something gyroscopic seemed to govern that truck; driving it was like maneuvering a bumper car, a lot of fruitless overcompensating and futile swings of the wheel against emptiness. With a load of wood on board, this uncorralled skating was slightly less deranged; even so, I decided to replace the steering box myself, salvaging a used one from a wrecking yard and installing it via guesswork, but this turned out to be a mistake, because after that you needed the shoulders of an Atlas to budge the wheel, and had to lift yourself off the seat and throw your weight left or right while pushing and pulling, with muscular zeal, just to change lanes. I felt safer at this end of the steering spectrum, though, and with a less dedicated effort could hold a straight line on the road.

Keith and I flailed away at alders no one wanted near Monroe, in woods where a subdivision was supposed to materialize, as we were told by Uncle Lynn, who said he knew the developer. We ran a pair of heavy, whining Homelites, wore greasy chaps and silver hard hats, and skidded logs with the stakebed and a rusty cable. Keith had to stop often and eat brownies or Rice Krispie treats. One morning, he nicked his boot open with his Homelite—you could see not only the wound in the leather but the scored surface of the steel toe underneath. Mostly, Keith liked to sit on a log with a radio on and a joint between his fingers. It's hard to say which was more tiring, cutting firewood or driving the stakebed, but fortunately Keith enjoyed battling my botched steering-box job so he could grimace theatrically while excoriating my mechanical abilities. I let him.

We served, mostly, the satisfied clients of Countryman remodelers. One of my uncles would transform a couple's bathroom and they'd be so delighted they'd call again about their kitchen, and after that it was an easy matter for Keith to work from a list he'd developed, introducing himself as a Countryman and marketing our firewood. He'd make the sale and get careful directions. I'd back the stakebed into a driveway, and we'd toss a cord out at high speed before collecting our check; or, for a little extra, we'd stack. It was fun to feel muscular in the presence of a householder standing by with his checkbook, or in the presence of any woman, or to be watched by children as if we were exotic. One day, while tossing wood into a driveway, I realized that the columns and widow's walk next door, beyond a low boxwood hedge, were Dorothy Worthington's, or had been Dorothy Worthington's before she died. There was a BMW in her driveway. There was also a late-model Econoline van, and now that I was paying attention to it I saw that its sliding door was open. A few minutes later, a guy wearing coveralls emerged from the garage carrying a crate, stowed it, and went in again, and a few minutes after that a Saab pulled up to the curb and Lucy Hatch got out. She was wearing jeans and a mid-length coat, and her silver hair was longer than it had been before, but no less lustrous. Lucy peered into the van's open sliding door and kept her head in there until the guy in coveralls reappeared with another crate. He stopped short. She spoke to him for a minute, her hands in her coat pockets. He set the crate on the flagstones, sat down in the van's sliding-door frame, and poked a cigarette between his lips. Lucy went into the house.

I told Keith, while we tossed wood, about moving the piano. I told him how rich Dorothy Worthington had been, and this made him wince. Then I asked him if he minded sitting in the truck for a few minutes, because I wanted to go next door to get an address.

Lucy let me in. She still had on her coat. I had to remind her about the piano first, and then I had to explain myself—that I wanted to write John William at Reed—before she relented and stopped blocking the door. I followed her through the foyer, then into the living room with its monumental furniture, and past the conservatory with its white wicker chairs. We passed the Ambrose Patterson and the Tobey murals. I noticed that Lucy's hair had a becoming inward flip at the back but was still perfectly coiffed. She said nothing, just walked with her hands in her coat pockets, until we reached the study, where a year and a half before she'd greeted John William and me from her post by the door while a fire burned behind her. Then Lucy said, "Let me dig out his info. You can have a seat."

I said, "I'm filthy. It's better if I stand."

She gave me a probing once-over now. "Hey," she said, "do I remember this right? You wanted to be a writer."

"Embarrassing."

"Why is that?"

"Everyone wants to be a writer."

She moved things on her desk with elegant fingers. I said, "I read in the paper about John William's grandma."

"Nightmare. Here it is. I'll write it down for you."

While she was doing so, another woman came to the door, older than Lucy but every bit as trim, and even more classy, tanned, with a strong chin. "Are you a mover?" she asked me.

"No."

"Then who are you?"

Lucy explained. "This is Neil Countryman, Ginnie. He's a friend of your son's."

John William's mother took me in with brazen scrutiny. I tried to take her in as well, without seeming to, and remembered her unibrow from the photo I'd seen of her with Ansel Adams, on the wall of her study. Her face was all planes. Her black—I want to say "raven"—hair was in a compact, glistening bun. She was dark-eyed, with flaring nostrils. There are women in their fifties whom young men recognize instinctively as sexually complex, and Ginnie was one of them. She made me nervous, and between her and Lucy, I didn't want to leave right away. "I'm getting his address," I said.

"Neil's been here before," added Lucy. "He helped move the piano for Dorothy."

John William's mother stayed in the doorway. She wore a small black sweater closed by a single button, hoop earrings, and a necklace of lacquered wooden beads. "Excuse me," she said. "The murals, Lucy. I need you to get me the paperwork."

Lucy said, "Ginnie, you know what I'm going to say."

Ginnie crossed her arms. She looked at me fleetingly. Then she said, "Say it anyway."

"You can't take the murals," answered Lucy.

Now Ginnie entered the room. Her gait was imperious. I stepped back and, thinking I should indicate this was none of my business, looked at the floor.

"I can too take the murals."

"Not according to Brent."

"Brent can call me."

"He already called you."

"Don't tell me what to do, Lucy."

"It's not what Dorothy stipulated."

"You're in my house."

"We're in Dorothy's house. Excuse me, Ginnie, I've got this address written out now." She beckoned, and I stepped up and took it from her.

"A friend of John William's," observed Ginnie.

"Yeah."

"I didn't know he had friends."

"He has me," I answered.

Ginnie assessed me with greater interest after that, before squeezing her hair bun, gently. The gesture was slow and made me even more nervous. She said, "How did you get here?"

"I was bringing firewood next door."

"And how did you meet my son?"

"I met him running track."

Her eyes narrowed, as if this answer was suspicious. "You didn't go to Lakeside?"

"I met him at a track meet."

"Noted," said Ginnie. "But where is he now? He's dropped off the map, apparently. I haven't heard a peep from John William."

"Me, neither."

"For months—*silencio*. Señor Silencio."

"Same here, but more like half a year."

Ginnie crossed her arms and held her biceps in her lovely hands. "So what do you think of my son?" she asked.

"He's a good guy," I told her. "You raised him well."

Ginnie tried not to, but she laughed at that, turning her head to one side and covering her mouth with her fist. Her hoop earrings swayed a little. She said, "Bravo," and laughed some more.

I said, "I have to go. My partner's waiting."

"Of course you do," answered Ginnie.

I scratched my cheek then, which is, in the parlance of our day, passive-aggressive. Ginnie mocked me by mimicking this gesture; no doubt she wanted me to see that I couldn't get away with it, that she read everything, and that my resistance, however minor, was as transparent as my attraction.

"Go," said Lucy. "Can you find your way out?"

I did.

I wrote John William. I said I'd heard about his grandmother. I explained about my firewood business and said I'd met his mother in Lucy Hatch's study. I told him about Jamie and described my trip to Europe. I said I'd gotten his aerogrammes. I said I was sorry I didn't get out there before it was too late—I told him getting out there hadn't been "in the cards," without mentioning my interlude in Portland. Finally, I asked about Reed.

I still have the two letters John William sent me from college. The first is rife with freshman mania: John William is interested in all of his classes, and, besides performing three hundred push-ups a day, five hundred sit-ups, and seventy-five chin-ups, he's taken to late-night long-distance runs and has limited his diet to fruits and vegetables. There's a description of the repaired mimeograph and of a zeal to change the world, or at least Reed College, by tomorrow. The urgency of this, he says, "precludes my coming home for Thanksgiving or Christmas, two drags anyway." He doesn't mention Cindy, nor is she mentioned in his second letter—written, I know now, on the heels of losing her. Instead, he urges me to drop everything immediately and devote myself strictly to the gnostic path. I should, he wrote, "confront the aspiration and restlessness of Neil Countryman's dissatisfied soul," and act on that, because "What else is there but this dream we endure, with all its miseries?" John William had tri-folded eight pages of cramped script. He wrote that there was "no good knowledge to be had in college," and asked me which I preferred, "death and darkness or light and life?"

Scary, but, as far as gnosticism goes, I'm not against learning a little more. Life could indeed be nothing but a dream, and at least some of the time it does seem miserable—if that's what Gnostics believe, if that's what John William believed, I'm willing to look into it, though it doesn't sound like something I agree with. Which is not to suggest I have my own metaphysics, though I do hold with, or at least have an affinity for, "There is no death, only a change of worlds," reputedly the final words of Chief Seattle's 1854 treaty oration. In the end, though, I would probably have to say that, in a way, my religion is home and all that attends it. I wouldn't blame anyone for feeling averse to that, because home is a place I eventually have to leave, and then what have I done, by giving myself to it, other than pave the way for my own suffering? No doubt I'll pay the price for love, too, in the end. Home and love—so unwanted, and wanted, by John William. There are some lines from the Buddhist sage Shantideva on this subject that seem about right. "While I am lying in bed, / Although surrounded by my friends and relatives, / The feeling of life being severed / Will be experienced by me alone." That's frightening, of course, mainly because it's true, but it might also be true that there is no death, only a change of worlds.

IN OCTOBER OF '74, I moved closer to campus and lived in the basement of a house. My monthly rent was equal to a cord and a half of firewood. My basement had windows, because the house was on a slope, and through them I had—like Emily Dickinson—a view of a cemetery: a spur to morbid thoughts, yes, but also a parklike vista. There were no faucet handles at my kitchen sink, but with a pair of channel locks I was able to get hold of the valve stems. I kept my chain saw just inside the door, on newspaper, because I worried that in the stakebed's cab it might get stolen. So my little rental smelled, as I did, of wood powder and oil. Or it smelled of dinner. I ate a lot of eggs, because I could buy them at a discount from my uncle Kevin, who kept a coop in his backyard—in fact, I could take a dozen for nothing if I cleaned the coop and fed the chickens—but I also simmered turkey legs and hamhocks and beans, and tried to make an orderly evening routine out of reading textbooks and recopying lecture notes. Lonely as all this was, I enjoyed myself. The fetish of discipline agreed with me, and I began to stay on top of the housekeeping. Before I'd moved out of his house, my father frequently came to my bedroom door to say, "You're a four-fingered typist," followed by, for example, "I'm still having to pick up after you in the kitchen," and I guess that now I was taking a futile revenge, or proving something to myself, by being meticulous. Mainly, though, I kept things clean because Jamie stayed with me in my basement, on weekends. She took the Greyhound to Seattle on Fridays after school and left again for Portland on Sunday afternoons. On her first visit, we took a walk in the cemetery visible from my windows as a hillside Arcadia. Jamie, as it turned out, was a reader of headstones, and called my attention to the fact that a number were inscribed with *"Dum tacet, clamat,"* and that all of these were shaped like tree stumps. We talked to a groundskeeper about this, who said that *Dum tacet, clamat,* meant "While he is silent, he shouts," and that the stump-shaped headstones symbolized membership in the Woodsmen of the World.

"While he is silent, he shouts," Jamie said later. "That's got to be the Woodswomen, right? It was the Woodswomen who put that on the headstones."

"Maybe."

"That's the kind of answer that makes you a Woodsman."

At Thanksgiving, Jamie went home to Pocatello. I was toasted by one of my cousins, before we tucked into our clan's spread feast, as "Joe College Countryman," but then someone added, "with wood chips in his hair," to let me off the hook. In early December, my unzipped sleeping bag caught on fire after spending too much time against a baseboard heater in the middle of a snowy night. I woke up while Jamie was throwing it out the door. We opened all the windows to let the smoke out and, with our coats on, sat on the couch watching the snow fall on the cemetery where the Woodsmen were silently shouting.

For Christmas, Jamie gave me a hundred bookplates with the

words "Ex Libris" and "Death Mask of Shakespeare" just above the bard's balding pate. Beneath was space for me to write my name after "From the library of." I gave her a botanical sketch—two sprigs of currants, framed. A couple of months later, I lost the clutch in the stakebed—it went out between deliveries, and Keith had to tow it to my father's house behind his pickup. The next afternoon, in the rain by myself, I cut my knuckles turning a wrench. It was cold, and that forced me to sit in the cab at regular intervals with my hands in my armpits in order to continue. I was doing this when John William, now bearded, got in on the passenger side, hit me on the shoulder, and said, grinning, "Countryman!"

"What?"

"Have you sold out?"

"No."

"Are you Joe College?"

"No."

"Is your girlfriend knocked up?"

"My fingers are dead."

"Don't knock her up," he said.

It was a Saturday. We went to see a double feature—*Reefer Madness* and *Fists of Fury*. The theater was nearly empty, and we sat in the back row with our feet up on seatbacks. I hadn't seen John William in a while, but nothing felt different. We got stoned, after the movie, in an alley, and went to a pool hall, and then we ate fat dollar burritos at a dirty table beneath posters of Acapulco and the Grateful Dead. It was 1975, but the Moody Blues were being piped in through mounted speakers. I said I was thinking of going into teaching, and John William asked, "What for?"

"To make a living."

"I thought you wanted to be Updike."

"Updike wants to be me."

"Teaching?"

"You think it's a bad call?"

"The stuff they teach you at school is just so they can own you," John William said, wiping his mouth. "But you already know that."

"Who's they?"

"Jehovah's archons."

This was irritating, but I didn't say that, and we went to the Last

Exit on Brooklyn. There was a Tarot reading going on. All the marble chess-tables were taken. We waited our turn, watching good players make authoritative moves and slap their timers in front of spectators. For some reason, someone was tuning the piano. About halfway through our first match, one of the Go players at an adjacent table looked up and said, "It's Karpov versus Spassky over here." "Shut up," said John William. I lost the first, played the second to a draw, then lost again.

At midnight, there were drunks on the Ave. We sat in an alley passing another joint, and John William told me he'd dropped out of school and, with part of his inheritance money, was buying an acre and a trailer on the Hoh.

"How come?"

"I like it there."

"You quit school?"

"I didn't get along with anybody."

Then, out of nowhere, he was crying again, with the heels of his palms against his eyes, and as always, I turned away from it.

THE DAY WINTER QUARTER ENDED, I drove to Portland in the stakebed. I remember that I pulled up the mat on the passenger side in order to watch the highway through the rusted floor, and that I had a battery-operated Zenith and an earphone for that trip because Keith had "borrowed" my dash radio. I also had a birthday present for Jamie, which was a very presentable set of antique dishes—or, rather, two dinner plates and two soup bowls—I'd found at a pawnshop in West Seattle. There was traffic as soon as I crossed into Oregon, and a warlike impatience on the Morrison Bridge, but at the Casablanca the mood was celebratory, because the tests and deadlines, at PSU, were just a few hours past. Music could be heard from across the courtyard—big speakers competing with each other. On the floor below Jamie's, a banner had been taped to an apartment window, "Spring Bacchanalia," and we went to that event after a dinner of crackers and wine, and then to a huge crowded party, where Gail Thornton had friends, and where the album on the stereo, when we walked in, was by the New York Dolls. "Are you having fun?" I yelled into Jamie's ear at one point that night, in a room full of people passing a bottle of tequila, in the bottom of which lay a chunk of ginseng root—as opposed to an agave worm—and she yelled back into mine, "Not really!"

Jamie, who'd just graduated with a degree in sociology, went to work for the Census Bureau. All spring she took the Greyhound to Seattle on Friday evenings, after work, and left again for Portland on Sunday afternoons, just as she'd done as a student. Then, one Sunday, after swimming at Matthews Beach, we walked slowly along the abandoned railroad tracks above Sand Point Way. I finally said, "It's after three o'clock," but Jamie only shrugged. She wore a racing suit, zoris, and a towel around her waist. Later, we sat on tie ends in a shady spot. When I told Jamie I'd been picking blackberries here since I was six or seven, she said that didn't mean they were native to the area; these were Himalayans, she said, doctored into their current permutation by Luther Burbank to grace English gardens, and after that, just persistent invaders. "I wrote a report on Luther Burbank in the eighth grade," she said, "so now I'm a Luther Burbank expert." Jamie sat with her arms against her knees, her chin in her hands. I thought she looked contemplative and said, "You're going to miss your bus," to which Jamie replied, "I missed it a long time ago." I took that literally and said there must be other Portland buses that evening. "No, wait," said Jamie. "I quit my job."

The next morning, we took the stakebed to Portland and collected her sofa, clothes, books, and so on. Jamie, on the way down, referred to the hole in the floor on her side of the cab as "natural air conditioning." Later, going home, I sat watching the road blur underfoot while Jamie grappled with the mortal question of steering. She clenched her teeth to change lanes, and lifted her butt off the seat like a bicyclist. She drove through a squall with the windshield wipers at high speed and once, reaching into the handbag beside her, produced some napkins, which she used to wipe the steam from the glass. A little later, she rolled down her window and, while adjusting the side mirror, said, "I used to be a trucker."

We put her sofa by my windows with their view of the cemetery. I explained about the channel locks at the kitchen sink, and the next day, while I was cutting firewood, Jamie bought handles. She also put her box frame and mattress out near the sidewalk with a sign, on a piece of cardboard, reading "Take Me." She got a part-time job in Youth Services for the Seattle Parks Department, and another part-time job filing reports for King County's Eviction Prevention Program. Riding buses to work, she carried her lunch in a box we found at Value Village and, most of the time, a paperback. We still didn't have a shower curtain, and we slept beneath a cheap and fire-retardant blanket. Jamie's shoes sat by the door, next to the saw. One evening, my father came by, and when I let him in, there was Jamie reading on the couch with her legs tucked under her. Dressed like a housepainter in white coveralls and a white T-shirt, my father told me he needed my splitting maul because he'd lost track of his sledgehammer. "I knew some Shaws growing up," he said, which prompted Jamie to tell him she was from Pocatello. "Or Poke," she said. "A lot of people call it Poke."

"These Shaws were fish people," my father answered.

I WENT TO SEE John William early in June. Near Lake Crescent, in the shadows, the sky was clear and the wind was blowing. There was still a little snow on Pyramid Mountain, but just enough to coat the trees. The logging trucks coming toward me looked caked with old mud. I had, on the passenger seat, Aubrey Williams' *Poetry and Prose of Alexander Pope*, and was supposed to be reading *The Rape of the Lock* and *An Essay on Criticism*, but the epic style of the former and the heroic couplets of the latter were both deadly to me, and I appreciated neither as I sat by a creek giving each a pale effort. There was no stomaching such a rigorous versifier in those particular mountains. I suppose there was too much wit packed into those cantos and couplets for my taste—at any rate, I wanted to throw Pope into a riffle, but it was too late now to drop the course without a penalty.

In the valley of the Sol Duc there was sunlight in the clear-cuts. I thought of driving onto a landing and scrounging cedar butts to sell as kindling, but I didn't, because my hair was too long for me to take the risk. Instead, I drove through Forks without stopping and turned east on the Hoh Road, where there were farms and pastures. I'm not going to say that this valley feels pastoral, but at least it's inhabited, if sparsely. There was even a general store, green with age, where a naked bulb was lit already, in the late afternoon, outside double doors. I stress again—this is not a place of country charms. The Hoh, despite its marketing by river-rafting companies and fishing guides, resembles mostly the scar of an excavation. The channels and cobbled islands on its floodplain have the sterile cast of an open mining operation. For long stretches, its gray pallor and gravel bars are broken only by logjams, and the root wads half buried in its silt look washed of color. Genteel it isn't, even where there are cows near its bank to make a case for that. The Hoh doesn't even have the attractions of rural dilapidation. There's bald destructiveness in the path it takes. Along its shores, the rocks sit like debris, and the cutbanks, of which there are many, suggest raw and open gashes. It often seems as if a storm has wreaked recent havoc on the river, or freshly rearranged its course. It looks, in sum, just short of appalling. There's too much evocative and obvious geology to be borne there happily by a visitor.

In this valley, upriver from the general store, after crawling up and down the road and peering down the potholed lanes, I located John William's mobile home, because his Impala was parked in front of it. There was also a lot of cordwood stacked close to its door, under a tarp. He'd bought a single-wide of the sort you sometimes see on the highway with a chase car behind it, and it probably goes without saying that its siding was mildewed, and that moss grew on its roof; anyway, it had been sitting there for a while, not catching sun. It was unskirted, so I could see what was stored under it: pipe, buckets, plastic sheeting, and lumber, all looking sodden and archeological. I also saw the shimmed piers the house was set on. The adjacent pasture had been chewed to the nubs and then stove in by hooves, and on this day it was hard mud with fog low against it, and behind that, beyond strands of cattle wire, was the kind of brush that grows in river silt for a few years before starving.

When I pulled up in the stakebed, John William came out to see who it was, barefoot and with his beard looking denser than it had in March, and stood by the cordwood defensively until he realized it was me. "Countryman," he said. "You're here."

"What's this about?"

"What do you mean?"

"You've gone trailer-trash."

"No, I haven't."

He was leaning in the passenger-side window now, taking in the cab with its floor-mounted stick shift, the chain-saw files in the ashtray, and the hole where my radio used to be before Keith borrowed it. "Alexander Pope," he said accusingly.

We went in and, sitting by his woodstove on aluminum lawn chairs, ate bread and peanut butter. John William kept the lights off and the stove door open, so that we could see what we were doing but also watch the fire. One way to put things regarding his trailer is that austerity ruled it. I once visited the fire lookout on the south peak of Three Fingers and at night, when the view was no longer overwhelming, had a little of the same feeling I had in my friend's mobile home on the Hoh. A paucity of objects makes a room feel bigger—that might be part of it. At any rate, besides the woodstove and lawn chairs, there was only a cable drum in John William's front room, serving as a table; a wood block with a hatchet sunk in it; an antiquated vacuum cleaner; and some kindling and firewood. Our plates were on the drum, along with a box of kitchen matches, an open lockback knife, a water bottle, and a book called *The Gnostic Religion*, by a Hans Jonas. I know this is the full list of items, because that night, on the floor, in my sleeping bag, I made an entry in my journal. The lawn chairs, the cable drum, the wood block, the open woodstove: it was camping without the out-of-doors.

John William in his lawn chair, shoeless, bearded, his hair in his face, adjusting his fire by prodding it with kindling—that's the picture I recall. And that we smoked our roaches through a hairpin that a former tenant of that mildewed hovel had lost in the pile of the carpet, and which John William had retrieved and saved. A college dropout who becomes a barefoot trailer-denizen, a child of advantage who turns to simplicity: that wasn't such an unusual progression in the era of Gerald Ford, when the American woods were still full of young philosophers—and Vietnam vets—some of whom looked like Johnny Appleseed. My friend's wool sweater was so filthy as to suggest, I thought, a freshly shorn fleece. It had been distended by wear into the shape of a loose hairshirt, or maybe a sackcloth, and its weave had segregated, and its sleeves had relaxed toward a conspicuous length that covered his hands, limply. But though John William had consolidated a look of self-inflicted penury, ultimately there was nothing to be done about the fact that his teeth still implied a white dinner jacket and mints. As for me, I was the current recipient of a higher education, someone who'd made a European tour, and a lover whose inamorata was an older woman, all of which meant, to me at least, that John William and I should recalibrate. But that wasn't something amenable to force. In a friendship, you don't so much change terms as observe terms changing. John William might have been barefoot in his lawn chair, but he still had intrinsic gravity and traction, whereas I felt weightless, as ever, in his orbit, even dressed as I was in fresh experience. In other words, what I'd done, or was doing, my friend seemed immune to; what mattered right now was his celebration of the gnostic scholar Jonas. Had I read Jonas?

"I'm reading Pope."

"You should read Jonas."

"I've got all this Pope I have to read."

John William held his stick of kindling like a scepter. "You shouldn't waste your time," he warned.

Though I regaled John William with a description of Pope's grotto, and of its associated tunnel beneath the London road—the vestiges of which my professor had photographed on a visit to Cross Deep—his interest in my consciousness remained less than perfunctory. What mattered was Jonas and, if I caught the gnostic drift of things, the cruel farce that was reality; to this the hunchbacked poet must play second fiddle. Later, we went outside to consider the stars, which are rarely seen on the Hoh, and I pointed out, cannabis-appropriately, how densely three-dimensional the Milky Way appeared, and how obvious it was to me that we were in it, but John William was immune to this celestial insight, too, and only stood there in his hairshirt, barefoot, and said, "That's a satellite. They're taking pictures for their files."

"Somebody told me they can see smoke off your joint."

"Satellites can see your thoughts, but not through rock," John William replied.

Was this crazy? In the newspaper reports on the hermit of the Hoh, an abiding derangement is the heart of the matter. That's wrong. My friend was just speaking in code about satellites— speaking in a language private between us. A vocabulary for intimates: some teens can talk between themselves so enigmatically that their shades of meaning are unavailable to—for example—me voyeuristically at the salad bar in the school cafeteria. "Satellites can see your thoughts, but not through rock," is like something they might say. In John William's case, it was conscious hyperbole and therefore commentary. At one level, it was reefer-inspired. It was partly for fun. It was other things, too—but not derangement. I give no credence to that interpretation, and I knew him better than anybody.

In my sleeping bag that night, with the woodstove ticking, I decided John William would tire of this seediness and eventually move on to something new—something full of suffering, if I had to predict, like crossing Patagonia with no food. I could also hear Alexander Pope calling. When would I read his many, clever couplets? That was his telepathic, intermittent complaint. "At your age, Pope was writing his *Pastorals*," my professor had said, on the day before I drove to the Hoh. (Hagiography and admonishment, in equal measure, were staples of her lectures.) I'd been thinking about that and feeling disheartened. I felt condemned, after high school, to deeper failures, of graver consequence—or, to put this another way, I was ambitious.

The next morning, in John William's Impala, we drove the Honor Camp Road, which crosses Elk Creek and rounds Mount Octopus, and then the Owl Creek Road, which parallels the upper Hoh below Huelsdonk Ridge. The potholes ended where a berm full of cobbles had been lofted by a grader, and where a hiker could set out on the South Fork Hoh Trail. John William put his car key in a snuff tin and, on the back side of a maple, hid it under moss, and then we stuffed some gear in our packs, tightened our boots, and made trail. There was sunlight on the alders, on the gravel bars, on the fallen trees at water's edge, and on the water itself, but still the way was in shade for the most part. Wind was present, intermittently, as noise—not just leaves and branches but furtive groans, of the kind that augur tree fall. Finally, we came to a place by the river where four segments of a spruce lay like wrecked train cars against a hillside. Scenes like this in the forest form the sort of tableau that makes route-finding John William's way—committing landmarks to memory—a little easier than it sounds. We kept a creek on our right, passed through cedars hung with withes, rested where John William and I had depleted his char cloth while failing to start a fire, even came on the scene of our stalemated chess game, but it was always a graphically fallen tree, or a boulder poised against another boulder, looking ready to topple—anything dramatic—that I remembered best and found reassuring. Corroboration was what I wanted, and now and then, when the map in my head and the configuration of the world converged on schedule, I felt comforted and vindicated, but more often I negotiated the terrain with doubts and moved forward taking compass headings and orienteering notes, in order to militate against an unmooring like the one I'd been through with John William before, and so we could turn back, if necessary, without relying on his recall of the country behind us. It made no difference, because he knew where he was going.

At the site of our blood pact, beneath the limestone wall and above our pool, John William announced that he was excavating a "cliff dwelling." He'd built some tenuous-looking scaffolding, medieval and crude—really just some lashed-up limbs with a pronounced rightward cant. There were chips of limestone on the forest floor beneath it, made, he said, by his pick. I told him he was crazy. I said he was a fool. I told him he'd give up when his back was broken. We rested for a while, with our boots off and our feet in the pool, and then I followed John William up the scaffolding, and, picks in hand, we considered the raw concavity in the limestone, which, he said, was his work of the last two months. I looked down at his camp—his fire ring, his lean-to tarp, a line of nylon twine on which his socks were drying, and the pool lined with rock and brimming with clear water. In my view, this was a tidy illustration from a scouting manual. There were a number of drum canteens, with shoulder straps, hanging from a limb in shade, and when John William went to get one I tried swinging a pick a few times, and made some dents in the limestone, or, rather, small chalky nicks. Of course, the recalcitrance of stone doesn't need elaboration. And there's a reason why dynamite's the tool of choice among miners. Limestone can be pulverized to make a soil amendment, but that doesn't mean it's amenable to force. A pick's point will fatigue in a long match with rock, and a pick, with time, comes loose from its handle. I keep a pick in our garden shed, which I bought when we decided to do away with our carport, thinking I would use it to go after the concrete, but I ended up, before long, renting a jackhammer, lacking not so much strength as patience. Frankly, I'm probably unsuited to a war with hard materials, or, for that matter, to any labor of attrition, but I helped John William excavate his cave that day, taking my shifts on his haphazard scaffolding while feeling all the while that the effort was absurd. There were fossils in the rock, mostly small bivalves—I could see the clear imprints of their scalloped shells—and now and then a nodule of flint knapped off in a way suggestive of accelerating progress, but as for interests or satisfactions inherent in this toil, these were as meager as you'll find in any project. "Like striking stone" is a simile for getting nowhere.

That evening, after John William used his fire drill, we sat by high flames. In the orange light against the rising rock face, his scaffolding looked even more primitive, like the apparatus of a night attack made by Goths on crenellated walls. I remember John William telling me that he'd driven to Port Angeles at one point in May to eat at the Elks Club and watch *Chinatown* at the Lincoln. It was clear that this humble evening constituted the apex of novel activity for him over the past sixty days. While I'd been cavorting in my apartment with Jamie, John William had mostly been chipping at rock, here in this gloomy forest. I think again of Basho— "The new year's first snow: / how lucky to remain alone / at my hermitage"—but is this luck or something grim? That question, or one like it, was with me that night, and led me into reticence while John William, making use of the firelight, picked at the calluses on his palms, I would have to say obsessively. Later, I stumbled around gathering more branches to throw on the flames, and from between the trees looked back at his scaffolding and at the cliff, too, in the burnished glow. From that perspective, from that small distance, my friend's enterprise appeared disturbing, partly because it was so small there, with so much darkness around it, and partly because the flickering of the fire caught the small facets and indentations of pick work but not the depth of it, and made it look even more futile than it looked when you saw it from close up, in daylight. On the other hand, I slaved over one of my unpublished novels for seven years. Is that more or less ridiculous than pick work?

In the morning, a light rain was falling against the tarp. At noon, we walked out—we headed toward the road—and near a swale full of downfall brush saw an elk moving away from us. We watched it go, and after a while it was clear that there were more elk, at least five, farther off and slowly retreating, too, unharried shadows, and I made some notes on this, on their red coats and "the furtive and even ethereal way" they disappeared and reappeared among the spruces. At the river we threw stones into the current, and I snared, on a stick, the carcass of a salmon, a fish whose remaining flesh hung "like a tattered ribbon"; there was also a lone merganser "flying low and frenzied between the gravel bars and cutbanks." My hands felt raw. My blood-pact scar, that crescent in my right palm, looked pink. We sat for a while by a bend in the water course and then walked the flats westward. The Impala came into sight. We caravanned into Forks and ate eggs and bacon in a booth. John William reprovisioned—including, I remember, two extra pick handles—and then I followed him to Port Angeles. At Swain's, he bought overalls and rubber raingear, and we took his old clothes to a Laundromat and sat near the dryers eating cheeseburgers and reading a newspaper someone had left there. That night, at the Lincoln, we watched *Death Wish*, with Charles Bronson as an architect who becomes a vigilante. It was a Sunday, and I was starting summer classes the next morning, but despite that we drove out to Ediz Hook when the movie was over and sat on rocks by the salt water, looking back toward town. Port Angeles sits between the sea and the mountains, and because of this appears transitory when you see it from a distance, or small in its context. That's what we saw, and light from the town illuminating a log boom. A lot of timber was floating in the water near a mill on the harbor. I said, "So what, exactly, is the deal with you?"

"What do you mean?"

"I mean, what are you doing?"

"I don't want to participate."

"Participate in what?"

"In anything."

His new overalls and flannel shirt, from Swain's, made him look like a character from *Oklahoma!* while he sat on his rock examining his hands with more rigor, I thought, than they warranted. Behind him was the Strait of Juan de Fuca, some stars, and a container ship. I said, "I don't get it."

"Don't get what?"

"I don't get you."

"I don't get you, either."

"What's that supposed to mean?"

"Idiot," said John William. "You've got your whole life in front of you, maybe fifty or sixty years. And what are you going to do with that? Be a hypocrite, entertain yourself, make money, and then die?"

"No."

"Neither am I," said John William.

In the morning, I took notes while my professor gave an overview, up through the transcendentalists, of literature in America—its Puritan beginnings, the period of the deists, and the transcendentalists themselves, with their optimism—my professor said—goaded forward by the land westward that remained unknown to them. The idea seemed to me dubious. It still does, because a lot of people are indifferent to the unknown, and some are terrified of it, too— unknown lands aren't by definition a reason to look on the bright side. So I considered this opening lecture a little unsatisfying and later, at the library, dug around about this question of transcendentalism in relation to the westward unknown, but there was so much there about related things that I couldn't keep my original question in mind and got sidetracked, and really, this has been the story of my life, this sort of digression from what I intended, a manner of living that's upsetting in a fundamental way, so that at times I've thought of striking out on a new path. But which path would that be? That's now my $440-million question. COUNTRYMAN—GET OUT HERE BEFORE IT'S TOO LATE. There was more to that than I realized.

5

ALL ABOUT THE BENJAMINS

I CAN'T SAY HOW MANY TIMES John William swung his pick in order to excavate his cave. I do know that I hiked there frequently with heavy loads, and most of the time found him swinging it. Once, though, arriving in the evening, I found him sitting with a book I'd left under his tarp called *One Hundred Poems from the Chinese*. Reading, John William looked like a character from the Brothers Grimm—the long hair and beard, the candle and book, the pool in the woods, the fire behind him and the cave overhead, the rising rock wall, and the dark trees. I said, "Some of those poems are good."

He put the book down.

Working on his cave, John William developed big arms and a hulking back. He didn't sweat as much as I did, but his sweat was gamier. One day, while helping him—or pretending to help him, because I still felt strongly that this project was folly—I suggested dynamite. I said we could pound holes in the rock and fill them with explosives. I was fantasizing about a way out because the work was so hard. I was also confronting a truly onerous tedium, which had come to include me against my will. In sum, I hated pick work. With pick work, each blow reverberates in the forearms, and as the day wears on, the curved head becomes heavier and the tool feels out of balance; whereas earlier there might have been a crushing exactitude, now there's only flailing. I think of the chain gangs portrayed in films, bent along roads or in dusty fields, dressed in stripes and slowed by leg-irons, generally beneath a terrible sun, and though they often wield shovels or hoes, it's the swing of picks that comes readily to mind as a natural feature of this celluloid image, because pick work is servitude, it's penitential; I can imagine a circle of hell about pick work, but not about hoeing or shoveling. Anyway, when a day of cave building was done, John William and I sat by our flames, eating, on a lot of nights, beans and rice. There were lime-stone chips everywhere—they crunched underfoot and here and there caught firelight. A bluntness inhabited my hands: they felt like clubs and lost discernment. We were bug-bitten and smelled of sul-fur. But we were also young and had our hot tub. Of course, this cave wasn't really my project, and I could quit anytime, though, on the other hand, I felt compelled, or obliged, by a bond, by alle-giance, and by the posture of service which, I admit, was the posture I took of my own choice toward John William.

But I was only there sporadically. My life unfolded in other places. I peddled firewood with Keith, attended school, and lived with Jamie. Gradually, I didn't want to go to the South Fork Hoh, or I wanted to go but not urgently enough, partly because this life in town appealed to me, partly because excavating had gotten insuffer-able, and partly because of the rule, newly instituted by John William, that we couldn't smoke dope until dusk. That fall of '75, I made the pilgrimage infrequently, though always with a pack full of food—I remember buying hamhocks, pinto beans, apples, rice, and cookies, and weighing myself with and without this load, which came to seventy pounds. I also brought, on one trip, shampoo, soap, candles, toilet paper, and a can of white gas, and I laid these out on the forest floor, near the fire pit, and after a while—what choice did he have?—John William accepted my offerings and put everything under his tarp.

There were signs of progress when I went up there in Novem-ber. He'd been at it for eight months now, and it showed. The chips of limestone under the cliff face had become a heap. The excavation resembled a recess for displaying classical statuary, and the rudi-mentary scaffolding had been buttressed and reinforced. What had earlier looked medieval in aspect now had the ambience of a credible prospecting or of a nineteenth-century mining operation. I got stoned in the morning despite the new rule, and then we took advantage of good weather for labor—cool and clear, dry with no wind—and banged away with our picks in alternate strikes that, late in the afternoon, produced intermittent sparks. There was no stopping John William, which meant I couldn't fold. We lacked room for two up there, but by ducking expeditiously and in precarious rhythm we avoided each other and, grimly, got results. For my part, I felt possessed by the dogged futility of pick work, tried feeding on its slow advance, and was half able to mythologize myself—which toil like this requires—but I still flagged before my friend, who had better torque, a more compact swing, and endless motivation. You could hear all these distinctions in our separate reverberations. His frequency sounded more productive on every blow. That limestone niche yielded to John William less stubbornly than it did to me. I suppose my private sentiments that day must have been competitive— I probably dissipated myself in this familiar vein. However it was, flaking and chiseling, we wore ourselves down—I felt, at least, like a candle going out—and finally put the picks aside and stripped and hit the hot tub. Afterward, I cut some of the apples I'd brought into chunks and put those in the pot with the beans and rice. John William had, in his camp, cayenne pepper, and a book I hadn't seen before, Huxley's *The Doors of Perception*, which I read that night, its pages lit by a military-surplus headlamp I'd found at a garage sale, while he replaced a snapped pick handle. We slept by the fire, and at dawn John William said he'd dreamed of being locked in a room with a dakini while pulling at a door that wouldn't open.

"A dakini?"

"A demoness."

"That's the dream?"

"There was someone on the other side of the door, trying to help."

"Too bad," I said, "because that's all you'll get out here."

"Listen to you," John William said. "You're pussy-whipped."

We hung our sleeping bags from the scaffolding and ate cookies for breakfast. At lunch, I went back to *The Doors of Perception*. John William had found a small skull in the forest, which he couldn't identify, and neither could I. He also had what appeared to be the thigh bone of an elk or a deer, a large mandible, and what he thought were owl feathers. We scrounged distantly for firewood and filled the canteens. That afternoon, my pick head came loose, and as it rattled with each strike, I wanted to go home.

At dusk, we sat with our feet in the hot tub, breathing sulfur mist. I had a raw, oozing spot between my thumb and forefinger, and open calluses on my palms. A fleck of limestone, struck off by John William, had lodged earlier in the corner of my eye, and I'd gone to pains to dig it out, using the mirror in my compass lid, but there was still some residual complaint there, and I couldn't see normally. I read some of Huxley, but the print was watery. We ate more rice and beans doused with cayenne, finished the cookies and apples, and lay down in our sleeping bags close to the fire. I said, at last, because I didn't want to come to this place anymore, "Why are we doing this?"

"No one's making you do anything."

"Sleep in a tent."

"I don't want to sleep in a tent."

"What do you want, then?"

"I want peace," said John William, "so help me out."

I came again at Thanksgiving. There was the semblance of a cave by then. In the *Seattle Times*, the hermit's retreat is described as "spacious": it had to be spacious for John William to swing a pick, or for the two of us to swing our picks alternately, in lesser arcs than from the scaffolding, but nevertheless with force. Inside, in the gloom, there was no room for an overhead swing; long side-arm arcs were necessary, and these made my ribs ache. I also felt crowded and oppressed by rock, and turned often toward the light. We emerged from there coated with limestone dust, like miners, kicking out the chips with the edges of our boots; sometimes we rested with our legs dangling from the entrance, eating cold beans or crackers. We worked by lantern light on my second night there, because John William felt we'd lapsed inexcusably by napping through an afternoon; he hung the lantern, from its wire handle, on the scaffolding, and while it hissed we toiled nocturnally, like demons.

Around midnight, we got into the hot tub and, in the manner of movie mead-hall thanes, ate the greasy drumsticks I'd brought wrapped in foil. "So this is your deal," I said.

"Yeah."

"You'll get snowed out."

"True."

"You could snowshoe."

"Snowshoes leave a trail for the Park Service or whoever."

I said, "You could walk in the river and up that side stream."

"Maybe."

"You could cache food."

It was the sort of advice you might offer a hobbyist. At that point I thought of John William as a hobbyist—obsessive, but a hobbyist nonetheless. How else would I see it? Why would I think otherwise? He seemed to me like other kids of means who take on grueling projects at the cusp of adulthood—though instead of building a cave they usually do something like sailing to Antarctica or biking across Mongolia. To me, the pick work in the woods was in this vein of extended, masochistic recreations.

The next morning, when I got out my journal, John William said, "So you still want to be a writer, I see. You still want to write the great American novel."

"Because I'm a cliché."

"You want to be famous."

"Superficial: that's me."

"You want immortality."

"A novel wouldn't make me immortal."

"No," John William said, "a little sustenance for the ruling class, that's what a novel comes to, in the end."

"Your family," I shot back, "must own a lot of them, then."

"Cruel wit," said John William. "They're honing you in the English Department."

I left in the morning, and for a month I didn't go to the cave anymore, or to the trailer on the Hoh, preferring my own life, preferring it unencumbered by any duty to my friend, or by the necessity I'd felt, for three and a half years now, to put up with him. Walking from building to building on campus, or reading at the library on a rainy afternoon, I thought I'd finally let John William slip into the past. Most friendships end with a whimper, not a bang, and I considered letting ours end that way, but this, as it turned out, was a fantasy with no force behind it. There was this loyalty I felt, however strange.

That December, Jamie bought a Crock-Pot, but after a while we decided there was no way to cook anything good in it. We also got a sourdough starter going and were dutiful about keeping it alive. Jamie bought a '63 Datsun with rusted fender wells, because she got tired of taking the bus. The stakebed's brakes needed an infusion of cash. I noticed that my right hip hurt when I ran and started taking laps in the intramural-building pool instead. My chain saw had a starter-rope problem: it retracted cruelly, and its coiled tension stung my hand. My lower back hurt, and I quit cutting firewood. Then, at winter break, Jamie went to Pocatello, and, mostly out of guilt, I drove the stakebed to the trailer on the Hoh. There was snow on the ground there. The wind was rattling the bare branches of the trees, and the moon's cold glow lay against the river. John William came out in a watchman's cap. We stood by the truck only long enough to acknowledge how good things looked, and then we went in and sat in the flimsy lawn chairs, by the heat from the wood-stove. There was an elk antler on the cable drum, and a book called *Reading Animal Tracks.* John William said that his work on the cave had been suspended by weather, and that the South Fork Hoh Trail lay under snow. He sat with his cap low on his forehead while we ate tomato soup. He also tended his fire, poking at the flames and adjusting the damper. He said that he went twice a week to Forks for groceries, and that he had permission to gather scrap wood at a mill—he cut mill ends to stove length with a bow saw there, and hauled them in the trunk of his Impala. I asked if his father ever visited. He said that the weekend after Thanksgiving he'd gone with Rand to the Hoh Visitor Center, which was closed, and hiked the Hall of Mosses Trail in the cold, Rand with his hands in the pockets of his Burberry and a pair of binoculars slung from his neck that bounced against him as he walked. "When I was your age," Rand had intoned, "I was in the Seabees." John William said, "I know." They'd sat in the parking lot with the car idling and the heater on, and Rand had asked, "So what are your goals?"

"I have one goal," John William told him, "and that's to be reincarnated as an elk, Rand."

We sat in his trailer laughing about that. Then John William got up and came back with his chessboard. I'd been practicing and wanted badly to beat him. There was a chess club on campus, and I'd been playing against fiends and aficionados in the Husky Union

Building and taking my lumps. At a used-book store near campus I'd picked up, for 35 cents, Rudolf Spielmann's *The Art of Sacrifice in Chess*, with its examples of sham sacrifices and real sacrifices from legendary European matches, and I thought I could defeat John William by pretending to lose while gaining good board position. He stoked up the fire and put the board on the cable drum. The hot light from the stove spilled over the squares and illuminated the black and white bodies of the chess pieces so that they looked like they would melt. John William tugged his beard. He took off his cap. Out came his king's pawn. It took only this to make me waver and to recollect an observation of Spielmann's: "The timid player will take to real sacrifices only with difficulty, principally because the risk involved makes him uneasy." The gambit of sacrifice suddenly seemed in error. As a result, I got caught between two strategies and, on the defensive, exerted myself over the course of a long battle to produce a draw. There was no pleasure in that. Four or five times, I was so deliberate about my next move that John William picked up *Reading Animal Tracks* to pass the time. This was arrogant, or seemed arrogant. He said, "Hard to get counterplay in your restricted position," and "Good move—keeps tension in the middle of the board." Of course, these comments irked and incited me. But what could I do? In silence I pressed. We played a second game to a draw, and then a third. John William went out for more firewood, and when he came back told me he was interested, lately, in flint knapping— the art of making stone tools. He was emphatic that learning to knap was hard and showed me where he'd driven a pressure flake into his thumb while attempting to shape obsidian. He also showed me some flake scars he'd made on a chunk of flint, but there really wasn't much to see.

In the morning, we took the Impala to the coast. We walked north, toward Hoh Head, in a heavy rain, and sat under trees on a bluff above the ocean. There were gulls in the sand, and a seal partly eaten by turkey vultures. I was a little surprised when John William, wielding a lockback knife, cut a strip of meat from this dark carcass in the sand and chewed it tentatively; he said it tasted like beef jerky and wanted me to try it, but I passed. We built a shelter out of drift-wood and sat in it in order to avoid the wind, which by noon had the force of a gale. I laid my head against a square of washed-up Styrofoam. John William, in his watchman's cap, fingerless woolen gloves, and a tattered yellow poncho, stood barefoot in the surf with his arms raised, yelling. I felt impatient. I wondered why we were suffering these particular elements. Later, we took shelter again in the relative protection of the shore trees, where John William, leaning against bark, stripped off his gloves so as to inspect his calluses once more. "I'm majoring in English," I told him.

"Why?"

"I like it."

John William said, "What's the point?"

"What's the point of anything?"

John William: "What's the point of reading a lot of dead Brits?"

We drank water and ate pilot crackers. We compared the scars on our palms, mine crescent-shaped, his longer. I suggested leaving, and after a while we walked down the beach to the mouth of the Hoh. "I remember this place from when I was a kid," John William said. "My mother got interested in native art. She had these Hoh elders from here recorded on tape, but then she flipped."

This April, at about the time that I was prominently in the newspapers, a Hoh elder spoke at our school. He wore thick glasses and a flannel shirt and stood on the auditorium stage with the American flag on his left and the Washington State flag on his right. He showed slides. He told the students that the Hoh used to eat what was on the beach—barnacles, anemones, sea cucumbers, seagull eggs, smelt, and so on—and what they caught in pitfalls and snares. He said that in the beginning the Hoh walked on their hands, but then were turned right side up by Changer, the better to dip smelt. He said it was interesting that no owls lived on the South Fork of the Calawah, and that some Russians stranded on the coast in 1808 were made into slaves by other tribes, but not by the Hoh. Eventually, almost the whole tribe died of smallpox, brought by the drifting people.

In my classroom that afternoon, after hearing from the elder, my students and I, with the lights off and the shades drawn, watched *The Great Gatsby* on a television wheeled in on a cart. I sat in the back of the room, looking over the tops of their heads, taking in this oft-repeated scene in my life—Room 104, with its blackboard and posters of Tolstoy and Eudora Welty, its flag in the corner, and its model of the Globe Theatre on a table against a wall—but, frankly, I had seen that movie too many times, it had staled for me, and I wanted to shut it off and ask my students what they thought about that term, "the drifting people."

A YEAR PASSED, and, despite myself, I went on helping my friend with his cave. Then, in March of '77, John William showed up in Seattle. He called one Friday around midnight, and I explained how to get to our apartment. Then I sat on the couch, not doing anything, just looking out at the dark reach of the cemetery, and when he knocked I threw the door open wide and said, "Hey—you shaved your beard."

"Well observed, Countryman."

"Are you getting a job or something?"

John William, ignoring this, said, "The lonely writer in his gloomy cellar."

"Not quite," Jamie called from our bed and, with the blanket wrapped around her, shook hands with John William—the long arm emerging the way an arm emerges from a toga.

We put records on, including *All Things Must Pass*—the Cindy Houghton Christmas gift John William had repulsed—and Jamie lambasted Maharishi Mahesh Yogi, who'd prompted George Harrison to take up meditation, saying that the Maharishi had propositioned Mia Farrow, which, Jamie felt, undercut him spiritually. John William said that, for him, Krishna and Jehovah were the same, a point Jamie wouldn't grant. She said that the dualism of the Hindus wasn't really dualism; John William replied that the origin of darkness was in God himself; Jamie shook her head and said, "That's out of left field"; John William plunged next into something he called "the Valentinian Speculation"—with what I once heard a school psychologist call, in reference to a talkative student we were discussing, "socially inappropriate enthusiasm"—anyway, this is why we were awake during the wee hours.

Eventually, I gave John William a coat to sleep under. Around ten, I woke up because I heard a mousetrap leap in the kitchen. On the floor beside me was a collection of Henry James's stories; I was supposed to be writing a paper on James, but hadn't started. So I read for a while. I scribbled in my journal. We ate bowls of cereal at noon, puffed rice with bananas, Jamie referring to this as "Apple Scruffs," though it included no apples. Then she turned up the heat, put new records on the turntable, and started arguing with John William again.

In the afternoon, I made a lentil soup. I baked soda bread with raisins in it, which my grandmother Cavanaugh called Spotted Dog, and we ate it with orange marmalade and butter. Our basement smelled like onions. Everybody read for a while—I read James; Jamie, Willa Cather; and John William, my copy of *Climber's Guide to the Olympic Mountains*, which had missing pages. He and I couldn't help ourselves and reminisced, while Jamie was deciphering *Death Comes for the Archbishop*, about crossing Mount Olympus from the Queets Basin. John William read aloud the descriptive text—"This route, across the northeast side of Mount Olympus, crosses three major glaciers and requires mountaineering skill, roped travel, and crevasse-rescue knowledge and equipment"—after which Jamie put down her book and asked us why we were laughing so hard. "We should be dead," John William answered.

He went to the shelf and, finding Ovid there, recommended "Baucis and Philemon" to Jamie before selecting, surprisingly, a haiku collection I'd bought at a moving sale, Kobayashi Issa's *A Few Flies and I*. He sat down with it on the couch and turned its water-stained pages. After a while he said, "Here's a good one:

> "Awakened by a horse's fart,
> I see
> a firefly in the air."

We laughed. It was getting dark, and we'd spent the day indoors. We let our soup cool and finished the Spotted Dog. John William put the haiku aside, took up his bowl, and said, "Jamie, what do you think of Countryman?"

Jamie answered, "Kind of introspective."

"What else?"

"Kind of righteous, but Mr. Dependable. It's a trade-off."

John William laughed again, and since he was holding his bowl of soup in his palm, some of it spilled in his lap.

We ate. Then, after dinner, John William abruptly put on his jacket and said, "When's your spring break?"

"April second."

"Come out then. April second. You come, too," he said to Jamie.

We said we would, but that wasn't good enough; he was firm about our visit. "Promise me you'll come on April second," he insisted. "Swear it." So we did.

At the door I handed him *A Few Flies and I.* He didn't want to take it, but I made him, pointing out that if he didn't want it I could always take it back on April second. "So you're coming," he said.

"You just made us promise."

"One more thing," said John William. "Let me see your scar." I turned over my hand, and he looked at it closely—a prominent white ridge like the Crescent Ranch brand. "That's good," he said, and left.

As soon as he was gone, we opened "Baucis and Philemon." An elderly couple living in a cottage, they're granted a wish by Jove. They confer in private before Philemon asks, "May one hour take us both away; let neither outlive the other." The wish is granted.

I said, "Simultaneous deaths? Why didn't they wish for eternal happiness instead? What else would anyone wish for?"

"They did wish for that," answered Jamie.

LAST EVENING, OUR OLDER SON came home for dinner. He rode up on his Vespa, shouldering a waterproof bike-messenger's sack, and brought us a loaf of rosemary bread and two large bottles of Hefeweizen he'd bought at a store called Bottleworks, in Wallingford. His hair was in a brief ponytail. We sat in the backyard with English pint glasses. There were bees among the lavender plants. The night before, our son had seen Al Gore's *An Inconvenient Truth,* and it seemed to him now that the high temperatures in England—where, he said, some roads were melting—were a sign of bad things to come. We went in and cooked dinner, the three of us, while listening to a CD mix our son had burned and given his mother for her birthday. We ate pasta—fresh linguine—with a red sauce spiked with vodka, the rosemary bread, peas from the garden, a salad of endive, and sliced mango with French vanilla ice cream for dessert. Our son, fresh from architecture school, was recently hired by a firm specializing in green design, and this is what we talked about after dinner, on the patio, in the twilight, each with our Hefeweizen. He told us he was working with an engineer on a scheme to produce methane from kitchen scraps in a high-rise; he was also working on a high-efficiency lighting system for a snowboard manufacturer, and on recovering rainwater for irrigation at a large-scale nursery. Our son is twenty-six. During college, he worked for an outdoor outfitter, maintaining rental snowshoes and cross-country skis and wearing a blue apron; at that time, he was an avid ice-climber, but this seems behind him now. He has a girlfriend, and the two of them play park-department soccer.

I've noticed, lately, that our son's doubts have eased. For a while he thought he might want to be footloose, and made plans, for example, to climb peaks in Chile, but rarely do I hear about such things now. He talks, instead, about building a house powered by a solar-cell array, Seattle neighborhoods that are still affordable— because he's adamant, so far, about not asking us for money—and his fledgling interest in Buddhism. He seems to want a calm and orderly life, and, although he doesn't say so, I'm sure he wants children. I'm also sure he's watching me age the way I watched my own father age—noticing all the sad physical changes and feeling glad they're not happening to him. As a child, I recall, he was terrified, for a while, about the prospect of a comet hitting the earth and obliterating civilization.

We sipped our Hefeweizen. Jamie went in for a sweater. Our son said he'd just read *The Seven Storey Mountain*, by Thomas Merton, merging this reading with his inquiry into Buddhism, with reports of Tibetan solitaries meditating naked in the snow, and with another book, by Alexandra David-Néel, who, he told me, had lived in a cave in Sikkim. Did I know that Merton, the celebrated monastic, had taken an interest in Tibetan Buddhism? Did I know that he'd met with His Holiness the Dalai Lama? Did I know that he'd died in Thailand, suddenly, electrocuted by a fan after taking a shower?

Our son listened to his cell-phone messages. Now the lavender glowed in the late twilight—the purple heads looked a little fluorescent. Our son put his pint glass on the arm of his Adirondack chair and asked me if I'd been to an alehouse in Ballard with an extensive list of artisanal Belgians; he extolled its pub fare and, on the heels of that, a record store called Bop Street, on Ballard Avenue. He asked me if I'd read *A Pattern Language*, a book about post-industrial architecture. He urged it on me. He said he would bring it the next time he came. He told me that the Vespa got sixty miles to the gallon and asked if I'd like to go for a spin. We went out to the street and, wearing my bike helmet, I got on behind him in my shorts and sandals. It was a small bike to double on, but we did it anyway, and there was something sad for me about his adult odor. My son drove carefully, out of deference to his father. At a stoplight, he turned his head to talk—did I want to go to Brouwer's, a brewpub in Fremont? I told him I didn't, not right now. They had, my son said, fifty taps. They served mussels and *frites*—the national dish of Belgium. Had I ever had mussels and *frites*?

We went home. Jamie was reading by an open window. No, she didn't want a ride on the Vespa—even though our son asked repeatedly, teasingly—but she did tell him how much she'd enjoyed speeding on a Vespa when she was twenty-one in Rome. Our son went online to check on something. He fed the dog after making her roll over, then poured a glass of beer, took it to the living room, and turned on the television. There were four fingers of Hefeweizen left, which I drank from the bottle. I sat listening to the dog lick her bowl, to her long tongue aggressively slapping the metal, and gradually became aware of other sounds—the refrigerator compressor, the furnace fan circulating air through the house, the automatic ice-maker dropping ice, the wall clock ticking. Then I remembered that the pint glasses were on the patio, and it seemed to me important to go get them, let the dog out, shut the tool-shed door, and collapse the garden umbrella. I did these things and also put our dinner scraps in the worm bin, stopping for a few seconds to watch the fruit flies, with their ten-day life spans, feed on wilted lettuce leaves.

In the living room, our son sat in the armchair, watching a few seconds in succession of every channel. I lay on the couch, and because I was there, he lingered on Steve Buscemi, in *Fargo*, attempting to bury a briefcase full of cash along a snowy roadside fence while his face is bleeding—the wound plugged with what looks like toilet paper—and I became conscious that my son and I, for better or worse, share about the same sense of humor. "So what are you going to do?" he asked, during an advertisement.

"What do you mean?"

"Are you going to change anything? Now that you're rich and famous?"

"I'm going hiking on Thursday."

"That's a Zen answer," said my son.

I walked him to his Vespa when the movie was over and, before he got on the bike, put a hand on his shoulder and thanked him for bringing the bread and the Hefeweizen. The last thing he said was that he couldn't go hiking with me on Thursday because of work.

Later, Jamie and I went to bed with the window open. I could hear our neighbors' lawn sprinklers, and the fan in their greenhouse starting intermittently, and because I couldn't sleep while listening to these things, I watched Jamie, in the light from the open curtains, twitch in the privacy of her dreams, and later put my hand just below her navel, where not only could I feel her breath rise and fall but, at the tip of one finger, read her pulse.

"A light he was to no one but himself"—that's a line from a Frost poem, "An Old Man's Winter Night," which a lot of students don't respond to very strongly. "A light he was to no one but himself"—I wouldn't choose that, and if I have to suffer it one day, because of circumstances, I'm fairly certain it will lead to my demise, because that cast, that illumination, is foreign to me—I'm finally saddled with my take on things as ineluctably as I'm slowed, and pained, by the neuroma in my foot. So be it. I have the beauty that I have, and none other, in the meantime. One thing has led to the next in my life, but like lines of a poem. I suppose I've thrown in my lot with love, and don't know any other way to go on breathing. I embrace this world—the world my friend hated—and suffer it consciously for its compensations, and fully expect to awake one day to the consequences of this bargain I've struck, since life, eventually, closes in.

APRIL SECOND ARRIVED, a Saturday of dubious weather, and I sat in the Datsun with a bag of potato chips on my lap while Jamie drove and fiddled with her radio until there were no stations left without static. I mentioned that my sister used a potato for an antenna, and Jamie stopped and impaled an apple on hers, and after that we got an AM station featuring a preacher whose subject, that morning, was chapter 37 of Ezekiel, which contemplates the resurrection of the dead. In the curves around Lake Crescent, Jamie reminded me how the Italians drive in the middle of the road when it makes sense, and honk their horns and flash their lights a lot—in short, "make use of all their tools and concrete," as she put it while driving in the middle of the road herself, in this region of RVs and logging trucks. A little danger put things in perspective. I'd gotten a C on my James paper and a B– in my James seminar. I was glad the quarter was over, so I could read what I wanted—Raymond Carver's *Will You Please Be Quiet, Please?* I had that book along on April second, with my "Death Mask of Shakespeare" bookplate pasted on its inside cover, and as Jamie drove I read Carver while feeling jealous of him. Jamie stopped to pee behind a tree, and when she came back she said that she didn't want to drive anymore, that she needed a nap, so I drove toward the Hoh while she slept. She woke up, when I slowed down in Forks, to suggest we buy eggs, milk, bread, butter, and syrup and make French toast for dinner. It was raining, so we ran into the store. I remember Jamie in a green corduroy jacket from the Salvation Army and with a wet face as we went down an aisle. The jacket had a wool collar and, also wet, it smelled like sheep.

The Hoh was running high that day. The lane to John William's mobile home was muddy in the low spots, and we slipped sideways once, into the nubbed grass. The tarp was partly off the firewood, and the rope gasket in the screen door had loosened and let the screen flop. The lights were off. The Impala was gone. We sat in the Datsun with the wipers and defroster making their racket until I turned off the motor. "What now?" said Jamie. We waited, me reading and Jamie sleeping, then vice versa, until it began to get dark. Finally, we knocked on John William's door—first me, and next Jamie, with greater force. I held a black plastic garbage bag over our heads because of the rain, and Jamie said, "You look like Dracula doing that," before trying the knob. We went in. Not only was there no John William, there was also no furniture or anything else except a broom, a vacuum cleaner, and a box of scouring powder. The place, which smelled of damp carpet, was neatly abandoned, featureless except for the woodstove, on top of which an envelope, made from a brown paper bag and tape, with BONNIE AND CLYDE written on it in felt-penned capitals, was propped against the flue and secured by a river cobble. The note inside said, BARGAIN BASE-MENT LOVERS: PLEASE COME GET MY CAR. THANKS—SIMON MAGUS. Jamie said, "What's he talking about?"

We built a fire in the woodstove. I told her what I hadn't told her until then—because it seemed to me that the circumstances implied John William's permission—about the blood pact I'd made with him above the South Fork of the Hoh. Jamie didn't understand "blood pact." On the floor that night, in her sleeping bag, she said that a blood pact sounded ridiculous. Later, I thought Jamie was asleep, but then, out of nowhere, she said, "Gnosticism is elitist." I said I wasn't the right person to respond. "In the end, they're like the rest," she insisted. "They think it's only them who have the truth."

In the morning, we drove toward the South Fork trailhead. The weather was better, bright and windy, with the young leaves wet in the trees. Jamie sat with her arms across her belly, humming at first, and then she said that a blood pact was a guy thing. We rounded Mount Octopus. There was still snow on Huelsdonk Ridge. Our road was winter-ravaged and full of potholes. I described pick work. I described the scaffolding. I described John William's fire drill. She said that, to her, the Gnostics sounded crazy. If the Gnostics thought God—if there was a God—was like a big, malicious prison warden, that was "at least as crazy," she said, "as all the other religions put together." We drove on. The river had blown a new swath through the alders since the last time I'd seen it. We stopped, filled a canteen, and skipped a few rocks. Jamie said it was less about technique and more about persisting in finding the right rock, and she was right.

Up the road, we saw the hind end of a deer disappearing into brush. Here the going was even worse—craters like an obstacle course, and fallen saplings to slip past. Once, Jamie had to get out and bend a limb so that, driving by it, I wouldn't scratch her car. New alders were growing in the drainage ditch. Rivulets had eroded the road-base hardpan. We came to the road end, and, sure enough,

there was John William's Impala, under the trees. It looked dere-
lict, probably because there were no other cars to legitimize its presence, and because the wind had blown twigs, needles, and branches
onto its hood. The wind was less now, but not done blowing, so
more pieces of the canopy, of a gentle variety, fell while we stood
there. "It's a Nancy Drew mystery," Jamie said.

I looked beneath the floor mat for John William's car key before
I remembered that he always left it behind a maple, pulling up the
moss between root clefts and hiding it in a snuff tin. When I told
Jamie as much, she said, "Vintage Nancy Drew," but this line of
humor came to a halt when, along with the key, we found, behind
that maple, under moss, a plastic garbage bag containing—we
counted carefully, twice—seven hundred of what some of my students call Benjamins: that is, seven hundred one-hundred-dollar
bills. There was also a note, again in all capitals, reading, KEEP THE
MONEY BUT TAKE THE CAR TO SAN DIEGO & LEAVE IT THERE. "Is this
part of gnosticism?" asked Jamie.

Money plays a big part, probably the major part, in the media
coverage of the hermit of the Hoh, and I noticed that money caught
the attention of certain students, who approved of me suddenly as
they might approve of someone in a gangster film. Once, when I was
walking down the hall toward the lunchroom this spring, somebody
made, for my benefit, a cheesy hip-hop move, saying simultaneously,
"It's all about the Benjamins!" and another time someone said,
"Loan me some C's, please, I got places to be, see," before laughing
so uproariously he fell against a locker. But best was a junior, notori-
ous for being small yet still the sixth man on our basketball team,
who, on seeing me walking toward the parking lot, shouted, "I'm
down with Bill Gates, I call him 'Money' for short, I phone him up
at home and I make him do my tech support!" Cast in this new light,
I'm a role model.

Jamie and I sat looking at the Benjamins and wondering what to
do with them. "Are there other weird friends I don't know about?"
she asked.

"This is very old Seattle money."

"It's still green," said Jamie.

I said, "He's a filthy-rich trust-funder."

"I thought you were his blood brother."

"I am his blood brother."

"Well," said Jamie, "he must have sized you up correctly, because here you are, right?"

"We're both here."

"True."

"He sized you up, too," I pointed out.

You have to understand how much money it was—$70,000 then had the buying power of $220,000 as I write—to get an idea of what Jamie and I felt. Or you'd have to imagine those seven hundred Benjamins spread out on the moss. They spoke for themselves. They were crass. I understood, in their presence, that my life was changed, and this understanding was not only poignant but tinged by—I suppose the word is—corruption. Yes, corruption; absolutely, corruption, because it's one thing to have a view of yourself, and it's another to be shown the money. I don't care who you are—try looking at all those Benjamins. When they're close like that, you want them. Or I did, and do, and I'm not that greedy. But obviously, inevitably, you'll make your own decision. In the silence of your thoughts. Just between you and you. Money equals x in the moral calculus of our time, and the equation comes out differently for each of us.

Jamie said, as we knelt by the money, "This is pretty interesting."

"What do you think?"

"I say we split it."

"Okay, we'll split it."

Jamie said, "Let's live in Italy."

"We'll lose our apartment."

"Let's give it to charity."

"We need to slow down."

"We need," said Jamie, "to blow it."

We moved the money around—picked up Benjamins and put them down in new places, made little mounds, made a pile. I counted again, and Jamie lay with her hands behind her head. Finally, I put all the bills in the bag and lay down beside her. She said, "You better hike up to wherever this place is and give it back to him."

I tried the key in the Impala and turned the engine over experimentally. Then I shut it down and put the key back in the snuff tin and the tin back under the moss behind the maple. There were some leftover eggs, and leftover butter, syrup, and bread, and I put all of that, *Will You Please Be Quiet, Please?*, and the bag of Benjamins in my pack. The last thing Jamie said, from the wheel of her Datsun, was that she looked forward to listening again to the radio preacher who knew so much about Ezekiel and death. I laughed at that, but on the trail by myself, almost immediately, I felt spooked and lonely. I'd learned to be superstitious about money from those moralizing stories in which money is a curse—I'd read *The Pearl* in the seventh grade; I'd seen *The Treasure of the Sierra Madre* at midnight in a nearly empty theater—and from hearing my father say, a number of times, "Money is the root of all evil." I rested a lot, leaning on my pack but careful not to crack the eggs I was carrying, and eating slices of buttered bread slathered with syrup in the forest of hoary cedars where John William and I had failed to make fire with a flint and steel three years before. Later, I sat behind a rock, rippling a wad of Benjamins as if it was a deck of cards. What a feeling, all those serial numbers flying past, and Franklin staring at me as if it was only an hour since he'd nearly electrocuted himself so famously with a key and kite. His dour face made me remember the $5,000 I got when my mother died, and the packet of *frites* I bought in Amsterdam.

When I walked into John William's camp, I tried acting nonchalant and said, "What happened to your scaffolding?"

"I turned it into firewood."

"What are you doing?"

"Weaving a mat."

"What is that stuff?"

"Cedar bark."

He set his handwork in his lap and looked at me like someone with something to confess. His beard was growing back, and his face looked grimy. He said, "Did you find everything?"

"I did."

"Then you ought to be south of Portland by now."

"I'm not."

"Don't screw things up," said John William.

He scrambled the eggs and fried the bread in butter. We didn't talk for a while. I let him eat. There were a lot of tin cans in his fire pit in stages of charred disintegration. I had an old packet of powdered cream-of-leek soup in my pack, and he poured that into boiling water and ate it with bread heels. "You're a food junkie," I said. John William had a cast-iron pan and a cowpoke's coffeepot, both fire-stained. He ate without talking, and when he was done he poured water into the pan from the pot and, after swirling it a little, drank the water. But there was still egg in his beard.

I said, "This is sort of Robinson Crusoe."

"Crusoe was a goatherd."

"There's a film called *Robinson Crusoe on Mars*," I said. "He had a monkey named Mona. It had the guy who played Batman—Adam West."

John William said, "Up yours, Neil."

He'd made a sort of pueblo ladder, but lashed with manila cord instead of rawhide. We climbed into the cave, me with my pack on, and John William turned around and pulled the ladder up.

He'd put in adzed timbers. They were toe-nailed with spikes and shaped like mine buttresses. There were two of these frames, and along them were more spikes, spaced like coat pegs, from which hung two rows of ditty bags—dry goods out of reach of voles and shrews, or so John William must have hoped. He'd also laid in a fat store of canned food: there were cans twenty deep at the back of the cave, stacked to my height—peaches in syrup, baked beans, etc. He had jugs of white gas, extra lantern mantles, a lot of toilet paper, and a lot of C batteries. He had books, about a dozen, all practical, all manuals—tanning, flint knapping, food preservation—except for *A Few Flies and I* by Issa. I said, "Nuclear-bomb shelter."

"You want anything to eat?"

"How many trips did you make?"

"Exactly ten thousand."

I said, "How come no real books but one?"

"Only real books."

"Why'd you bring Issa?"

"Issa's not a sellout."

We sat on our sleeping bags. I didn't mention the money. I thought, at that point, that he'd stay just till winter. But in this I was like someone who believes the world is flat—I didn't want to look at the evidence.

I said, "So what's this San Diego?"

"What do you mean?"

"Why San Diego?"

"So they think I went to Mexico."

"Which 'they'?"

"Countryman, don't be dumb. Just find a canyon or a parking lot down there and ride the bus back for me."

I said, "Then what?"

"What do you mean?"

"What happens next?"

"They'll figure I'm in Mexico. That way I can stay up here without being hassled."

"You want people to think you're in Mexico." .

John William: "What's your IQ?"

After a while, we climbed down. John William tried to show me how to make a mat, but I got frustrated with the slow handwork, and after a while took up a crosscut saw and made rounds of firewood instead. I split and stacked. I filled canteens. I made kindling with a maul. John William went on weaving cedar bark. I said, "Nice job cleaning out your trailer."

"You liked that?"

"What happened to the lawn chairs?"

"I left them by the highway."

"What about the cable drum?"

"I turned it into stove wood."

"Your chess set?"

"Still got it," John William answered.

In his ragged sweater with its singed, unraveled cuffs, he wove his strands of bark like a mental patient in an arts-and-crafts session. Why he preferred this to the $70,000 in my pack seemed a perfectly reasonable question, and so, with the maul in my hands, I said, "What makes this better than seventy thousand bucks?"

"Look around," said John William.

"But you could have this and the money."

John William stopped weaving and said, "No, you can't. Money ruins things."

"Then why are you giving it to me and Jamie?"

"If you don't want it," said John William, "give it to charity."

"We are giving it to charity."

"Good."

In the morning, I put *Will You Please Be Quiet, Please?* next to his other books, and got my pack on without having told him the money was in it. The last thing I said before heading out of those woods was "You've gone off the deep end." He looked like Ishi, the last of the Modocs, who was found in a slaughterhouse corral in 1911 wearing a covered-wagon canvas re-envisioned as a poncho. He said, "Just get my car down to San Diego, that's all I ask."

JAMIE AND I KEPT the $70,000. It was hard not to. In fact, it turned out to be impossible not to. And we have no regrets, because with that money we eventually bought the house we live in—or, to put it another way, we didn't waste it. It was a little complicated not to show up at our banks with $35,000 in cash each, but by dividing it into more innocent-looking portions—amounts you might get paid for selling a car—and opening checking accounts around Seattle, we got it laundered.

But first we drove John William's Impala all the way to San Ysidro. Jamie told her boss she had to take a few days off to help a friend in need, which was true. Before we left, we hid the money, or most of it—$69,000—in my father's basement, inside an old television I'd gutted, years before, to hide dope in. Jamie thought this seemed a little sordid—my pot supply and all that cash inside a television. No matter. We spent a night in Medford, Oregon, in a motel, and a second night in Fresno, also in a motel, and we made it a point to drive at or below the speed limit, because a cop stop would leave a paper trail for the private detective Rand Barry was sure to hire when the abandoned Impala, still registered in his name, was recovered near the border not long after John William withdrew $70,000 in cash from his trust-fund account. Jamie and I used our headlights and turn signals, we yielded when we were supposed to yield, we came to full stops at stop signs. But no problems, smooth sailing, air-conditioned rooms and swimming pools, restaurant meals and late-night movies, and, best of all, everything paid for with Benjamins. In the end, Jamie parked behind a McDonald's in San Ysidro, and we walked away with our sunglasses on after wiping the fingerprints off the steering wheel, transmission lever, parking brake handle, and door handles. Two gringo kids near the border, with backpacks.

It was a hot Greyhound trip northward. We passed it in a miasma of sleep and sweat, rousing ourselves every once in a while to eat oranges and play shaky games of Gin, or to read while California went past, but then we couldn't take it anymore, not happily, and why should we? San Francisco, hailed in song as a good town for lovers, was imminent. What an easy decision for two vagabonds on a lark. Rashly, we squinted at ginseng in Chinatown. We went to the Haight, even though this was the year, 1977, that the Village People launched. In the Haight, we visited a used-record shop where I bought a three-LP box set—*The San Francisco Sound*—for $6.50 as a souvenir, breaking a Benjamin to make this transaction and hearing about it from the clerk: "You're wipin' out my change, big spender." So we loosened up. We went on a spree. We took our money up to Nob Hill, feeling like Bonnie and Clyde—as in John William's trailer note—or, rather, like Faye Dunaway and Warren Beatty as Bonnie and Clyde. We might have said, if we were going to talk about this trip, *You should have seen our hotel room—Italian marble in the bath!* The gilded Mark Hopkins, for which we weren't dressed, with its terra-cotta and its uniformed doormen, was not opposed to cash when flashed, and so we waltzed in, laughing on our way through the lobby and in the elevator to the twelfth floor, where we got off, turned the key, donned the bathrobes, ordered room service, ran the bath, slept through the afternoon, woke up, drank wine, and when we went out in the dark and came back in the dark, the hotel exterior was lit like a film set.

And now that I'm confessing to all of this, let me also describe our dinner at Jack's, with its off-the-charts prices and rarefied menu—how we asked the Mark Hopkins concierge for a recommendation, no expense spared; how he made us a reservation and ordered our cab; how Jamie wore her fake Ph.D. spectacles that night; how we drank a bottle of—this is in my journal, which I kept open on the table, as if I was an unabashed restaurant critic—a Barton & Guestier Pouilly-Fuissé after dismissing the sommelier's California suggestions; how we paired our Pouilly-Fuissé with distinctly the wrong dishes, which in retrospect I realize ruined our act: what came to the table, for both of us that night, were entrées in rich, complicated sauces. No matter. We giggled our way through every course. It was like being in a play. We had expensive digestifs and smelly cheeses before I laid down another Benjamin, and we kept our faces straight as our waiter carted it away on a gleaming tray.

So it was all about the Benjamins in the City by the Bay. But then we were on the bus again, our spell broken, back inside our skins and jointly rueful, reading purgative paperbacks between bouts of sleep and conversation, Jamie with her Virginia Woolf and me with a new edition of Carver I'd found in a Russian Hill bookstore. Cinderella after midnight—that high, thin diesel drift, so slowly nauseating and fundamental to Greyhound; suspicious bus vagrants slumping, sulking, and leering; cigarette fumes at bathroom stops; highway droning; torpor; gum bought from a machine. In this way, California got behind us, but it took a while. Strangely, it wasn't until Oregon that I had this regret: there I was reading Carver when I realized that, in San Francisco, I'd failed to check out the storied haunts of the Beats—Kerouac's rail yards, Ginsberg's *Howl* flat, Ferlinghetti's bookstore, and so on. I mentioned this to Jamie, and she made a good point—she said we could always go back.

Of course we can—but we haven't. For one reason or another. So we've yet to see Gary Snyder's Zen cottage in Berkeley, or William Everson's Kingfisher Flat near Santa Cruz, or the Six Gallery—the Six Gallery is gone, but nevertheless—where Ginsberg first read *Howl*. In fact, we haven't been back to California, but that's something we're mulling changing soon, because it might be worthwhile to see the Joshua trees, visit friends in San Jose, and take hikes in the Sierras. At least we think it might be worthwhile.

SURE ENOUGH, a private detective found me. I came out of my basement one morning to walk to campus, and there he was, leaning against my stakebed, wearing an open leather blazer and running shoes. He had very dark skin, like Idi Amin, but a disheveled-looking salt-and-pepper shock of hair. He was athletic-looking except for a tidy paunch, and his mustache was that thin, little gigolo's stripe certain aging Lotharios incline toward. When he saw me, he stopped leaning against my stakebed, roused himself like someone warming up to run, flashed his PI card—blurry in its bifold sleeve—and said, "Mind if I walk with you?"

It was a line from *Columbo*, a show my father fell asleep in front of religiously. I wanted badly to say, "It's a public sidewalk," in deference to my role as the guilty antagonist, but instead I said, "No."

He had an upbeat gait. He said his name was Vance Reese. He said that he worked for someone named Bledsoe, and that this Bledsoe had been hired by "your friend John William Barry's next of kin" because John Barry was "of late a missing person." I said, "You're kidding," and he said, "Do I look like I'm kidding?" We walked past a sorority and a lot of beer cans in a gutter, and Vance Reese said, "Do I?"

"No."

"So where is he?"

"I couldn't say."

PI Reese nodded. He picked up his pace and walked backward in front of me, skipping a little. He said, "Y'all see Mr. Bojangles?"

"No."

"Y'all see Buckwheat?"

"No."

"Okay, then," he said. "All right, then."

He fell in at my shoulder. I had the impression he was giving me time to think it over, but I didn't say anything.

"What class you going to?"

"History class."

"History of what?"

"European Exploration of North America."

"What week is this?"

"First week of the quarter."

"First week of the quarter," said Reese. "So what you do with spring break?"

"I went camping."

"Where at?"

"The Duckabush River."

"Where's that?"

"In the Olympics."

Reese said, "You must like that."

"What?"

"That outdoor business. That getting-bit-by-bugs business."

"Yes."

"What you mean, yes?"

"I like it—camping."

Reese plunged ahead and walked backward again. He said, "So who you go camping with?"

"My girlfriend."

"The one who come out this morning, or another one?"

"The one who came out this morning."

"What's her name?"

"Why do you need to know?"

"What's her name?"

"Jamie."

"Jamie what?"

"Jamie Shaw."

We crossed 45th and went along a leafy path. There were other students, all with books, most walking fast. Reese said, "You didn't go to California?"

"No."

"When's the last time you heard from your friend?"

"Last fall."

"What he say?"

"I went to visit him where he lived."

"Where was that?"

"Out on the Hoh River."

"Last fall?"

"Yes."

"What he say?"

"What do you mean?"

"What he say about *missing*?"

"He didn't say anything."

Reese gritted his teeth. He shook his head. He stroked his eyebrows flat. "Another white boy of few words," he observed.

We came to the Quad. People were hurrying now to make their nine-thirties. "I have to go," I said.

"You seeing to business," said Reese.

"My class is in this building."

"All business," said Reese. "That's smart." And he fluffed his wild hair with a cake cutter.

I never heard from the Bledsoe Agency again. But at the time I felt cowed and, that morning, couldn't concentrate on European explorers. After class, from a booth in the HUB, I called Jamie at work and told her that we'd gone camping on the Duckabush during spring break, in case anybody asked, but nobody did, and nobody checked our bank accounts, either. Why would they? John William had disappeared in Mexico.

6

LOYAL CITIZEN OF

HAMBURGER WORLD

I WENT TO SEE John William after getting back from California, setting out in the stakebed after classes on a Friday, irritated with Keith for stealing my radio and fretting that Vance Reese might be—to borrow a phrase from the PI genre—tailing me. My brakes felt too forgiving, so every half-hour I topped off the fluid and pumped up the pedal while watching, surreptitiously, my rearview mirrors, and imagining Reese just over the hill, behind the wheel of a sedan, with a cup of coffee and a glowing cigarette. I turned onto a side road and pulled over around a bend to wait for my nemesis, but he never materialized. My paranoia waned after that, and, idling by a hayfield, I ate a leftover square of cold lasagna off aluminum foil before getting back on the highway. It was the time of year when a lot of bugs die against your windshield. Twice, crows intent on road-kill refused to scatter until I loomed too large to be ignored. Around Forks, the mills were blowing smoke, and the yards beside them were decked high with logs. I laid in some groceries—I spent more of John William's $70,000—and then drove to the South Fork Hoh trailhead, where I let my shoulders rest after battling all that friction in the steering box. The place felt sinister, though. Your imagination can get the better of you where a road ends against a forest. It's easy to feel trapped with your back against trees. Vulnerable to all of this, I got on the trail and tried loving my solitude, but this was a futile and self-conscious effort. I didn't want to be there, by myself, while the sun went down. I didn't want to be hiking in such a tense silence. The maple leaves were youthfully green, but that didn't ameliorate my nervous view of things. Before dark, I bivouacked, tentless, by the river, banking up a fire in front of a boulder and basking in its heat with my journal and *The Collected Eliot, 1909–1962*, which an excitable professor had asked me to scour, and although all of that might sound pleasant enough, or not a bad way to pass evening hours—especially with the din of water on the gravel bars and my view of stars illuminating silhouetted hills—I didn't enjoy being there. I suppose you could say that my aloneness got the better of me, or that I felt fear that night, by the river, by myself—but fear of life, and not of animals or the forest. "The Hollow Men" didn't help, because I couldn't disown its mood, or break its hold on my thoughts, as I lay in my sleeping bag by those smoking coals, and though this temper made me tired, it also left me agitated enough to prod, more often than I needed to, the sticks I was burning. I mostly felt wistful. I didn't want to have behind me, already, some experiences I couldn't have again. Reading Eliot by flashlight was like deciphering runes, and made it more difficult to sleep.

In the morning, I ascended to John William's cave, feeling, strangely, like a supplicant. It seemed to me I had a plea to make without knowing what it was. John William greeted me with a rock that missed my head by inches. Standing by the fire pit, holding another rock beside his ear, barefoot and grinning, wide-eyed with feigned malice, he looked more disheveled and bedraggled than before, but his teeth were still conspicuously white, and he still had that upright, English fell runner look, that ebullient physicality and stalwart expression I'd loathed on that May afternoon, five years earlier, when he'd gripped my hand earnestly after beating me in the half-mile. Now his wool pants and limp sweater both had burn holes, brown-edged and smaller than dimes, that must have been made by flying cinders, and the ash in his hair, beard, and eyebrows made him look ghostly, or ceremonial in the tribal sense, as if this ash was ritually cosmetic, but he also resembled a downed RAF fly-boy surviving on wits, derring-do, and a stiff upper lip, maybe in the

Schwarzwald. My friend had no mirror and didn't know, probably, that with his stains of leaden ash, his smudges and grime, he further brought to mind a Day of the Dead celebrant, an Ash Wednesday penitent, or—especially with that rock in his hand—a character from *Lord of the Flies*. "You missed," I said.

"Same old Countryman."

"What's that supposed to mean?"

"You're here."

I got out of my pack and threw the Eliot at him. He caught it, looked at the cover, and said, "I overdosed on T.S. in Althea's class," meaning the Mrs. Mastroianni who'd given him an F for forty-seven opulent if misguided pages on "Cosmology of the Gnostics: Penetrating God's Illusion," the Mrs. Mastroianni who'd petted her Abyssinian while discussing Chomsky with him in her apartment, the Mrs. Mastroianni who believed all her Lakeside students should read, reverently, as John William put it, "that most overrated poem of all time, 'The Outhouse.' "

"I don't know 'The Outhouse.' "

"It's also called *The Waste Land*."

I'd brought T-bones, catsup, mayonnaise, and iceberg lettuce. Within ten minutes of my arrival, John William was frying the meat in mayonnaise while packing his mouth with all the lettuce it could handle. He ate that head the way other people eat an apple, by cleaving it in two, except that he poured catsup and mayonnaise into the exposed leaf folds and doused them with salt, pepper, and cayenne. He doused the burning steaks as well, and flipped them repeatedly with darting fingers, and after slopping more mayonnaise—also with his fingers—into his smoking and spitting skillet, cut a chunk of half-cooked beef, charred and fat-rimmed, and ate it from the spear point on his pocketknife. I noticed, again, that dozens of flattened cans lined his fire pit, slipped under one another like roofing tiles—clever heat-reflectors that, with time, were degrading into rust-hued powder—and that some of his fire-ring rocks were heat-cracked. His camp, nevertheless, retained its vaguely military fastidiousness. His canteens were neatly hung. Socks were drying on a line. The heads of his hand tools sat on stone, not dirt. The limestone chips that were the refuse of his cave building had been swept under trees, and the hot tub, enlarged, now included a flat, stone bench.

"Hey," John William said, "how was San Diego?"

"San Diego? I thought you said Vegas. I thought you wanted me to sell your car in Vegas. Didn't you say Vegas?"

John William, who'd finished off the lettuce already, said, "These steaks are done enough," stabbed one on his knife, and tore into it. "What's T.S. say about meat?" he asked, close to unintelligibly, because he wouldn't take time away from chewing.

I said, "Eat both."

While he did so—noisily and with shiny chin whiskers—I discovered cedar bark floating in the hot tub, rolls of inner bark knotted with their tapers, and dangled my feet among them. These packets suggested my friend's woodland prowess and occasioned in me a glandular resentment. They were so neatly done, so adroitly crafted, that I felt bad about myself just looking at them. Here he'd been going competently native, under these trees and in these woods, while I'd been analyzing "Gerontion" in a college library carrel.

When John William was meat-sated, we climbed his pueblo ladder. He'd driven two spikes over his cave entrance to support a stripped sapling on the horizontal, and wrapped around this, like a roll-blind, was a cedar mat he could unfurl like a curtain. He left it where it was, though, to let forest light in. We sat on cedar mats and under cedar mats: three were hung, from spikes and cord, like banners. They weren't so much festive as civilizing, though the work was crude and absent of design—not the sort of thing you'd see in a gallery alongside ceremonial masks, but not bad, either, tightly woven and, in the main, square. Sprawled under them, I rested while John William tried unraveling his rat's nest with a 59-cent comb I'd brought.

He was eagerly talkative. No doubt he hadn't spoken for a while, except to birds who didn't answer, or to squirrels who squeaked at him from trees. He tried to show me how to make three-ply rope out of cedar bark by twisting to the right, but I told him I didn't need to know about this, since I could buy rope. A few minutes later, he put in my hands a cedar basket he'd woven, delineating his technique as if he was guest basket-maker on a Sunday-afternoon public-television show, and stressing how useful this item would be for gathering whatever he was gathering. Not changing my tune, I reminded John William that five-gallon plastic buckets were free for the taking behind paint stores.

His cave felt improved. The subterranean gloom of those lime-stone facets was now concealed by the warp and weft of his mats, which insulated, too, dispelling drafts. You could loll meditatively without feeling claustrophobic, because the banners, in squaring off what was shaped like a mine shaft, hid tomblike indentations and made the air less dank. This was not so much a dungeon now as a room in one of those Japanese teahouses I'd seen in *National Geographic*. This was the secure, well-stocked, and shipshape nest of a survivalist whose bona fides were apparent in his mats, baskets, canned-goods larder, how-to manuals, and ditty bags of sundries hung like pelts. It was easy to be impressed by my friend's industriousness and preparatory efforts—he'd been making like a squirrel getting ready for winter—but I couldn't help thinking, at the same time, that things would change when his food ran out.

I said, "So what happens when the cans are gone?"

"I'll have more room."

"You'll walk out of here."

"No, I won't."

"You'll go up to Forks for bacon and eggs."

"No."

"You'll start thinking about hamburgers and have to come out."

"That's you," said John William. "You're thinking of yourself. You're a loyal citizen of hamburger world."

I DID WHAT I had to do—which is to say, I visited my friend a lot, hauling offerings on my back—powdered milk, toothpaste, Fritos, shampoo—none of it, I stress, at his behest. At the same time, he didn't reject these artifacts from the real world the way he'd once rejected Christmas presents, because in the end he couldn't reject them and go on with his hermitry. Was that hypocrisy? I brought him gloves, socks, lantern mantles, and white gas. I brought him *Playboy* and *Penthouse*. I brought him chocolate malted-milk balls, weed, scissors, a deck of cards, and M&M's. He knew, of course, what all this meant—that, like everyone else, he was dependent on hamburger world—but what could he do about the fact that he was human? Nothing except try to get supremely woods-wise, which is what he spent his time doing. My visits, though, were vacations from this regime: we played Blackjack with M&M's in the pot, drank Jack Daniel's, and turned the pages of *Penthouse* and *Playboy*. Occasionally, John William would blurt something like "Miss June's most recently read book is *All Things Wise and Wonderful*," or "Miss July likes to listen to KC and the Sunshine Band while washing her Corvette." If I laughed, he'd say, "She also likes to listen to the love theme from *A Star Is Born* while pleasuring her dog," or "In her spare time, she repairs sluggish vibrators." In other words, he could be as puerile as any twenty-one-year-old boy in the exercising of his wit. And so could I.

So—I stress this—we had fun up there. Yes, it was perplexing to see my friend this way—as a lonely woods-dweller, as a filthy forest troll—but we still liked to smoke dope, play cards, and, in short, treat the whole matter as a Huck Finn–like vacation. For a while, we indulged in heavy gambling and passed long nights with a deck of cards and straight faces. John William was a credible and practiced bluffer who could relax through a ruse and not betray himself. I found this to be true in our Blackjack tournaments, epic bouts in the dirt by the fire, or on cedar mats, by candlelight, in his cave. He played as if he was ahead and betting my M&M's even when he wasn't, and this gave him an ease I didn't feel. He had gambler's cool, and his confidence was natural. At first I thought I knew what was up—for example, if his eyes went to his chips on the flop, it meant he had a winning hand—but I was wrong. Fortunately, most of the time we were just playing for candy, although on one trip, determined to defeat him, I suggested we play for more meaningful stakes. We took a hundred toffee-covered peanuts each and, after settling on an ante of five, agreed that he whose stock was first depleted would suffer thusly: if I lost, I would have to dig enough cedar roots out of the ground with a yew stick to fill one of his baskets; if he lost, he would have until my next visit, two weeks hence, to memorize *The Waste Land* and recite it flawlessly. The two tasks seemed about equally abhorrent. Naturally, I got in trouble right away by bluffing. The set of my chin and the aggressive way I dropped a lot of toffee-covered peanuts into an already scary pile was about as subtle as showing him my down card. I got my expression under better control but couldn't help shifting around a lot when investing in a paltry hand, and again John William lit me up for more peanuts. Down to nearly nothing, I started talking off the cuff, thinking this might make him waver, but instead it made things worse, because my silences now meant something. In short, John William knew what I was holding more than 50 percent of the time, and it didn't take any more than that to clean me out. As it unfolded, digging cedar roots with a yew stick was arduous. My back couldn't take all the stabbing at rocky soil. The roots snaked around stones, and since our deal was for straight roots—because those were the ones good for baskets—I pulled a lot of roots I couldn't deliver. To keep my word within a reasonable duration, I had to work by the river, where the digging was easier and the roots were straighter, and so the cruel reality of my defeat was that I not only dug roots, I carried them uphill.

During three days in August, we played a lot of chess, and this tournament was notable for the gravitas that flavored it when it became apparent to John William that I'd been practicing. I beat him in our first game by making sacrifices aimed at penetrating his castled position, and then, after a loss and a draw, I beat him again by sacrificing in the early going so as to get a rook file open. We sat on cedar mats, fending off gnats, drinking cherry Kool-Aid, and, at first, deriding each other's gambits, but by game five we'd fallen silent and were both eyeing the board as if the stakes were mortal. I won that one, too, again via sacrifice, and then we settled on twenty-one matches as appropriate to our circumstances. In this marathoner's mood, we played a trio of draws. John William twisted his hair while he brooded. Neither of us would capitulate during lengthy end-games. The next day, I blew the morning's first match by attacking eagerly and, as it turned out, transparently, but came back by employing my signature—sacrifice—in this case a rook for two pawns. It worked, and for the rest of that day I hit him with variations on my theme, gulling or beguiling him with irresistible give-aways. John William could be duped, I found, if I let myself look stupid—but not if I let myself look too stupid.

Day three of Barry versus Countryman. We both knew that he was the more sophisticated player but that an upset was potentially in the making. After lunch, I dared an end-game exchange sacrifice, a rook for a knight, and thereby, and roundaboutly, promoted a pawn, which I parlayed to a go-ahead victory. That closed it out, because all the remaining matches were attritional bouts, which took patience on my part, since John William knew what was happening and did everything in his power to obstruct my conservatism and force the board—but still I got the draws I desired.

When the last match was done, John William shook my hand and said, "You've got it dialed in, Neil."

"What's that?"

"Sacrifice."

BEFORE HIS FIRST WINTER, I tried coaxing John William out of cave dwelling. I went to see him on the day after Thanksgiving, bringing with me leftovers packed by my aunts—including two slices each from four different pies, and a Tupperware container of mashed potatoes—plus twenty packets of dried leek soup and a hundred bouillon cubes. There was snow on the ground, but not a lot, and almost none right under the trees. The needles on the spruces looked waxen and brittle, and the canteens, when shaken, sounded sandy. In the cave, steam billowed from our mouths, and I, for one, wore a hat and kept my hands in my pockets. While John William bolted sliced turkey from a plastic bag, I emphasized that when the road got snowed in I wouldn't be able to bring supplies. He shrugged off this news. He licked his fingers and started on the pie. I counted his remaining cans and reported the result—seventy-seven—but this made no difference to him. Nothing made a difference. All talk of winter and its meaning was useless. I decided to leave him my sleeping bag, gaiters, gloves, stove, and parka in lieu of pleading.

When fall quarter ended, three weeks later, I drove out in the stakebed with the heater on high, a pack full of food, and tire chains and a shovel, but there was no getting up the Owl Creek Road when it began to climb Huelsdonk Ridge. I tried walking it on snowshoes but gave up after four miles, in the main because I'd warned John William about this and felt that let me off the hook. It didn't. That night, in the Forks Motel, I drank a lot of bourbon, then fell asleep with my clothes on and the thermostat at seventy-five. There were steelhead fishermen in an adjacent room, and I heard them get up at four-fifteen and drive off, snow crunching under their tires.

All morning the snow fell. I didn't feel like moving and read

Chekhov stories in bed. Finally, there was nothing for it but to face hamburger world. I walked down the street in someone else's tracks and, at the café, ate pancakes and patty sausage while reading the morning paper. I did the crossword puzzle, too, and then I just sat. The thermometer outside the window read twenty-three. I walked back with the wind and snow coming toward me, and a state truck, dropping sand, went past with a muffled rumble and tire chains rattling. It was bitter getting my own chains on, but when I was done I turned the key to my room and ran hot water over my fingers.

When I got home, Jamie said, "At least you tried." She had a head cold and was wearing the striped pajamas she'd given me for Christmas the year before, and she had her arm across the couch back behind me, a book in her lap, and a box of graham crackers on the side table. The cemetery full of Woodsmen looked Irish in the night glow, and on 55th, a car, sideways in the steep street, rested against another car while teen-agers rode inner tubes past it. I said, "I give up. I'm calling his old man."

"Okay," said Jamie, "but give it twenty-four hours."

The next afternoon, we went Christmas shopping at Northgate. I got my dad a coffee-table book on the castles of Ireland, and Carol a sheepskin car-seat cover. We went to *The Last Wave*—Richard Chamberlain as an Australian lawyer going mad. Afterward, we got a table at India House, and while we were sitting there sipping mango lassis, Jamie looked at her watch and said, "Twenty-four hours."

"Yep."

"Are you ratting him out?"

"Nope."

"How come?"

"He'd never speak to me again if the Park Service came for him."

"He'll also never speak to you dead," said Jamie.

We ordered three curries, knowing we'd end up taking some of each back to our apartment. "He isn't going to die," I said. "He's got food, two sleeping bags, water, and a hot tub."

"When did you decide all of this?"

"During the movie. I used the whole twenty-four, Jamie."

She said, "I always try to use the whole twenty-four, especially when the question's a big one."

"All right," I said. "Will you marry me?"

"Give me forty-eight," Jamie answered.

BEFORE JOHN WILLIAM gained fame as a hermit, there was a Bulgarian near Darrington who made the news in modest fashion
because he lived in the woods for seven years. According to reports,
the Bulgarian inhabited a hole in the ground covered with brush and
sod spread on a tarp. He also built a shelter near a creek in fishing
season, and no doubt he ate berries, but his primary survival technique was serial burglary. Whenever his situation became dire, the
Bulgarian would walk out of the woods and break into a cabin. He
often left mud behind, on the floor and on beds. He was legendary,
like Bigfoot, as far as Darrington was concerned; there were people
who left canned food for him on their porches, alongside supportive
notes. A tracker finally pinpointed this invisible local hero, who, it
turned out, looked like Cro-Magnon man and was still fierce at
sixty-eight. He was arrested after a prolonged wrestling match with
two law-enforcement officers and an attack dog. Later, his hovel was
located on a hillside. There was a seep nearby, and some Mason jars
filled with water. He had binoculars, rope, string, bits and pieces of
flashlights, several rifle barrels, a slide mechanism from a shotgun, a
burned rifle forearm, a .22 Hornet, a foreign-made automatic pistol
and a hundred rounds for it, a box of twelve-gauge shells, and a coffee can full of transistor-radio parts. He had three fishing spears and
a lot of pencil nubs, but no paper to write on, and no books. After his
arrest, he was diagnosed as paranoid. He ended up in jail.

   Is there a difference? The difference is that I bought a used snowmobile which I could run up a corrugated aluminum ramp (donated
by Keith, whose ATV and dirt bike were both permanently dis-
abled) and secure to my stakebed with cargo straps. I dropped Inter-
mediate Short Story Writing and Late 19th Century American
Literature, substituting for them Renaissance Drama and Greek
Lyric Poetry, so that my Fridays were free for winter quarter.
Rescheduled, I drove to Forks on the second Thursday in January
1978—John William's first winter in the Olympic Mountains—
stayed in the motel, and, on Friday, at first light, drove as far as I
could toward the South Fork Hoh before running my snowmobile
down Keith's ramp and blitzing toward the trailhead. This was my
first ride on a motorized sled. The machine wouldn't track. It was

loaded with my pack, snowshoes, and a large box of tools, and its windshield was scratched. It kept wanting to turn sideways, and its shocks needed a rebuild. Its muffler was shot, but that didn't matter, because no one was around in those woods but me, and I had on the earmuffs I used with my Homelite. At first, I felt precarious through every road bend, but then I discovered the foot pockets and, throttling up, found my balance. Cutting through all that untouched snow while sitting on a hot engine made me giddy. It also made me think of the scene from *Dr. Strangelove* in which Slim Pickens rides an H-bomb out of a B-52. At a midnight show a few years before, as Pickens, holding his hat and whooping like a cowboy, plummeted toward Russia, John William leaned in and told me that his father was one of the engineers responsible for the B-52's wing design. I thought of that, too, screaming along on my snowmobile, but mostly I was busy trying not to ski off the road.

Walking in, at first, wasn't bad. I traversed, downhill, to the riverbank, and snowshoed the gravel bars—the sort of open-country travel, in sun, near water, that is, to quote Wordsworth again, full of glimpses that would make me less forlorn. No one but me had touched that snow, other than birds, elk, and a bobcat, lynx, or cougar—I couldn't tell which. I'm not good at reading tracks, but these, whatever they were, looked as well defined as diagrams, and the paths they took, toward the water or forest, were interwoven with, I imagined, hunger and wariness. I realized then that my tracks were graphic, too, gigantically so, and my thoughts, as I shoed, became ponderously shrewder, less inclined toward ambience and more toward evasion, though at the same time I couldn't take seriously the prospect of someone's tailing me. I thought of Vance Reese, James Bond–like, on skis, slipping through the woods above with binoculars, and dapper in a Swiss parka and mirrored glasses. But then back to the serious problem at hand, which was how to disappear when every step I took had a spotlight on it.

I've mentioned before that place by the river, mentally marked, where four segments of a spruce lay like wrecked train cars against a hillside, and that this is where, keeping a tributary on my right, I characteristically left the trail to climb to the cave. Not this time. This time, getting out of my snowshoes, I crossed the tributary on a log, buckled in again, and shoed up the South Fork Hoh another mile, to where a dozen or more spruces, gouged from a bank, had collapsed, roots and all, into the water. If someone was interested—and I didn't think someone was—they could brood over my disappearance amid such debris, but that brooding wouldn't lead them to John William Barry, especially if I walked on the snowy downed trees until my boot prints composed a kind of labyrinth.

I did all of that, and then I backtracked in the water. I waded. I stayed off the snow. I got wet. I only knew what I knew, and what I knew was from television. You throw dogs off your scent, escape cops with flashlights, evade vigilantes, befuddle the infantry, and, basically, outsmart all the stupid people in the world who want to treat you badly, by wading. So that's what I did. I slogged back downstream with frozen feet, carrying my snowshoes, in the South Fork of the Hoh, and then, where the segments of spruce lay against the hillside, I slogged up the tributary a quarter-mile, and sat on my pack with my feet wrapped in a sweater before changing socks. This whole morning, from my snowmobile charge up an inundated road to my watery deception, was fun and lonely.

I shoed into camp at midafternoon and dropped my huge pack on the snow. In the cave entrance, the cedar curtain was dropped, but as I stood there wiping the sweat from my face it rolled up a little and John William popped his head out. "I thought you were a bear," he said.

"Bears hibernate."

I explained my ruse. I told him about the snowmobile. He looked at me the way the doorman at the Emerald City looked at Dorothy while she pleaded for admittance. Then I opened my pack and tossed up to him a box of chocolate-covered cherries wrapped in cellophane. "My sister gave me those for Christmas," I said. "She buys them on sale at Pay 'n Save."

John William said, "A snowmobile."

"It was fifty bucks."

"You know you have to wade back to those downed trees on your way out."

"Fine."

"Chocolate-covered cherries?"

"I ate your Almond Roca about an hour ago. But I still have this." And I tossed up a bottle of kirsch.

He put the ladder down, then pulled it up after I'd climbed in. We sat wrapped in sleeping bags with a lit candle between us, drinking kirsch from the bottle and eating the candies. John William had a scab on his cheek about the size of a prune. His fingernails were bitten down. His sweater was unraveling. He had on his hat, and his bag was pulled so tightly around his neck that only his face showed, with its scraggly beard. Otherwise, things remained fastidious—his gear and supplies, his hand tools and ditty bags: all was in tidy order. I counted cans again: twenty-eight. They were arrayed in a pyramid, its base seven twenty-four-ouncers of SpaghettiOs. On the other hand, John William still had most of the leek soup and all the bouillon cubes. I gave him the half-dozen hiker's freeze-dried meals Keith had given me for Christmas (which I could tell came from the discount bin at Outdoor Emporium). I gave John William rice, pinto beans, powdered milk, pilot crackers, dried apricots, and a bag of carrots. I gave him the book I had along, which was a paperback edition of *Robinson Jeffers: Selected Poems*. Finally, I gave him the special holiday issue of *Penthouse*, with its cover photo of a brunette in black lingerie drinking champagne from a tall glass, and its lead article on "The Real President Behind Carter." I shook all of this out of my pack and onto a cedar mat, as if I was a trader. John William went for the carrots.

For hours, we lay in our sleeping bags, talking. It was cold, but no colder than most winter camping, and there was always the hot tub. We nursed the kirsch and smoked hash. John William wolfed down a lot of pilot crackers and dried apricots. I asked him if he knew what day it was, and he said no, so I told him it was Friday, January 13, 1978, to which he replied, "Paraskavedekatriaphobia."

"What?"

"Fear of Friday the 13th."

I said that, while he'd been in the woods, ABBA had set the record for albums sold. We mulled whether a computer could ever beat a chess champion, John William pointing out that chess demanded not only computation but a sense of irony. I confessed to spending some of the $70,000 on the hash we were smoking before giving him an account of my laundering scheme. First Seattle Dexter Horton and Best Trust and Savings—the banks founded, respectively, by his paternal grandfather and his maternal great-grandfather—were now repositories of laundered cash, and John William was glad to hear about this, that some of the money had been parked in those institutions, right under the noses, and in the account books, of his "weaseling, demonic forefathers." "So what happened to charity?" he asked.

"I can't exactly walk into the Red Cross with a bag of cash."

"You're giving it to the Red Cross?"

"Not necessarily," I said, and immediately his fresh use of the word "weaseling" came to mind.

He got up on one forearm to light the hash pipe with the candle. Then he lay back, waited, and exhaled toward the ceiling while tugging at his beard. It was so cold in the cave that, between the hash smoke and his vapor, John William was like a human fog machine. His exhalation looked like a jet's contrail. He said, "Give it to a Buddhist monastery."

"How come?"

"Those guys need it."

"What for?"

"They want to row us to the other side."

Later, we had our fun with the *Penthouse*. "Miss December's most recently read book is *Jonathan Livingston Seagull*. She's currently a spokesperson for the Sisters of Mercy. She enjoys big-game hunting in a thong." And so on. We finished the kirsch, and after that, standing in the cave entrance and unzipping to relieve myself, I fell ten feet into the snow. My lip got cut, but otherwise it was the kind of fall you can have when you're drunk—painless and exhilarating. "Whilst alive," wrote Basho, "I enjoy my wine and keep repeating to myself 'tomorrow, tomorrow,' until I'm rebuked by the sages." John William sent the ladder down for me.

I PUT MONEY into the snowmobile, and kept it under a tarp. Keith liked tinkering with it, and replaced the track and a cracked engine mount after he'd borrowed it for a weekend. I took it up the South Fork Hoh at the end of January, and this time I brought John William a pair of bearpaw snowshoes, a garage-sale bow saw, a can of white gas, toilet paper, and as much food as I could stuff into my new expedition pack. It had snowed more, my old tracks were gone, and this time I had with me knee-high waders big enough for two pairs of socks. More spruces had come loose from the bank, and the pile in the river looked impossibly snarled. I'd bought a copy of *Reading Animal Tracks*, and though this was useful, what I really needed was *Reading Animal Shit*, since I couldn't make much of the scat I found on the hard, icy snow in the shadows. It snowed while I herringboned, sweating in my rain pants and track jersey. I was so heavy under my back-breaking Sherpa load I postholed constantly, despite my snowshoes, and left deep shafts behind after crawling out. In camp, I dropped my pack as though it was a bag of cement and sat on it, wiping my face with a bandanna, until John William climbed down his ladder, wearing the parka and gloves I'd given him. "You fool," he said. "It's snowing." We stood around eating salami, cheese, rolls, broccoli, oranges, and Reese's Peanut Butter Cups. Then we dug out the fire pit, started a blaze, and shoveled free a wide swath of ground. For an hour, we soaked in the hot tub like Finns, getting out every once in a while to toss wood on the flames, and dunking now and then to clear the snow from our heads. In fact, pale, bearded, and in need of a shampoo, John William looked a little like a Finn—like one of those cadaverous, long-ago Finns in the illustrated *Kalevala*. He looked archaic, and so white you could see the blue map of arteries beneath his skin. You could see the points of his breastbones, too, because he'd lost so much weight. When I told him I thought he looked like a pencil-neck, he said that he felt fine "trimmed down like this," that he never got sick now, that winter agreed with him, that the cold and the dearth of food had cleared his head, and so on. Nevertheless, he appeared raw and chafed, and ghostly in the sulfurous mist. He might have been a pauper in Helsinki, if Helsinki had paupers, someone who'd gathered enough coppers together for a rare visit to a public bath.

I said, "The average person would go crazy here."

"I'm going crazy."

"So throw in the towel."

"I don't throw towels, Neil. I never throw a towel. Put my head in a wringer, I wouldn't throw a towel."

John William lowered his face into the water. When he came up he said, "You do what you have to do, but no one's getting me. Life's short. Eternity's long. I'm going to slip past God—he can't get me."

"Slip past God?"

"To the mother of us all."

"You sound like a loon."

"No," said John William, "that part's clear."

It was this sort of thing that was starting to worry me in a way I hadn't worried before. He'd been in his cave for ten months now, and he was beginning to sound like a street-corner mystic or a midnight caller to an AM talk show. But I didn't tell him this. I bit my tongue, hoping that it was a phase, and that with warmer weather he might do better. And I went up there a lot. By March, there were new trees across the trail with branches full of melting snow, but I kept going, clambering over obstacles. I carried the old shortwave radio I'd hauled around on my shoulder the summer my mother died, but from the cave we couldn't get reception on any of its bands. I packed it out again, and brought up, instead, on my next trip, with extra batteries, a portable cassette player, plus The Band, The Knack, The Cure, The Doors, and four lectures on modern physics. I kept John William in porn, I bought him new underwear, I scored pot in his name, I gave him Neruda's "The Heights of Machu Picchu" and William Carlos Williams' "Spring and All." In late April, I saw two anglers standing in the river, intent-looking sportsmen in separate bends, but they didn't see me; other than that, my only company on those heavily laden journeys were the gray jays, ravens, and squirrels.

Jamie and I got married on June 17, the day after I graduated with a B.A. in English, in the small Arboretum gazebo. Erin read from Frost's "The Master Speed" (". . . life is only life forevermore / Together wing to wing and oar to oar"), and my father, because we asked him to, from Heaney's "Glanmore Sonnets." Afterward, there was a reception at Tillicum Village, lavishly hosted by Jamie's parents, neither of whom was happy about the fact that this wedding wasn't held in Pocatello. The Countrymans made their long-winded toasts, and the party lined up for salmon and red potatoes, and later for the wedding cake, chosen by Jamie's mother, which was five tiers of fondant topped with sugar roses. Keith caught Jamie's garter with a lunge, wore it as a wristband for the rest of the night, and, while dancing recklessly with Pocatello belles, shook it like a tambourine above his thick Irish head. At the microphone, arms tightly around Jamie's shoulders, Walt Shaw noted that his daughter was independent, had a mind of her own, was headstrong even as a girl—as "a tyke"—but now seemed to have succumbed a little to someone called Neil Countryman. "Not so," cut in Jamie. "No succumbing."

The next day, we drove the Datsun to Anacortes and rode the ferry through the San Juan Islands to Victoria, where we stayed at the Empress, took afternoon tea, and ate a slow dinner on the veranda. In the morning, we drove to Tofino, where we'd reserved a cottage. We slept in the afternoon there, and walked the trails, and rowed to Meares Island to look at the harbor seals, and then we went home, and except for the rings on our fingers and our new possessions—kitchen gear, fluffy towels, vases, etc.—nothing was different.

I remember that one evening, shortly after returning from Tofino, I had dinner with my father, and heard him say, because I didn't have a job, "With an English degree and a nickel you can get a cup of coffee." I told him that coffee was more like a quarter now. I didn't say that I was flush with cash and planned to spend the summer writing. That spring, I'd started sending short stories to literary periodicals with a cover letter describing myself as unpublished, and that summer, I started getting them back. I wasn't ready to give up, though, and started keeping a chart to track where I'd sent what. I also got distracted by visits to used-book stores, especially Shorey's, which no longer exists but was once a place of close-shelved magnitude and of occasional good deals if you were willing to dig, which I was, because I liked it in there, cool and dark as it felt on a hot day. Shorey's was a warren, and it smelled antiquarian; half a million titles were arranged there with no real logic, and after spending an inordinate amount of time lost among them, squatting in corners and perched on scarred stools, I liked to go to the Athenian for a dark beer spiked with Peychaud's Bitters, pull out my notebook, and write self-consciously, like Hemingway in *A Moveable Feast*. Still I got rejection notices: "There's a strong sense of passivity in this that I think is due in large part to the heavy reliance on the subjunctive/ past conditional," and "One hopes for some forward movement, Earl working through to his redemption." These went in a file. I started a novel but quit ten days later. Near the end of August, I walked from our apartment to the UW's College of Education, and applied.

That fall, while I was taking Introduction to Pedagogy, Developing Curriculum, and Strategies in Evaluation, John William was—for example—approximating soap out of fire-pit ash, grease reserved from a salami I'd brought him, rainwater, and salt. I remember pulling into his camp on a Saturday and finding him at this effort. He said it was his third try; rodents and insects had gotten one batch, and his recipe had been off for another. His beard was full of ash as he leaned over the fire, hair falling dangerously close to the flames, and measured out grease and lye water. On a flat rock nearby were lined up empty cans, into which he planned to pour his mixture.

In his second winter in the woods, my friend got chilblains and a toenail fungus. I brought him a half-dozen pairs of fresh socks, a bottle of Benadryl, new felt-lined pac boots, and a vial of anti-fungal cream. Bearing these interventions on a day of deep snow, I found him with his hair cut down to the nubs; his scalp itched, and he'd thought a close clipping might help. Did he have ringworm? I wasn't sure, looking at the little bald patches and red, irritated areas on his skull, but since it couldn't hurt, I suggested he try some of the anti-fungal cream I'd brought for his toenails. I had it in me to play doctor, I guess, though my aptitude was limited to pulling splinters and delivering specious diagnoses, two services I provided to John William. He benefited also from my pharmaceutical-supply service, which included codeine, ibuprofen, cortisone, some amoxicillin I'd been prescribed for an infection but didn't use, dandruff shampoo, mercurochrome, and psilocybin.

That's right—we tripped up there. Psilocybin mushrooms are so ubiquitous in Seattle that you can pluck them from the grass in the shade of trees at Ravenna Park, for example. Roosevelt students used to do exactly that, and probably still do. We could be deliriously stoned and still ID 'shrooms because of the way their stems turned definitively blue about a minute after they were picked. It was best to be selective and take the richly hued ones with veils breaking loose if you wanted a potent trip. Psilocybin not only froze well in baggies, it was also prized as a trade commodity by users too clueless to pick their own but flush with bud, coke, or hash. Do

I sound like an expert? I am one. That old guy at the front of the class, pointing at the word "synecdoche" on the blackboard while wearing orthopedic Birkenstocks: you should probably suspect that he used to trip, because, no matter what he looks like today, he probably did.

John William's mushroom trip was cousin to his acid nightmare. He got the shakes, got sick, turned green, and started panting, and then crawled into his sleeping bag and tried to ride it out by keeping his head covered and mumbling to himself. As for me, everything was funny. I'd try not to laugh at nothing, but it couldn't be done. Later, I got deeply into the weave of my friend's mats. Next, I put the ladder down and wandered through the forest, looking at trees. The long branches of the cedars with their voluptuous greens were the spirit of the Miss December who enjoyed hunting in a thong. I lay in moss, emitting foghorn notes. Creeped out by lichen where it hung like fake cobwebs, I wove my way through it in a delicate dance, thinking that made me invisible to spirits. Finally, I went back and checked on John William, first by poking him with a stick through his sleeping bag, then by manipulating his head from left to right and right to left while pulling on his beard. Feeling him move, I decided he wasn't dead. Next, I mopped up his vomit with the remains of a sweater and flung it out of the cave. For a while, I sat with my knees up and my back against a wall, making those foghorn notes I'd made in the forest but with an interest now in the cave's sonic architecture, its tomblike acoustics, listening to my reverb, and remembering the Roman catacombs I'd visited the summer I met Jamie. I'd been chanting for a while when John William said, between notes, "Please stop."

"Are you okay?"

"I'm dying, Neil."

"You want water while you're dying?"

"Just stop that weird noise."

I got a canteen and put it by his head, but he didn't drink, so I had to uncork the canteen, pull him upright by the beard, and pour water between his lips as best I could. A lot spilled. His face and hair got wet. When I dropped him again, I said, "Try to go with it or something."

"Never again—they're punishing me."

"Right."

"I'm seeing too clearly," John William mumbled. "I don't want to see this clearly."

"Okay."

"Jehovah," he wept. "Jehovah's got me."

I DID MY STUDENT TEACHING at Garfield High (the Bulldogs), which I knew, mostly, as the school Hendrix never graduated from. For some reason, I was assigned to teach English as a Second Language to kids newly arrived from "Indochina," even though I had no idea how to do this. On my first day, in a sweltering portable, I stood at the front of my class and, with ten fingers against my chest, said "Teacher," and then wrote "teacher" on the board and repeated it, and next went up and down the rows making these kids point at me and say "Teacher," and as they did I shook hands with each and looked each in the eye and smiled, thinking this was the right thing to do. As it turned out, all of them knew what "teacher" meant, not to mention a lot of other words, even whole sentences, and so they rightly felt what we were doing was a waste of time. I found out about this at the end of my third day as "teacher," when a group of girls, maybe six or seven, pushed a student named Quyen in my direction and stood behind her, looking at the floor or peeking at me from behind Quyen's shoulders, while Quyen said, as boldly as she could, "Mr. Countryman, you teach *harder*."

One day, one of my students said, "Mr. Countryman, why bad scar on your hand?" and I told the class I'd made a blood pact when I was younger, and tried to describe a blood pact in simple language, the cutting of the palms and the mingling of blood, the solemnity surrounding this masochistic ritual, but it didn't seem to me that the concept was understood, and the only comment I got from a student was "Dangerous—you get hepatitis." After Thanksgiving, I decided that they should memorize poems and recite them in class, and that by this means we could work on the cadences of English and the subtleties of its American inflection, because these were sticking points for them. So as not to overwhelm anybody, I started with haiku, which, I had to explain, was a Japanese word, but that only caused new layers of confusion. Discombobulated, I tried to define scansion, but this was obviously completely off the subject and prompted Quyen to observe, using a word I hadn't taught her, "You intellectual today, Mr. Countryman." "Year after year / on the monkey's face / a monkey face," I said, getting deeper into scansion, but of course that left them more stumped. I gave up on haiku and tried hitting them with quatrains—"In Canada's North / It is very cold / Eskimos go forth / But there is no mold"—before giving up on poems and turning instead to movies. We would watch a short scene three or four times in succession, from *The Christmas Coal Mine Miracle* or *The Adventures of the Wilderness Family*, and then I would hand out mimeographed scripts and, after pairing up students, force them to re-enact. Mimicry ensued.

One night, Jamie suggested Dick's Drive-In in Wallingford for French fries and tartar sauce. We sat in the Datsun lobbing fries onto the hood for combative pigeons while listening to AM radio and watching the Dick's crew, in white paper hats, orange company T-shirts, and grease-fouled aprons, work madly behind glass to meet the burger demand. In short: hamburger world. The parking lot smelled like a deep-fryer. It was summer, eleven-thirty on a Friday, and there were a lot of stoned teen-agers lined up at the windows. I went to get some extra napkins, and while I tried to work them free of their dispenser, a Sid Vicious look-alike leaned down and sideways, so as to be heard more clearly through the half-oval pass-through. Over a microphone, his order was succinctly repeated, and when he tipped his head in confirmation I heard, "Two chee fry Coke!" in a female voice, and then "Two chee fry Coke!" repeated by a male. I got in the car and told Jamie about this, that I thought "Two chee fry Coke!" was high comedy, and she said, while finishing her fries, "Guess what? I'm pregnant," and wiped her fingers on my jeans.

Our funds were consolidated. We started going to open houses, learned real-estate lingo, took cards, but avoided agents. The search for the right home always left me with bad feelings. I would read the literature handed out at an open house and feel antagonized. "Quiet, woodsy setting." "Spacious slate entry." "Custom upgrades." "Designer touches." If we asked enough questions, a listing agent might say, looking us over as we stood in a foyer, "Do you think you qualify for financing?" Then, in the car, I would complain to

Jamie—"Do you think you qualify for financing? What's with that?"—and we'd move on to the next house, me disdainfully, Jamie with either morning sickness or a yearning for fries. In this mode, we discovered our bungalow. "Bungalow" sounds Raj, or British Civil Service, like iced tea on the veranda while a Punjabi domestic in baggy white cotton waves a palm leaf and calls you "sahib." Our bungalow, though, has horizontal siding and no frills. When we came on it in 1979, the sellers had recently added a ranch-house carport that was already so mildewed their agent wrote "Could easily be turned into a full garage" on the promotional circular. The house had been rehabbed in the mid-sixties with some "Colonial Revival" modifications, mainly a second floor and a gambrel roof, but still, in character, it remained a bungalow—that is, unadorned, maybe even homely. What made us buy such a motley excuse for architecture? We bought it because we could buy it outright with a little left over for property taxes, and because we fancied ourselves capable of converting this "promising fixer-upper" into something wonderful—or, as they say in home decorating, "It had good bones." Plus, we were suckers. "Our" bungalow—it was ours before we bought it—had a modest veranda we thought of as charming. We could imagine sitting there in rocking chairs after dinner while passing the baby between us. It usually doesn't take any more than that to sell a house. One matching myth and you're ready for escrow. Everything else can be rationalized later. That's what we did.

On the Wednesday morning after Labor Day in 1979, I walked out the door of our bungalow at seven, unlocked my new ten-speed from where it was cable-locked to a veranda support, and rode to school in my dress shoes and sweater vest with a hulking briefcase from Value Village strapped to the rat-trap by a bungee cord. Thirty minutes later, I took over Room 104 from a teacher named Janet West, an Elizabethan specialist who'd been good enough to leave behind her files, and who sent me postcards that fall—delivered to my teacher's box—from Aruba, Reykjavík, and Ulan Bator, the capital of Outer Mongolia. On each she wrote, "Wish you were here," followed by, successively, "Aspirin is our friend," "Have you tried Scream Therapy?" and, finally, "Are we all happy in our chosen profession?"

I had to miss school on the day in April when our son was born, but other than that I never needed a substitute, and garnered a reputation as an eager beaver who started when the bell rang and wouldn't allow bathroom trips. Someone would say, "I have to go to the bathroom," and my answer would be, "I do, too," and, without further ado, I'd return smugly to Melville. Then, one day, a girl shot back, "You don't get it, C. I really have to go. It's a girl thing," and walked out. A few minutes later, a boy raised his hand and said, "C, I got this boy thing," and walked out, too, and after that I decided not to have such a hard-and-fast policy about bathroom trips.

My second semester, I taught Modern English Literature, a class I've mentioned already. I was supposed to start with Hopkins and teach through Pinter, but there was some room, in between, for a few narrow choices—Sassoon or Owen, for example, or Kipling or Conrad, because there wasn't time for both. My preference was for Conrad, but when I read the Kipling story in *England in Literature*— "The Miracle of Purun Bhagat"—I changed my thinking. A Brahmin of no small accomplishment and acclaim drops everything, takes up a begging bowl, and wanders into the Himalaya, where he inhabits a deserted shrine to the goddess Kali, who, a footnote in *England in Literature* explains, is "malignant . . . the black one, garlanded with skulls." He's fed corn, rice, red pepper, fish, bannocks, ginger, and honey by villagers, until he dies, cross-legged, with his back against a tree, and then these villagers build a temple and bring offerings, "but they do not know," Kipling concludes, "that the saint of their worship is the late Purun Dass, K.C.I.E., D.C.L., Ph.D., etc., once prime minister of the progressive and enlightened state of Mohiniwala, and honorary or corresponding member of more learned and scientific societies than will ever do any good in this world or the next."

Was this fair of me? I had my own reasons for choosing Kipling over Conrad, but no one knew this, and I could discuss "The Miracle of Purun Bhagat" with my students as if our discussion was an exercise in literary history, instead of a veiled way for me to ask myself if John William made sense. I taught Kipling every year for two decades.

· · ·

IN MY FIRST YEAR of teaching, I began making it my ritual to read, annually, the National Book Award winners in poetry and fiction. I also began bringing these books to class when I'd finished them, a "Death Mask of Shakespeare" bookplate in each, hopeful that students might borrow and return them if I left the books conspicuously displayed. My first year at this, I set two hardbacks in the chalk tray, wrote on the blackboard READ THESE BOOKS, and drew an arrow from those words to each title. They disappeared, and, despite the Death Mask of Shakespeare, I never saw them again. After that, I changed tactics and started buying used paperbacks, so many that Jamie had to get me, for my birthday, more bookplates, and these titles I kept in a conspicuous bookcase on the east wall of Room 104. Some came back, some didn't, but either way I had an excuse for used-book-store browsing. If I went to the right shops and bought the right books, I could keep to my budget of $300 a year and buy about a hundred titles.

Nineteen-eighty: William Styron's *Sophie's Choice* in fiction and Philip Levine's *Ashes* in poetry won National Book Awards, but, looking at the list, I couldn't help noticing that the winner in Religion/Inspiration was Elaine Pagels' *The Gnostic Gospels*. I bought John William all three, but it was the Pagels, of course, that excited him. It was like I'd brought him the Dead Sea Scrolls or the Rosetta Stone. He dropped everything else and read it while I was there, and so I read something, too, and this was a pleasant interlude, I thought, like a kind of Sabbath, except that every once in a while John William would mar the peace by blurting out a sentence from Pagels, like "The creator caused his Mother to grieve by creating inferior beings, so she left him alone and withdrew into the upper regions of the heavens," or "The world originated when Wisdom, the Mother of all beings, brought it forth out of her own suffering." I'd nod at him and say, "That's great," or "Wow," and then return to my own pages, but he didn't get my message and started paraphrasing instead of quoting, which was lengthier and therefore worse. The next day, which we spent setting traps meant to catch small rodents, hauling wood into camp, and filling canteens, we were able to talk about other things by about the dinner hour, but when we were in our sleeping bags later that night, and all conversation had ceased, and I, for one, was moving toward sleep, John William, as if it was a bedtime prayer, broke the silence with "And Jesus said, 'Let him who seeks continue seeking until he finds. When he finds, he will become troubled. When he becomes troubled, he will be astonished, and he will rule over all things.' "

"Great memorizing."

"Shut up, Countryman."

I turned toward him and said, "What if I don't want to rule over all things? What if I don't want to be troubled and then astonished? Why would I want to rule in the first place? What if I just want to sleep?"

John William said, "You're already asleep."

"That's so deep," I said, "O Your Royal Profoundness Swami Laurelhurst."

"You're sleepwalking through your life."

"The problem with living in a cave is that you risk turning into a guru, and then no one likes you anymore."

"The problem with living in hamburger world is that you risk turning into an idiot," John William answered. "Didn't you say you want to write books? You can't do it with a cheeseburger in your hand."

I said, "I disagree. The only way to do it is with a cheeseburger in your hand."

"How many have you written?"

"I'd have a book by now if I wasn't always bringing you toilet paper."

"I never asked you to bring me toilet paper."

"I bring it anyway."

"Why is that?" John William said. "Why is it you're always bringing me toilet paper instead of writing the Great American Novel?"

"You tiresome ingrate."

" 'Tiresome ingrate,' " said John William. "You've got a dainty vocabulary now. You're ready for a cocktail party with 'tiresome,' Countryman. Your 'tiresome' is a nice touch. *Touché*."

"All hail Lord Barry."

I could hear John William scratching at his ringworm, or at whatever the problem was, in his scalp and behind his ears. "This is driving me nuts," he announced.

"Use that stuff I brought."

"I'm out."

"I'll get you more."

To put it another way, I was like Purun Bhagat's villagers with their corn, rice, red pepper, fish, bannocks, ginger, and honey. The Zen master could slap me across the face, and instead of leaving the monastery behind I'd fetch his rice with a terrible eagerness.

OVER THE YEARS, things changed. Parts of the trail were washed out by the river, and there was so much tree-fall every spring, when the water was too high for me to walk on the gravel bars, that the trip in became a bushwhack. I often scratched myself getting through with my expedition pack. Once, while struggling in a slash-filled ravine, I scared up a herd of elk, who crashed away so thunderously they scared me in return, because at first I thought they were an avalanche bearing down at just the moment when the rain forest had me throttled. On that same trip, I ran into three climbers with ten-day packs who were headed for the Valhallas. They were openly curious about a solo hiker with a load bigger than any of theirs but no rope or crampons, and I had to tell them that my plan was to waltz up Mount Tom and Hoh Peak, and from there to dabble with the possibility of penetrating northward to the Hoh's main fork. In other words, I styled myself an inveterate bushwhacker as a means to explain my dearth of climbing equipment, and then sat around with this trio trading esoterica on the territory so as to seem legitimate. I don't know if they were impressed, but I felt confident they were thrown off the scent of what was in fact a supply run. I was bringing food, soap, towels, socks, underwear, candles, and a host of cassettes from the Great Lectures Company with professors holding forth on particle physics, Victorian Britain, great battles of the ancient world, etc., so I made it a point not to open my pack while we sat by the river, these climbers and I, examining a map. John William, I should say, had by now a sizable cassette collection and an ample library, but he'd incinerated the *Penthouse*s and *Playboy*s I'd brought, because—he said—he didn't want them "taking up space in my head." I chided him for this. I described Rebecca De Mornay in

Risky Business and Maud Adams in *Octopussy*. "Countryman," he said, "poontang's the bait in Jehovah's trap."

One spring when I showed up in his camp, my friend was smoking strips of elk meat in a miasma of smoke and blue-bottle flies. He looked skinny, dirty, scabbed, bruised, and scratched, and he had blistered lips, cold sores, and an infected eye. There was the smell in the air of singed flesh, and a peculiar odor I later learned was elk brains, with which John William planned to tan the hide. Bones, antlers, hooves, teeth, haunches of bloody meat, a bladder, some sinews—the pile of parts beside him was explicit. My friend was processing a five-hundred-pound mammal, which, when you think about it, is no small trick. By the butcher's art, what was once whole is split, but not without a lot of gore, stench, and, if you've never seen an animal parted out before, news about anatomy. I sat upwind of the animal in question while John William's foray as an elk smoker went poorly. He'd built a rack out of lashed branches, hung the meat from it by cedar cords, and set it downwind of his fire, and now, while keeping green wood on a cool blaze, was frustrated by his lack of temperature control. The fire would get so hot the meat would cook; then it would get so cool and smokeless the flies would descend. One rack of meat had already turned too black to eat. I tried some, but, as John William warned me, it tasted the way you would imagine cinders taste. We stayed up all night, modulating the fire and manipulating the distance and angle of the rack. As water left them, the strands of flesh shriveled and twisted. We made a few taste tests, but otherwise we stayed busy gathering green branches and, with prodding, aspiring toward a steady, cool smoke. I dried out at a slower rate than the meat did, and when I put my wrist to my nose the smell was of tinder. After thirty hours, John William was satisfied. We moved the meat onto a tautly strung line for air cooling, reloaded the rack, and smoked again, this time trying backstrap sliced thin as prosciutto and salted more heavily than the prior batch. Things went better, but it was still necessary to be constant at the fire, and to sleep in alternating snatches.

John William had found this elk, he said, in the woods to the north, in a dark hemlock forest, down on its flank and with two puncture wounds in its neck, but still warm. After milling beside it for forty-five minutes with his ice ax in his hand, he felt confident that its killer—it had to be a cougar—had chosen deference.

Satisfied, and making guesses and a lot of mistakes, he'd quartered the elk. He'd rolled up its antlers, teeth, bladder, hooves, and sinews in its hide. What he carried out first was a forequarter raggedly split off along the backbone and cut between the third and fourth ribs. When he came back, an hour later, toward dusk, to make a second run, a hindquarter was gone, and the liver and heart. John William hung the other hindquarter out of reach on a rope he'd brought, and tied up the hide as best he could, but when he came back the next morning, the hide had been nudged about twenty yards north of where he'd left it, turned over, and pawed at. His hung hindquarter was intact, but the other palatable remains were gone along the route of an obvious dragline, and there was scat nearby, the smell of cat urine, and flies working the offal.

His elk jerky, meant to last the winter, didn't last until July. Nor did his "pemmican," which was just a lot of pulverized elk flesh mixed with rendered elk fat and some yellow raisins we dried in the sun and tried to crush with a stone pestle. It went bad even faster than the jerky. John William thought he might have burned the fat, or not used enough of it; however it was, his "pemmican"—which looked like wax and sawdust—tasted rancid by June. As for the hide, I have to give John William credit. It turned out to be at least a modest success. He went at it the way he'd gone at building his cave. If his *Guide to Wilderness Living* advised him to remove the hair and epidermis with overlapping strokes a quarter-inch wide, he did that without cheating, and so did I, taking my turns. We fleshed, soaked, grained, and membraned; we stretched the hide, threw it in the hot tub and weighted it there with rocks, dragged it out and wrung it with twists, pulled it like taffy, bounced a stone on it as though it was a trampoline, beat it with a stick, rolled it over a rope between trees, and worked it over the base of a pick handle. We mixed the elk brains with water, and I ended up, later, at home, needing an antibiotic, because I didn't wear gloves working brain mash into the hide. When I came back two weeks later, John William had made some inept-looking moccasins. They were so bad you could see his toes poking out of them. I brought him some glover's needles and thick nylon thread, and he made himself an ill-fitting shirt. His tailoring was laughable. The shirt caught him at the armpits and puckered at mid-back. Some of its decorative fringes were wrongly placed and quickly burned to scorched nubs in his fire. To me, he looked like someone in a frontierish straitjacket, but he insisted on wearing it. It was at about this time that I began to realize how sad it was to see him. To pull into camp with my load of M&M's, Top Ramen, Rye Krisps, Crest, and Evereadys, and find him yet again a little more devolved, a little more like one of those hominids I'd read about in Introduction to Physical Anthropology, was increasingly distressing. With his head coarsely sheared, his foot-long beard, his buckskin shirt, and his rudimentary moccasins, he was so flagrantly absurd, so filthy, so post-apocalyptic, and at the same time so evocative of the early-nineteenth-century American West as portrayed in a bad museum diorama, that anyone with the poor luck to come across him could not be blamed for assuming he'd gone comically mad, or maybe dangerously mad, or, if seeing him distantly, through trees, say in mist—say while crouching fearfully behind a log—that he had to be a figment or a flashback. But he was real, and, as I say, sadly so to me, because he seemed diminished and lacking in his prior fine luster. The fell-runner posture and the Gatsby-esque teeth were things of the past. His gums were swollen. His shoulders were small. I would find him in his cave at midday, in his sleeping bag, doing nothing at all, just picking at his cuticles and calluses and hawking spit; or I would find him sprawled by the fire with his head on his arm; or sitting under a tree as if he thought he was the Buddha. He argued now that there was a lot to be said for "conserving body fat," as he put it, and for "the art of doing nothing," but from my point of view he was just depressed. Which, I thought, reflected poorly on his mission. It hadn't led to happiness.

That winter of '84, I saw that in the empty spaces of his books he was making small drawings. If there was an available end or front page, he used it, or if a chapter started halfway down the page, he drew in the upper half, or if a poem ended with its final verse on an opposing page he filled the white space below it. His paint, or ink, was wood ash mixed with watered-down spruce pitch, and with this he could get shades of gray or black—though I noticed that his drawings were always of one color—and his brush was a raven's wing bone tipped with elk hair bound to it with nylon thread. In my sleeping bag, with my headlamp on, I leafed systematically through his library. In none of his drawings was there anything like a direct representation of an object in the world, but, on the other hand, they weren't abstract. The dots, dashes, lines, and daubs converged to imply, say, mountains in mist, or trees, or cliffs, or moving water. There were no human forms, and no symmetry or dynamism, just monochromatic still-lifes by suggestion, with the white space always put to work, and the paint applied supplely, like calligraphy ink. I thought this development, John William as artist, was at odds with how I knew him, but what would be the point of saying so? Even more unexpected was coming across this, written on the end page of *Rabbit Is Rich*, right after Updike's illustrious bio:

> Raven in my cave,
> Mosquitoes whining at dusk—
> This is what I have.

The next day, it snowed. We sat in the cave entrance wearing our sleeping bags like robes and watched the flakes float and wander. Snow began to settle on the forest floor wherever the canopy didn't stop it. The shapes it made against the dirt were like a map of what was overhead. Arcs formed, articulating the lay of limbs. You could see the sweep of foliage in the undulating patterns. I'm obviously drawn to moments such as this, and don't forget them, but, for better or worse, I'm equally drawn to words, so I said, sitting in the cave entrance with John William and watching snow fall,

> Raven in my cave,
> Mosquitoes whining at dusk—
> This is what I have.

"I agree."
"You want to play chess?"
"No."
"I brought dope."

"I've become a bad tripper. Dope gives me nightmares."

I shuffled through my pack and found the National Book Award winner for fiction in '84, Ellen Gilchrist's *Victory over Japan: A Book of Stories*. "They dropped poetry," I said. "I don't know why."

John William stretched a hand out as if to gauge the snow, or just to feel it melt against his fingers. He said, "This is bad."

"What?"

"I'm going crazy up here."

"Leave, then."

"Leaving's crazier."

"That loses me, Barry."

He didn't answer.

I handed him *Victory over Japan*, because I didn't know what else to do, but he said he didn't want it and set it on the cave floor. I said, "I think you should bag it. What's the point?"

He rubbed his eyes with his knuckles, chuckling, then laughing, then laughing harder, as if whatever he was thinking seemed funnier all the time. He had to sigh and say, "Oh," a few times to make his laughing stop, and then he said, "How could there be no poems this year? That's insane."

"I can always bring poems."

"I mean, with all the crap in the world, and they cut poems?"

I said, "Name your poet."

"Galway Kinnell."

"Go out when I go out. Hike out with me."

"*The Book of Nightmares*. Isn't that a great title?"

I said, "Please."

He gave me the finger. "You're their emissary," he said. "You're the oldest trick in their book—a traitor."

"Which 'their'?"

"The Archons."

"This is what I mean," I said. "You need to bag it."

"Bring poems by women," said John William. "I want to know what women think. I want to understand women."

"Meet one."

"I do. You remember my dakini? The one from my dream?"

"Try to hear what I'm saying. Listen to me for once."

"She's blessed me with fear," he said. "Fear's my way out."

I HAD TWO SONS by the winter of '84. I was teaching Orwell in Modern English Literature—it was a good year for retrospectives— and I was adviser to the Chess Club. Jamie and I were installing a woodstove. I'd learned a few things about bicycle maintenance. We were short of money. Sometimes, on Saturday or Sunday afternoons, I sat in our bedroom with a yellow legal pad and worked longhand on short stories. Sometimes, instead, I raced strangers around Green Lake. One Sunday, in February, at dusk, I saw a runner far ahead of me moving at a rapid clip, fast enough that I'd lose sight of him in bends, so fast I grew disheartened in the straightaways about gaining enough ground to make him aware of my existence. It was getting dark. The wind was blowing from off the lake. Some overwinter- ing ducks, in silhouette, fluttered in the reeds. I felt obstructed. It was not so much that he was pulling away as that I was receding. I thought he was wearing a sleeveless white singlet, warm-ups, and a headband, but he kept disappearing and reappearing, and anyway, in the gloom it was hard to tell much about him. My hope was that I would wear him down, but this didn't happen. He ran the lake twice, and so did I, but I was always too far behind to feel like I was racing. We were running in darkness now. I tried to make a push near the bathhouse, but this was a delusion I believed in only briefly. Even so, I pushed myself until I lost control of my footing on a patch of ice and broke my left ankle. The next day, I taught sitting in a swivel chair, my cast on a coffee table borrowed from among the stage props in the school theater, and my crutches in my lap, so that I could use them when needed as a long-distance pointer. In American Studies, we were reading Thoreau, and one of my students, a girl who went on to Yale and now works for the State Department, was loudly amused by the image of Henry David tossing out his rock paperweight when he discovered he had to dust it. She said, "What a granola-head," and "Why are we reading this?" An argument ensued about abun- dance, leisure, work, nature, and what a second girl kept calling "the American way." When I asked her what she meant by "the American way," she said, "Basically, the destruction of everything—the world, your happiness, your soul, everything. The complete package. Evil and war. That's who we are, Mr. Countryman."

JOHN WILLIAM DIED. I'm not going to indulge anyone's interest in forensic details. If you're fascinated by charnel-house specifics, the vocabulary of coroners, or the undertaker's daily bread, forgive my reticence. I'll say plainly that I found him on May 4, 1984, after having overdone it on my not-quite-recovered ankle. I shouldn't have made the journey, but after eleven weeks, I was worried. And rightly so, because he was facedown across his fire pit, with his midsection charred and his arms in front of him as if reaching for something. He'd burned in his own fire, why or how I'll never know, though I could speculate that, weakened by hunger, he'd stumbled, maybe, and that—maybe, or maybe not—this stumbling was suicide. Does it go without saying that writing this is hard for me? Regret for what you did or didn't do, said or didn't say, after someone dies—I have that and expect I'll always have it. I should have spoken up, if not before I broke my ankle, certainly after, because I'd known—sitting on the couch at home, correcting essays, with my casted foot on the coffee table—that John William's situation was dire. Yet I couldn't turn him in. There was a part of me, at twenty-eight, with a wife, two kids, a house, a dog, and a job, that agreed with him, and so I couldn't make the call. I started to, a couple of times, but then I convinced myself that dying up there was preferable to granting Jehovah another victory, and set the phone down. Jamie didn't agree. She wanted to call Olympic Park and tell someone about the maniac in the woods who was up there, right now, starving to death, but I asked her not to do that, and, to her regret, she listened to me.

Alone in the mountains, I was spooked by my friend's corpse and had to sit for a long time at a considerable remove, not looking, looking, then looking away again, and, amid all this, wondering why I wasn't crying. There were five ravens in the trees. I'm not going to say what work they'd done, only that they were eyeing me with inscrutable patience. After a while, I moved closer to the remains and stood there with my left arm across my gut and my right elbow resting on it so I could keep my palm against my mouth and my thumb and forefinger pinching shut my nostrils. I could see how he'd been sitting by his fire, reading, and had stood up and fainted—

maybe—because beside his legs was a canteen, and out in front of his hands, in the dirt, was *One Hundred Poems from the Chinese*. Even this didn't make me cry, the thought of John William, at the hour of his death, reading Tu Fu or some other Chinese poet who'd been dead for a thousand years. To the contrary, it was something I was glad about.

After about an hour, I accepted things as they were. What choice did I have? When I thought of walking away from what was left of him, it felt wrong, so I stayed, climbed the ladder, and got a shovel. I took apart his ring of fire stones and threw the smaller ones at the ravens, but they didn't fly off, only moved to other branches. Determined not to disturb John William's remains, I shoveled out all the partly burned wood I could get at without touching him, spread the ashes I could reach, and groomed the forest floor nearby. I put his canteen, book, and shovel in the cave and came back with a cedar mat, which I laid out close to his left side and wriggled and tucked under him the best I could. But now I had to sit at a remove again, for another ten or fifteen minutes. I got my gloves out of my pack, and a bandanna, and I tied the bandanna across my nose and put the gloves on, but still I sat at my small distance, with my back against the cliff, my elbows on my knees, and my swollen ankle hurting, and said his name a few times. Inured by this, or a little inured, I got up, reluctantly, and did what I thought I should do, which was to shove John William's remains onto the mat and roll them up, and while I was doing this I finally cried a little. Shoving him like that, no matter how respectfully I tried to do it, injured my sense of funereal propriety, and the feel of his weight against my gloved hands, the way he seemed to push back, his mass, the glimpse I had of his beard, of an ear, of the whorl of hair at the crown of his head—these are the images and sensations I remember. I had to shut my eyes and rudely assert myself, unceremoniously, the way you might with a roadkill deer, to get him where I thought he should go. After that it was a little like rolling up heavy carpet, except that making that first turn, rotating his weight until he was shrouded and gone, was like the moment when my mother's coffin began to descend. The literal disappearance is, for me, the worst part of a funeral.

He fit. I cinched him up with his handmade cedar cords and

made a bound bundle. It was like tying down a sleeping bag in the era before stuff sacks. Then I had to sit some more, at a distance again, and look away from John William's cylindrical sarcophagus and let expire from my hands the feeling of pulling knots tight against the pressure of his corpse. The ravens were gone now. I wanted to walk out and be on the road with the radio playing and the dash lights glowing before night fell, but, again, it was necessary to accept things as they were. I made myself look at the lozenge I'd constructed, and then I made myself sit close to it and felt frightened of the supernatural, of the possible but impossible resurrection of the dead, and of the woods themselves. So it was a long time before I put a hand on the rolled mat, and then my other hand, and bent my head to it with the bandanna over my nose, through which the smell of cedar now muted some of the other smells, and with this step-by-step approach I was eventually able to lean the side of my face against my friend's bark coffin and rest like that, if rest is the word for what I was doing. I can't tell you exactly what I was doing, but, once again, it seemed right.

After a while, I trussed the bundle even more rigorously by running a line under my knots and seizing up all the cords, so that pulling it could only make everything tighter, and, raising dust and making noise, I dragged my friend away from the last ashes. There might have been a more reverent approach, but I couldn't think of one and had to accept the self-loathing that went, for me, with the rudeness of my undertaking. Skidding one's friend across the earth as if portaging a canoe over ice was not how it was supposed to be done—this is what I told myself while doing exactly that, while just managing when better was called for. But I was alone, a solo pallbearer, the only mourner. And now I had the question of what to do next and had to guess what his preference might have been in this matter, for burial or for burning on a pyre? I sat some more. I took off my left boot and rubbed my ankle. It occurred to me that I'd rolled him up too fast, that I should have cleaned his body or anointed it with water from the pool, or pressed his eyelids over his eyeballs, or combed his hair, or that I should have done all those things, but it seemed too late for any of it now, so on top of everything else—including anger—I felt regret about my handling of my friend's last rites.

It got worse when I remembered that a cave is probably the most ancient of crypts. Jesus was entombed in one. So, after a while, I put down another mat and skidded my burden to the base of the ladder. I tilted John William upright in the slow, careful way you might raise a heavy log onto its end, laid him against my chest, and climbed rungs facing outward until, with a lot of grunting, and using one foot at the last to keep him balanced, I had John William propped against the rungs below me. It would be easy to see something darkly comic in all of this unless you were there to witness my haplessness and renewed crying. Then I hauled him to the lip of his cave on the sluggish conveyor of his handmade ladder. It was like hauling a large fish onto a dock. It was taxing, crude, low-tech, and within my means. Still, I didn't want to drag him over the hard limestone edge, and had to fumble again while the ladder fell to the right, to get all of him into his cave without a complete collapse of dignity. When I had him in far enough, I said his name again, and then I dragged him under his cedar banners, among the things he'd collected—teeth, bones, feathers, antlers—and amid his tools, clothes, books, cassettes, and so forth. As they used to say on television, he would need all these things for his journey to the happy hunting grounds.

It was a rough night for me. I lit all the candles I could find, and tried not to panic about sitting with a dead body in a cave, which was hard at 3 a.m. As I understand it from *The Tibetan Book of the Dead*, which my son urged on me about a year ago, and which I read so we could talk about it, the period of passage from one life to the next is forty-nine days. But I didn't know this then. I'd heard of spirits hovering in a room, of the soul leaving the body in the form of vapor, of the dead close by but unable to communicate, and of the efficacy of prayer in the presence of a corpse, but I wasn't much on prayer and couldn't bring myself to say one with sincerity. I knew a little about wakes from listening to Cavanaughs and Countrymans on the subject—how the body is laid out and washed, and how a crucifix is set against the breast and a rosary placed between the fingers. I'd heard about the hanging of sheets, the keening and crying, the whiskey, stout, clay pipes, snuff, tobacco, and wine, the stopping of clocks and the turning of mirrors toward the walls, the twenty-four hours of visits, the kneeling and praying before the corpse, and the party in one room and the dead person in another, though always attended. And I was also aware of the Bean Sidhe—the Banshee— who, my mother once said, was an old woman who stood in front of a house a few hours before someone inside was to die. You would know her by her long red hair. She'd be pulling a comb through it. It would cover her face. And you would also know her by her unearthly wail. Consider yourself lucky to hear it, said my mother, because the person about to pass never does.

So I sat with the dead. I've heard there are monks who do this regularly, who sit in bone yards, cemeteries, or crypts, in order to make friends with eternity. I don't know about this. I'm not sure I could break bread with the reaper. So that was a long watch for someone like me. After a while, without prayers to say or anything to do except feel scared, I started reading from John William's books of poems, silently at first, and then aloud.

I read until it got light. It surprised me that Kinnell's *Book of Nightmares* sounded, at the end, like something from *One Thousand Poems from the Chinese:*

Sancho Fergus! Don't cry!

Or else, cry.

On the body,
on the blued flesh, when it is
laid out, see if you can find
the one flea which is laughing.

I'm reminded now that I'm asked to read a poem each year, on Thanksgiving, to the Countrymans. This comes after the spate of toasts we make to every dead Countryman we can remember, which we all know is partly an excuse to drink more than we should. That's not a good reason to invoke the dead, but there's a primal satisfaction in saying their names while reeling a little and in- dulging, one more time, our private apprehension, our lonely thoughts of being snuffed, like them. At any rate, I almost always choose something Irish, because fine words about the hard dirt of the old country still have an appeal to the Countrymans, especially after all those toasts, or at least that's my theory. . . . "Mullahinsa, Drummeril, Black Shanco— / Wherever I turn I see / In the stony grey soil of Monaghan / Dead loves that were born for me." Something of that ilk, and then we eat, as if an Irish poem was a dinner blessing.

7

NINETEENTH-RICHEST PERSON
IN WASHINGTON STATE

LAST EVENING, JAMIE AND I went to a reading that was also a tasting of locally produced foods: cheeses, figs, artisan breads, crostini, an iced tea that tasted strongly like chocolate, and herb-crusted salami. We—the nibbling audience—were introduced by the bookstore manager to a young cheesemaker, who said a few words about the products we were sampling before introducing Erin's husband, Wiley—Wiley was sponsoring this reading/tasting in his capacity as owner of eatlocalfoods.com—who rose to say he felt a little embarrassed about the shameless self-promotion he was anyway engaging in by calling our attention to his business and Web site, dedicated to the marketing of local foods, in the guise of hosting, in Wiley's term for it, a literary evening. I like Wiley, but I have to add that his midlife crisis took a turn I didn't anticipate. Shortly before turning forty-nine, Wiley quit his job in human resources at a large insurance company and, after working with some high-school students for a few months on an electric car they wanted to enter in a clean-fuels contest, told Erin he was going to Italy. A marriage counselor said it was significant that Wiley had chosen the scene of Erin's crack-up for his retreat; at any rate, off Wiley went, ensconcing himself in a villa near Rimini, where, said Erin—after visiting him—

he passed his time taking walks, perusing food markets, sitting in churches, and preparing late dinners. When he was done with all of that, he came home and started eatlocalfoods. "We're doing good work," Wiley told us, an audience of about fifty, before introducing the author of *Food Made Simple*, "and I'm happy to be part of tonight's event."

The author stepped forward. She spoke engagingly, and then took questions on, for example, butter. Afterward, Jamie and I, with plastic cups of the chocolate-tasting iced tea in hand, milled with Erin, who told us that her son, who'd majored in economics at the University of Chicago, was currently in India, where he worked for a nonprofit bank dedicated to rural development via loans to villagers. Her daughter had what a doctor thought was mono. Erin and Wiley were planning a trip to the Canadian Okanagan, which, Erin said, was now "the Napa of the North." Did we want to go? Did we need a getaway? Were we burned out yet on all the hermit hoopla?

Wiley joined us, carrying, on a small paper plate, four slices of seedless watermelon. He doled them out, and then he used his new nickname for me—Joe Celebrity—as in "So what's up these days with Joe Celebrity?" This sort of thing has been happening to me for a few months now, and I've learned to say things like "Joe who?" For example, Jamie and I went to lunch this afternoon at an Italian restaurant, and our server, who recognizes us because we've eaten a lot of meals there recently, insisted, cheerfully, that I should know about a blog in which I was, at this moment, along with the hermit of the Hoh, hotly discussed. "Hermit of the what?" I asked him.

Last weekend, Carol and her husband threw their annual summer "rendezvous," which is a wine, beer, and barbecue convention for the Countrymans and Weismans. In the past, they've sent out comic invitations and served salmon and chicken off their backyard grill, but this year they sent out an Evite instead, and hired a caterer who trailered a cylindrical barbecue into their driveway and set up a buffet—barbecued beans, potato salad, spare- and babyback ribs. Needless to say, we went through a lot of napkins and drank a lot of pale ale and red wine. One of the Weismans had brought along his dog and showed me, on the patio, some tricks it could do before asking me what it was like "for just an average guy to be getting so much coverage." I moved on. My brother-in-law had installed a

Mosquito Magnet at the edge of his patio, an electrical device that, he complained, didn't work as advertised, and so, wielding a grill lighter, I helped him light citronella candles in clay pots around the yard. "You ought to get a Man Friday," he said when we were putting the Mosquito Magnet in the garage. Later, I sat on a bench with a cup of pale ale and listened to my cousin and his second wife bicker: "At least one person in this marriage is not an idiot" got said, which prompted me to point out that, strictly speaking, this statement could mean there were no idiots in the marriage at all. My cousin took this as an opportunity to ask me if I wanted to invest in an apartment building.

Anyway—I'm famous in this mildly taxing way. It hasn't meant much so far, other than some awkwardness now and then. Other than that, the tone of my life is the same. I'm still, in the main, a burgher with a fly swatter. I still get out of bed at night to look into things when our dog barks. And last night, around three, she barked unrelentingly. It turned out that a raccoon had overturned the worm bin in order to get at the vegetables inside and was eating on the porch with an air of proprietorship. Jamie got up and put the dog in the bathroom. I opened the window and said "Leave," but the raccoon only looked at Jamie and me, two faces in an open casement, as if we were curiosities, and, not changing pace, ate more. Jamie said, "Do you understand English?" and "I'm talking to you!" but it took me, opening the door and holding a broom, to motivate this raccoon down the stairs. My point is that Jamie and I were up at three this morning, drinking tea in the living room and talking not about the hermit hoopla or what to do with all our money but, no surprise, about our sons, with an emphasis on the younger one, because Jamie is worried about him lately, and has a hard time doing what she and I are supposed to be doing at this stage—namely, backing off. Our younger boy, a tattooed and sun-cured twenty-four-year-old, appears, this summer, to be following in the footsteps of other Countrymans—that is, swinging a hammer and drinking copious hard liquor. Jamie's concerned about the drinking, of course, but more immediately about our son's thirty-two-year-old girlfriend, who looks like Nicole Kidman and is from New Zealand—Jamie's afraid that our son will marry her and move to the Southern Hemisphere. So, at three in the morning, she and I had a familiar discussion: me wondering if we should be worrying about things we can't control; Jamie wondering if we made mistakes as parents; me with my bromide on "letting go"; Jamie saying, "She isn't right for him"; me with "They have to make their own decisions"; Jamie asking why he chose someone thirty-two. There was no solution, of course, to the riddle of our son, except talking about him until he didn't seem like a riddle. Then Jamie went to bed and, with more tea, I climbed to my garret.

It was hard to know what to do so early in the morning, so I read some poems by Han Shan, who lived twelve hundred years ago in a cave in Chekiang Province. A colleague of mine in the English Department gave me the Han Shan after reading, in the paper, about John William—she left it in my box with a Post-it attached saying, "Might be apropos—keep it." Since then, I've read these poems in snippets, feeling irked sometimes, because they're dissonant in a way that can't be the translator's fault but must be part of Han Shan's intention, just as a Zen master, in answer to the question "I read in the Sutra that all things return to the One, but what does the One return to?" might say, "When I was in the province of Tsing I had a robe made which weighed seven chin." Anyway, I took up Han Shan around four this morning, before it grew light:

> A hermit's heart is heavy
> he mourns the passing years
> he looks for roots and mushrooms
> he seeks eternal life in vain
> his yard is clear the clouds are gone
> the woods are bright the moon is full
> why doesn't he go home
> the cinnamon trees detain him

And I felt irritated. Because, for me, this so-called hermit hoopla isn't fun. It isn't fun because so much has been co-opted—with my participation—and because I remain, in my own mind, unexonerated. That I rolled up John William in a cedar mat and left him in a cave by an uncharted mineral spring seems to me permanently unaccountable. I've passed twenty-two years now without putting it to rest, and with an urge to speak about it the whole time. A decade ago, when our sons were young, we took flashlights, candles, and a lot of extra batteries, and went into the Ape Caves near Mount Saint Helens, and while we were down there, sitting in a dank niche and eating sandwiches, I wanted to tell the boys about John William. I also wanted to say something to Pete Jenkins when I saw him at the Mountaineers Club after a slide show on the Andes in '92—Pete nearly shook my hand off, and greeted me with such overwhelming goodwill that I spilled my punch. Yes, I remembered *Desolation Angels;* yes, I remembered eating a squirrel; yes, I understood, like Pete, that John William had been missing for years and was presumed dead in Mexico. "Out-of-control guy," Pete summed up, and I agreed.

I saw Rand Barry on the first Saturday in May about fifteen years ago, the first Saturday in May being the opening day of boating season in Seattle, which is annually celebrated with a nautical parade. I was in a rental canoe with Jamie and the boys, all of us in lifejackets, holding water a little east of the Montlake Cut so we could watch the sailboats and yachts go by, when, at close quarters, Rand cruised past at the helm of a *Cornucopia III*, with a man and two women in the cockpit behind him, all possibly in their sixties, all holding highball glasses and wearing visors. The boat's chrome-plated rails shone, and on a halyard overhead an American flag rippled. The trio in the cockpit looked bored but festive. Rand had grown his silver hair longer but still wore his Buddy Holly glasses, and still had the slightly precarious posture, a little like a heron's, that suggested trouble with his center of gravity. He held his glass with exaggerated care, elbow thrown out, like someone at an English garden party, and while I watched he turned to look at the other man on board, who gave him a sort of general thumbs-up, as if to say that their voyage was successful, which Rand acknowledged by raising his glass and regaling the parade of boats with his foghorn. There were answers all up and down the column. There was a minute-long consensus of foghorns. The boredom in the cockpit of the *Cornucopia III* briefly lifted as the members of the party enjoyed the cacophony and, I could see, Rand's role in inciting it. Rand brought his glass to his lips, drank, and then ate what might have been a corn chip.

"Rand—your son's dead in a cave on the South Fork of the Hoh!"—I didn't yell that across the few yards of Lake Washington separating us as the *Cornucopia III* motored past. I was a father myself now and felt bad for anyone whose child had disappeared without explanation, but still not a word escaped from my mouth. We paddled into Lake Union and beached our canoe at Gas Works Park so our boys could play on the old machinery, eat sandwiches, and fly the kites we'd brought. I sat on the hill with Jamie, watching, and told her that I'd just seen John William's father, and asked her what she thought I should do, if anything, which was a question I'd put to her many times before, and to which I already knew her answer. Sure enough, Jamie said, "I've told you a hundred times what I think," "You've made it clear it isn't up to me," and "I've learned to live with how I feel about it."

Two years ago this month, I climbed Mount Anderson with an English Department colleague—a dyed-in-the-wool classicist—who enjoys that sort of thing. We're good friends, close enough to speak intimately, and together we outlasted four principals, two remodels, and three strikes. On the summit of Mount Anderson, my colleague the classicist took pictures and a nap while I gazed down on the Linsley Glacier, where John William and I had passed a night in a snow hut, smoking hash and eating candy bars while sitting on our packs, in '72. And again I wanted to say something, and thought I might to this colleague, because he's such a trustworthy friend; but, as always, no words came, and he and I stumbled down the mountain, walked out to the trailhead on wobbly legs, and drove to Port Townsend for a celebratory dinner of Stella Artois and panini.

I also went up to the Valhallas once, with two mountaineering friends who shared my interest in those peaks. We passed our first night at Camp Stick-in-the-Eye, not far from where, years before, I'd disconsolately read Eliot by flashlight. I wanted to tell these friends everything. I imagined showing them the cave, but instead we made camp in a high, damp meadow and climbed as many spires and pinnacles as we had time for, and slid around in chutes full of scree, and sat under the stars late at night arguing about politics and talking, as I recall, about lightweight hiking equipment. These were two guys I'd met through the Mountaineers who were not too serious about technical climbing and whose company I enjoyed, but, still, I didn't tell them how much time I'd spent in this region, or why or how I'd spent it, and, the last I heard, one of them had rheumatoid arthritis and was no longer hiking, and the other had moved to Phoenix.

There was a time when we had a membership at the Pacific Science Center. It was cheaper that way to take our sons to the exhibits, the Planetarium, the IMAX movies, the Tropical Butterfly House, and the laser shows. We've seen robotic dinosaurs, played virtual soccer, posed at the Shadow Wall, tested our hand-eye coordination, and eaten lunch at the Fountain Café and in the Brown Bag Court. I would say that, a dozen times over the years, Jamie and I shelled out pennies and nickels and watched the boys make wishes before they tossed their coins into the pools. When I told Jamie about the harvesting I'd done there, in these same pools, with John William, she laughed and then, with no warning, hit me in the solar plexus.

We took the boys to Fort Clatsop once, years ago, between Christmas and New Year's, to see where the Lewis and Clark Expedition had overwintered at the western terminus of their slog. "Fort" seemed very much the wrong word for the modest, palisaded hovels replicated there by the National Park Service, but we were able, despite that, to glean a little of the feeling of a winter in those woods under duress. A volunteer dressed in period clothes demonstrated the firing of a powder musket, which made an unimpressive bang and left a singed smell in the air. Then our sons tried writing their names with quill pens, and started fires, or tried to start fires, with flint, steel, and char cloth. Of course, during all of this I thought of John William. The candle-making demonstration and the short course on tanning hides hit me, that day, with all the force of bad dreams. Afterward, we drove to Tillamook, toured the cheese plant, and ate ice cream from waffle cones at a table outside the souvenir shop. I took comfort in this—when the boys were young, I took comfort in them because they gave my life a shape. So it was discomfiting to see them reach and then surpass the age at which I met John William. I had to collect the boys once, a few years back, after they'd gone out to Kalaloch with two friends, one of whom had managed to roll his pickup into a ditch. All four of them looked hungover when I arrived on the scene. It made me think of getting lost in the North Cascades in '72.

Before they were married, Wiley and Erin decided to climb Mount Rainier. Wiley insisted on a "shakedown cruise" with his equipment, and since he was eager to see the rain forest, we hiked up the main fork of the Hoh together while Jamie and Erin went to

Portland. On the trail, I heard about Wiley's first marriage, which technically wasn't over, and about his children, a girl and a boy, who lived with their mother in Georgetown. "Why would I ever want to be the cause of someone else's pain?" Wiley said, meaning his kids, but he was also of the opinion that the woman still technically his wife was a "horrendously poor listener who deserved what she was going through." I wanted to say, "Over that ridge, on the other side of the river, my friend lies dead in a cave, Wiley," partly because we were there, and partly because it's hard to keep a secret like that when someone else has let his guard down the way Wiley had let down his. But in the end, and maybe ridiculously, there was that oath over swapped blood, and so, instead of mentioning John William, I asked Wiley how old his kids were.

The closest I came to breaking my pact with John William was in Room 104 during Modern English Literature. I'd moved things along that quarter so as to leave time for stories by Frank O'Connor and Alan Sillitoe, and so we read "The Loneliness of the Long-Distance Runner," and came to the paragraph where Sillitoe writes, from the point of view of a reform-school boy in a long-distance race:

> I could just see the corner of the fenced-up copse in front where the only man I had to pass to win the race was going all out to gain the half-way mark. Then he turned into a tongue of trees and bushes where I couldn't see him anymore, and I couldn't see anybody, and I knew what the loneliness of the long-distance runner running across country felt like, realizing that as far as I was concerned this feeling was the only honesty and realness there was in the world and I knowing it would be no different ever, no matter what I felt at odd times, and no matter what anybody else tried to tell me.

And, of course, this made me think of John William, which I told my students for no good reason. I told them that I had raced like this myself, with something like that kind of loneliness, against a boy from Lakeside who subsequently became my friend. I said we'd found a hot spring in the mountains and made a blood pact not to reveal its location. They looked at me as if wondering whether this digression had a point, and so I read Sillitoe's passage aloud a second time, and we pondered it together. One student thought Sillitoe was interested in "the terror at the heart of nature"; another thought Sillitoe was telling the reader "that once you see the truth about things there's no turning back." This latter emerged as the interpretation of choice. We added the English castes to the mix. I told them about the "Angry Young Men." Someone, naturally, brought up Camus. I miss having conversations like this with teen-agers—I'm done teaching now; it's summer and I won't be going back—but it would be better if a teacher didn't have so many papers to correct. It's the papers that make teachers think twice.

I WAS AT SHOREY'S. Shorey's had moved to Fremont and wasn't the same, but the booksellers there were as moody, impolitic, and distracted as ever, and still made a point of not noticing anybody. A coffeehouse had been attached, with a stained-glass window and an antique couch, so now the line between book browsing and coffee drinking was blurred—I would see someone standing in front of a bookshelf with an espresso, and it would break the spell I was under. But no matter. My zeal for the esoteric author and the strange title remained intact. And I still enjoyed the unraveling of purpose I felt around decrepit volumes. But my keenest enthusiasm was for little-known poets. Their chapbooks, limited editions, and self-published pamphlets held promise. I thought I might find something unappreciated but inspired on a page I hadn't looked at yet. And so, on this day in '98, at about the time when the lead news story concerned impeachment proceedings against Bill Clinton, I was in a book-lined cubbyhole at Shorey's, hopefully perusing a collection called *Chronic Obsessions* by a poet named Robert Leventhal. It had been self-published, on excellent paper, in '74. It was noted, in the back, that *Chronic Obsessions* was a letterpress printed in a limited edition of 250 copies. Fifty copies had been bound in cloth and boards.

Robert Leventhal didn't suffer from the fatal flaw of many poets, which is a surfeit of self-regard. His trick was to write in the persona of a woman whose sensuality was tinged with sadomasochism, so that for the reader—or for this reader—the thought of a Robert Leventhal behind the words was an invitation to distress. I read his first poem and felt provoked, I would say, by this sense of an alter ego at work, or of someone obfuscating. On the other hand, I imagined Leventhal arguing that provocation was his purpose, and I pictured him as an academic, rail-thin, with a three-day growth of beard and a morose lecturing style. In "Santa Fe Interregnum" he wrote:

I made the journey to Santa Fe.
There I followed the sisterly example and observed complete
     celibacy
But could not hold to this and became a painter of landscapes.
In the sun I took a hirsute lover.
I scourged him with nettles and dug in my nails.
In return, he abused me.
And so we made love to our shadows each morning
In transcendent light. Hairy kundalini satyr invented by Eros—
I called him this and other names with
Twenty layers of irony. Soon we walked on our
Hands to Taos. I painted nude men with diminutive
Cocks while they appeared at odds with themselves.
That moment when the guilt cult of Thanatos
Could be seen in their faces—I tried to catch this
After midnight. As it turned out my Theravadan was
A happy bisexual. He thought I was a beguiling creature from
Wealthy Corinth. But I had been impregnated by the
Errant seed of Encolpius, and as I swelled, my satyr enjoyed
Me up into my sternum while urgent to touch the
Growing alien. That I was carrying someone else's
Genetic complement made my lover
Insane with pleasure. I painted my
History for his benefit and because, as he said,
It was part of his metaphysics. It was my life before
Santa Fe he wanted to possess while dabbling in
Tantra. This lover put an ear to my pubis and listened to
My parasite while I told him how Priapus had struck,
At 3 a.m., with no advance warning,
In the form of bladder-blocking semi-tumescence.
How after five seconds of missionary enthusiasm it was

Over, except for our separate trips to the
Gabinetto, where I earnestly failed to douche free
His seed. And so I am with child while my lover
Knives me. It's wonderfully strange.

Sitting on a stool in my cubbyhole at Shorey's, reading this
Robert Leventhal poem written in the voice of a pregnant Southwest landscape painter, was like seeing Norman Bates as his mother
near the end of *Psycho*. The wig falls off and the dress falls open, and
then, after a psychiatrist explains Norman's warped psychology, his
dual personalities, we see him in a chair with a blanket on his shoulders, talking to himself in his mother's voice.

I turned a page in *Chronic Obsessions* and read "First Words":

After my grandmother went earthward
In unflattering regalia
I spied in the distance
The man who would be my husband.
Why did I pretend to have an errand?
The cups by the cut-glass bowl of lemonade needed
Straightening and I straightened them
While the Negro at the
Serving ladle didn't watch.
He kept his hands behind his back and looked into
The middle distance. "Just ignore me," I said, and
In reply he dipped his head to one side.
Around the back of the gazebo I "bumped" into
The man who would become my husband.
He cupped a hand over my shoulder in an effort to
Hold me upright. Chevrons were stitched
On the arm of his summer dress jacket.
I slipped my shoulder free
But his raised hand stayed as if to signal
Pure intentions. He raised it further, as if taking an
Oath. He raised the other, like a fugitive at
Gunpoint. He did these things humorlessly. Then he
Stood in a posture of obeisance that was a little
Reminiscent of my current lover,

Male couchant, with his eyes rolled back in his head.
My husband-to-be now began to
Teeter. His five o'clock shadow was a matrix of
Tiny pinholes. He seemed to have a pointed
Breastbone, like a bird. His manner included no detectable irony.
"I'm sorry," he said. "I didn't mean to touch you."
Those were my husband's first words.

I wasn't much impressed by Robert Leventhal, partly because I couldn't hear his music, and partly because he read like soap opera. But I knew from other chapbooks I'd opened through the years that there might be a gem where it wasn't expected. So I read, next, "I Torture Myself":

> For fun. This must be said: for fun.
> And when I am done for the moment with
> Torturing myself
> I torture him as a sacrifice to the
> Goddess of resentment.
> I like to pin him to his altar.
> My shame at this is worse than
> My husband reading the paper
> After work. He folds each section,
> Feet crossed at the ankles,
> And wonders, because he has to, about
> Eisenhower's health.
>
> There are fine forms of
> Torture. A subtle art, and nuanced,
> Rooted in the beginning of time,
> Torture is Eros. One form of torture
> Demands doing nothing while another demands
> All. Let your victim weep
> Both ways. Let your victim
> Bleed: never staunch a fresh wound.
> If you hear him crying, for no reason,
> From his chamber, be happy
> Because it was so easy, this

Torture via absence, this torture in not doing.
Let him torture himself.

The days are long this way.
This torturer knows ennui.
I need to be doing the
Work that has chosen me—
The incitement of pain.
But since this prison is for
Both of us he stuffs my ears with
Agony. How do I tell him that
My choices are bad
In this era of limitation?
That the lonely torturer behind the
Mask hates him so much it
Feels like love?

Baby—please don't blame me.
Hurt for my sake, be Christ-like,
And suffer as I suffered when you
Tore through my womb.

I would have slid *Chronic Obsessions* back in among the other
chapbooks if I hadn't happened to notice, in its table of contents, the
title "Alki, 1851," which was also the title of the poem I'd read
twenty-six years before, in Ginnie Barry's study, after smoking weed
there with John William—the poem Ginnie'd had printed as a broadside and then displayed, framed, with her name on it as poet, behind
her writing table:

They oared ashore through rain,
And though they were egregious in their long-distance purpose,
Kamogwa didn't suck them under in his gyre,
And Thunderbird, on high, watched.

Their friends hanged Bad Jim.
At the Mad House, Sawdust Women plied for coin.
Eskimo Joe cut timber in a union shirt.

Ikt papa ikt sockala Tiee—one pope and one God—or so it was
  proclaimed.

Next came the box-houses and lectures on phrenology,
Faro and Little Egypt, dancing nude,
Bunco, vaudeville, nickelodeons, ragtime,
Pantages, jugglers, graft.

Then donkey engines turned bull teams to beef.
The wool dogs of the Squaxin went quietly extinct.
It rained on the tree farms and on the monuments to loggers,
And the Utopian Socialists surrendered.

The *Minuteman:* they built it.
The engineers in the football stadium:
It's they who dreamed up Dyna-Soar,
Awake beside sleeping wives.

So I cast this prayer on the Ocean of Compassion:
O rising phallus on the plain above the waters,
Be as you are, germ seed of the future,
Help me to count what cannot be counted,
World after world,
And anchor me in Anchorless Mind,
Until I cease.

  This same poem was in "Robert Leventhal's" chapbook. In other
words, John William's mother had a pen name.

I SAW VIRGINIA BARRY twice after her son disappeared. The first
time, a middle-school art teacher we know invited Jamie and me to
an opening at a gallery in Pioneer Square that was exhibiting his
work, and so we went, and milled uncomfortably, and drank wine,
and looked very closely at my colleague's oil paintings, most of them
done on modest canvases. This gallery was only a little wider than a
hallway, so it was impossible to linger over the art without having
someone pass between us and it every few seconds. It was shoulder
to shoulder in there, and loud, because a lot of people clearly knew

each other; there were dozens of conversations under way, and a lot of light striking wineglasses. In short, our brick-walled vault felt cramped and chaotic. Since our friend had drawn an overflow crowd, I was able to speak to him only briefly before it was someone else's turn to greet the artist. After that I wanted to leave, but instead I found Jamie again, and we made a second jostling circuit of the paintings. "I'm not sure this is me," she observed.

Later, someone silenced the crowd with an insistent fork and wineglass. It took me a while to realize that it was John William's mother who wanted to address us. Her hair was black and silver now, and she wore it pulled so tightly back it seemed to lift her forehead. On the other hand, she hadn't gained a pound since I'd seen her, thirteen years before, standing near the doorway of Lucy Hatch's office with her fist against her mouth, trying not to laugh after I'd said, about John William, "He's a good guy. You raised him well." If anything, Ginnie looked even more sleek. She'd aged in a glamorous and enviable style and was striking the way women in their sixties can be striking. Ginnie handed off her wineglass and opened her palms as if to bless the gathered art-lovers. "Welcome," she said. "Many of you know me, but for those who don't, I'm Virginia Worthington, owner of this gallery, which is so remarkably managed by my friend Nora Friedman." Applause, plus a smile and a wave from Nora Friedman. While this was unfolding, Ginnie reached back and took the measure of her chignon, turning her head slightly down and left-ward. In profile, under track lights, wearing an embroidered bolero jacket and leather pants, she looked, I thought, self-possessed.

We heard about my colleague's work—how his oil paintings evoked "discrete units of entablature and, at the same time, stained glass." We heard about the "mandala motif in many of these paint-ings and the recurrent theme of the Uroborus as seen in Mexican calendar stones." Ginnie mentioned some pamphlets on a table, urged all of us to enjoy the Chenin Blanc provided by a vintner from the Yakima Valley, and then, with spread hands, turned us loose once more "to look deeply into these glorious works of art." After-ward, I told Jamie who'd just spoken—that Virginia Worthington, as she called herself, reclaiming her locally respected maiden name, was John William's mother. Jamie said, "She looks like a matador in that two-million-dollar jacket." And she did look like a matador. That was the right image. Ginnie looked flamboyant, if economical, making small talk. Once, in that packed gallery, I drew close enough to see her tiny earrings, and to hear her say, as I passed voyeuristically, to a man and two women, "The Arias Peace Plan for Central America would certainly be a boon for the arts." Surprisingly, I felt no urge to tell Ginnie what had happened to her son. She left me, I suppose the word is, numb.

The second time I saw Ginnie was in 2002—four years after I'd bought *Chronic Obsessions* for $5 at Shorey's. She was now an octogenarian and had endowed, at the University of Washington, the Virginia Worthington Poetry Series, designed to bring three poets a year to Kane Hall for readings and lectures. On the night I went, with my colleague the classicist, to hear Joseph Powell read, Ginnie was introduced by the dean of arts and sciences as "a true friend to the university and a lover of the arts whose generosity, grace, and philanthropic vision now bring to our campus the gift of fine poetry." He preemptively took Ginnie's hand and touched the padded shoulder of her suit; then Ginnie went to the podium, bent the microphone toward her brightly painted lips, pulled her jacket smartly down, and rubbed her palms together while we applauded. Reaching back to touch her hair, as she had fifteen years earlier, in her art gallery, she thanked us for "that kind and heartfelt greeting" and acknowledged the dean's "words of praise." My classicist friend leaned toward me and said, "It's a Worthington Worthington, as in money," and later, "Quintessential harridan." Ginnie had become regal in her advanced years and carried herself like a dowager, leading with her chin, and addressed her audience with icy beneficence. She looked, I thought, like a film star at dusk—like someone loath to move out of the spotlight. "I am gratified to share fine poetry with you," and "The stellar constellation of poets this inaugural season bodes well for the future of the Virginia Worthington Series," and "I have insisted on reasonable ticket prices in perpetuity," and "At lunch today with Joseph Powell, I let him know just how entirely pleased I am that he has joined us for this debut." When Powell came forward, wearing a droopy mustache and cowboy boots, she called our attention to him with the open hands of a magician who has just produced something implausible.

Of course I thought, seeing her this way—so aged but indomitable and so self-reverential—of *Chronic Obsessions*. I didn't see the benefactor with deep pockets and a love of poetry the dean of arts and sciences had proposed; instead, I saw a woman who'd poeticized badly. I saw Robert Leventhal. I saw someone who felt that torture is Eros. I've more than once, for a variety of reasons, had to impress on my students that "you can't tell by looking." I'm there in my sweater vest, cleaning my glasses in front of the blackboard, sweaty with my passion for Basho or Shakespeare, chalk on my fingers and squinting at the clock, and I know they don't know, for example, who Neil Countryman is. Dickinson hardly published, I might say, by way of an example. Most of her neighbors had no inkling she wrote poems. Robert Frost was notoriously enigmatic with biographers. The amiable New Englander, the laureate and sage, was also his secretary's sadistically charged lover. How wonderful that the hoary and sinewy Virginia Worthington had endowed this promising poetry series. She seemed so remarkably clearheaded, even wise, and entirely in command of her moment at the podium. She seemed so worthy of our praise.

HERE'S WHAT HAPPENED.

One day this spring, I read, in the *Seattle Times*, an article called HUMAN REMAINS FOUND IN OLYMPIC NATIONAL PARK. This sort of thing gets reported sometimes—a hiker or climber will go missing for years, and then a femur is found, or a skull and some plastic, and two or three paragraphs will appear in the local section with the words "unidentified" and "investigation" and a description like "twelve miles west of Quilcene" or "seven hundred feet below the summit of Mount Constance." The article this spring, though, was more thorough. It used the term "federal law enforcement officers" and the phrase "in a remote area of the park near the Hoh River." I showed this to Jamie, and she said, "I think you might be busted, Neil," and, "Don't worry—I'll visit." In other words, she didn't believe, after twenty-two years, that this article had anything to do with us, and neither did I.

The next morning, though, there was a longer article in the *Post-Intelligencer*, with a byline and the heading PARK REMAINS PROMPT QUESTIONS. It included "evidence of long-term habitation," "potential foul play," "National Park Service criminal investigators," and

"Armed Forces Institute of Pathology," and it reported that the human remains in question were discovered by "park personnel engaged in field research on the South Fork of the Hoh."

I went to school, but it wasn't my best day of teaching. And just as I feared, they were waiting for me, outside Room 104, at two-thirty, when the bell rang. There were two of them, a man and a woman, both younger than me by at least ten years, and they didn't appear threatening, grim, or intimidating. I confessed, "I know why you're here," and then, sitting on the table at the front of my class-room, I gave them all the detail they wanted. When that was done, I said, "Can I ask you one question? How did you find me?"

"Your name was in his books," they said in tandem.

The *Seattle Times* assigned an investigative reporter whose style—and I mean this as a compliment—might best be described as "grip-ping narrative." It was rich raw material: the son of so much local wealth, a Lakeside grad, missing for twenty-nine years, turns up in a cave as a mummy who's been rolled and bound in a cedar mat. One *Times* article begins like true-crime noir, with the discoverers of John William's cave, two cougar researchers tracking "a radio-collared juvenile female in the lush darkness of the rain forest," stumbling on a scene so strange—the dug spa and the cave in the wall—"it was as if they were characters in an episode of *The Twilight Zone*." A forensics doctor comes off like a horror-movie bit player while explaining mummification, adding, "The chemicals in cedar, specifically plicatic acid, are a potent preservative," and "It's possible to do an extensive autopsy on mummified remains," and "Condi-tions like these even enable us to get fingerprints after more than two decades." A wilderness-survival expert is quoted: "His gump-tion was only exceeded by his foolishness." Lakeside weighs in: John William is described by former teachers as "a conspicuous academic presence," "one of my top three classical philosophy students of all time," and—Althea Mastroianni—"brilliant but eccentric and dis-turbed." A Lakeside classmate: "He wrote a lot of angry letters to the *Tatler*. People basically stayed away from him." His Scoutmaster: "He was a wonderful Scout and in so many ways a good example to the younger boys." The owner of the general store on the Hoh River Road: "I told him not to come in if he wasn't going to wear shoes." A former air-force survival instructor who now runs a wilderness school in Oregon: "This guy had to have been highly motivated to stay in the woods that long."

In Part Two of the *Seattle Times* investigative series, we read that Rand Barry filed a missing-persons report with the Clallam County sheriff in late April of 1977, after finding his son's "slatternly, dilapidated trailer on the main fork of the Hoh River abandoned." Rand also contacted the Washington State Patrol and, later, the National Crime Information Center and the Friends and Families of Missing Persons and Violent Crime Victims. The Bledsoe Agency—Rand's private investigator—gets a brief mention (but not Vance Reese). The *Times* reporter, sleuthlike, follows the trail to California, where the Highway Patrol impounded John William's Impala near the San Ysidro border crossing in early April of '77. "The missing boy's father," Part Two tells us, "brought his son's disappearance to the attention of Senator Henry M. Jackson, whose office contacted the U.S. Embassy in Mexico City, but nothing came of this high-profile effort." Et cetera.

Part Three—this is where I show up, wearing that mustache in my annual picture, and depicted—it seems to me—as Mr. Chips crossed with John Muir. I'm of "North Seattle, blue-collar, lunch pail origin" and "a well-liked high school teacher with twenty-six years of classroom experience under his belt." I'm the father of two and live in a modest home not far from where I grew up. Jamie is "a real estate appraiser and a volunteer youth advocate with Boys and Girls Club of Seattle." According to the *Times*, I'm contemplative and answer questions slowly. I ride my bicycle to work and rarely use my car, a '92 Honda Civic. My friend the classicist says about me, "Neil is dedicated. He never misses a day of work." One of my former hiking partners from the Mountaineers says I'm "persistent on the trail and knowledgeable in the woods." My sister: "Neil's a generous soul and has always been determined." My mother's untimely death is mentioned, as is the fact that my father passed away in '98. There's plenty from me about the packloads I carried, and the backtracking in snow, and the elk jerky, and so on, but probably the best quote the *Times* reporter got from me, while we sat by the South Fork of the Hoh together, was "I let him down."

Part Three, though, is mostly about John William's "Early Years." There's a quote from an elementary-school teacher ("Precocious, but I suppose you would say socially inept without posing a classroom behavior problem"), and a carefully written description of Laurelhurst ("architecturally notable postwar ranch houses interspersed with striving Tudors behind foliage"). We're given some color—that in the sixties the Barry family attended dinners and barbecues at the Seattle Yacht Club; that John William played Pop Warner football and Little League baseball; that his mother, for a brief period, chaired a neighborhood gourmet club; that the family enjoyed summer sailing trips to the San Juan Islands and Desolation Sound; that John William liked canoeing in the Union Bay Marsh, built a telescope from a kit, and joined the American Association of Variable Star Observers at age fourteen. His parents separated and "eventually divorced." His mother "became prominent in the Taos art scene." His father's Boeing career "was highlighted by the test launch, at Cape Canaveral, of BOMARC, a combination pilotless airplane and missile whose development he was largely responsible for."

Before Part Four could be published, I got a call from an attorney, saying—to my message machine—that he'd read about John William in the paper, and asking me to call him "with due speed regarding important news." He said his name was Mark Sides. He was terse, I thought, and in his terseness evasive, especially in his reference to John William as "your intimate friend, and I'd guess the term is, uh, uh, my posthumous client."

I Googled Mark Sides. He was a partner at a Seattle firm called Berman Piper with "extensive experience in civil litigation, land use, and environmental law" and had been named in '98 by *Washington Law & Politics* magazine, a "Super Lawyer." There was a photograph of a slim, nearly drawn man about sixty, wearing a blue blazer and graying at the temples; he was a member of the American Water Resources Association, the Downtown Seattle Association, the Planning Association of Washington, and the National Association of Industrial and Office Properties. His undergraduate degree, from Berkeley in '68, was in the political economy of natural resources. He'd gone to law school at Stanford and had graduated in '71, Order of the Coif. Sides had clerked for a U.S. Court of Appeals judge in San Francisco and had lectured, in '03, at the University of Washington on the Model Toxics Control Act. He was on the board of directors for the Vashon–Maury Island Land Trust and provided pro-bono legal services to Powerful Choices, "a nonprofit organization serving women's empowerment and self-defense needs and supporting witness protection for Bosnian rape camp survivors." I followed a link to the *Puget Sound Business Journal* and read an article from its November 3–9, 2004, issue on Sides's successful handling of a lawsuit brought to determine who should pay for the clean-up of contaminated property. I also read his tips for choosing an attorney, written in a dry but striving style, employing the phrase "unvarnished counsel" and warning potential clients that "the law is a thicket demanding careful negotiation." In sum, his Web page served its advertising purpose: Sides seemed credible and inspired confidence, and his Berkeley degree in something radical-sounding was sufficiently mitigated by his subsequent narrative and by the particulars of his impressive CV.

But how boyishly sixty he was in person, on the seventy-first floor of the Columbia Center—Seattle's tallest building—in his corner office with its panorama north and east and its immediate view of the rooftop communications array and of the zigguratlike concrete terraces in the upper reaches of the Seattle Municipal Building. It might have been a problem, in the professional sense, to look as young as Sides, or to look so reedlike and easily pushed over; on first impression, he struck me the way I'm struck by photos of adolescent congressional interns who, posing beside senators, peer into the camera looking eagerly pliant and, in proximity to political power, happy to have no point of view. Would this work at the bench, or in the Berman Piper conference room we'd passed on the trek to his office, with its voluminous rosewood table? This vague calling forth of George Stephanopoulos with a shorter haircut? The color of his belt matched his cordovan loafers, and, without a jacket or tie, dressed in chinos and a white pinpoint oxford with carefully rolled sleeves, Sides looked like one of the older models in an L.L.Bean catalogue. There was a framed photo on his office wall of Sides and another man, both in flimsy nylon shorts and sweat-soaked bibs and chips, crossing the finish line at the Seattle Marathon, Sides with his thin arms raised in painful exhilaration in the end zone at Memorial Stadium. There was another, more moody and contemplative black-and-white of Sides trail-running, with the light glinting in the well-defined, if slim, quadriceps muscle of his leading leg as he passed under alder trees in what looked like early evening. Noting my eye turned toward this portrait of a runner—of a solitary man captured in a brooding, poetic training moment— Sides said, "That was taken on the Middle Fork Snoqualmie by my wife, eleven years ago next month."

Generally speaking, Sides's office was in disarray, with document boxes and a pair of shoe rubbers under his desk, wine gift-bags stuffed into a corner, and, in the slant of morning light through his southeasterly window, food crumbs and dust on the small pedestal table holding down the center of the room. This was no show office. Instead, it had the feel of an air-traffic-control tower, with its banks of uninterrupted floor-to-ceiling windows, treated with anti-reflective glare, about a thousand feet off the ground. Sides was frank and said that sometimes, gazing out, he wanted to be mayor of Seattle. He couldn't see the Rainier Valley, the Industrial District, or the port, but otherwise he was poised like Zeus above the city, and from his desk took in not only Puget Sound but the rooftops of lesser towers, four lakes, two mountain ranges, and the eastward suburbs installed in their low green hills. We were literally twice as high as the Space Needle, that erstwhile symbol of Seattle's quaint ambitions, which from here looked like one of the extraterrestrial tripods in the 1953 version of *War of the Worlds*—in other words, from the vantage of the Columbia Center, the Space Needle resembled a B-movie prop.

Sides's guest chairs, in vinyl, weren't ergonomically correct, as I found when he invited me to sit in one. From this lower perspective, my view was of the sky and of Sides swiveling in his lounger. "Okay," he said. "So why are you here?"

I said, "Right."

Sides chuckled, crossed his arms, and stuffed his fingers in his armpits. He even leaned to his left a little and affected a look of rank skepticism. "You're Neil Countryman," he observed.

"True."

"What's your birthdate?"

I told him. Then Sides produced, from a desk drawer, a small tape recorder, at which I nodded. "This is new," he said. "I'm not good at it yet. I lost the old one in Atlanta last month. I'm lazy about longhand and tend to dictate." Another chuckle as, looking stumped, he fiddled with his recorder. "Yep, it's true—I tend to dictate," he said. "You can verify that with my wife."

"I think you have the wrong guy," I told him. "I'm a teacher."

"You're a teacher," he said, "but not a teacher in trouble. In fact," he added, "it's the opposite of that—you better hold on to your chair." And he held on, demonstratively, to his own chair.

This was toward the end of my twenty-sixth year of teaching, thirty-four years after I'd met John William, and twenty-two years since he'd died in his campfire. This was on an April morning during spring break, so cloudless and promising that I'd pedaled my bicycle downtown and locked it to a rack in front of the Columbia Center before coming up to see Sides. My plan, at that point, was to pedal home in stages, visiting used-book stores along the way and stopping somewhere for a sandwich. I also planned to go to Trader Joe's and Rite-Aid. In other words, my day had a shape I looked forward to. But now here was Sides in his Naugahyde saddle with his fingers linked behind his head, seated under his six tall windows and at the intersection of his two wall-desks with their law books, brown accordion folders, and three-ring binders. Here was Sides before a sky of cobalt blue, vastly spread, saying, "Did you ever think you'd be rich, Neil?"

"No."

"Well, you are," he said. "In fact, right now, as we speak, you and I, you're the nineteenth-richest person in Washington State. Give or take," he added, "your net worth is four hundred forty million dollars."

I said, "Who's the joker?"

Sides chuckled a third time. "Your friend Barry," he answered. "He named you in his will."

I didn't answer. I sat there thinking, like an English teacher, that even $440 million didn't stand between me and annihilation. "Feature this," urged Sides. "Right now your projected investment income for '06, from dividends and interest alone, is twenty-two million."

I laughed—or should I say I snorted skeptically. Sides plucked a document from his desk and, after sliding on glasses, read, " 'I, John William Worthington Barry, a resident of Clallam County, Washington, and a citizen of the United States, declare this to be my Last

Will and revoke all my prior wills and codicils.' Et cetera. He leaves you everything."

Sides put the will back on his desk, set the glasses on it, joined his hands in his lap, and, swiveling again, smiled at me. "Forget about the recorder," he said. "I can't make it work."

I said, "You're sure about this?"

"Trust me, Neil."

"Have you told anyone?"

Sides pointed toward his door, next to which hung a framed reproduction of a World War II poster, a stark, Cubist depiction of a burning ship half beneath the waves above the tongue-twisting and cautionary caption LOOSE LIPS SINK SHIPS.

I said, "So do you do a lot of wills?"

"I don't do wills at all."

"But this will is good? Because you hear about 'bad' wills. You hear about contested wills. You—"

"As in Anna Nicole Smith," said Sides. "But you're not Playmate of the Year."

A jetliner was passing behind him now, and because I was in the Columbia Center, or not merely in the tower but on its seventy-first floor, I felt the presence, or convergence, of terrorism icons. I also noticed on the sill to Sides's left a plastic box of golf balls. That's when it hit me—that Sides was the lawyer from Eugene who'd freed John William from Seaside's jail in the summer of '74—that he was, according to an aerogramme I got in Europe that August, John William's "pro-bono savior." I even remembered John William's phrase about him—"pissed about the right stuff." Now I watched Sides brush the dust from his loafer; maybe the advance of morning light had brought this dust to his attention. I said, "Ivan Gempler."

"You're definitely the guy," Sides replied. "Those are some magic words."

BESIDES *Federal Environmental Laws 2005*, the 2004 *Revised Code of Washington*, and *Salzburg's Federal Evidence Update*, Sides kept on his desk a fake oversized martini stir stick complete with fake plastic olives. This he rotated between the fingers of his right hand while telling me how he'd met John William. "Summer of '74," he said, "I went to work for the Oregon Wilderness Coalition, out of Eugene. Mostly what we did was keep clear-cuts on hold during back-and-forth appeals. You know, paper warriors—we kept trees standing for an extra nine months. Anyway, we were constantly sending students out to inventory timber sales and roadless areas. I did a lot of leg-work myself. I was involved in inventories of the Rogue and Ump-qua. A bunch of us worked out of the Survival Center at U of O. I started in organizing—I was a field organizer all up and down Lane County. This turned out to be my talent—bringing people together. I signed up recruits, which was easier than you might expect in a community where you could get fifteen hundred people out to a save-the-trees march. To bring you to my point, it was through my work as an organizer that I met your guy Barry. I found him in a jail cell," he said, "on the coast near Seaside, and I gave him a lift to Eugene. You got it right—he called himself 'Ivan Gempler,' and did Ivan Gempler ever smell bad. And talk a lot. Rabid. I mean, to the point that I regretted having him in my car." Sides slumped a little farther in his chair, with that far-flung sky behind him. He said, "I dropped him off at this tepee and got him work counting deadwood. I got him a paying gig building trail through some old growth where we wanted to get politicians in to see the trees. He was good. He was reliable. He was into it. He got the point. Lane County Audubon needed some spotted-owl counters, so they could challenge a timber sale under NEPA regulations, and I sent them Gempler. I sent him to the Wilderness Society. I even got out there with him once on something, but you know what? He drove me nuts. His mouth was always open. There are people who like to have conversations, and then there are people who like to talk—your guy was the latter. I mean," said Sides, "you're in a tent after a long day of putting miles on your boots, and your tent-mate has to sit yogi-style on his sleeping bag so he can lecture you at two in the morning about whatever's in his head—except, for whatever reason, your guy didn't *have* a sleeping bag. Instead, he had a blanket that was more like a hairshirt, and scary, because it looked loaded with lice; hygiene was not your guy's specialty."

"No."

Sides slid his chair forward. "What was it with 'Gempler'?" he asked. "How do you explain him?"

"I don't."

Sides smiled. "But you'll take his money."

I shrugged, and Sides added, "I mean that in a good way. Because you don't have to get him to be his heir, do you? He just has to get *you*."

Sides nodded as if in affirmation of his own point and said, "Off the subject. I lost contact with 'Gempler.' I didn't see or hear from him for two and a half years. I got involved with some things in San Francisco, and then I joined a firm up here. We were in the Hoge Building, on the fifth floor, and Gempler comes to see me. Unannounced, right? I get a call from the receptionist saying there's an Ivan Gempler. No beard now. No appointment. This is March of '77. This is twenty-nine years ago or thereabouts. I come out to the foyer and he says, 'Found you in the phone book.' I tell him fine and try to work him out the door, try to get him to see I'm a big-deal lawyer. No dice. We end up in my office. He's got all these documents in a bag—birth certificate, driver's license, bank stuff—and he shows them to me, so I find out he's not Ivan Gempler."

"Okay," said Sides. "It's John William Worthington Barry's twenty-first birthday, and he wants a will. I tell him I practice environmental law—I don't do wills. But he's got this thing about me. He doesn't want somebody else. So"—Sides threw up his hands—"I did it."

"His will."

"Here it is," said Sides. "All kosher. Two witnesses. No holes. Very simple. I've held it for twenty-nine years."

But it was still hard to believe. And I couldn't think of anything to say anymore. Who were the eighteen richer than me, besides Bill Gates and Howard Schultz? I thought of checking Forbes's list. I said, "Isn't there some kind of stair race here?"

"Leukemia and Lymphoma Society," said Sides. "Top time right now is in your age group. Believe it or not, a guy named Wigglesworth, who has it down to under eight minutes. Last year, we had a guy age ninety-nine do it in twenty. But look—just pay someone to do it for you."

I said, "I've never been here before. But I did read *The 9/11 Commission Report*. This building was targeted."

Sides shrugged. "I know why they hate us," he said. "I hate us, too." And he added that this particular Columbia Center was soon to be outstripped in height by a new one being built in Manhattan, which would include not only an architectural spire but a wind turbine, LED lights, and a gray-water system. "It doesn't change anything," he said.

His screensaver, on dual monitors, roiled like the colored mineral oil in the lava lamp Carol used to keep in her bedroom. I said, "So what's the next step?"

"You celebrate," said Sides. "And then I cultivate you as a client until you put me on retainer."

"Okay."

"Welcome to my world," said Sides.

8

PERIODIC IRRITABLE
CRYING

As it turned out, no prosecutor was angry with me for failing to report the death of a missing person or for interring my friend in a cave twenty-two years ago, so I was rich with no strings attached, and print syndication loved the figure involved: $440 million. I was even in tabloids, which Jamie calls "comeuppance": in fact, MUMMY BEQUEATHES MILLIONS! is now framed and hung on the wall of my garret. By May, at school, my nickname was Bling. One student asked me if I was going in for a grill and suggested platinum caps and princess diamonds. I was encouraged to change my ride, too—to get off my bicycle and get in an Escalade. A foreign-exchange student from Serbia-Montenegro asked me for a loan, explaining that his mother was dying and that he needed a plane ticket. Wiley started letting me pay for pizza after tennis. Carol urged me toward international travel—she suggested a trek in Nepal, or a visit to the Lake District for a dalliance with Wordsworth. My friend the classicist harangued me relentlessly with predictions about my "sybaritic future." Someone I went to high school with called to say we should have lunch, on him, at a sushi house near his brokerage. My cousin Colin asked me to consider investing in a short plat. I invited him over, and we sat in my garret drinking porter and talking about

Keith, who died two years ago, at fifty-three. We also discussed my father's 1950 Westcraft trailer, which Colin wanted to rebuild with a friend in the sheet-metal trade and pull behind his truck during deer-and-elk season. Inevitably, we got tanked. Colin said I'd won the lottery. He asked if I'd heard of Billie Bob Harrell, who committed suicide after winning $31 million in Texas. The next morning, I Googled Billie Bob Harrell and ended up printing a Web page— "Tips for the Latest Instant Millionaire." There were ten, and the last was: "Move away. And not just out of town. We're talking out of state, possibly out of the country. You can't expect to keep a lid on your secret forever; information wants to be free. Maybe buy a modest house with a good alarm system in a gated community with a private security force. That ought to minimize the solicitors at your door. Also be sure to get an unlisted phone number."

I forwarded this to Jamie, who in the face of so much money is like me—surfing for cautionary tales and worried about the dark side of luck. "Big question," she said. "Do we just laugh it off? I'm leery and sort of paranoid now. Not as screwed up as this Billie Bob guy, but leery, you know, because, basically, I've been happy without a private security force."

It must be said again, though, that she's stopped appraising real estate. As for me, as of the first week of September, I'll be— technically—on leave from teaching. It's a one-year arrangement, meant to keep the door open, although I'm 99.9 percent sure I don't need it open. And that's fine. I did my stint. Someone else will take over in Room 104, and really, it won't matter very much to anybody except me.

Meanwhile, the ringers are off on our phones. The dog barks when someone knocks at the door. I have a post-office box now, and I'm careful with my e-mail address. I've also been reading more about the Gnostics, and have made it through the Hans Jonas book John William once pressed on me, though not, I confess, with complete understanding. "Dread as the soul's response to being in the world," Jonas says, "is a recurrent theme in Gnostic literature." It's a theme for me, too, even though each day, doing nothing whatsoever, I make over $60,000.

Yesterday I went to Rite-Aid and deliberated for a long time on whether or not to buy nonprescription glasses good for reading fine print. They were under $10. I'm guessing—I haven't calculated it—that I made at least a hundred times that in interest during the time it took me to decide to buy the glasses. I could go on, but the point is, I'm still a skinflint and a bank-book watcher. For me, no risky investments. I don't mind staying even with inflation—in fact, it's all right with me if I lose ground. Nothing tangible has changed, except that I have time now, to write, walk, and think, and a new set of things to worry about, like what money's going to do to our sons.

A few days after the *Seattle Times* ran my picture, I got a letter from Lucy Hatch—now Lucy Hatch-Myers—the woman with the silver pageboy who had once been Dorothy Worthington's *chargé d'affaires*. "How glad I am," she wrote, "to see how things turned out, as I am the executor of Dorothy Worthington's estate and have followed her instructions as scrupulously as possible, despite her daughter's lawyers. . . . The fact that there was no death certificate for John William denied them leverage. . . . I will admit to holding that money in trust in part to thwart Ginnie, since Dorothy was adamant that her daughter not see a dime. . . . It was my plan that upon Ginnie's demise I would allow the trust to go into probate. . . . She absolutely loathes me. . . . I hadn't expected that John William's remains would be discovered or that a will would emerge. . . . I do hazily remember you moving the Bösendorfer. . . . My only regret is that Ginnie succeeded in corralling the majority of the artwork. . . . The entire Highlands collection was spirited off to Taos. . . . At any rate, the majority of Dorothy's estate remained intact and is in your hands now. . . . Incidentally, my niece had you for Modern American Lit. her junior year. . . . How very bizarre this is, bizarre and wonderful."

REMORSE—AND NOTORIETY—finally led me to Rand Barry. I called him right after the news broke about his son, but his reaction was so geriatrically cryptic—"What did you say your name was again?" and "I have no idea what you're talking about"—that I immediately wrote him a letter, too, explaining my role in what happened to John William and apologizing for what I'd not done and done, right down to raiding his liquor cabinet. No reply, but then came the news about my millions, and it seemed important to call

Rand again. This time, he said he welcomed the chance to talk to me, so one day, after school, I pedaled downtown and met with him—an old man bent beneath a buzzardlike dowager's hump—in a private den at the Rainier Club. We had to dodder indecisively first—the leather armchairs of the Curtis Reading Room? the well-lit ambience of the Kirtland Cutter Room?—before settling on our discreet lair at the end of a hallway. A white-jacketed server, a college kid with the well-bred look of someone imagined by Ralph Lauren, led us there, then patrolled our retreat for empty glasses and to see if the mixed-nuts bowl needed filling. Otherwise, this zone of wainscoting and overstuffed couches, gilded portraiture and highbacked chairs, inspired—in me at least—a midafternoon sleepiness, and lent our proceedings an air of machination. Its well-conditioned air was oppressively inert, and from its walls a gallery of pitiless faces, both painted and photographed, seemed somehow to urge both profiteering and snoozing. These were Seattle's past financial leaders—Hemphills, Millers, Stimsons, Winns, Boyds, Shorts, Prices, Bests—most looking grim about posterity. Among them stood Ben Ehrlichman in ten-button spats, alongside his nephew John Ehrlichman in short pants—the John Ehrlichman who would one day direct Nixon's "plumbers' unit." So we were watched over, Rand Barry and I, by capitalists and at least one crook.

Mr. Barry, short of breath merely sitting, tried to straighten his tie by rummaging through the folds of his shirt front. I couldn't help noticing the brevity of his torso, or its rounded collapse; his slacks were pulled high so that the distance from his wattles to his belt buckle seemed a matter of inches, and this shirt swath, which included part of his tie—the lower two-thirds was pooled in his lap—appeared rumpled in a way he couldn't address. The futility and blindness of his effort, the absentmindedness of it—you would guess that as a younger man he hadn't been handy, that screwing in a light-bulb might have tested his dexterity (though I did know already how much he'd loved a boat's tiller and, by inference, the complicated trim and tackle that goes with sailing). Such native haplessness was in his face, too, though his face was most prominently stringent and severe—and, in default, torqued by consternation. Those spots old people suffer, from too much sun? Mr. Barry's had been burned off, leaving crimson silhouettes on his cheeks and temples, shades of aborted precancerous lesions (but their removal might also have been due to vanity). His eyebrows, like Pierre Salinger's, looked steel-wool-ish, a feature that ought to make a man appear merry but that made Mr. Barry seem irrational and fierce, ready to deliver a reprimand or an order. Finally, by some dermal distress, his earlobes were scabbed, and his skull, scrimmed by a few well-pomaded hairs, was liver-spotted and knotty. The picture of age, decline, and desiccation, and though there was nothing to be done about it all, the hand befuddled and restless at his shirt front belied a soul who raged against that, however feebly. Yet to no avail. Mr. Barry's Argyle dress socks had slipped, and a sliver of his purple shins showed. His ankles, where they disappeared into his shined and buffed wingtips, put me in mind of stilts.

His infirmity seemed to me an opening. On the other hand, he'd been a Boeing executive—a vice-president in sales late in his career, and before that a project engineer—so some tincture of past authority still clung to him. Sure enough, while I vacillated, Mr. Barry took the initiative, insisting that I run down the facts of my life, which I did, in brief, beginning by reminding him that I'd chatted with him in his backyard in the summer of '74, and ending by giving him the name, at his request, of the school where I worked for twenty-six years. "English teacher," he observed. "I myself am not well read. I did recently complete *In the Heart of the Sea* by an author called Nathaniel Philbrick, which is a wonderful account of the whaleship *Essex*, and before that I enjoyed reading the book by Alfred Lansing on Ernest Shackleton's voyage to Antarctica in 1914 and '15. So I do read. Not often novels. But I am not an illiterate philistine entirely. I got out *Main Street* last March and took a stab at it and found it enlightening and entertaining, and earlier this spring I completed reading the Arthur Miller play *Death of a Salesman.*"

I told him I'd never been to the Rainier Club before. Mr. Barry took this as a cue for genealogy: on his mother's side, he said, they were the Fosters from a Tacoma investment house and the Colemans in logging—not members of the club, but one of the Fosters had been mayor of Tacoma, and one of the Colemans had been a lead engineer at Grand Coulee Dam. On his father's side, though, they'd all been club members, starting, of course, with his father himself, and including his great-uncle James Barry, who'd owned the Acme Fish Company, and his great-uncle Langdon Barry, founder of Western Sand and Gravel. Mr. Barry didn't stop there: Dexter Coleman, on his mother's side, was vice-president of Meyer Brothers, the company responsible for logging most of southwestern Washington; Thaddeus Coleman was a partner at Coleman & Denny and a legal adviser to First National Bank of Commerce; Younger Foster financed hydroelectric projects; Toby Foster was a majority partner in Foster Shipyards. At last Mr. Barry paused, possibly to consider if he'd forgotten any family luminaries, but also to grapple more vigorously with his tie and to sip from the Sprite with ice our server had delivered, on a pewter tray, with my coffee and a fresh bowl of mixed nuts. "By the way," he said, locating a cashew, "I congratulate you on your enormous good fortune. You could join the club, you know, if that was what you fancied."

There was a roar—air conditioning starting up—and with it came the smell of supper: the daily buffet was being prepared for service in the Heritage Dining Room, which we'd peeked into, with its wall sconces and Rococo chandelier. Mr. Barry chose this moment to extricate a monogrammed white handkerchief from his coat pocket, ball it between his fingers, and pat his nose. He also checked his watch, and I recalled that he was looking forward to Hospitality Hour downstairs; when I'd met him in the lobby, with its timbered ceiling, he'd stopped to scrutinize a readerboard schedule with a hint of anxiousness coloring his mien. John William once told me that his father stopped drinking, every year, as a Lenten regimen: forty days of prohibition Mr. Barry endured to justify indulgence through the rest of the calendar. After Easter, no cocktail would be poured in the house until five, except on weekends, when noon was the rule. I supposed this explained the glass of Sprite Mr. Barry held now, as well as his agitation as he'd scrutinized the lobby's readerboard—he was holding back and looking forward simultaneously; he wasn't indulging at the moment, with me, so as to enjoy hospitality later with his friends.

"It's hard to see myself as a member of the Rainier Club," I said. "Did you get my letter?"

"I did," he answered, "and I'm very appreciative of your sincerity, Neil, but I would also advise you not to be too hard on yourself, because you're not to blame for a thing."

"But I am to blame, if blame's the word. I—"

"Right there," Mr. Barry said, and pointed at me. "I've noticed a tendency with your generation—the difficulty it has in assigning blame. With responsibility. With things that aren't gray but instead black and white." Mr. Barry spilled some pop and added, "I believe it has to do with Vietnam. That was the problem for your generation. When I was with the Seabees on Munda, we knew what we were doing there. We were going to stop the Japanese, because they'd attacked Pearl Harbor. It wasn't complicated. So let me tell you who's to blame insofar as my son is concerned. His parents are to blame. Virginia and myself. We did a very mediocre job of raising him."

I said, "He'd still be here if I'd—"

"I don't believe that," said Mr. Barry. "That poor boy was in trouble from the get-go. First of all, he had no siblings, because his mother had the operation done that prohibits future pregnancies. By the way, this wasn't something she and I conferred on, that John William would be an only child. This was unilateral on her part. I heard about it after the fact. You have two children, so you know that the exchange between them, the interplay between siblings, is extremely important. I felt we should have had more children, but my point of view was dismissed."

He sipped from his Sprite. "Another thing," he said, picking up steam now. "So you don't blame yourself, Neil. John William had a terrible colic. I used to put cotton balls in my ears. Do you want to know what his mother did about it? She planned a schedule. And she implemented a regime I didn't approve of. Her thought was that the boy should not be deferred to—she characterized his crying as a test of wills: who would break first, the mother or the child? There was a hell of a lot of crying in that house as a result of this ridiculous campaign of hers. I'm not sure where she came up with this plan, or if a pediatrician recommended this strategy, but her idea was to sit in the corner of the living room with her nose in a book while the boy was crying in his crib and not to go to him no matter the duration. We were at odds about that, because I did not feel it was the proper approach at all to a child's crying. I used to feel sorry for him, but my hands were tied, and I was not allowed to meddle in this business of his crying. You know, I wasn't there very much. I worked for the

Boeing Company from June of 1948 until August of 1989, so I was not in charge of child-rearing. We had roles. I was the breadwinner, and I was a more-than-adequate breadwinner, but I couldn't walk in the door at five-thirty p.m. and take command or make decisions regarding this crying that my son was doing. So I put in the cotton balls. That was my strategy. That was how I dealt with things. I came home, said hello, and put in cotton balls. Now, would you do that?"

I shrugged ambiguously. "You wouldn't," said Mr. Barry. "But I was a very busy man then. My work was demanding, but I liked my work because it was so challenging and . . . stimulating. Frankly, I preferred work to being at home, with all that crying going on."

Mr. Barry fiddled some more with his shirt front. "If you want to blame someone," he said, "blame the psychologist B. F. Skinner, because Virginia believed in this B. F. Skinner, that you didn't want to positively reinforce the negative behavior of crying by offering comfort, that was her argument. Incidentally, there was no speaking with Virginia about this or anything else. She was always smarter than me and always correct—she was correct as a matter of course. Personally, I thought it best to console the boy. There were reasons for crying. This was his way of communicating, he had no other. From time immemorial, women have taken babies to their bosoms in response to crying. Wasn't this obvious? Let me tell you something I remember perfectly. If I was making a point, Virginia kept her nose in her book. My points were so negligible and unworthy that she could read while I made them. Now, I saw the scorn in that, of course, as I know she meant me to. She would read while I was talking, and she would talk into her book while she was responding to me. Which was she talking to, the book or her husband? Here was all this crying, and then Virginia taking her position so adamantly. I'm going on a bit, but my point is, I'm sure it had an impact on John William. What if your first experience of the world is to cry and cry and get no response? I'm not a psychiatrist, but I have made my own cursory forays in the area of psychology, reading a little about these things, and everyone who is an expert on the subject agrees, you can't mistreat an infant like that and afterward have a reasonable expectation that all will go right in adulthood. It doesn't work that way. It's basic. It's fundamental. Do you agree with that?"

I said I did.

"Blame," said Mr. Barry. "As far as blame is concerned, I have to say that a measure of mental illness enters into the equation as far back as 1956, the year John William was born, even though Virginia wasn't hospitalized for this condition until the summer of 1967, eleven years later. I would say that her actions, from the time of his birth, did not proceed so much from logic as from difficult and irrational emotions. I'm certain I first noticed this about Ginnie at about the time John William was born, and I remember being disturbed to realize that the woman I married, I don't know, was *off* somehow, if that term makes sense. Does it? Of course, it was obviously politically that Virginia was not in the mainstream, and that she fancied herself as among the left wing, at that far end of the political spectrum, even an anarchist, but strictly in theory—because she liked to live well and did live well, enjoying fine dining and so forth, nice vacations, and sailing trips, as much as she could— but let me make this other point now, that Ginnie was also just mentally *off* for many, many years before it blew up and became a self-evident, material mental illness demanding my intervention. What do I mean?" Here Mr. Barry lifted his left hand in a fist, out of which popped his little finger. "I mean, first, that she was sometimes very adamant and forcefully committed to an illogical course of action, as I have pointed out in describing her techniques of child-rearing in 1956, and I mean, second, that she was a terrible insomniac from the time of our wedding until 1967, when a doctor prescribed her with the right medication. Third was environmental phobias. I couldn't paint a stair railing without her making a stink over toxins. There were just so many perturbing and difficult things that were part of her makeup, I had to throw up my hands and keep my mouth shut if I was going to survive. And I did keep my mouth shut," said Mr. Barry. "I was mum in the face of Virginia's mental illness, and that was just a terrible mistake."

I have to say I was surprised by his sudden cogency and by the turn our afternoon had taken toward confession. He was so forthcoming that I asked about it, to which he replied that he had prostate cancer—"the slow kind"—and was interested in seeing "that the record reads accurately. You know," he added, "I mentioned to you earlier my interest in reading, not literary reading most of the time but books I enjoy, and in this vein I've read, oh, at least a half-dozen biographies that are sensationalistic, and let me tell you, these kinds of authors are coming out of the woodwork. Have any of them contacted you, Neil? Two have contacted me."

"No," I said. "What did you tell them?"

"That I would never cooperate regarding that sort of thing."

"In that case," I said, "I should probably tell you that I'm . . . fiddling with a book about your son."

Rand seemed unruffled by this bit of news. "Well," he said, "you were his friend, if the newspaper is correct, and friends have an interest in the truth."

"Truth's like blame for my generation, though. It doesn't mean anything clear."

Rand said, "Personally, I think it's interesting, the truth. I think readers would be interested in hearing what happened."

"What happened?"

"His parents happened. Virginia and I. I'll give you an anecdote," added Rand. "I'll give you a representative 'for instance.' "

TRUTH? AFTER A DAY at the Boeing Company, in mid-July of 1956, Rand came home to find the house in disarray and poured himself a Dewar's and water. The kitchen smelled like spoiling food, and in the bathroom, on top of the ammonia of baby urine and the lidded bucket of soiled diapers incubating its stench of infant stool, there was the odor of Ginnie's houseplants. Meanwhile, in a corner of the living room, Ginnie sat blithely reading in her favorite chair, a Chippendale turned toward a garden window. (This was before her revelation about "modern," when everything in the house would be summarily carted off and replaced by furniture Rand didn't care for.) And, of course, the baby was crying. It was all oppressive in the extreme for Rand, standing in the kitchen doorway and assessing Ginnie in profile, Ginnie with her reading glasses and her book of poems by Lawrence Ferlinghetti (he couldn't quite see the cover from his distance, though it looked like the book by this Ferlinghetti she'd been carting for the last three days). Rand tucked the *Post-Intelligencer* under his arm and swirled his drink. He knew better than to say "dinner." Beset by domestic facts, he gathered soda crackers, a cutting board, a knife, and a wedge of Swiss cheese. "I'll be on the patio," he said.

"Perfect," called Ginnie, without looking at him.

Outside, Rand opened the sports section. His rhododendrons were well past their prime, but the lawn was thistle-free and green for midsummer. Three weeks until the Gold Cup, but already the paper was reporting hydroplane news, and there was an article by Royal Brougham on Pete Rademacher, "blood cousin to Wrong Way Corrigan," who'd boxed in the *P-I*'s Golden Glove tournaments and was now training for the Melbourne Olympics. A plane flew overhead, and Rand knew from the sound of it, muted as it was, that this was the Boeing 367-80 with its four Pratt & Whitney engines. The Littletons were barbecuing; their hornbeam hedge shielded this activity from view, but not the smell, the tinkle of their glasses, or their voices. Rand sliced his cheese. There was a wasp nest under the eave he hadn't noticed until now, evening stragglers making return flights to its portal. Rand watched avidly. He shut his eyes for thirty seconds, but then the baby cried louder. Or shrieked. "Shrieking" was the right word. Two and a half months in, and Rand was thoroughly familiar with the term "periodic irritable crying" and with the diagnosis "hypertonic baby." Sometimes the problem seemed to be colic, and sometimes it seemed to be generalized fretting, but either way what issued from John William's throat was an insufferable caterwaul. Rand struggled out of his chaise longue, panicked, and went into the kitchen to refill his Dewar's. Mute irritation welled in him while John William wailed, up and down the register, changing octaves now and again, and pausing only to gather more oxygen. A tempest of angry need, a storm of unmet desires, a railing against helplessness—or just plain shrieking. Rand was about to stuff cotton balls in his ears, but then Ginnie called, from her post in the Chippendale, and in a tone of stringent and weary insistence, "He has everything he needs and is crying for no reason. I don't want you even thinking of going in there."

"It's sure loud," said Rand.

"Please. Just take your second cocktail out to your deck chair."

"This is just a splash of Dewar's, you know."

"Whatever it is, take it out."

Higher decibels from the infant John William. "I'm going to tell you this because I have to," Rand said, abrogating his principle of marital muteness. "A child doesn't cry for no reason."

Ginnie tossed her book to the floor—now he could see that it *was* by this Ferlinghetti, a volume called *Pictures of the Gone World*. She twisted in her chair and yanked off her reading glasses, but a shriller shriek now emanated from the nursery, and she had to wait for that to subside before she could castigate her husband. "Something's wrong," said Rand.

"If you'd like to take over my job," said Ginnie, "just say the word and it's yours."

Rand knew this was the perfect moment to redeploy his tongue-biting policy—except that the baby was still bawling. "That sounds different to me," he said. "Couldn't he be stuck by a diaper pin?"

Ginnie slapped her forehead. "A diaper pin," she said. "You're not here all day the way I am, are you. This? What you're hearing? It's the garden variety. It's the everyday crying. It's the feed-me-whenever-I-want-you-to crying. If you go in there now, you'll undo all my efforts. You'll undercut my ten weeks of discipline. I absolutely, positively won't have it."

With that, she fitted her earplugs into place—the rubber sort used by swimmers. She preferred them because of their fit in the ear canal, because their small flanges created perfect seals; these were what she wore in bed while John William screamed away the wee hours. Every night, at 2 a.m., the alarm went off and Ginnie rationed out five and a quarter ounces of evaporated milk diluted by water—but from then on, until 6 a.m., let John William wail: she would not respond.

Rand retreated. Back on the patio, a late wasp had found the cheese. He stuffed in his cotton balls. The past-their-prime rhodo-dendrons looked bedraggled. In the glow of evening, they also appeared dour. A breeze came up, and Rand smelled Lake Washing-ton. It was the ripe odor of foul chemistry, and it reminded him of Munda—mud, innocent American colons racked by coconut milk, and a perdurable, painful dysentery. Laurelhurst, when the wind was right, smelled like a makeshift navy latrine. Rand plugged his nose. The wasp crawled into a crater in the Swiss, which at its cut edge was already hardening and yellowing. It was clear, too, that the eaves needed painting, that he'd fallen behind on his flower-bed weeding, and, finally, that his cotton balls were acoustically insufficient. Because there was that yowling and whimpering still, muted but no less incessant and irritating. There was that railing against unjust circumstances. Rand's son *in extremis*, desperate for attention. Actually, it was how he himself would cry if crying was at this stage a credible option. It wasn't, and Rand didn't have three hands to stop his ears and nose at the same time. He understood that to a hypothetical observer he would look tranquil in his segmented chaise longue, a Laurelhurst householder sipping a cocktail with the newspaper beside him and a water view, and yet, between the putrescence of the darkening lake and the lament of his baby—not to mention his spouse—he was in turmoil. He was enduring, he felt, intolerable conditions. Rand stood, downed his Dewar's, went inside, and waved his arms at Ginnie, who was again at her reading. He pointed at his chest, mimed a driver at ten and two on a steering wheel, waved goodbye, and fled.

Rand drove his Bel Air convertible out of Laurelhurst and north on Sand Point Way. He'd bought this model in the main out of curiosity about its high-lift camshaft and four-barrel carburetor—both new for '56—but also because of a *Car Digest* story in which a Chevy engineer drove it up Pikes Peak in under eighteen minutes. Rand had gone whole-hog: power-operated top, fender skirts, and whitewalls. The salesman was an old fraternity brother, Carter Lodge, already as lustrously bald as his father, who owned the dealership and looked like Daddy Warbucks. Rand kept the Bel Air waxed, but not scrupulously. There wasn't room for that in his schedule, and it was the sort of thing—the bent posture of polishing—that made his lower back stiffen on the right side. He did buy high-octane gasoline, almost always at Larry's Chevron near Five Corners, and he changed the oil every two thousand miles, a job he enjoyed. He would listen to Husky football (Hugh McElhenny was gone but they had Dean Derby), Seattle Rainiers baseball (Elston Howard behind the plate), or Seattle U basketball (the young Elgin Baylor jumping over everybody) while inscribing tune-up notes in a binder on his workbench. Rand gapped his points and set his timing with a strobe light, decompressing with a bottle of Pabst's Blue Ribbon; now, driving, he measured the precision of his latest tune-up by the timbre of the Bel Air's hydraulic lifters, a hum with substance behind it, a flawless concordance of engineered parts that could be heard and felt. He liked driving, particularly in the countryside— driving for no reason other than to appreciate the engineering of his car. On this evening, the farther north he went—top down, follow- ing the lakeshore—the better he felt, and as the July twilight deep- ened into moodiness, he began to enjoy, with self-destructive glee, his seditious escape and bold flight from domesticity. Though there would be hell to pay, eventually, in one way or another. His mutiny couldn't stand. Ginnie would win in the fullness of time. But— that came later. For now, capriciously and happily on the lam—if a bit guilty to have left his son in torment—Rand toured. He trav- eled east on new but badly engineered arterials. More of "Lake City," as this area had come to be called, had been clear-cut since the last time he'd motored this direction. There was obviously no oversight of the manner of development. No foresight, either. A lot of haphazard construction along the contours of ravines, homes slapped up on stump-riddled hillsides, insufficient municipal infra- structure, and a lack of storm drains. Rand saw dollars with little wings attached, bags of coins with helicopter props disappear- ing into the distance, as he wended through "Lake City." And gloaming—was that the word? Chintzy new "ranch houses" going purple *in the gloaming*. Night was falling, and no citizens were about. Rand realized it must be the case that many of them worked for Boeing.

He wound up the Bel Air's 280 horses and drove by the North- gate Shopping Center. Its vast plain of parking was empty at this hour, except near the theater, which had on offer *Forbidden Planet*, with Anne Francis. Rand had seen her the year before in *Battle Cry*, looking good smoking a cigarette and wearing a chipper beret. *Bat- tle Cry* had left Ginnie cold, though; it was sappy, she said, on the rainy drive home from it, and full of "war clichés." What she liked was a movie he found interminable—James Dean in *Rebel Without a Cause*—and also *Invasion of the Body Snatchers*, which to Rand seemed just another black-and-white B-movie. "Group-think," said Ginnie. "Conformity." But what he saw was Dana Wynter, leading with her breasts, fleeing in sham terror. Ginnie said that was a metaphor.

They'd argued about it, though in the spirit of exhaustion. "It isn't worth the effort," Ginnie said. "You're not going to get it anyway." But two days later, she hadn't forgotten and still needed to be right about *Invasion of the Body Snatchers*. Conciliatory as always, Rand "admitted" he was still thinking about it.

Rand turned south. It was unbelievable how blighted Aurora Way was north of 85th, the city limit. What might have been a parkway of trees and lawns, like the section of Aurora passing near Green Lake, was here a corridor of callous disregard for the standards of Rand's city. A strip of commerce fashioned out of plywood and vinyl, gaudy signage and aluminum window sashes, with the sort of hot tar roofs that smelled noxious on a sunny day, then cracked in winter. In a twenty-block section there were eight real-estate agents with oversized readerboards announcing lots for sale in "Shoreline" and "Lake Forest Park," and four "motor courts" with neon lights and vacancies. Rand passed Chubby and Tubby's, Hamburger Heaven, Rudy's Value-Save, Zisko's Insurance, Colby's Lawnmower and Small Appliance Repair, and Petterson's Paints—did he know these Pettersons? There weren't a lot of Pettersons, he supposed. The ones he knew had married into Byrd money, made selling cheaply bought railroad right-of-ways to timber companies in the twenties. Byrd's heir, a girl named Elvira, had married a Petterson, and then the money moved over, and pretty soon Byrd's railroad fortune was dispersed among too many lackluster or wayward Pettersons. Now—it made sense—one of them was selling gallon cans of latex to the do-it-yourself-ers mortgaged for life in "Mountlake Terrace" and "Firdale." Rand recalled that his own eaves needed painting. But it was hard to find painters you could trust.

Rand parked his Bel Air by the Green Lake Bathhouse and opened the glove compartment. Inside lay a flask of Bond & Lillard, which he put in the pocket of his summer-weight chinos. (B&L was straight Kentucky bourbon, bottled-in-bond and 100-proof, which Rand's Boeing colleague Brad Sisk extolled with the zeal of a sales rep, taking names at the office for fifths and ordering a case every other month.) The flask was something Rand had picked up at a Maritime Society Silent Auction; it had gone to sea for a dozen years with the captain of the two-masted schooner *Equator*, Robert Louis

Stevenson's ship to Samoa in 1889. Rand tipped and nipped with reservations—he had a 9 a.m. meeting with Defense Department planners—recalling Stevenson's stirring epitaph: "Home is the sailor, home from the sea, / And the hunter home from the hill." Exactly, he thought, and dosed himself more fully. Those phrases made death more appealing than life. The adventurer in his eternal easy chair. Not to mention Polynesian bathing beauties—unsurpassed, in Rand's estimation.

Warmed, he got out, raised the convertible roof, locked the car door, and walked the lakefront promenade. The lake reminded him of an illustration of Loch Ness in a children's book he'd once cherished, the sort of Victorian watercolor drawing that implied the lonely presence of a monster. Yes, Green Lake tonight was both silvery and ominous, but everything was ominous right now to Rand, whose mental refrain and litany through the evening had been, and was, Am I ready for tomorrow? He had on board Ted McCallum from the Industrial Products Division and a team of preliminary-design engineers to outline a new guidance system for BOMARC, but they hadn't met to coordinate and were just going to wing it in the presence of the air force. Unknowns. Plus, Ted was touch-and-go in the clinch. Two of the engineers were pointyheads from the Michigan Aeronautical Research Center—BOMARC was a joint venture—and Rand hadn't met either of them. Worse, so far BOMARC, meant to shortstop Russian bombers, couldn't hit sluggish drones that should be sitting ducks. One problem was accuracy of calculation, another was complicated circuitry. The main problem was that BOMARC, a hulking hybrid, was both a rocket and a pilotless airplane. Could it be both? That was the question haunting Rand. Plus, there were guys on the accounting side calling BOMARC "SLOWMARC," because the project was now two years behind schedule. The previous BOMARC had crashed at Cape Canaveral in '54, and Dick Nelson, the lead engineer, had to go to D.C. to explain it to the secretary of defense. A million bucks up in smoke, a plume above the Everglades, and Nelson was transferred to manufacturing, where he could do less harm (though word was he'd improved things down there). Now it was Rand's turn to walk point on BOMARC, which, he'd been told, had better become GOMARC. With a chuckle, okay, but he understood.

Rand recalled that, at this very minute, he was missing the Seattle Yacht Club Summer Sail he and Ginnie had made annually before the birth of John William. Members went north in a well-organized flotilla, moored at Roche Harbor, ate, drank, and were persistently convivial. They moved from deck to deck to flirt, borrow ice, or just stay in motion while the boats rocked under them, hopping over gunwales with a box of crackers under an arm or a bottle of vodka hoisted like pirate's booty, sunburned and salty, windblown and randy. Babies had been absent from those maritime revels, but not prepubescents, and especially not teen-agers, kids who inhabited the same boat space but in a different dimension, in their own closed universe, only rarely making eye contact with the likes of Rand while they giggled, ate, and just plain looked good. But a baby? Out of the question. What would you do with an infant, after all, when it was time, around midnight, to row ashore in a courtesy boat and descend on the swamped bar in the Hotel de Haro, ostensibly for a round of festive libations but in point of fact to ogle winsome strangers? Unknown. Out of focus. Anyway, Rand would be home tonight instead, a landlubber in Laurelhurst, awake in bed with cotton balls in his ears.

Rand sat on a bench when his left ankle started throbbing, as he knew it would, within a half-mile's walk—this from long bouts of tennis in his twenties—and enjoyed a last round of tippling. This was good. Summer leaves in their fullness, and the smell of loam and lily pads. A furtive, woody haven, an arboreal respite. Here his B&L, at long last, dulled him. Summer nights in Seattle are not often warm, but this one was, with the breath of lindens. Rand melted into it, finally done with restiveness. A leaf-edged, gentle, shrouded vista, a view of the serene urban lake of his childhood, where he'd waded, swum, hunted frogs, rowed, and felt his wet worm turn watching girls in damp bathing suits. "Home is the sailor, home from the sea, / And the hunter home from the hill."

After a half-hour, Rand got up and, pitching a little as he negotiated the promenade, made his way back to the Bel Air. He put the flask in the glove compartment and lowered the top. Traffic had dissipated. The streets were lonely. Weaving toward Laurelhurst on Ravenna Boulevard, he caught "Irish Pat" McMurtry on the radio, pounding Ezzard Charles in round ten at the Lincoln Bowl, and in his state of more-than-mild inebriation, he felt roused by the manic description of blows and by the violent enthusiasm apparent in the crowd's roar, a partisan crowd with a weakness for McMurtry and a racial disdain for Charles.

Rand drove pointedly. He felt a burgher's loyalty to Laurelhurst and wished to avoid the impropriety of sideswiping a parked car. In the strictly spaced pools of streetlamp light, though, the world appeared ghastly, and an accident seemed probable. The streets were narrow, and the hedges emphasized a diminishing perspective. Rand spied a '56 Jaguar in a driveway. Someone had parked a boat trailer at curbside. The Bel Air convertible passed through a zone of rose-garden scent that was tropically viscous, and then, subsumed by the fetid plume from Lake Washington, gone. A black Lab trotted down the sidewalk, sidewinding as if to command the street on a whim. The night felt humid, and the humidity was enervating: Rand felt a headache coming on. There came the decision in favor of McMurtry, received by the gallery with unfettered delight, and this made Rand want to honk in affirmation. Instead, he snapped off his radio, the better to concentrate. At the intersection with NE 33rd, he slowed for an oncoming car, which, as it made the corner, heading east far too fast, he recognized as Ginnie's Buick Century four-door sedan— and there was Ginnie fervidly at the wheel, her stern, sculpted face close to the windshield.

Ginnie? But it couldn't be. She would be reading her Ferlinghetti in bed right now, ears stopped and wearing a linty nightgown, the planes of her cheeks rubbed pink with expensive cold cream. She would be thumbing through *Collier's* and perusing the ads with her head propped against three pillows. She would be peering down through her beatnik glasses and nursing untold grievances while maintaining a freighted and female silence against the advent of his return. Rand idled. To be paralyzed by an unusual turn of events— that was him, and he knew it, much to his chagrin, but the way he liked to think of this was *native caution* and *due deliberation*. So he denied what he'd seen and mistrusted his blurred perception, yet the fact remained that Ginnie had passed by—recklessly—at this odd, late hour. It could only mean one thing: emergency. And, if he was further deductive, infant emergency. Rand thought again of his diaper-pin hypothesis. Maybe John William had impaled himself and then, in his writhing, driven the point into his colon, or punctured a major artery. If so, then he, Rand, would be right, right in a way that meant purchase on Ginnie, leverage, and a marital upper hand, and though he wouldn't choose an emergency involving John William as the trigger for such an advantageous posture, he also saw this potential outcome—this skirmish victory in the war of his marriage—as a silver lining to what might be a black cloud, and as a long-term, sunny side-effect.

Convenient to Laurelhurst was the Children's Orthopedic Hospital—a complex of buildings mammothly institutional and notably out of scale with the neighborhood—and Ginnie careened toward it, down 42nd, with the breathlessly intoxicated Rand in her exhaust stream. He caught up under the emergency-bay klieg lights in time to see her in the door of her Buick. Ginnie emerged with the tempestuous John William, and though foremost in Rand's thoughts was the well-being of his son, immediately beneath that was loathing for his own existence—for his bilious wife, for his ear-splitting baby, for BOMARC and his meeting in the morning, not to mention the fat against his belt and the ceaselessly returning weeds in his flower beds. John William! thought Rand, running at a speed he hadn't ventured since giving up tennis, and aware of how clumsy his gait had become, how undependable his legs, how pincered his lungs were by lack of exercise. He was thirty-six.

The infant in the hospital parking lot was crying, but that wasn't new; in tenor and intensity it wasn't any different from crying Rand had heard many times before. The klieg lights revealed the same strictured face, yowling and choleric, that greeted him each time he peered, from a furtive angle, surreptitiously, into John William's crib. Or maybe it was redder, but it was hard to tell with certainty. Rand didn't trust his take on things. There was something kaleidoscopic about the way he was experiencing the world right now. Between the adrenaline and the B&L, he only knew it in fragments—there was no continuity. But he did note that, for once, Ginnie seemed off her game. She was palpably panicked—the moment had gotten her. Shadowy armpit perspiration showed on her tunic, and her face was blanched by anxious effort. She didn't even have the wherewithal to castigate him for being suddenly present. It was as if she didn't have time to register his existence, much less engage in vitriol. With the baby in her arms, she hurled herself at the hospital's automatic door, which opened with a pneumatic exhalation, as if separating pressure fronts, and he followed. It was a quiet night in the emergency ward; the foyer had the feel of silent anticipation, of a stage set before Act One. Rand was struck by this. That there was no drama. The only drama was theirs, and they'd brought it with them as if in search of an audience. Ginnie advanced like the star of the show, and with the determination he'd seen in her when she confronted their neighbor's dog by blending stampede with lecture. Which animal is more alpha? was the only question.

The emergency-ward desk nurse lacked a sense of urgency, and to Rand her flippant manner seemed outrageous—gum-snapping, slow with a stapler, averse to eye contact, inappropriately dreamy; she was in her mid-twenties, and her lower lip looked wet and lazy. Rand stopped to explain, but Ginnie didn't hesitate; she disappeared with the baby behind a pair of swinging doors—the kind with small windows that reminded Rand of portholes—and left him behind with the paperwork, which seemed to him a secretarial task and further undermined his sense of command. Yet, filling in blanks, he felt himself relax a little—the business-as-usual atmosphere in the anteroom subdued his desperation. He had time to think now. He was aware of his inebriation. He was aware of how menial and subservient he must seem to this sultry receptionist, whose bouffant was dark and lax. At best, he realized, he was an afterthought to her. He didn't register; he didn't give off scent. Rand acknowledged his feeling of being unmanned by time and marriage, a sensation he worked hard to keep in the background. It occurred to him by way of consolation that he did rise in stature on board the *Cornucopia*, as master of the tiller, where Ginnie, disturbed by the sea, was diminished. (It was a big part of what he liked about sailing.) This reversal—Rand waxing while Ginnie waned—was rare, but also occurred around jumper cables—because Ginnie was irrationally afraid of electricity—and in moments demanding celebratory elocution: for all her education and classes in rhetoric, Ginnie was tongue-tied at wedding receptions, whereas he, dumb Rand, offered toasts to happiness with ease. He'd always believed that this shortcoming of hers arose from a lack of feeling. Why was it that after weddings she invariably detailed for Rand the reasons to expect failure? He's a cretin, she's a bimbo, he lacks drive, she's ineffectual, he's devil-may-care, she's "repressed . . ." Rand had his wallet out. He was fumbling through the plastic dividers, and this awkwardness deflated him further. He wasn't skipper of his ship, he didn't exist.

In Room 2, he found Ginnie and a Dr. McAfee, who looked startled, Scottish, and, despite his youth, old-school—tufts in his nostrils, dark hairs on his fingers—while rotating on his stool with his hands in his lap and the earpieces of his stethoscope at the back of his neck. As Rand entered, McAfee was using the phrase "further cardiac and vascular evaluation." He stopped to introduce himself; Rand was certain McAfee smelled liquor, and that made him self-conscious and ashamed. Ginnie's strong throat was conspicuous in the light of this room, and there was a heavy female smell of exertion, an exudate of hormone—frankly, thought Rand, the smell of Ginnie's sex, which was always on hand when she exercised. Rand perched on the examination table. In McAfee's manner, he thought he read the thrust of things—naturally, he and Ginnie had overreacted, in the way of most parents. There was no real emergency here. The doctor had seen this hysteria before; the atmosphere was of a misunderstanding. Yet Ginnie looked subdued and circumspect. If he was giving her the benefit of the doubt, he would say that the night's events had exhausted her and rule out any other explanation. But—tellingly, he thought later—she wouldn't look at him, and there was a hint of guilt in that.

"I've been telling Mrs. Barry," said Dr. McAfee, "that far and away the most common cause of infant loss of consciousness is breath-holding. Isn't that simple? It's very scary when it happens, but actually quite common. Sometimes an infant will cry in a way that sounds progressively more hysterical until breath-holding sets in, but just as often an infant will start to cry and then, immediately, he holds his breath and— Does that make sense? As a simple explanation for why your son passed out? About twice a week we see a baby in here just like yours, and I'd say that only about one time in five hundred is it something other than simple breath-holding. Which is not to say that the parent seeing this for the first time would not be concerned. Of course you are. The child has lost consciousness. You're bound to react with legitimate panic. But did he quickly come to again? Yes. Is he entirely animated, alert, and lively? Absolutely.

And I would say, in this case, with *very* healthy lungs." Dr. McAfee winked at Rand. "We've given John William a sedative," he explained. "But really he's a normal and healthy child. Except," he added, "there's something that concerns me, and that's evidence of bruising at his neck and around his throat. I've looked at it closely, and, yes, bruising, or might I call it formative bruising. You should expect some subsequent discoloration over the course of the next several days."

In the face of this, Ginnie blanched. It was a hard thing to feign, this reaction she wanted to enact of concern devoid of guilt, yet there was nothing she could do about the color draining from her face, and it gave the lie to her pose of maternal consternation and nothing more. Of course, this is what Rand saw, so it could be—and would be—argued in the days to come. And Ginnie, predictably, played the B&L card to maximum effect in countering him as he exhorted her to acknowledge a misdeed. "Bruises," he would say. "They don't come from nowhere." "Plastered," she would answer. "You've got no ground to stand on." Back and forth like this: for him, the bottom line remained the bruises; for her, his alcoholic fog that night impaired his memory. The sad part was—Rand had always known this to be true—even when he was right, he was wrong.

In fact, by the next evening, Ginnie had cornered him into this admission: that he only *thought* he remembered Dr. McAfee saying "bruising at his neck and around his throat." "Formative bruising," Ginnie emphasized. "Meaning bruises that are not yet bruises. Marks that look as if they might become bruises. Marks that are not yet bruises. Ergo, marks that are not bruises. Dr. McAfee didn't call them bruises. And lo and behold—did they turn into bruises? You've been looking as closely as I have. Are they bruises? Really? What is a bruise? I object to this whole line of questioning, Rand. I object to the accusatory tone you're taking. It's clear to me you're engaged in a witch hunt. Don't pretend it isn't so—you're after me, you want to blame me. I told you before, I told Dr. McAfee, I've explained this, and here I am explaining it again—I shook him. Okay? I shook him in a panic. I took him by the shoulders, and in a panic I shook him." Ginnie mimed the action she was describing, exaggerating the gentleness with which she shook John William. "Shaking," she said. "It's a normal reaction. Dr. McAfee concurred with that. Maybe you don't remember, because you were drunk. Who, by the way, is really at fault here? You come home from work, you drink for an hour, and then you waltz out, and the next time I see you, you're tripping on your own feet and stinking of bourbon. How helpful were you in this terrible emergency? You—"

"I *do* remember," Rand retorted. "I remember that you couldn't give a clear answer when he questioned you about this shaking. Shoulders?" said Rand. "There were no bruises at his shoulders. You can shake a person all day at the shoulders and it won't produce bruises at the neck and throat. How come, if you had him by the shoulders . . ."

On and on. Yet her energy in self-defense remained prodigious. She wouldn't admit to what Rand suspected: that her frustration had flowed over; that she'd momentarily strangled John William. "On a baby," she argued, "you can't just grab shoulders, they're too small; the insides of your hands, your thumbs, they end up closer to the throat; that's the mechanics of the situation." "But," countered Rand, "there aren't marks on the shoulders." "We've covered this ground already," said Ginnie. "Shoulders are bony, the throat is softer tissue, so which is going to bruise more easily? And why is it I'm still defending myself? I won't do it a single moment longer! Go pour yourself a Dewar's and sit on the patio! Go read your sports news! *Go!*"

He gave up. He decided to live with it, hoping she might be chastised by this episode, hoping that its aftermath might be penitential, and for many years it was, or seemed to be, because there was nothing like it again, nothing quite so disconcerting. But then, one night in 1968—in between Ginnie's mental-ward incarcerations—he stood in the doorway of John William's bedroom feeling helpless while Ginnie said, with her hands on her hips, "Look at me, John William. I want you to look at me while I speak to you, John William." She was holding a sheet up, carefully, by a corner, as if it was poisonous or radioactive. "Did you think I wouldn't notice?" she sneered. "Well, I notice *everything*! I notice every one of your sickening semen stains." Her expression deepened, and the nascent crow's feet by her eyes became fissures. "I can't tell if you're listening to what I'm saying," she said. "Please acknowledge me when I speak to you, John William!" And then she took him by the chin.

"Now, listen," she said. "I'm the one who has to clean up this semen. I'm the maid"—But she *has* a maid, thought Rand—"I'm the one doing the disgusting work of scrubbing your semen out of this sheet, and I don't want to do it anymore!" At this, the boy shook his jaw from her clutch. He looked left, toward the floor—it was defensive, Rand saw, the plate of his skull exposed, but also submissive, demonstrative cowering, if spiced by anger. "Okay," said Ginnie. "That's terribly disrespectful." And she dropped the sheet over his head, under which he struggled like a netted animal. "You sit like that. With your sheet—stop squirming. You sit like that with your sheet on your head until I give you my permission to take it off." And there he sat like a Halloween ghost for the next forty-five minutes. Was any of this normal? Rand didn't think so. The boy was just the victim—the chief victim—of his mother's mental problems. Rand was angry but didn't say a word—everything about his family life was so ambiguous and twisted, so contorted and convoluted, that he finally felt speechless. A lot of nights, he came home from work to strained silences and ill tempers, but he didn't say anything, because he felt intimidated. In the secretarial pool he passed through at Boeing each day (trying to look chipper for the duration of each journey, top-of-the-morning and entirely squared away) there was a freshwater aquarium, and Rand had noted a number of times how the fins and tails of certain fish were gouged, torn, chewed, tattered, and otherwise severely abused. He felt like these fish looked—a secretary would find him one morning belly-up and bloated, white around his edges, and have to fetch the little net and flush him down the drain. What should he do? Kowtow or rebel? Slap Ginnie across the face or fix a Dewar's and water? He did nothing, as usual. He feebly registered discomfort on occasion; he sometimes railed but consistently to no avail. Either way, he was pathetic in the mirror he was always holding up to himself; the reflection he saw, of a limp noodle, of Walter Mitty without the dreams, was both depressing and reinforcing. "I tell you that I wholeheartedly disapproved and did not participate," Rand Barry told me in our lair at the Rainier Club, "but I won't deny my culpability, in that I was listless and did not stand up to her as I should have. I confess to this shortcoming— I ought to have been different. There should have been more strength in me. That's easy to say in retrospect, but at the time? It was a dif-

ferent . . . era. A different time in my life. I let it happen. That's
wrong in itself. It's the old cliché about the German population. At
the very least, they acquiesced. They stood by. They didn't object. I
mean, regarding Hitler. That was me in my own home, that's an
accurate comparison. I deferred. I turned a blind eye. I stood aside,
I bit my lip. I let these things happen—these things that couldn't
have been good for John William. That makes me guilty, to some
extent—I don't know exactly how much, but to some extent. I fully
accept that. My wife was mentally ill, and I didn't do enough to pro-
tect my son from it."

Rand rapped the side table a few times with his Sprite glass, but
carefully—he didn't want to break it. Was this the rap of regret? Of
anger? Of self-loathing? Of blame? Or was he merely settling his
ice, the better to drink without spilling?

"I'm not your judge," I said. "I've got my own guilt."

"BUT I WOULD ALSO like to accentuate the positive," Rand told
me that afternoon. "Here I've been emphasizing certain factors
which I feel contributed to my son's . . . unhappiness. But, on the
other hand, there were many happy times. There were sunny days.
We were an ordinary family. You couldn't pick us out from other
Laurelhurst households. I could tell you about excellent summer-
vacation journeys—our trip by car to Edmonton and Calgary in the
summer of 1966 was a highlight; now, that was a wonderful time
together. In '65, we drove to Yellowstone. In '64, we sailed as far as
the Queen Charlottes. We had a nice group of friends, some of
them with children who were John William's age, boys and girls
both, fine boys and girls, and we were very active socially speaking,
at the Seattle Yacht Club. This was a lot of fun for us—I'll empha-
size that. I mean that you had the Valentine Costume Party, and
dances for the teen-agers, and every Christmas a Poinsettia Ball—
and Laurelhurst. Laurelhurst was a wonderful place to come of age.
There was a well-organized football program, on top of very good
Little League baseball, and our park was well kept. You could go
there on a Saturday morning to play tennis and all of the leaves
would have been swept from the courts. I also remember that the
gym at the grade school was kept open on Friday evenings so that

the neighborhood boys could play basketball there together. Wasn't that nice! And I felt good about the fact that things were well supervised. There were a lot of responsible adults who took an interest in children, and who took the lead in organizing and monitoring activities. Our kids were not made to fend for themselves, and if they said they were bored, as kids often do, an adult could point to any number of opportunities to get involved in good things that would fill their hours. It's amazing to me, when I think about it now, that people had the time and the commitment and enthusiasm for so much activity outside their employment. Is it like that now? Of course, this was before so many of our women entered the workforce, so things were different. But what's my point? To accentuate the positive. To say that John William grew up in a wonderful neighborhood, in a wonderful era, with all the advantages you would expect were entailed. You can paint a picture any way you want, and I see now that the picture I've been painting up to this point, which is mostly about how troubling my wife was—I see now that this isn't one hundred percent fair. Yes, I'd better back up and do justice here, and tell you that, on the bright side, Virginia chaired, for about three years, the Laurelhurst Neighborhood Gourmet Society. This was a monthly theme dinner in somebody's home, with wine and friends and interesting recipes. And some of these people were also part of a once-a-month bridge club, which eventually became a Saturday-night bridge group we were regularly involved with in the early sixties. She could actually be a very charming woman, Virginia. She was more sophisticated than other women, often admirably so. For example, she invited a Jewish family, the Mayers, who had just moved in on Laurelcrest Drive, to join the gourmet circle. Others hesitated, and we could see they were uncomfortable, but Virginia, she liked the Jews and the Greeks and the Italians, the warm Mediterranean peoples, not just their cuisine but their style, their ways, and in this she was ahead of her time.

"Myself, I was active as a Scout leader. I was not able to make the time commitment required to be a Scoutmaster, but nevertheless I attended Monday-night meetings and, I would say, about every other month was able to go along on troop hikes. I attended the Jamborees. Due to my nautical background and my stint with the Seabees, I had some facility with knots, and so one of my responsibilities was to help the new boys feel at ease and learn the small tricks associated with knot-tying. So this was my way of giving something back to the community. The hiking—I've sometimes wondered just how much influence the Scouting experience had on John William, and if it was formative in some way, because, as you know, he became so interested in wilderness. All those hikes we did, you see. Did you know that John William was an Eagle Scout? That he was Senior Patrol Leader, which is the highest rank a Scout can aspire to? He was. He was serious about it, too, the Scouting. I want you to understand what a highly ethical young man he was—again, looking on the bright side. 'To help other people at all times; to keep myself physically strong, mentally awake, and morally straight'— that's from the Scout Oath, which the boys said at the beginning of each meeting. Some of the boys, you could see, were facetious. They were smart boys and had a tendency to be sarcastic at their age. But John William wasn't like that. I think he was glad to have this serious ritual. We didn't go to church, because I am a lapsed Catholic and Virginia is an atheist, so for our son this was the only real ritual in his life, this reciting of the Scout Oath and the other rituals of Scouting. Do you know very much about Scouting? There is a lot of ceremony. It is a little bit too solemn for my taste, but I was happy for my son to be involved in this activity. I remember when he made the Order of the Arrow, which is reserved for boys who are the cream of the crop, who rise to the top by virtue of their achievements. This was a ceremony in the basement of a church with the lights dimmed and a color guard on hand, and a father dressed up as the Indian sage Akila, and the point of all of this was the presentation of a badge in the shape of a primitive arrowhead. Well, I'm not much like this, but even me, if you didn't look out, you could break into a grin during something of this nature. Not John William. He was nearly in tears. In retrospect, putting two and two together, that makes me a little uncomfortable. He seemed so admirable at the time, such a high achiever as a Scout and elsewhere in his life, but in retrospect it's clear that my son was, the term might be, *over the top*. Such intensity! I liked it a lot, and so did other adults, but you would have to say now, looking back and seeing what's happened, it was a sign I missed, this intensity. No, I was just grateful that he did so well at everything, and so this *force*, which I felt was largely responsible for his achievements, was something I celebrated. And how was I to know differently? Really, you should have seen John William on these Scouting trips, showing the younger boys how to build a crisscross fire or lash together sticks. They respected him, and, frankly, so did the men, and so did I, because he was so responsible about these things, such an exemplar of Scouting at its finest. I remember seeing him make a sundial once and thinking, Where did he learn that? Because certainly he hadn't learned it from me. I was not very particularly an outdoorsman when it came to the hills and mountains, you see—I was a man of the sea, I guess; I liked to be under sail. Now, John William, he liked the mountains, but he also liked to go canoeing in the Union Bay Marsh, which we did when I had the time. Do you know this area of the city? Do you know where the large parking lot is behind Husky Stadium? There was a canoe house down there, with nice rentals available. For fifty cents an hour you got a handsome canoe and a pair of very nice paddles made of ash, and off we went together, exploring in the channels. What a lot of fun that was! We had a bird book and two pairs of binoculars, and I would bring along a big bag of peanuts or potato chips. And—we identified plants. Out there in the tulies. You have your cattails and your lily pads, of course, which most people know, but after that there is quite a variety of vegetation, and this struck John William's fancy. In fact, he made a marsh-plant identification poster for his Nature Merit Badge, and, later, a marsh-plant identification scrapbook with notes, et cetera, for his eighth-grade science class. We used to paddle to a place called Gadwall Cove where, it goes without saying, there were gadwalls and the like, but of course our big hope was to see an otter or a beaver or a muskrat or a mink. So that was one of our hobbies—something we did together. I like to think back on it, because I'm a birder, and it was uncanny to see such avian life in such an urban setting—for example, we saw a few Virginia rails, and—do you know this bird?—the northern phalarope."

"I don't."

Mr. Barry clutched at his tie's knot. He had fixed on the idea again of starting at the top and smoothing his tie downward. "This is a bird a bit like a tern but, oh, smaller than a killdeer," he said. "*Too Late the Phalarope*," he added. "Alan Paton. I mention that title because you're an English teacher. Not many people read *Too Late the Phalarope*, but I have, because its title attracted me, and I can tell you, it isn't about the phalarope at all, which doesn't mean this novel doesn't have its merits. But the phalarope makes a small appearance only. It isn't about the phalarope."

We had that settled.

"John William liked the soft drink called Dr Pepper," Mr. Barry said, "so I always brought bottles of Dr Pepper for us to drink in the canoe. He also liked to go to the Burgermaster, which I point out to establish that fast-food items were part of our cuisine. We ate hamburgers, Kentucky Fried Chicken, Swanson's TV dinners, fish and chips from Spud on Green Lake—all of that. Because, number one, Ginnie did not like to cook, and, number two, she was hospitalized on three occasions for extended periods, during which John William and I fended for ourselves by eating what I would term 'convenience' foods.

"By the way, I have to say that there was this matter of the ongoing dissension between Virginia and myself in John William's life. He was certainly aware of the carping and nastiness. Let me tell you something. On more than one occasion, I moved out altogether. Did John William share that? In fact, on three occasions I packed a suitcase and left the house for periods of varying duration." Mr. Barry gouged his forehead with a knotty forefinger. "I still have a fairly good memory," he said. "The first time was in August of 1962. On that occasion, I stayed temporarily with my brother Walter before reconciling and returning. Then, on the Tuesday before Christmas in 1968, I left again, and again I stayed with Walter for three and a half days. On the final occasion, which was in June of 1970, I checked myself in at the University Tower Hotel on 45th and Brooklyn, in the University District. That hotel has since been remodeled, and you wouldn't recognize it, but in 1970 it was very traditional, close to the freeway and not far from the Seattle Yacht Club, where I had a slip leased for my boat. As I recall, I spent most of the month of June living there, and, frankly, in many ways, I enjoyed that. I could read the newspapers and go to ball games and drive out to the horse races at Longacres after work if I so pleased. This was a very nice life, free but, quite frankly, lonely. I wasn't prepared to abandon a wife who was ill after I'd made the vow 'in sickness and in health,' and I absolutely couldn't abandon my son and therefore leave him bereft of a male role model in the home on a daily basis. A lot of men I know who have been divorced, as I have been divorced, have made a much easier transition. Not me. I have felt considerable guilt, and, to get back to what I set out to say, I just couldn't leave John William in the lurch while I was living the carefree bachelor's life at the University Tower Hotel in June of 1970. And so I called home often. I spoke with him daily. And do you know what? He was very mature about it. In 1970, John William had just turned fourteen years old but he comported himself like a young adult in the course of those conversations. I was embarrassed to have to acknowledge to my own son the wreck of my marriage and my domestic failure. I gave him to understand that I was at a loss and uncertain about my future. You should have heard him in response to his father. 'Don't think of me,' he said. He said, 'I know that when adults get divorced they worry about how it will affect the children, but don't worry about me.' Does that characterize it for you? Again, in retrospect, it was over the top, but at the time, I just felt fortunate that my son was so mature about this and everything else." Mr. Barry gouged again at his forehead. "Years ago," he said, "I had season tickets to the Seattle Repertory Theatre, and so I was fortunate to see the marvelous play by Paul Zindel called *The Effect of Gamma Rays on Man-in-the-Moon Marigolds*, which was eventually made into a movie starring the actress Joanne Woodward. Do you know this play? The family in this play is a mess in every way, the whole thing is a lot of testimony to what a mess they are, but somehow the child, or one of the children, a girl, turns out to be wonderful despite that. And it goes to show, you can't predict. Environment isn't everything, genes play a bigger role—in my mind, the major role. A child can turn out perfect despite a lot of bad experiences. I used to think John William was that way. The saving grace of my life was that, no matter how awful my marriage seemed to be, and other things, my son was absolutely golden, just perfect. Smart, athletic, mature, gifted, polite, sincere, hardworking, golden. That's how I thought of him.

"Something else," said Mr. Barry. "As you know, I was an engineer, and as an engineer, I tried to nurture in my son an interest in the sciences. Well, we subscribed to a few magazines that I felt were useful to this effect, such as *Popular Mechanics*, which is very well known, and *Science & Mechanics*, which is less well known but in many ways superior, and it was from one of these that we got the idea to build our own telescope, which you could do from a kit—and then, when we had done one of these, which was just a rudimentary matter of assembling parts, we got more ambitious and embarked on a mission to build a fairly sophisticated and powerful telescope on our own, or, should I say, John William got ambitious. He used to take the bus downtown to the Seattle Public Library on Saturday mornings to do his research, and he brought home from there copies he'd made of pages from articles in, I don't suppose you've heard of it, *Popular Astronomy* magazine, to which, by the way, I got him a subscription for his thirteenth birthday; it's now defunct. 'The Poor Man's Telescope'—that was the article that intrigued him so and got him started, because it detailed how an amateur telescope buff had made a concave mirror, at home, in his workshop—good, hard information on how to make a very sophisticated mirror, one that could see into space. John William brought back from the library a book called, I think, *The Amateur's Telescope*, a title of that nature, by a Reverend Ellison, that I do remember—sometimes it's the title and sometimes it's the author—who we subsequently discovered was the director of the Armagh Observatory in Northern Ireland, and also an expert in the making of telescope mirrors. It evolved that John William, age thirteen, had convinced the Seattle Public Library to order this book from a library in *London—at age thirteen*.

"But I would have to say that his primary source of information was simply *Scientific American* magazine. *Scientific American* had undertaken to popularize the hobby of amateur telescope-making. They had an ongoing series, so there was plenty of information there, a lot of technical data and food for thought, which John William imbibed. What amazed me most was that my son was not daunted. Telescope-making is a scientific hobby—it isn't just building soapbox cars or putting together a go-cart. You don't have to be an Einstein, but you do need better-than-average intelligence, an innate grasp of the principles of physics, considerable patience, a lot of determination—what I would call 'grit'—and, finally, some handiness, which, by the way, I did not have—I wasn't good with tools—

but John William did. That boy liked to tinker. He liked to look at things closely. He wasn't turned aside when success required a diligent effort and very fine tolerances. In glass work, flaws are magnified. With the lens of a telescope, you need to work within a millionth of an inch of perfect. So you had better be motivated, and John William was. He spent a lot of late nights on his telescope project. Why was that? is an excellent question. You know, I think astronomy and astrophysics are among the more romantic of the sciences. Deep space and the mysteries of the universe—they're pretty intoxicating. It was just the same thing with me and flight. I used to marvel as a young man at the sight of an airplane. How did an object of that size and weight get off the ground? It seemed impossible, and the impossibility of it, going higher, bigger, faster, the more impossible the better, the more they said it couldn't be done—all that intrigued me. So this is something I know a little about—how the scientific inquiry can dominate a young person and start him on an exhilarating journey."

Mr. Barry paused. He seemed aware, suddenly, that his glowing report on his son's youth was at odds with the fact that John William had grown up to live—and die—in the woods. But his hiatus was only a hiatus, not a transition. His tone remained celebratory. "John William cut his teeth on a six-inch 'scope," he said, "made his errors, learned from them, and then went on to a twelve-inch project. He did both without dimensioned drawings or hard specs, although I did help out with a lot of preliminary calculations, and I walked him through some models. This was hard stuff—a lot of advanced algebra and work with parabolas and conic sections. The theory of the mirror, its mathematical basis—this isn't a business for just any thirteen-year-old. But he had a high IQ and that intensity I mentioned. He understood what it took. He was willing to do all the grinding and polishing. He was patient in working with carborundum—something I found laborious. You know, it was impressive, but again, I see now, over the top. Because he was too much the boy wonder, too much the young genius—and I didn't see, and neither did Ginnie, how this might have what you would call a dark side." Mr. Barry stopped again, poised over the phrase "dark side," which momentarily stilled the hand at his tie. "I remember once, around two a.m.," he said, "I got up to do something or other and I could see that there was a light on in the basement. Two a.m. The house was cold. I went down the stairs, and there was John William kneeling on the floor, and he was busy with something called the Foucault knife-edge test, which is a way of determining if a mirror is spherical. A lot of people know about Foucault's pendulum but not about Foucault's knife-edge test. This is the French physicist who is justly famous for demonstrating the rotation of the earth on its axis, but what people forget is that Foucault was avidly interested in light—light, more than gyroscopes and pendulums, intrigued him. And his knife-edge test is truly ingenious. You can use it to measure the smallest mirror imperfections, but all you need is a light and a razor blade. Of course, Foucault would have used a kerosene lantern, but John William was using an electric lamp. So the basement was dark except for this one light source. John William had devised a sort of chimney from a loose piece of tin, and since the lamp was shrouded in this sleeve, I guess is the word, not chimney, the light in the room was dampered, muted. With the exception being a tiny pinhole my son had made with a sewing needle. The light emerging from this hole was considerable, and it was aimed at John William's mirror-in-progress, a mirror he'd been grinding and polishing for a week. John William was kneeling, as I've told you, and he was using the razor blade, which he'd mounted on a popsicle stick, to act as a line cutting through . . . it's hard to follow, this business. Hard to describe. And I suppose the science doesn't really matter right now—but believe me, Mr. Foucault knew what he was doing. And so did John William. 'It's two o'clock in the morning,' I said. 'You have school tomorrow.' And so forth. And what he said to me in response was strange. For a thirteen-year-old. Who you think would worry about getting in trouble or being disciplined by his father. He said, 'I'm going to stay up and do this. This is what I want to be doing. School is a waste of time. Most of what other people think is a good way to spend your time is a waste of time from my perspective. Other people can do whatever they want. I'm going to do this. It doesn't matter to me if it's two o'clock in the morning.' Words to that effect. Mildly rebellious. I don't quote verbatim. Except for this one statement, which made an impression on me and stuck with me word for word. Which was, quote, 'The stuff they teach you at school is just so they can own you.' What did that mean? You've been in education, Neil. But it was two in the morning, and I was too tired to ask him questions. I had to get up and go to work in a few hours. Probably I told him to go to bed or something, but I didn't enforce whatever it was I said. I walked away. I left him there with his shadowgraphs. He was making curvature notes. It was a lot of geometry—the kind of geometrics with mouth-filling names."

" 'The stuff they teach you at school is just so they can own you,' " I said.

"That's right," Mr. Barry said. "Strange."

FOUR-FIFTY-FIVE in the afternoon—five minutes until Hospitality Hour began in the Rainier Club's Kirtland Cutter Room. In June in Seattle near five o'clock, it's possible to tell, from a south-facing window, that the sun has dropped in the northwestern sky, because its light at that hour flares in the glass of skyscrapers, but only in the upper reaches of northward façades—and this was visible from one of our den windows on the third story of the Rainier Club. Our white-jacketed server was now gathering up our nut bowl, my coffee cup and saucer, and Mr. Barry's Sprite glass. Try as he might, he couldn't be inconspicuous, because in juxtaposition to the decrepit Mr. Barry—and to me—he moved with ease. So there we were. But we were not going to talk about the hermit of the Hoh in front of this boy-god. Then Mr. Barry looked at his watch and mentioned the men's room. So my cue had arrived; our meeting was over. He began collecting himself for the effort required to rise into a standing position. He was figuring out the physics of the moment—what to lean on and what to push from, which limbs to involve and how—when our server intervened. He extended a hand, as if Mr. Barry was a fallen football comrade, while behind him, on his outstretched other—dramatically high and slightly tilted—he poised his loaded busboy's tray, and all of this with a white-toothed smile, a bow tie, a dimpled Anglo-Saxon chin, blue eyes, and no trace of facial hair.

Mr. Barry just persisted in his mechanical difficulties. He was a bit like a wind-up toy running down as he clawed at the armrest of the sofa, at the sofa seatback, and at the coffee table, his futility increasing with every manipulation. He made a first ill-ventured stab at rising, which ended with him back on his cushion. "I don't need any help," he said, but he did, and before long, humiliated, he took the boy's hand. Upright, he felt for his tie and, at long last, straightened it. Our server backed out of the room.

Mr. Barry maneuvered toward the fireplace, the better to survey the financial leaders whose images hung on the wall. The dozens of painted portraits and formal photographs there commanded his attention; he wanted to gaze into them before he left—some he leaned away from with his glasses in his hand, others he examined with his glasses briefly perched, others demanded a glasses-on, then glasses-off approach. I joined him. A gathering of the Seattle Bond Club, its members in tuxes, its officers seated, the whole lot looking tipsy. A. O. Foster of Foster & Marshall, a file folder in hand, standing in the complicated-looking doorway of a bank vault and leading with his chin. Hal Sampson, Ron Adolphson, Bill Rex, and Fred Paulsell planning something or other at a boardroom table. Mr. Barry leaned in particularly close and then, with one wing of his glasses, tapped the glass of a photo and said, "That's my father there, second from left."

A formal photograph of the nine partners in Diversified Securities, shot in 1927 and hand-tinted in sepia, so that they looked more faded than they had to. For some reason, all nine had chosen an expression of humorless sobriety. There was nothing in the photo save them, no backdrop other than a black curtain. They might have been justices of the Supreme Court without the robes. Mr. Barry's father, William Danforth Barry, had one hand at the lapel of his coat and—I'd seen this in the Boeing photos of his son—a bright, nervous expression. A lot of men of that era looked like gangsters, with their hair slicked back and parted in the middle, but W. D. Barry had an earnest look instead, and stood out because of it; he was also taller than the others, and gazed over the tops of their heads like the only basketball player present. "He accumulated a lot of wealth," Mr. Barry said. "He was very, very good at making money."

"How?"

"He invested in everything. He had a hand in any number of ventures, from logging to aircraft. He invested in aluminum. He made a fortune in iron ore and coal. He was very shrewd about downtown real estate. For a while there, his timber holdings were extensive. He funded the Washington Power Supply Company while it developed hydroelectric. He knew everybody. He was a major shareholder at First Seattle Dexter Horton National, and they were very big on war bonds. They spent a lot on their financial infrastructure, and he never balked at that. As a result, they were one of the first banks to go statewide, and after that, he got interested in agriculture. He made a lot of money on commodity futures while First Seattle was busy assimilating a lot of those little hayseed banks you used to have. And let me tell you, when the state went into hydroelectric in a big way, there was my father. He made a killing while a lot of other venture capitalists were going under."

"Interesting."

"And now, as I understand it, you're richer than even he was."

In the elevator—Mr. Barry on his way to Hospitality Hour, me to my bike—I asked him what his plans were for the summer. "Scandinavia," he answered. "The second Mrs. Barry and I are going to view the icebergs near Greenland and the Scandinavian fjords. A very good cruise line that, as far as I know, does a wonderful job."

In the Rainier Club's lobby, we shook hands. I held on to his a little longer than he liked—his hand was mostly bones, and cold—and while I had him like that said, "You were very candid in talking about him. I thank you for it."

"Well," said Mr. Barry, feebly pulling his hand away, "put 'Rand Barry' in your acknowledgments, will you? Right where Virginia will see it."

9

ALKI, 1851

PEOPLE BEGAN TO COME OUT of the woodwork. Old Lakesiders chimed in with what they thought was important. A former teacher from the Bush School, where John William spent eight years, sent me a sheaf of handwritten pages—"Bush, in those days, was forward-thinking," she wrote. "It's still operating today, and it still has nothing to do with the two George Bushes who have been presidents of the United States." I liked this start to things and checked the envelope for her name: Helen Grant, it said, on a return address label bearing Amnesty International's logo. "One day, during recess," wrote Helen Grant,

> John William stayed in and sat at his desk reading *Silent Spring*. Can you imagine a second-grader reading *Silent Spring*? I went about my business, and he called my name. "Miss Grant," he said, "it says here that a lot of people my age will probably die when they are older of environment-related health problems." I urged him not to worry. I assured him that Rachel Carson didn't mean to frighten anyone. I suggested that *Silent Spring* might be a good book to read when he was older and in a better position to understand it. I was going about my business once more when again he called for me. "Pollution is causing a lot of kids to be retarded," he said. "It's bad for birds, too. I read in another chapter where the insects are dying. And the frogs and stuff. Because of DDT in the surface water. Do you think this is real?" he asked me.
>
> I said I didn't know. I suppose it was the wrong answer. Looking

back, and now having read about John William in the *Seattle Times*, I feel it was indeed the wrong answer. I want to tell you that two things strike me, knowing what I know today. The first is that *Silent Spring* makes a kind of sense it didn't before. I hope that my snippet about *Silent Spring* gives you a measure of insight into your friend—that it is new information. The second is to mention his very distraught tears when I said I didn't know if Carson was accurate. Poor little John William was completely inconsolable. He buried his face in his hands and wouldn't remove them. I had to call the school nurse for a sedative.

THE *Seattle Weekly* put John William on its cover: a mugshot, post-arrest, in Seaside, 1974, in which he looks like Charles Manson with a lower hairline. Stamped across John William's face, in a font eliciting a Bureau of Prisons stencil, is THE WORLD SUCKS, and underneath, much smaller, THE HERMIT, SANS PROZAC. The *Weekly*'s reporter, it's quickly apparent, views the "interlude at Reed" as the crux of the matter ("Not that Reed is Granola University, because its curriculum is as conservative as any in the country—you don't graduate from this school without reading prodigiously from a lot of tried and true Greeks and Romans") and there dug up a former mental-health counselor named Gayle Griffin, who'd seen John William for "symptoms of anxiety and for the evaluation and treatment of a stress-related psychological disorder." John William had come to see her with "pain behind his eyeballs, sleeplessness, palpitations, weight loss, incessant weeping, and generalized hysteria." (These symptoms came on the heels of John William's estrangement from Cindy Houghton, but he seems not to have divulged this crisis of *amour* to Griffin, who, absent this information, speculates that his malady stemmed from "a well-advanced oedipalism, with extreme hostility toward authority figures and with delusions of grandeur.") Griffin had Valium in her repertoire—other Reed students used it, and she knew a doctor who would prescribe—but she couldn't convince her patient of its efficacy. Engaging John William in talk therapy, she'd noted "an unusually keen intelligence coupled with a striking degree of megalomania." The *Weekly* quotes liberally from her psychiatric reports: "Patient exhibits symptoms of intellectual obsessiveness . . . drives counseling toward the theater of ideas and away from psychological investigation . . . highly prone to emotiveness . . . Arrives on time for sessions but without shoes . . .

Patient queries me about contact with parents; I'm repetitively asked to assure him of the privacy of our proceedings . . . Patient shows concern for the integrity and security of his counseling files . . . Patient is an only child with subsequent egocentrism and exhibits difficulty neutralizing aggression toward parents . . . I am now experiencing a well-developed and highly negative transference . . . Patient has apparently left Reed College 3/12/75."

The *Weekly* also dug up Reed professors of the era—Marvin Leedy in philosophy and Howard Jaffe in religion and humanities— who stressed that John William, despite his strangeness, was an excellent student. The *Weekly*'s focus, though, was on a Ronald Metzger, decribed in its pages as "a roving professor and ecopsy-chologist now retired and living near Arcata, California," who remembered John William as "a highly politicized radical and, just briefly, a personal friend." Metzger had taught at Sierra and Skid-more before Reed, and at Humboldt State afterward; in his photo for the *Weekly* (caption: "Metzger at Vulture Valley Hojo") he appears as a robust and handsome man of seventy with a rich crop of silver hair, a silver goatee, and a prominently strong neck showing at the throat of his chambray shirt; he looks earthy, tousled, sun-burnished, and agrarian. "We hung out," Metzger told the *Weekly*. "John William had read my books and was eager to talk ecology. And talk we did, which I enjoyed." (The books Meztger refers to, according to the *Weekly*, are *Entropy and the Post-Industrial State*—"an accessible critique of modernity"—*Cosmology and Ecology*—"musings on transcendence, animism, and mythos"—and *Mind, Soul, and Nature*—"Metzger's argument for ecopsychology.") Metzger also reported getting postcards from John William in '75 and '76 (they were signed, in the absurdist vein John William employed when he was feeling comically effusive, "Mother Enithar-mon," "Zosimos the Panopolitan," "Moloch's Pawn," and "Simon Magus"). "I question the questioning of his sanity," says Metzger. "To me, he was simply passionate about the right things. He had a valid critique of the world and made it. If that's insanity, something's wrong. Personally, I think there's something wrong. With the world and not with John William."

. . .

I ASKED LUCY HATCH-MYERS for Ginnie's contact information. I tried the number Lucy gave me, got voice messaging, and, after three days, heard back from a Bill Worthington. He asked me to imagine a family tree. On one side is Ginnie's father, Cyrus Worthington, and on the other is Cyrus' brother, Stanford. I was to draw a line straight down from Stanford and insert the name of Stanford's son, Stanford, Jr., and under that, of his grandson, Stanford III, and under that, the name of the guy I was talking to, Bill Worthington— "in other words, and I know it's complicated, I'm the grandson of Ginnie's first cousin."

Bill Worthington's tone, I thought, was more condescending than it needed to be. He spoke the way John William once spoke: as if he deserved to be listened to by definition. I said, "Grandson of Ginnie's first cousin," and he answered, "It's a hassle to explain. All those Stans. Anyway, I'm returning your call."

I said I thought I'd called Ginnie. Bill said I had. He said he had power of attorney on behalf of "Aunt Ginnie," which meant he managed her affairs, since Ginnie had Alzheimer's. "She's eighty-five," he explained. "We think it must be Alzheimer's. I didn't catch it from the message—tell me your name."

"Neil Countryman."

There was the pause I'd come to expect in recent weeks when I said that. I'd learned how to fill it. I said I was sorry to hear about Ginnie. I mentioned having seen her in good health at a poetry reading, and that I remembered her as lucid and vibrant at her gallery. I said, "Alzheimer's is very hard on families."

"Is it, now."

He was being uncivil, so I said, "None of this was my doing, you know."

"I don't know that."

"I didn't call to argue."

"Of course not. You're rich."

I said I wanted to see Ginnie. "Ginnie doesn't know a knife from a fork," Bill replied. "She can't meet with you. No way."

"It's more for me than for her," I said.

"Exactly," Bill answered, and hung up.

. . .

I CALLED BLEDSOE. They advertised in the Yellow Pages as "Seattle's Oldest and Finest Investigative Agency, with 43 years of service and results." The next day, an investigator called to say that Ginnie was in Room 11 in "the dementia ward" at Harbor House, on Harbor Drive, in West Seattle. I asked what he meant by "dementia ward" and he answered, without sympathy, "The basement." Dementia ward in a basement—it sounded medieval. But as it turned out, Harbor House had a wide view of Puget Sound, which on the summer afternoon I went to see Ginnie was sun-addled, shimmering, and stippled with sailboats. The institutional grounds, though small, were parklike, with some relatively tall Douglas firs and a grove of wind-bent alders. In the lobby, through tall windows, I saw a container ship pass closely by—the *Korea Maru*, forty-eight thousand tons—negotiating the last leg of its pan-Pacific trade voyage and looking pestered by pleasure craft. All this not far from Alki Point, where the twenty-two members of the Denny Party, including Ginnie's great-grandfather, went ashore to found Seattle.

I gave them the truth—I was a friend of Ginnie's son and wanted to visit her. I was pointed toward an elevator and told to push the "B" button. A number of residents basked in the wide hall, some in wheelchairs, some with walkers, some with canes, some in slippers. They made me feel more interesting than I was. Gawked at, I thought I could smell pablum. Mostly what I saw was my own possible fate, which left me defensive. In the elevator, going down, I heard the silence of doom.

An odd elevator arrival. I'd expected a reception, a greeting, a waiting area, or someone in charge, but instead the door opened on the sort of lonely cul-de-sac that makes a person think twice. Was I on the wrong floor? Maybe I'd used a service elevator in error. I appeared to be nowhere. But after scouting around two corners, I gained confidence. Room 1: Ruth Middleton. Room 2: Elizabeth Blair. At Room 3 I said "Hi" to Margaret Casey. She was parked in her doorway, monitoring the foot traffic, which at this point was me.

Virginia Worthington wasn't in Room 11, but her door was open, so I could see the cot she slept on, and her television—which at the moment showed static—and I peeked into her private bath, which had a wheelchair-accessible shower and a floor drain. Since this was a daylight basement, she had windows, but they looked onto a service road at approximately the level of a truck's axle. Ginnie's room had none of the accoutrements of retirement—no books, knitting needles, crochet hooks, etc.—and that made me wonder what she did all day. There wasn't even soap in the bathroom.

Farther along the hall was what I think is called a "station," and here, at a long counter, sat a black woman in an orderly's uniform—it looked like green crepe paper—and arrayed around her, leaning on the counter or standing nearby, were other orderlies, also black, also looking as if they were wearing crepe paper, and surrounding these orderlies were about two dozen old white people. They were variously immobile, and, as with the people upstairs, their interest in my presence seemed inordinate and, I have to add, in some cases aggressive. I was spoken to and yelled at. One woman, as if reciting a mantra, reeled off her name, her son's name, and his phone number. I was also thought to be a doctor.

Ginnie was eating with a walker beside her in a dining area named for a donor. She was alone, and mostly bones now—bones and the garish makeup of a tart—and her hair had been cropped and moussed. No more chignon, leather pants, or bolero jacket; no more glorious art; no more fine poetry. Now she had a bib, and when I sat down across from her she looked up from her macaroni and steamed carrots and said, "You."

"Me."

"They told me you left."

"Who told you that?"

"I thought you were at school."

"Which school did they tell you?"

"He went to Barnard."

"Who went to Barnard?"

"Guy Benedetti," answered Ginnie.

I put my elbows on the table and leaned on them, toward her. "Mrs. Barry," I said. "I'm Neil Countryman, John William's friend."

"I know who you are."

"I knew him in high school."

"At Barnard he had herpes."

"I knew him in the seventies."

"It was Broadway and West End."

"I knew him in Seattle thirty years ago."

An orderly checked on Ginnie. I said we were fine. Ginnie said, "She's Ethiopian. Her parents live in Gondar."

She ate for a while. Then she said, "Don't you dare think I'm stupid."

"No."

"Or let me give you the Freudian retort. It was forever the queen's gambit declined, make a note of it. Or the trapper trapped. Or thrust and counterthrust. It was very much the naked queen's defense. Why don't you cruelly repeat that?"

She opened wide her mouth, so that I would see the carrot mush inside. There was a quality of flagrant insult to this. I waited until she was done with that, and then I said, "What I came to say is that I'm sorry."

"You shouldn't have seduced me."

"I really hope you understand that I'm sorry."

"Satyr."

"I should have said something, Mrs. Barry. A long time ago."

She lifted her fork as if to strike me with it. As my friend the classicist had observed: quintessential harridan. It occurred to me that she might live for a long time, that her breath didn't want to leave her lungs, and that she was afraid.

She said, "Dr. Spock encouraged bedtime reading."

"Do you understand me?"

"Your generation is awful," she sneered. "You used to call me your Seattle box-house baby. Don't you remember that?"

"That wasn't me."

"Let's not pretend."

I gave up. She ate some macaroni. She said, "You remind me of an egret. A perfect egret. You have a pointed breastbone. I ought to trim your wings."

"Anyway," I said, "I apologize. I should have told you."

"You should have paid," she said.

I took Robert Leventhal's *Chronic Obsessions* from a bag at my feet and turned it toward her so she could read the title and look at the line drawing, on the cover, of a woman's naked, headless torso. "I brought you this," I said. "It's a gift."

Ginnie put her fork down and, turning her head to one side, touched her hair lightly. I said, " 'Alki, 1851.' On the wall of your study. In Laurelhurst."

"Don't you dare think I'm stupid."

"I don't," I said. "But I thought you might like to have this copy, in case you don't have one anymore."

"You're a shadow," hissed Ginnie. "You're his shadow. Get *out*."

"I'm sorry," I said, one more time.

Some very credible people believe that everything important happens to you before you're six years old, but who knows? There are things lost to history with no eyewitnesses, and there are also the unjustly accused. To put this another way, *Chronic Obsessions* might not mean anything, and Rand might be lying. Or maybe the truth is that truth is too complicated. If I extrapolate from myself, there's a lot of deceit in the world without a beginning, middle, or end. The way it really works, a lot of the time, is that you suffer from the weight of what happened, from what you said and did, so you lie as therapy. Now the story you make up starts to take up space otherwise reserved for reality. For phenomena you substitute epiphenomena. Skew becomes ascendant. The secondary becomes primary. When it's time to confess, you don't know what you're saying. Are you telling the truth, or do you confuse your lies with reality? The question is comical. The answer is lost in the maelstroms of consciousness. It's even possible to pretend, eventually, that the question wasn't asked. You've been kidding yourself about yourself for so long, you're someone else. Your *you* is just a fragile fabrication. Every morning, you have to wake up, assemble this busy, dissembling monster, and get him or her on his or her feet again for another round of fantasy. Is this what some sutras by Buddhists are about? Maybe. The book-length bromides on mental health? At times. The biographies on politicians? Take Nixon or Clinton. Anyway, I don't know anything about Rand or Ginnie. I don't know if anyone tried to strangle John William. I don't really know who tormented whom, or why, or if anyone was even tormented at all. I don't even know much about myself. I only know that Ginnie protested with *Chronic Obsessions* pressed against her bibbed chest. Then she kicked me out. That was it for me at Harbor House. As I was walking away, she said to my back, "If only you knew the first thing about torment! I was born in the wrong place and time! I was trapped!"

. . .

JAMIE AND I TURNED IN the '92 Civic and bought a hybrid, which we recently took to the Canadian Okanagan—the Napa of the North that Wiley and Erin told us about. We walked, swam, biked, sunned, tasted wines, ate well, bought pottery, and watched the sun go down, and though all of this was fun, none of it made us happy. We both wanted something else that was unnamable. It might be forever unnamable. In this regard, money changes nothing, which Jamie and I knew before we had it.

When I think about John William now, I think about someone who followed through, and then I'm glad not to have followed through, to still be breathing, to still be here with people, to still be walking in the mountains, and to still be uncertain—even with all this cash on hand—in a way I seem to have no choice about. I'm a hypocrite, of course, and I live with that, but I live.

TODAY I WENT to a used-book store on Admiral Way. It's crammed, because its owner recently closed a second shop, in Greenwood, and consolidated the collections. Half the titles are in boxes, and these boxes are everywhere, one on top of the next, which frustrates me, since I can't look into them. Still, one thing I like about having money is that I feel looser in a used-book store. I'll buy a title just so I can look at it more closely before giving it away. For example, I recently bought *Cocktail Shakers, Lava Lamps, and Tupperware* for $6.98. I wouldn't have done that before. Too much of an indulgence. In fact, I'm now struggling with a tendency to collect. It's been liberated by money. I bought a first-edition hardcover, in good condition, of Dr. Benjamin Spock's *Baby and Child Care* for $39.98, which is absurd. Why did I need to have it? I've been looking at it lately, though, since Spock was influential. His points of wisdom and advice are numbered 1 through 805:

1. You know more than you think you do.
2. Parents Are Human—They have needs.
3. Some children are a lot more difficult than others.
4. At best, there's a lot of hard work and deprivation.
5. Needless self-sacrifice sours everybody.
6. Parents should expect something from their children.
7. Parents are bound to get cross.

And so on, to the final line of the book, which is "It's not the words but the music that counts."

My purchases are piling up now. *Literary Hills of San Francisco. The Rights of Hospital Patients. Jesus and the Lost Goddess. The Travels of Lao Ts'an. Poems by Ko Un. The Drama of the Gifted Child. Boeing in Peace and War. Taking Stock: A True Tale of Seattle's Investment Community.* Back issues of *The Mountaineer.* Back issues of *Popular Mechanics.* They all wait for me, and I'll never get to most of them. I read somewhere recently that there are at least thirty-two million different books in the world, and that most are out of print. The ones that aren't are read by a very small percentage of the world's population. Most people have never heard of most authors, much less read them. Golden ages of literature have come and gone without our knowing anything about them today. Forgive me for teaching—it's so hard to stop. It's just that I hear, sometimes, about a writer achieving immortality. Shakespeare, for example, who wrote, "Imperious Caesar, dead and turned to clay, / Might stop a hole to keep the wind away."

ALLY KRANTZ CALLED, because *Seattle Morning* called her, and she said this was a conference call with a publicist from a good publisher—a publisher who might want to be my publisher once they got a look at my John William book—and this publicist said that I would be crazy not to do it, that it's not a good idea to turn down television.

A limo got arranged, but since it arrived at 5 a.m., my neighbors didn't see me get into it. Then there was the makeup, and someone mussing my remaining hair to and fro before giving up on trying to make it look good. Then there was the greenroom, with its muffins and grapes; me; other guests; and a television, surrounded by tropical plants, airing *Seattle Morning.* Quadruplets, the healing power of dogs, Seattle dentists in Jamaica, a home make-over, and "the four-hundred-forty-million-dollar man!"

At the right time, I was escorted onto the set. Under bright lights, a young woman ran a microphone wire up my shirt. Here were my hosts, whose names I didn't remember. They were attractive in a way I thought of as scary. We hobnobbed painfully. I was asked what it felt like to be fabulously wealthy, but when I started to answer, someone said, "Save it." Then we agreed that the dentists in Jamaica were doing a good thing and that their story was amazing. Thirty seconds. We groomed. One of my hosts said that if I was nervous it didn't matter, because I'd still get to keep the money either way— wink. The other said, at the last second, under her breath, in a seductive whisper, "Here we go."

All this sudden wealth. It must feel so strange.

You were a schoolteacher.

So how has your life changed?

What next? Staying at the Ritz?

Tell us about the hermit. What kind of person was he?

Not your average Lakeside student!

You must have been surprised.

What a generous friend.

Best of luck to you, Neil Countryman. We wish you happiness.

ACKNOWLEDGMENTS

THE AUTHOR wishes to thank Robin Guterson, Mike Hobbs, John Wolfe, Bob Fikso, Mike Drake, Ralph Cheadle, Joe Powell, Robin Desser, Anne and Georges Borchardt, Lisa Sanders and the Lakeside School, Judy Lightfoot, Joel Hardin, Danny Wickstrom, and Terry Zaroff-Evans for their assistance during the preparation and writing of this book.

PERMISSIONS ACKNOWLEDGMENTS

ALSO BY DAVID GUTERSON

EAST OF THE MOUNTAINS

When he discovers that he has terminal cancer, retired heart surgeon Ben Givens refuses to simply sit back and wait. Instead he takes his two beloved dogs and goes on a last hunt, determined to end his life on his own terms. But as the people he meets and the memories over which he lingers remind him of the mystery of life's endurance, his trek into the American West becomes much more than a final journey.

Fiction/Literature/978-1-4000-3265-5

OUR LADY OF THE FOREST

Ann Holmes is a fragile, pill-popping teenaged runaway who receives a visitation from the Virgin Mary one morning while picking mushrooms in the woods of North Fork, Washington. In the ensuing days the miracle recurs, and the declining logging town becomes the site of a pilgrimage of the faithful and desperate. As these people flock to Ann— and as Ann herself is drawn more deeply into what is either holiness or madness—*Our Lady of the Forest* seamlessly splices the miraculous and the mundane.

Fiction/Literature/978-0-375-72657-6

ALSO AVAILABLE

The Country Ahead of Us, the Country Behind,
978-0-679-76718-3
Snow Falling on Cedars, 978-0-679-76402-1

VINTAGE CONTEMPORARIES
Available at your local bookstore, or visit
www.randomhouse.com